The Homeschooler's Software Guide

2001 Edition

By
Dan & Tammy Kihlstadius

Published in the United States of America by
Homeschool Advisor, Inc.
10424 Ewing Road
Bloomington, Minnesota 55431

We dedicate this book to our children, Anna, Bethany, Charity, David, Elijah, Philip, Geremiah, and baby Joseph, who waited patiently (and sometimes not so patiently) for mommy and daddy to finish "the book."

If you would like additional copies of this book,
check out our web site at:
www.homeschooladvisor.com
or write or call us at
Homeschool Advisor
10424 Ewing Road
Bloomington, MN 55431
952-835-0063
We are also available to do
software and computer workshops.

The
Homeschooler's Software Guide

By Dan and Tammy Kihlstadius

Part I
Using a Computer
in Your Homeschool

Chapter One
Starting On A Firm Foundation: Our Purpose And Criteria

Chapter Two
Choosing Software

Part III
Computer Hardware

The Homeschooler's Software Guide

ABOUT THE AUTHORS

We are a homeschooling family, just like yours. We have eight children and the oldest six are homeschooled. We review computers and educational software for families and advise them in using computers at home. We don't see what we do as a business but as a ministry. Our goal is to help parents make the wisest decisions in purchasing a computer and educational software from the vast choices available. We do this from a greater perspective than just what has the best educational value; we also look at every title from a conservative Christian perspective, as you will see in our "Criteria" section. If the program contains any objectionable material or goes against Biblical principles, we will not recommend it. In addition to reviewing software, we speak about computer hardware and software at curriculum fairs around the country, and we are long-time contributors to Mary Pride's *Big Book of Home Learning* and columnists for Mary Pride's magazine *Practical Homeschooling*.

OUR HISTORY

Way back in 1990, our oldest child Anna was six years old and just learning to read. At the time Dan used a Mac computer for his business. This little Mac had only a nine-inch black and white screen, but Anna just loved it. We had only two games she could play: *ReadingMaze* and *NumberMaze*. Then we bought *Reader Rabbit I* to help her learn to read. She loved it! Shortly after this, Bill and Mary Pride came out with *Pride's Guide to Educational Software* in 1992. It contained over 750 software reviews in over 500 pages. Tammy was so transfixed by it; she read it cover-to-cover in one day. She was blown away, not only by the plethora of educational software available, but also the enormous future potential of this new teaching medium. Through just these two simple little black and white programs, we saw how software had the ability to transform learning from a "Do I have to?" into "I want to." We were so impressed with the educational effect of these two little black and white programs that we decided to start a business reviewing and selling software to other homeschool families. We knew computers would cause a paradigm shift in the future of education. We sent a copy of one of our first catalogs to Mary Pride; she hired us on the spot to write reviews for *Practical Homeschooling* magazine. Since then we have literally looked at nearly a thousand educational software programs, tested them out on our own kids, and researched well over a thousand more. We still love using our computer in our homeschool and hope you will too!

In February of 2000, we sold the catalog business to another homeschool family here in Minnesota. This gave us the time, freedom and motivation to focus 100% on reviewing software: the good, the bad, and the ugly. (And believe me, there is a lot of UGLY out there!)

Your Servants in the Lord,
Dan & Tammy Kihlstadius

Section I

Using a Computer in Your Homeschool

Chapter One

Starting On A Firm Foundation:
Our Purpose And Criteria

WHAT IS OUR PURPOSE?

This edition of *The Homeschooler's Software Guide* was created as a resource to give you enough information to make the wisest purchase decisions possible for your homeschool computer needs. We have labored literally tens of thousands of hours in research, study, writing and in the printing of this guide. As just mentioned, we personally examined nearly 1000 software programs worth well over $30,000 to come up with these suggestions. Our hope and prayer is that every family reading this book will benefit from our investment of all this time and money. We trust it will save you money by helping you to avoid bad software and save you countless hours of time hunting down good software. We trust the software that you do choose will be a positive contribution to the education of your children.

What we do review:

We try to review most of the educational software available. We stick to what you will see in the stores and on Internet sites. More obscure titles that are used primarily by public schools are usually not included because most of these titles are prohibitively expensive for homeschoolers to buy and use. However, we do research these titles and if we find a gem that homeschoolers should buy and use, we include it.

What we do not review:

As a general rule, we do not review utility, word-processing, business, printing, or personal productivity software. However, we do include a few kid-sized word processors in our reviews. We also do not include every title possible; especially if we feel better titles are available in that same subject area. How many typing tutor programs should one homeschool own? One should be sufficient. We also don't review Barbie, most Disney movie programs, Barney, most storytelling programs, or role-playing and sports games. The bottom line is this: If we thought it was relevant and useful to homeschooling, we reviewed it. If it wasn't relevant, we didn't review it.

As you read this Guide, keep these thoughts in mind...

There is a lot more that we could have added to *The Homeschooler's Software*

Guide if we had more than 24 hours in a day. Sure, we could have spent another month or so checking out three or four-dozen software programs so that we could find maybe ten more worth recommending. For that matter, if we did NOTHING else but find and test software, we could probably put off sending this off to the printer for another six more months.

This Guide was not written to teach you how to use a computer, it was written to help you get the best use out of your computer for your homeschool. Although we include many tips, hints, and suggestions for using software and computers in your homeschool, this book is not designed to teach you "how" to homeschool. (That might be the next book we write! J)

Furthermore, the computer is not a substitute for Mom, and most software programs are written and designed as supplements, not core curriculums.

We cannot guarantee that everyone will love every title, nor can we guarantee that no one will find anything objectionable. What we do guarantee is that all titles are described as seen through the eyes of a Christian, homeschooling family. What you won't get is the hype from some high-priced advertising agency, designed to get you to open your wallet and spend money on something that you might not even want. Keep in mind, those fancy boxes on the store shelves are designed for corporate profits and are no guarantees of quality content. We say this from the perspective of being strong capitalists ourselves. (We are all for profits.) But not at the expense of our children's education. If you are going to be rewarding the balance sheets of software companies, then be rewarding those that are producing quality educational content with good character and values.

Note: All Bible references and quotes are from the King James Version of the Bible.

OUR CRITERIA

No matter how good or popular a program is, we will not review it if it is occult in nature. This is one of the most important criteria that we use in screening software to be included in our book. Is there any magic performed anywhere in the program? Do any of the characters have any supernatural powers? So important that it is the focus of the entire next chapter *(Software and the Occult)*.

In addition to the occult, here are other criteria (in descending order of priority) we use in screening what we will or will not recommend.

1. Do the characters have good or bad character?
2. Does the program have true educational value?
3. Is the program easy-to-use and does it offer customization and record keeping?
4. Is the program truly fun and enjoyable?

Character

If they were real, would we allow them into our home or allow our children to play with them? If the characters were rude or obnoxious, we passed on reviewing it. If the characters were polite, kind and generous, that was a plus and we mention that in the review.

Educational value

As to number 2, we look for programs that have a high proportion of educational value relative to game play. If you are going to use it in your homeschool, a program should offer a fair amount of worthwhile learning. Our top picks usually have at least an 80/20 ratio of educational content to game content; some even have 100% educational content further maximizing the program's value.

However, some "experts" are even questioning whether software programs have any educational value whatsoever. There has been much press lately claiming computers are a waste of time for children. In Jane Healy's book, *Failure to Connect*, she makes a compelling case against computers for young children. However, if you read carefully between the lines, it comes down to what software these children are allowed to use, how much time they spend on the computer, and how well the teacher incorporates the technology into the learning environment. The Alliance for Childhood (www.allianceforchildhood.com) claims there is little evidence to prove a connection between computer use and academic achievement. However, the *2000 Research Report on the Effectiveness of Technology in Schools* profiles more than 50 independent studies that show a positive relationship between technology and student learning. The latter has been my experience as well. As long as the software is of high quality, the child monitored, and time limits are in place, computers can offer a great deal of learning potential. See the section on the *Top Ten Ways to Use a Computer in Your Homeschool* to open your eyes to the potential benefits of a computer in your homeschool. On the other hand, just because you don't have a computer, doesn't mean your homeschool is a failure.

There is a right way and a wrong way to use a computer in your homeschool. The wrong way entails buying only arcade games and letting your kids consider the computer as their personal entertainment center a la Game Boy. The right way requires Mom and Dad to choose appropriate software and actively supervise computer use.

Oh, and by the way, the American Academy of Ophthalmology says working on computers will not harm your eyes.

Easy-to-use?

We look for software with easy-to-use menus and interface. The screens should be easy to read with clear and eye-appealing graphics. The screen layouts, menu bars and icons should be consistent throughout the program. Labels should be logical and icon based with auditory assistance being a plus. The program should allow instructional choices so that the teacher can customize the program to fit differing curriculum needs and difficulty levels. Good software allows one to save levels and offers an easy exit procedure. Friendly documentation with teacher helps or even a teacher guide is a big plus. The program should supply auditory, tactile and visual cues to enable all types of learners to better remember content. A truly versatile program will offer the ability to use alternatives to a mouse such as a joystick, trackball or touch screen. Some of the best programs offer the ability to create your own customized content, games, or activities.

Is It fun?

This last criterion was not essential in a program getting thumbs-up from us. For example, if the program was very effective in teaching and great for homeschooling, it did not have to be a lot fun. In fact, a program can be no fun at all and we may still recommend it—if it can fulfill specific homeschool objectives. An example of this is *PhonicsTutor*. It is probably the most boring program reviewed in this guide, but it is also the best phonics program we have ever seen. A homeschool family created PhonicsTutor. They looked at all the phonics software available and realized all of it was inadequate. We actually consulted with them back in the fall of 1993 through the early development stages. What they developed was so good it is the only phonics and spelling software program we use daily in our homeschool. The fun factor is not high on our list of must-have features. Keep in mind, however, most kids find doing anything on the computer preferable to doing anything in a textbook or workbook! For more on this so-called "crucial" fun factor, read the "But Mom! It's BOOOORING!" section.

SOFTWARE AND THE OCCULT

What is wrong with a little magic?

Some of you may be thinking, what is wrong with a little magic? As long as it isn't demonic or black magic. After all, Cinderella is such a great story! Why should our book be screening software for every spell, wizard, and act of magic?

We would assume most parents do at least some degree of screening of what goes into the lives of their children. Obviously, the younger the child, the more you screen things. Any parent who is interested enough in their children to be checking out computer software is obviously concerned about what goes in their heads. You check out what goes in their bodies at mealtime; you try to screen their reading material, movies, TV, music, friends and more. Is it because you are cruel, heartless, and you want your children to live nothing but dull, boring, empty lives? Obviously not, it is because you want the best for them and you want to protect them.

We trust that the very reason that you are reading this book is because you want to screen out the junk and buy only the best quality software for your children to use. It is our goal to help you accomplish this more successfully.

The number one goal in software that most parents are screening for is educational value. The second thing that parents need to look at—and more importantly in our opinion—is the character of the characters in the program. "Would I let my children play with people who act like this? Is this an example I want my children to follow? Is there sinful behavior in this program? If so, what kind of consequences does it have (if any)?" However, even more importantly than all this, there is what we feel is a far greater, but far more subtle issue: Spiritual themes. Whether or not this is an issue to you does not change the fact that spiritual themes exist in much software aimed at children. To illustrate the point, we'll share an experience in our own life.

When the light came on

One day our children were watching a VERY popular children's video. Dan was doing other things, so he just passed through the room every now and then. In one of the scenes, the main character slid UP the banister, defying the laws of gravity. (Before we go any further, we must point out that we are not opposed to fantasy, as in imaginary talking animals. Imaginary, impossible events and characters are not the issue here, as we will elaborate.) On another trip through the room he noticed objects floating (read that "levitating") around the room. Then it struck him.

At that moment, it was as if a light was turned on and he could see more than just the scene on the TV, but also the powers that really made things happen. This lady in the movie was far more than what she seemed. To the viewer she was a wonderfully sweet, loving, and sympathetic lady with incredible (and of course, imaginary) powers. Then the light went on in his head and he saw her in a different light than the one meant for the viewers to see. He saw her for what she really was—a witch. Sweet, lovable, friendly, and full of good intentions, but she was still a witch. No way around that fact.

Then another thing hit him; did he want his children to grow up emulating a witch in their play times when they are role-play-

ing?!?

Some time later our children were watching a video with a mermaid as the main character. The more we watched, the more problems we began to have with it. For starters, the cartoon seemed to justify and even glorify her stubborn and rebellious ways. But that was not the message that disturbed us the most. The movie implied that there were two types of magic - good magic and evil magic. Even worse was the message that the magic was simply a neutral power and that the good or bad of magic was only based on how that power was actually used.

Is that kiddie cartoon a wolf in sheep's clothing?

This incident was where this issue crystallized for our family. We realized that there are no neutral magic powers. In reality there are only two powers, one being evil and one being good. Furthermore, we realized that even more insidious, was that most often the evil power does NOT come as dark, terrifying, or wicked; but rather evil comes disguised as good. NOT wanting to reveal its true self, NOT wanting to reveal its true intentions or motives. The classic analogy is the "wolf in sheep's clothing". Evil usually comes disguised as being sweet and innocent, hoping to deceive the ignorant and naïve. A well-known FBI profiler pointed out the fact most serial killers look like the average guy. Most people think incarnate evil would be recognizable but most of these evil people look and act like your average next-door neighbor.

Yes, certainly there is an obvious side to evil—crime, violence, hate. If someone comes walking down the street towards you, they look like a crook, and they are carrying a gun, you are able to put two and two together and decide to stay as far away as possible from this person. Thus avoiding any of many possible disasters. But, does the con artist use a gun to steal your money? Does he make his intentions known? In Dan's previous occupation, he had a great deal of contact with very many people who had been swindled out of their money. Never did these victims describe the culprit as someone who seemed to be evil, terrifying, wicked, or someone that a person would want to avoid. Usually, it was just the opposite. At first, most of these victims even refused to believe they had been deceived and swindled!

The Con Artist

Dan personally knew one of those people who turned out to be a con artist. By the time his scam fell apart, he had cheated people out of tens of millions of dollars. Did he seem evil to Dan? No. In fact, he seemed quite the opposite. His family was involved in church; he was friendly, and very intellectual. Did he seem like someone that would eventually be convicted of numerous crimes? (He is still sitting in jail.) Not at first. However Dan can still clearly remember the day this man told Dan an absolute lie while giving Dan the friendliest, most cheerful smile he could. After enough lies, half-truths, and attempted deceptions, Dan realized that it would be best for him to have nothing to do with this person. Yes, for a while, Dan had also been deceived. But he was one of the first to realize that man was a con artist.

All right, already. so what in the world does all this have to do with educational software?!?

Either nothing or everything. If you don't believe that Satan exists, if you don't believe that he has a well-constructed strategy to keep as many people as possible out of heaven; if you don't believe any of that, then all this has nothing to do with educational software. However, if you DO believe in more than just "good" and "evil" energy forces affecting "man's" actions; if you do believe Satan exists with a desire to trick, blind, and deceive, in order to send as many people to hell as possible, then all this has everything to do with educational software. If a person is "saved" and eventually on his way to heaven, does Satan give up on that person and go on to the next? Of course not. He is still constantly there trying to deceive us regarding other areas of our lives. Trying to distract us, trying to ruin our witness, trying to get our focus off our Lord Jesus and the Bible. Whatever it takes; whatever works. And THIS is why this all has everything to do with educational software.

Christians have become blind to this type of message in popular culture. As Douglas Groothuis, (Ph.D., Associate Professor of Philosophy, Denver Seminary) put it in the forward of the book, *Harry Potter and the Bible*:

"Spiritual discernment in America may be at an all-time low, both in the Church and in the world. The idea of "spirituality" - now all the rage in our postmodern times - is deemed a subjective, relative, pragmatic pursuit of personal enjoyment apart from considerations of truth, rationality or objective reality. And far too many Christians have failed to develop their critical faculties concerning the enticements of a post-Christian culture. Moreover, in our fallen world, many forms of evil masquerade as innocent, harmless and fun. They are often accepted with little evaluation or criticism, especially when they are popular and entertaining."

Parents are always concerned about what friends their children associate with. Do you want your children playing with someone who practices witchcraft? (Folks, let's call 'magic' what it is—witchcraft.) Do you want your children playing with someone who encourages your children to practice witchcraft? Do you want your children practicing witchcraft? Since the Bible expressly calls witchcraft "sin," we would not want our children pretending to act out in a sinful manner, whatever that sin may be. As you read these Bible verses, think about which of these activities you would desire for your children to participate in. Galatians 5:18-21 states, *"Now the works of the flesh are manifest, which are these; adultery, fornication, uncleanness, lasciviousness, idolatry, witchcraft, hatred, variance, emulations, wrath, strife, seditions, heresies, envyings, murders, drunkenness, revelings, and such like: of the which I tell you before, as I have also told you in time past, that they which do such things shall not inherit the kingdom of God."*

Obviously, not a single one of these activities is acceptable to a child of God of any age.

If you think we are being a little extreme on this issue, let's look at it a different way. We are certain that you would not let your children use educational software that involves killing or stealing as part of the activity, would you? You would *never* say, "Hey, it's only imaginary, what's wrong with a little pretend raping, pillaging, and burning? After all, they are learning a lot of good educational things and they are having fun too!"

A little poison won't hurt anybody

Either the Occult exists (and it is wrong) or it is pure fantasy (in which case my whole concern is completely erroneous and we—Dan and Tammy Kihlstadius—believe a lie). Is just a little magic okay? Would you drink from a glass that had just a little poison in it? People, this is not a gray issue! In the Bible, there was ZERO tolerance of ANY form of occult or witchcraft. It was seen for what it was—the tool of Satan—even where it was used for what seemed to be for apparent good. Example: Saul consulting a witch to "try" to discern God's will (I Sam 28:7-9).

It is our belief that Satan is the primary force behind many things for children that look sweet, cute, innocent and fun on the surface. But do you think that God thinks these things are cute and innocent? They are really just attempts by Satan to get and keep your children's attention and focus off Christ, and one of many steps towards Satan and his compromising ways. *"For such are false apostles, deceitful workers, transforming themselves into the apostles of Christ. And no wonder; for Satan himself transforms himself into an angel of light."* (II Corinthians 11:14) … not a red-horned demon with a pitchfork.

Harry Potter and the Bible

Recently, a new series of books has captured the mind and interest of literally millions of young readers. While I knew that the Harry Potter stories contained magic, I did not know exactly what the books contained. However, what little I did know was enough for me to choose not to let my kids read the books. I then decided I needed to read at least one of the books so I would be able to quantify my criticism. After reading the first book in the series, I felt led to warn my fellow brothers and sisters in the Lord about these evil books. The entire book is based on learning and using occult practices along with lying, revenge, deception, and stealing to get ahead in the world. Twelve-year-old Harry Potter attends Hogwart's School of Wizards as if it were just another boarding school. His classes teach potions, spells, broomstick flying and wand wielding instead of physics, geometry and English. "Normal" people, people who do not have the ability to use magic, are called "muggles" and are looked upon with disdain and distaste. He and his friends regularly break rules, act cruelly to those they dislike and basically show very few if any fundamentally Christian values. This fact alone is enough to eliminate these books from your reading list.

I just finished a book called *Harry Potter and the Bible*. The author, Richard Abanes, brought this whole message home when he said,

"What do the words and images in Rowling's Harry Potter series communicate? There may indeed be a few "good" messages scattered throughout the books, such as: 1) remain loyal to your friends; 2) do not commit murder; and 3) share your snacks. But the underlying lessons communicated through Rowling's novels are far from positive:

* *Lying, stealing, and cheating are not only acceptable, but can also be fun.*

* *Astrology, numerology, casting spells and performing "magick" can be exciting.*

* *Disobedience is not very serious, unless you get caught.*

* *Being "special" means you deserve to escape punishment for behaving badly.*

* *Adults just get in the way most of the time.*

* *Rules are made to be broken.*

* *Revenge is an acceptable course of action."*

I highly recommend reading this book.

Please, parents, do not allow your children to read these books! It is just another one of Satan's ways to make witchcraft seem wonderful, harmless and fun.

Pokemon

Another major hot fad is collecting and playing with Pokemon cards. When I first heard about Pokemon it was in a major news story about a cartoon shown in Japan that induced seizures in some of the children watching it. "Oh, that sounds weird," I thought. Apparently, the rapidly flashing pictures and lights had some sort of affect on the brain. Later, they brought the cartoon to USA. Next came playing cards with the cartoon characters on them. Kids started collecting and trading them via a complicated card game. At first glance, the Pokemon fad may seem harmless enough, but upon closer examination, I discovered it is full of far-eastern mystical religious practices.

Do we live what we believe?

To those of you who are my brothers and sisters in the Lord, if you believe that the Bible is true and use it as the primary guide in your life, then we would exhort you to cleanse your home. Not just software with any occult themes in it, but please eliminate everything else with occult: movies, books, games, pictures, statues, or anything else involving any form of supernatural power deriving from an deity or "force" that is not from Jesus Christ. That includes Pokemon, Star Wars, Harry Potter, Cinderella, Aladdin, and the rest. If we are to obey the Bible, we must resist these *powers* that exalt themselves over God, *"Casting down imagi-*

nations, and every high thing that exalts itself against the knowledge of God, and bringing into captivity every thought to the obedience of Christ." (II Corinthians 10:5) Every thought—not just some—but EVERY thought! To do this we must take hold of God's plan of defense, *"For the weapons of our warfare are not carnal, but mighty through God to the pulling down of strong holds."* (II Corinthians 10:4)

To those that don't believe, will you get conned?

As for those of you who have not turned your lives over to the creator of all existence, the Lord Jesus Christ, for your sake (not mine), PLEASE, grab a Bible and read what IT has to say about the creator and about salvation in the books of Acts and Romans. Furthermore, think about it this way. How WOULD Satan WANT you to respond? Who are YOU going to listen to? Before you answer, just remember that Satan appears to Man, NOT as a scary Red Devil with pitchfork in hand, but as the Great Deceiver—a wolf in sheep's clothing and an angel of light. He comes NOT to scare, but as the *ULTIMATE* CON ARTIST wanting to steal away your most valuable possession—your soul for eternity. In the end, will he have conned YOU?

How about some balance to all this ultra-conservatism?

Lest you think the Kihlstadiuses are so narrow-minded that we have thrown out the baby with the bath-water, we thought this would be a good place to give this whole subject at least a little bit of balance.

We don't have a problem with imaginary things like flying people (such as Superman, and as opposed to "levitating" people) or

talking bunnies (or talking mice or talking trees.) We do know from our own personal contacts that there are Christians who do have problems with such things. To them, if it is not possible in the real world (like talking animals) then it is wrong. As the right-wing-extremist-wacko as you might want to label us, I guess this is kind of where we draw the line. We deeply respect our Brothers and Sisters who hold those beliefs and convictions, even if we don't share them to the same degree. We even try to assist them in finding software that is acceptable to them. We just don't take our own convictions to that level. And, of course, when we all get to Heaven, God will be able to definitively settle this issue for us all.

Back on the subject of flying men (e.g. Superman). When imaginary characters do things that are impossible in the real word, we try to examine the "implied" source of these extraordinary abilities. In the case of Superman, the sun on the planet he was born on was different than our sun, so it gave him different abilities. Ok, sure, that is an incredible stretch of reasoning. But nowhere is there an implication that the source his powers come from some supernatural or magical force or ability, such as that of a "flying carpet's" source of power. Talking bunnies are just that. Certainly not real, but the animal's abilities are not acquired through demonic forces.

I hope this reasoning all makes sense to you.

In the case of Snow White, yes there is magic. However, the magic is clearly portrayed for what it is—EVIL! In the end, the battle is shown between good and evil and in this case, the good conquers the evil. Contrast this with Star Wars where it is a battle between good magic and evil magic.

Neither "Force" acknowledges God or Satan. The message is very clear that the "Force" is neutral, it is how one uses it that makes it good or evil.

Learning to discern

When it comes to magic, there are some programs that are borderline. They are fine programs, but somewhere in the program there are some images of magical items. An example of this is the program *Storybook Weaver Deluxe*. This program is like an electronic flannel graph or colorforms with dozens of backgrounds and 1500 built-in images to allow children to illustrate, write, and even add sounds to their own stories and booklets, in a fun and creative manner. It really brings out creativity and motivates children to write stories. Our children love it! The problem is a few of the choices of objects are magical characters or items. Children can choose any object to use or not to use, at their own discretion.

So in the case of "bad" objects, they can choose not to use those objects in their story. Also, the objects are "static", meaning that the objects don't do anything—they are just still-life pictures. Using this approach, we have taught our children to identify (discern) wrong things and make the right choice not to use them.

Digressing on discernment

We feel lead to digress for just a moment to take this "discernment" issue one step further. We would like to share something with you that has been extremely helpful in teaching our own children how to apply discernment along with making wiser choices in all areas of their playtime. However, before we do, we need to explain something that has been of even greater benefit in training our children in nearly every area of life.

We learned a VERY valuable piece of parenting advice at a Bible seminar that we attended. (More on that seminar, later.) It was that if you teach your children rules without teaching them the principles behind the rules, they are far more likely to eventually break those rules and disregard them. This is especially true for when they become adults. They need to understand the principle behind the rule if it is to have life-long meaning and application for them.

Back to the discernment part. As a parent, we could come up with a list of about 1,387 or so rules of exactly what our children can and can't do. And doesn't it seem that no matter how long of a list we make, some creative child does something obviously wrong that they claim innocence for doing and their defense is, "You never said I couldn't do it?" Well, we came up a principle what covers a lot of area. This is a playtime principle that was worked EXTREMELY well with even our youngest children. And the Biblical principles behind it are pretty obvious. We have taught our children that they are not allowed to play or do anything imaginary that would be wrong to do in real life. An example of this rule is no pretend shooting at anyone. This same rule works very well for helping them understand what software they can and can't use. With nearly 1000 titles for research and review in our house, and four computers, sometimes we just can't police what every child is using every moment.

We do not teach acceptance, compromise, or tolerance. Using these methods of discernment and making proper choices, we have taught our children (in a setting of our choice) that there are *many* things in this world that are totally accepted, and even embraced by most people; but these things are wrong for people who have committed themselves to choosing God's ways first. Using this approach, our children as young as age four have developed a sharp sense of what is right and what is "bad" in the area of the occult. We are able to generally trust them, when they are not with us, to choose wisely and correctly. (Now if they would just obey everything else we tell them!)

OUR GOAL: TO ENCOUR-AGE YOU AS YOU HOME-SCHOOL

Thinking about homeschooling?
...Tired of homeschooling?
...Ready to throw in the towel?

(In this section, I am deviating from the main focus of this book. I want to encourage Christians to start or continue homeschooling. When we ran our mail order business, we fielded many phone calls from parents thinking of homeschooling, beginning homeschooling, or just burning out from homeschooling. We felt then, and still do, a burden to encourage and exhort Christians to keep up the good work of training their children.)

Consider the following:

If you are thinking about homeschooling and your children are currently in a government school (or even Christian school) or if you are ready to give up homeschooling, keep the these things in mind.

A significant number of those in the teaching profession are there, first and foremost, for the purpose of indoctrinating the next generation of children with their own morals, values, and political beliefs. Teaching academic skills and excellence is purely secondary to those teachers' agendas. Now this is fine IF you SHARE those same morals, values, and political beliefs. Remember who is teaching your children in these schools. By sending your child off to be taught by someone else for 8 hours a day, five days a week, 40 weeks of the year, you are essentially handing over your children to be indoctrinated by the enemy. You are placing them under false teachers and the Bible expressly forbids listening to false teachers.

As bold as this next statement sounds, I firmly believe it with all my heart. God will hold millions of Christian parents accountable for turning over their children to God's enemies, for allowing those same enemies to turn those children away from their parents and, even worse, away from God. My Brothers and Sisters in the Lord, I exhort you here. Satan is alive and well on planet Earth, and one of his favorite, most successful training zones is our public school system! Are you really willing to place your children in Satan's hands?

II Peter 2:1-16: *"But there were false prophets also among the people, even as there shall be false **teachers** among you, who privily shall bring in damnable heresies, even denying the Lord that bought them, and bring upon themselves swift destruction. ...And many shall follow their pernicious ways; by reason of whom the way of truth shall be evil spoken of. But these, as natural brute beasts, made to be taken and destroyed, speak evil of the things that they understand not; and shall utterly perish in their own corruption; And shall receive the reward of unrighteousness, as they that count it pleasure to riot in the day time. Spots they are and blemishes, sporting themselves with their own deceivings while they feast with you; Having eyes full of adultery, and that cannot cease from sin; beguiling unstable souls: an heart they have exercised with covetous practices; cursed children: Which have forsaken the right way, and are gone astray, following the way of Balaam the son of Bosor, who loved the wages of unrighteousness; But was rebuked for his iniquity."* Please think a minute about what God means by these words.

Government schools definitely have an agenda to teach, and that agenda is often different in various schools. But wherever you go, there is one thing that is certain: no matter what public school you check, you can know with full certainty what their agenda is *not*. It is *not* to train your children to become Godly adults who love and obey the Lord Jesus Christ. It is not to teach your children Biblical principles and morality. In fact, if they do any teaching of any form of morality, it is usually morality that is contrary to Biblical principles. Pick almost *any* Biblical topic or subject. I challenge you to see what your local public school is teaching on that topic. It is always taught apart from the Bible and is far too many times the *opposite* of what the Bible teaches. Most public school morality teaching is based on how you "feel" about something, do what "feels" right to you. Instead of teaching abstinence, they hand out condoms. The teaching is like, "If it feels right to have sex before marriage, go ahead—just make sure you use your condom. If it feels right to love and marry someone of your own sex, go right ahead; just make sure you use your condom." This is the sort of hypocrisy the Bible is referring to in II Peter 2:19 *"While they promise them liberty, they themselves are the servants of corruption: for of whom a man is overcome, of the same is he brought in bondage."* (Equally evil, government school will almost never condemn anything.) You can hardly find anything that government teachers will draw a hard line on and say, "This is absolutely, always wrong." They almost never are willing to take a stand for truth, morality, or what is right and what is wrong. If you do not believe that government schools have an anti-Christian, anti-Bible agenda, *please* research some of the resources at the end of this article.

Our Biblical responsibility:

God instructs each parent to raise and train his or her own children. Ephesians 6:4 admonishes us to bring up our own children, *"And, ye fathers, provoke not your children to wrath: but bring them up in the nurture and admonition of the Lord."*

Children are like our arrows and we must fashion them to be straight and true; and when they are ready, we will aim them at the enemy to fight the battle. (I speak in a spiritual sense.) Psalm 127:3-5 *"Lo, children are a heritage of Jehovah; and the fruit of the womb is his reward. As arrows in the hand of a mighty man, so are the children of youth. Happy is the man that hath his quiver full of them: They shall not be put to shame, when they speak with their enemies in the gate."* When one goes into battle, one is best prepared with as many arrows as God would provide us. By sending our "arrows" off to the government schools, we are allowing non-Christians to aim them for us; and if they come back, aimed straight at us, we have no one to blame but ourselves. (This analogy courtesy of Gregg Harris. Thanks, Gregg!)

Our children are with us for a relatively short time! When we send them off to school for seven to eight-hours a day, five-days a week, we are losing so much time with them. Time we could be developing a deep relationship with each of our children. Time we could be developing their character by working with them in day-to-day chores and responsibilities. Time we can train them in Godliness and obedience. Time we can never get back. Our children will face such an evil world; they need all the Biblical training and protection we can give them.

Training in obedience is so important in raising children. One mom told me that her child "would never listen to me and do her schoolwork. So I could never homeschool." I told her that she had a far more serious problem if her child would not obey. Sending the child off to someone else to deal with the problem will only postpone the inevitable—full-blown rebellion. Winning and keeping the heart of your child from age five through eighteen will produce a confident, obedient, and Godly young adult. I know this because I see it every day in homeschooling circles. Of course, there are the rare homeschooled teenagers who rebel and wreak havoc with the family but that is the exception not the rule.

I urge you to seriously seek God's will in this matter and pray for strength and wisdom. When it gets hard and looks impossible, just remember, none of us can do God's will in our own strength and flesh. My husband and I are not perfect homeschoolers, nor are we special in any way. However, we trust God to provide all we need to fulfill His will. We look to God for grace and homeschoolers seek it in bucketfuls. We are all weak vessels fit only for the Master's use. When you feel like it's just too tough to homeschool, remember, there are home-schoolers out there who have it tougher than you and they keep on. One of my best friends has six children at home, all under age twelve: one is autistic (eight-years-old and still wears diapers), one has Down's Syndrome (two years old and still crawling), and she is going through chemotherapy for breast cancer after losing a breast last year. Furthermore, her husband works long hours as a full-time pastor. If she can homeschool, anyone can. Another mom in my home-school support group literally homeschooled on her deathbed. Not until she *died*, did she stop homeschooling her two youngest boys. When these women (and I) are praised for their successful parenting, they can only point to the Lord and give Him all the glory! If you need more information on the how's and why's of homeschooling, check out the recommended homeschooling resources at the end of this article.

LAZY MOM'S GUIDE TO HOMESCHOOLING:

I know we are not lazy, but we need to be more relaxed about homeschooling. Here are a couple of tips and a warning that will help you get through the next year.

First the warning: You will burn out. Many homeschooling moms do, especially first-timers. They try to do too much at once. Keep in mind, you don't have to teach a full 8:00-4:00 day with 8 different subjects each day. In fact, it may surprise you, but your children can grow up to be fully functional, intelligent adults without having learned the 50 capitals of the 50 states in their first year of homeschooling. Yes, you can go a whole year without any history. I wouldn't recommend it but you can. (I realize this will not go over well with some of the super-organized, super-structured experienced homeschooling moms, but this isn't your first year!) Just concentrate on the basics: reading, writing and arithmetic and then add in additional subjects as your confidence grows and your time and energy allow. Even more important than the three R's, is building your child's character. Spend time with Bible training and learning obedience. Set aside time daily and/or weekly for family worship. Some days at our house are entirely spent cleaning house and working on the children's attitudes. That is real life, folks.

Exploit!

Use what I refer to as the "exploitation method" of teaching. (Some homeschooling experts refer to this as a "Delight-Directed" method.) If your child has absolutely no interest in history this year, but is fascinated by science, then go super-easy on the history and go crazy with science. Sure, your child may fall a little behind in history for this year, but look at the trade-offs. That child might cover two, three, even four or more years of science instead, and his absorption and retention will be so much more significant than it would be with lesser motivation. Two or three years from now that same child may have little or no interest in science but suddenly find history rich and alive instead of dead and boring.

Another important consideration is Dad's support. Homeschooling is far more successful when Dad is on board. Not that he needs to participate in the actual instruction, but he needs to support Mom and back her up when she sets up chores, schedules and responsibilities for each school day. He needs to make sure she has enough financial resources to buy quality homeschooling supplies and materials. If the budget is too tight, re-evaluate your spending priorities. (Do you really need that new car? Maybe your vacation this year can be closer to home.) I know most homeschoolers are living on one income and have already trimmed the budget as far as possible, but homeschooling can be done with minimal finances if mom is resourceful. Use the library; rent or check out at the library educational videos. Go to a used curriculum sale. I try to buy curriculum that is reusable or resalable. For example, I have had four different children use my Saxon 5/4-math book already; but I did have to shell out $45 the first time. I know some parents who swap materials back and forth between families as their children pass through the grades. Ask for educational books and materials for Christmas presents from Grandparents. The Lord will often provide exactly the materials you need when you need them. Last year, my tenth grader needed a science book. Another mom brought a box of Abeka (one of the top producers of homeschool curriculum) science books to our homeschool meeting last year and there was an entire package of all the materials for a high school science course—free! Now my tenth grader is using it this year. Other homeschool parents can tell of similar testimonies.

Another tip to help avoiding burnout and to save money is to stick with the basic "3 R's" until you start to get a better handle on homeschooling. There is one subject that I would add to the "3 R's" and that is "thinking skills". (See the section, *The 3 R's and 3 C'S*.)

Must-have essentials

There are one or two books that are absolutely essential for the new homeschooling mom: Mary Pride's *Big Book of Home Learning* Series and/or Cathy Duffy's *Christian Home Educator's Curriculum Manuals*. These are the best books that describe the various (non-computerized) curriculums, books, resources, games and other products available for teaching your children at home. If you don't already have at least one of these books, you should strongly consider making it your very next homeschooling purchase.

Another important tip for you beginning and veteran homeschoolers: (You will hear this from many other sources, but here goes anyway.) Educate yourself about different learning styles and tendencies in children,

and try to figure out what your child's learning style is. Then, try to find educational materials that cater more to that learning style. This principle is as true for computer software programs as it is for any other teaching material.

Finally, when it seems the darkest to you, if you get frustrated and feel like you are failing, just remember this: it's hard to do much worse than the government schools.

Homeschooling resources

Beyond Survival: A Guide to Abundant -Life Homeschooling

By Diana Waring

This is more of a touchy-feely type of book with lots of encouragement and insights into the why's and how's of homeschooling.

Street price $12

Diana Waring - History Alive!
122 W. Grant Street
Spearfish, SD 57783
302-369-9176
www.dianawaring.com

The Big Book(s) of Home Learning: 3 Volume Set

By Mary Pride

Mary Pride's dry wit, personal touch, and down-to-earth style make us all want to have 9 kids and homeschool all-year-round! Reviews and describes curriculum with teaching tips and how-to's. This set of books is essential for all homeschooling families, especially those new to homeschooling. Even as a veteran homeschooler, I found this series absolutely invaluable for planning my homeschooling purchases, lessons and schedule.

Street price $69/3-volume set

Home Life
PO Box 1250
Fenton, MO 63026
800-346-6322
http://www.home-school.com

Christian Home Educators' Curriculum Manual

Elementary Edition 2000

Jr. and Sr. High School Edition 2000

By Cathy Duffy

Cathy Duffy reviews and describes many types of curricula available to homeschoolers. Describes teaching methods and learning styles. A must have for any home educator.

Street price $20 each

Grove Publishing
16172 Huxley Circle
Westminster, CA 92683
714-841-1220
www.grovepublishing.com
E-mail: info@grovepublishing.com

Educating the WholeHearted Child: A Handbook for Christian Home Educators

By Clay and Sally Clarkson.

How to use real books and real life to make your home a vibrant center of living and learning for you and your child. I really enjoy this book's homey feel.

Street price $21

Whole Heart Ministries
PO Box 67
Walnut Springs, TX 76690
254-797-2142
www.wholeheart.org

Dreamers of a Godless Utopia

By Michael Chapman.

If you have any doubts that the government schools have an anti-Christian agenda, this book will convince you. Extensively researched, this book examines current school curricula and textbooks and exposes the blatant bias and revisionist history. The one example that really stuck in my mind was the quote from a 5th grade textbook that said, "There is less poverty [in Cuba] since Castro gained control." That is a blatant lie and just one example of how communism is glorified in current secular textbooks. Many other examples show extensive anti-Christian bias as well. Other textbooks promote pagan religions. *World Adventures in Time and Place*, a 6th-grade social studies textbook, instructs the child to read aloud this prayer in a section on Egypt: "Hail O Nile, who comes to give life to the people of Egypt. Created by the sun-god to give life to all who thirst…" Dear brethren, this stuff *is* in the public schools, please do not ignore this. Homeschooling will save our generation because instead of allowing our children to be "brainwashed" with the errors and lies of Satan, we will be able to wash our children's brains (and souls) in the Word and in truth.

Street price $10
American Heritage Research
PO Box 1291
Minnetonka, MN 55345
Fax: (952) 974-1445

The Right Choice

By Chris Klicka

This book will give you all the right reasons and statistics to start homeschooling and stay homeschooling. Excellent ammunition for disarming those doubting relatives.

Street price $12

Noble Publishing Associates
PO Box 2250
Gresham, OR 97030
503-667-3942
800-225-5259 (orders only).

The Ultimate Guide to Homeschooling 2001 Edition

By Debra Bell

Street price $16

A great book for beginners. Lots of "how-to-do-it" and "where to find it."

Debra Bell's Home School Resource Center
1425 East Chocolate Avenue
Hershey, PA 17078
800-937-6311
www.hsrc.com

HOMESCHOOL MAGAZINES

Practical Homeschooling

This is Mary Pride's magazine and you can tell! Packed with comprehensive and witty reviews, this magazine focuses on understanding and using multitudes of homeschooling resources and materials. They review tons of top-notch homeschooling products, new and old. Resources are listed with places to find it all. They also have a large section devoted to computers and homeschooling and cover a vast array of subjects in each issue, including online courses and services, editorials, web sites, software and hardware reviews, computer news, and more. Also included are web site, distance learning and online academy reviews. PHS reviews are substantial, often filling whole pages rather than a few short paragraphs like other magazines. I highly recommend subscribing. The subscription price will pay for itself in helping you choose computer resources wisely. (It con-

tains enough information to fill a paperback book with each issue.) Also check out their web site for links to other homeschool resources. Call (800) 346-6322 and please tell them Dan and Tammy Kihlstadius sent you!

$19.95/year 6 issues.

Home Life
PO Box 1190
Fenton, MO 63026
800-346-6322.
www.home-school.com.

Home School Digest

This is the magazine that claims to be for "the serious homeschooler" and it is. Addressing issues such as courtship, discipline, and more, this quarterly magazine offers solid Biblical teaching for all aspects of raising and educating children. I really enjoy this magazine, but it is really convicting to the heart. If you sign up for a subscription for yourself, you can subscribe for a friend as well at no extra cost!

$18/year 4 issues.

Wisdom's Gate
P.O. Box 374-www
Covert, MI 49043.
E-mail: wisgate@characterlink.net
www.homeschooldigest.com

Homeschooling Today

This magazine is excellent for those homeschoolers who enjoy unit studies or literature-based studies. It includes resources and guides for these types of studies. One of my favorite features is the inclusion of a beautiful print of a famous masterpiece and a study guide (by David Quine) for the artwork and artist in each issue.

$14.99/ for your 1st year, $19.99 for

every year after.

Homeschooling Today
PO Box 1608
Fort Collins, CO 80522-1608
970-493-2716
www.homeschooltoday.com.

The Teaching Home

This magazine has the feel of a support group meeting with a lot of advice and encouragement. Not many curriculum reviews, but much practical how-to advice. Great for first time homeschoolers! Don't be discouraged by the picture-perfect family on the cover! The staff carefully screens advertisers, and only allows ads from companies they personally approve of so you can order from advertisers with a higher level of assurance of quality and the ability to deliver on product claims. Order the magazine online and save 25%!

$20/year; $30/2 years; 6 issues/year.

The Teaching Home
PO Box 20219
Portland, OR 97294
503-253-9633
www.teachinghome.com

Homeschool organizations

Homeschool Legal Defense Association

Every homeschooler should belong to this organization. When you become a member for $100/year, they guarantee to represent you in court if you are ever in any homeschool legal battles. Even if you don't think you will ever go to court, think of your membership as helping the home-schoolers who do and an investment in the ministry to keep homeschooling legal.

Homeschool Legal Defense Association
PO Box 300, Purcellville, VA 20134

540-338-5600
www.hslda.org

NATHHAN: National Association of Challenged Homeschoolers

This organization is dedicated to helping homeschoolers who have handicaps. Topics covered include: Down's Syndrome, blindness, ADD, ADHD, deafness, and more. A lot of practical Biblical advice and resources. I highly recommend their newsletter.

$25/year 6 issues of their newsletter and membership

NATional cHallenged Homeschoolers Associated Network
PO Box 39
Porthill, ID 83853
(208) 267-6246
E-Mail: NATHANEWS@AOL.COM
www.nathhan.com

Chapter Two

Choosing Software

INTRODUCTION TO CHOOSING

There are thousands of educational programs, all claiming to be the best. Let's examine criteria for judging software value, choosing software, specific software recommendations, and using it in your homeschool.

Good software is not cheap. The old adage "You get what you pay for" is VERY true. "Shareware" software is cheap, but very little comes close to the quality of commercially available software. (Shareware is software distributed free or for a minimal fee, but then obligates to pay a set fee ranging from $10-$40 if you like it and want to keep it.) On the other hand, commercial software has more features, better sound and quality graphics. Remember, when choosing commercial software, most software companies back their programs with a 100% satisfaction guarantee. If for any reason you don't like it, send it back to the manufacturer within 90 days of purchase and get a full refund! One company, Knowledge Adventure, allows you to return product up to a year after purchase.

Where to find and who to buy it from

When you are ready to purchase any of the titles listed in this Guide, check the Appendix of Software Resellers. The companies listed are all owned and run by Christian homeschool families. Please try *The Home Computer Market* first. They try to have all my top ten titles in stock at all times. They usually have most of the other titles in stock or can special order them for you. They offer competitive pricing, phone or online ordering and top-notch service.

If you cannot find a particular title from a reseller, your next best bet is to call the company directly. See the Appendix of Software Publishers for their phone number and web site. Most offer online ordering as well.

Consider your children's learning styles: would they prefer more visual interaction, audio stimulation, or hands-on interface? Most software can teach to all learning styles. Look for software that is age-appropriate and doesn't push the child to master skills for which he's not yet ready. Many of the better software programs have adjustable skill levels designed to accommodate the differing abilities of different children in the same family. On the other hand, make sure your children won't outgrow the program too soon.

Find software that is easy-to-use or intuitive, (meaning that the goals and methods in each program are somewhat self-explanatory to the user.) Some software is so intuitive that your children can work independently without you "holding their hand." On the other hand, some software is best used with the teacher sitting right there. The *Mighty Math* series is an example of software designed to be used by the teacher to demonstrate and explain concepts. Software should also be flexible with regards to how the child interacts with the program, allowing them to use a mouse, the keyboard, or an alternate device—whichever is easiest for that child. Touch screens and voice-activated computers are available for children with special needs. Autistic children are communicating for the first time using computers. We personally know of a 17-year-old boy, once considered unreachable and a mental vegetable for most of his life. He is just now communicating, exhibiting remarkable intelligence, and reaching out to his family for the first time ever—through the computer keyboard! If you have questions about what's available for handicapped children, read the article on special needs.

When it comes time to choose software for special-needs children, ask questions about the program's features and ease of use. Seek out counsel from other families with computers. We strongly urge you to check out Mary Pride's magazine *Practical Homeschooling* for current educational software reviews.

SOFTWARE COMPANIES

When we first started reviewing software, there were only several dozen educational software companies and only a few hundred educational software programs worth looking at. Almost eight years later, this small industry has exploded into about 700 software companies with over 5000 software programs. Most of the industry leaders of ten years ago are still here, although some may have new names or have been bought out by bigger publishers. About half-a-dozen major publishers now dominate the market; and each one has different philosophy and a different market strategy. To help you select software, we wanted to let you know the track record and personality of each of these companies. Some companies consistently produce winners; some are hit or miss. Some have a near-perfect track record for producing wholesome, Christian-homeschool friendly software; some rarely produce anything Christians would want in their home.

The Learning Company

The Learning Company, or TLC, is one of the granddaddies of educational software and is the developer of the classic, but extremely successful, Reader Rabbit series. TLC also owns, as its subsidiaries, other well-known software companies: Mindscape (*Mavis Beacon*), Princeton Review, MECC (*Oregon Trail*), Creative Wonders (*Sesame Street* and *Madeline* titles), Broderbund (*Carmen Sandiego),* Parson's Technology (*QuickVerse*), Cyan (*Myst*) and more. Overall the company produces good titles with a few must-haves in the bunch. For wholesomeness, you can't do better than *Reader Rabbit*, but a few of the other titles may contain objectionable items. All

Learning Company software carries a 90-day, money-back, 100% satisfaction guarantee and can be returned directly to the company for a refund. Just don't lose your receipt. Tech support is good but not toll-free.

Knowledge Adventure

There once was a dad who wanted his kids to have educational software that was high quality but fun software to play with. So he made a program called *Science Adventure* and another called *Space Adventure*. They were sorta fun and sorta educational. But what he did differently than other software companies was to guarantee that your family would *love* them or you get your money back up to a year after your purchase.

Urged on by the success of the first two programs, he came out with *JumpStart Kindergarten*. A group of age-specific and entertaining activities, this program was an instant hit. Suddenly, parents wanted more of this grade-specific software designed to entertain their public-school-burned-out kids. Knowledge Adventure (KA) complied and produced *Jumpstart First Grade, Preschool, Toddler, Second Grade* and so on. All were big hits. To expand Knowledge Adventure's domain, the company bought Davidson, a veteran of school oriented educational software, older then KA itself. The owner, Jan Davidson, was a teacher at heart and in past occupation. She had developed some classic, kid-pleasin', teacher-pleasin' software including *Math Blaster* and *Kid Works*. If you buy a Knowledge Adventure title, you have an entire year to decide if you like it! Just return the program to Knowledge Adventure with your receipt to get your complete purchase price back! Tech support is good *and* toll-free.

Edmark

Edmark (now owned by IBM) consistently produces the highest-quality educational titles in the market (in my humble opinion), as well as the most wholesome titles you can find. *Kid Desk* is one of their titles. The brains behind Edmark are primarily educators dedicated to high-quality development and production. Most of their titles are primarily designed for school use and are also very adaptable to special-needs kids as well. They also make the *Touch Window*, a product that allows children to interact with programs by just touching the screen. If a title is from Edmark, you can bet it's worth buying! One feature we see consistent in every Edmark title is that all of the characters exhibit the best and most polite manners. Phrases such as "May I please" and "Thank you" are the standard rule between the player and characters. We actually spoke with the people at Edmark about this and they said that kindness and good manners are a standard that is built into every Edmark title! And it shows! Tech support is good but not toll-free.

Dorling Kindersley

Although Dorling Kindersley products (both software and books) are sold through party plans (like Tupperware) they are some of the best out there. The company is based in England but distributed widely in the USA. Most of their CDs are jam-packed with information, games and activities. They are also colorful, engaging and fun. We recommend quite a few of their titles.

Humongous Entertainment

Humongous Entertainment titles do not stress education as their primary purpose; they stress good, wholesome fun. They have developed some of most lovable software characters: Putt Putt, Fatty Bear, Spy Fox, and Freddi Fish. My kids love all the titles and there is not a bad one in the bunch in terms of quality. Now Humongous has added Blue's Clues as another character to round out the favorites. Great graphics, stories and sound are hallmarks of Humongous Entertainment.

Disney Interactive

I don't include many Disney titles because most are related to their movies and most of their movies revolve around magic (a.k.a. the occult). (See our article on Software and the Occult.) However, I am a big *Toy Story* and *Winnie the Pooh* fan and have reviewed some of those titles. Not a lot of educational value, but enjoyable.

SECRET SOFTWARE SCAM (RECYCLED SOFTWARE)

The secret scam of the software industry: recycled software

These past few years I have noticed a new trend in the software industry: recycled software. Recycled software is software that was once sold under another name. Exact same program, just re-named and re-packaged. Sometimes the program is slightly upgraded; sometimes it is exactly the same version. Another tactic is to bundle it with another program and rename the whole bundle. This pumps up sales on a stale product and brings in new buyers. The stores think they are getting fresh product but it in reality, it's one week old bread put in fresh new wrappers with current dates. In fact, some

of it seems to be a little moldy inside. Do consumers benefit? Absolutely not! In fact, this can be very confusing and costly because they can end up buying software they already own!

Why do they do this? Two reasons:

1. Retailers don't want to keep selling great classic software. They want something new on the shelves continually. So software companies are forced to take old stuff and make it "new."

2. Retailers also charge software companies money to put their titles on the store shelves. You would think it would be the opposite but it is not. The Learning Company, for example, has to pay Best Buy or CompUSA up to 25% of the cost of the software to put it on the shelf. Therefore, not a whole lot of money is left over for research and development of new titles.

The Learning Company is the biggest culprit with dozens of repackaged titles. Let's trace the evolution of just one title:

Reader Rabbit

Reader Rabbit 1

Reader Rabbit Reading 1

Reader Rabbit Reading ages 4-6

Reader Rabbit's Learn to Read With Phonics

Another company guilty of recycling: Knowledge Adventure. Their biggest recycled title: *Math Blaster.*

Math Blaster

Math Blaster Episode 1: Search for Spot

Mega Math Blaster

Math Blaster 6-9

Math Blaster Third Grade

Math Blaster 6-9 (again)

Another tactic company's employ is taking a series of older titles and repacking them into a completely new series. For example, Knowledge Adventure took their older versions of top-selling Jumpstarts and a few other older Davidson titles and re-packaged them into the *Learning Center Series. Learning Center Series: Toddler* is just the original 1996 version of *Jumpstart Toddler. Learning Center Series: Math Ages 7-9* is the original 1996 version of *Math Blaster Episode 1: Search for Spot.* The Learning Company did the same with some of their older titles, repackaging them into the *Leap Ahead Series. Leap Ahead: Reading* is the same *Word Munchers Deluxe* we have been recommending for years. *Leap Ahead! Math Ages 6-9* is *Treasure Mathstorm*, a program from 1996.

In our reviews, we try to list any previous names of the program so you know what you are getting. Sometimes you can get the exact same version in older packaging for less. Sometimes you can get a new bundle with two programs for the price of one. For example, *Reader Rabbit's Learn to Read With Phonics* includes both *Reader Rabbit 1* and *Interactive Reading Journey.* Both are great programs and a lot cheaper in this bundled set.

When shopping, remember this tip: check the back of the box in the fine print. If it is recycled, it should say, "Previously sold as XXXX." Or something similar. But be forewarned, not all recycled software is labeled as such. Also, check our web site: homeschooladvisor.com for updates.

Here are the recycled titles we know of now:

Leap Ahead 2nd Grade is *Treasure Cove*

Leap Ahead Phonics is *Kid Phonics*

Leap Ahead Kindergarten is *JumpStart Kindergarten*

Leap Ahead Math 6-9 is *Treasure MathStorm*

Learning Center Series: Toddler: is *Jumpstart Toddler* (1996 version)

Learning Center Series: Spelling and Grammar: is *Spell It Deluxe* and *Grammar Games*

TYPES & FUNCTIONS OF SOFTWARE

Do you want to target a specific subject area or do you want a comprehensive or integrated program that can teach a variety of subjects and skills, e.g. math, science and logic? The subjects available are plentiful: phonics, math, algebra, music and piano, physics, foreign and classical languages, geometry, logic, history, geography and more! How do you want to present the material? Each educational program has a different way of "interfacing" with the student. The main modes of interface are drill, arcade-action game, research & reference, simulation, kid-size word processor, discovery and tutorial.

Drills...

A drill-based program will most likely test on and reinforce material your child has already learned. These types of programs offer the ability to customize exactly what type of material your child will practice, and the ability to track your student's progress. They may also offer the ability to design your own games. Some drill titles include *PhonicsTutor* (which teaches as well), *NumberMaze Challenge* (elementary math), *World Discovery Deluxe* (World and U.S. geography) and *Reading Mansion* (reading). The best drill titles, such as these, are designed to present the material so effectively that the child is learning these topics as well. These are among the best in educational software and well worth the investment.

Reference & research...

A reference or research program will contain activities or games that encourage research and investigation into several topics via a mini-encyclopedia or textbook integrated into the program. We recommend *ADAM: The Inside Story* (Anatomy) and *Eyewitness Encyclopedia of Science 2.0* (Jr. and Sr. High science) from Dorling Kindersley. Most of the Dorling Kindersley titles even have built-in quizzes to test learning retention.

There are full-sized multimedia encyclopedias, dictionaries, Bible study packages, atlases, and many other major reference materials available on CD-ROM. The best multimedia CD-ROM encyclopedias for homeschool use include *World Book* and *Compton's. Compton's 3-D Atlas* is also a fine resource for the homeschool. These resources can truly enrich the homeschool learning experience. One title we do not care for is Microsoft's encyclopedia *Encarta*. Unless you are specifically looking for content that is politically correct, environmentally correct, evolutionary, anti-Christian with a morally liberal slant, we suggest you avoid this program.

Simulation...

Simulations are programs in which you are in control—you're the designer. For example, in *SimCity 3000*, you design an entire city from the ground up: the roads, the electricity, the lakes, where the residential, commercial and industrial zones go, the taxes, and more. These types of programs involve highly complex artificial intelligence (this means the computer does some heavy-duty thinkin'!) to project outcomes based on your actions or decisions. In *My Amazing Science Explorer*, conduct your own science experiments!

In *Oregon Trail 4*, wise decision-making is critical to success in the program. You are in charge of a small party of pioneers on your way out west. When you need to cross a wide river, you are faced with two choices: should you take the ferry or float your wagon across the river? It costs precious money to take the ferry, but floating across is free. As the player eventually learns, if you take the risk floating across the river, you may tip over and all drown! You never know when because the events happen randomly based on a probability of them happening. This part of the program makes for a good object lesson—that our actions have consequences, sometimes good and sometimes bad. In this case, the wrong decision can actually cost the lives of some of your make-believe family. Simulations allow students to test ideas and theories without the fear of failure (or loss of life and limb...or even your kitchen table!) or large amounts of liability insurance.

Discovery...

If you have little ones, discovery programs are the best. In this style of program, the child chooses and "clicks on" an item or character on screen with the mouse or on screen cursor and something happens. For example, a character or object moves, talks or initiates activity with the child. There are several very educational and enjoyable programs available that will entertain, stimulate and teach your young ones. We recommend any of the *Putt Putt* series, *Busytown*, *Reader Rabbit*, *Sammy's Science House*, and *Millie's Math House.*

Word processing...

There are several "kid-sized" word processors that can help your child get their ideas and thoughts onto paper. *Imagination Express* or *Storybook Weaver Deluxe* are for ages 5-12 and will motivate almost any child into writing and illustrating story-books. For actual word processing and creating school-like reports, *The Ultimate Writing and Creativity Center* is our favorite for ages 7-13. If you have older kids, *The Student Writing and Research Center* will enable your student to easily design, edit, produce and publish first-rate reports, letters, stories, newsletters and even booklets. Also check out the desktop publishing software that came with your computer, most likely Microsoft Works or Word. Each will allow the student to choose formats (2 column, 3 column etc.), fonts, font sizes, and pictures. Some wonderful homeschool projects using word processors could include writing letters or e-mails to relatives, congressmen, and missionaries; or creating small booklets. Create a family newsletter and scan in some favorite family photos; publish works on your own homemade web site. The Internet gives students an ever-wider audience, thus adding incentive to their efforts at written communication, by making the publishing and distribution process much easier.

Computerized curriculums...

When we ran our software mail order business, hardly a week went by that we didn't get a call from somebody requesting a computerized school curriculum for his or her child.

Unfortunately, up until recently, we have had nothing to offer them. Then Alpha Omega Publications came out with *Switched-On Schoolhouse* (Available for 3rd-12th grade), which is essentially the *Alpha & Omega LifePacs* curriculum on computer. For the benefit of those of you who are unfamiliar with *Alpha & Omega*, it is a Christian-based, workbook-formatted curriculum for the subjects of math, science, history and geography, language art, and Bible.

With a few exceptions, most things that call themselves a curriculum, course or tutorial are not. Or at least they are not as seen through the eyes of parents trying to use it to actually teach a child. Most computer programs don't actually thoroughly teach fresh, new concepts that a student doesn't already have some basic understanding of. Very few of these self-proclaimed computerized curriculums have the ability to take subject matter that was previously totally unknown and teach it in a way that the student will be able to independently fully grasp and comprehend. Most such programs operate under the assumption that the student has already been introduced to the material and/or is already working with some other core material and/or full curriculum. Such software programs usually simply review and drill on what the student has learned elsewhere.

The *ALS (Advanced Learning Systems)* programs from American Education Corporation are a basic computerized curriculum series for grades 1-12. They teach the bare essentials of a subject level and are a barebones curriculum. ALS presents the lesson, offers a practice test and then gives a 10-question test; thus it is basically an interactive computerized textbook. Subjects available include world and US history and geography, science, reading, English grammar and vocabulary, and more. Another exciting option in *ALS* is the ability to "author" your own lessons. With *ALS* you can write up the material, add pictures or diagrams and design your own questions. *ALS* is an excellent and inexpensive option for moms who don't have the time or the confidence to teach these topics, but want to be sure all essential curricula areas are covered. If you do consider using *ALS*, keep in mind it was developed for use in public and private schools, though I have not seen anything objectionable in the material we have used and/or reviewed.

Before you can best utilize a computer program, you need to understand what type of program it was designed to be. There are some wonderful multimedia reference programs that would not work as a core curriculum, but would make a great supplement to an existing curriculum. On the other hand, there are some good programs that make a basis for a curriculum, but either aren't multimedia enough, or lack the depth that most parents expect in a full curriculum. By combining both types of programs for a more balanced curriculum, you can get the best of both worlds.

An example of this would be using the *ALS* series as a core curriculum. Each unit is well structured as a course or curriculum. These programs have a broad range of material covered within each topic and are well organized in covering most key areas. Their weak points are that they are mainly text with a few graphics. Whereas the depth maybe sufficient enough for public school usage, most homeschooling families prefer greater depth, variety and rigor.

At the other end of the spectrum, the

Dorling Kindersley programs offer wonderful multimedia coverage with sound, videos, animations, and vivid graphics. Each item is usually thoroughly covered in great depth and detail. Also, the programs make great use of built-in links to related topics.

For those of you not familiar with the term "links", a link is a highlighted word, usually in a different color, that, when clicked on with your cursor, will take you to a different screen which has that highlighted word as the main topic. Your child might start out studying about "X". While studying the main topic "X", they see something about "Y". They click on "Y" and from "Y" end up at "Z." At this point the child ends up at "Z" with a total fascination of the new material. Had you assigned "Z" as a topic from the start, your child's interest and retention of material would probably be significantly less compared to their studying "Z" as a result of following their own natural curiosity.

This method of teaching works so very well with what we refer to as the "exploitation method" of teaching. (Remember, you heard that term here first!) You are exploiting children's natural desire to explore and learn on their own. With this method you use the outline of a general curriculum while studying in depth those areas of your child's greatest interests. As you well know, an interested, motivated child learns and retains far more than one who is not interested.

Tutorials...

Most importantly, there are tutorial programs that will teach an entire subject step-by-step. A tutorial is different than most computerized curriculum because a tutorial fully teaches the subject. A computerized curriculum is primarily a workbook on a computer with automatic grading. Contrast this with the foreign language tutorial *The Rosetta Stone* which blends sound, pictures, and artificial intelligence to *train* students in speaking a foreign language without needing any additional supplementation. However, some computerized curriculums, such as *Switched-On Schoolhouse*, are so good that they can pass for computerized tutorials as well.

Some examples of tutorial-type programs

For pre-readers, *Let's Go Read: An Island Adventure* will teach and drill simple phonics. Small children love the colorful, sharp graphics, engaging interface, and clear, accurate voice and phonics sound. This program could essentially teach all the beginning phonics you'll need! *Let's Go Read: An Ocean Adventure* is this program's sequel and teaches letter blends, alphabetizing, building words and rhyming words. For more intensive phonics fun combined with a typing tutor for older (6-9) children, we find *Read, Write and Type* from The Learning Company very effective.

PhonicsTutor is a comprehensive tutorial patterned after Sam Blumenfeld's phonics, reading and spelling program *Alpha-Phonics*. Designed to sequentially teach a student of any age phonics, reading, capitalization, punctuation, and spelling; this program can truly be your entire phonics and learn-to-read curriculum! It is probably the most thorough and comprehensive computer program on the subject. (See *PhonicsTutor* review on page 101.) *PhonicsTutor* is a little on the 'dry' side (text and speech only, like electronic flash cards—no hopping bunnies or animation), but it is among the best for what it covers. It is the only phonics software we use everyday in our homeschool. Right now I have three children of three different age levels using it everyday!

All agree that typing and keyboard skills are essential these days and your computer can best teach you how. *Typing Instructor Deluxe* is a highly rated, proven program that teaches typing to any student age 8 and up! Proficient typing skills can give a job applicant an edge in a competitive job market.

Despairing over not being able to supplement your child's schooling with piano lessons? Want to learn piano yourself? Take a look at the *Piano Discovery*. This program comes with one year's worth of thorough, step-by-step piano lessons (additional years can be bought). Hook up your MIDI keyboard and away you go!

For high-school level we find *Math Teacher* for Algebra, Calculus or Geometry to be wonderful, step-by-step tutorials, incorporating graphics and diagrams to fully teach each subject. In addition, there are excellent foreign language tutorials available. The foreign languages available include Vietnamese, Japanese, Latin, Polish, Hindi, Korean, Thai, Arabic, Hebrew, Swahili, Indonesian, Turkish, Chinese (Mandarin), Russian, Welsh, Portuguese, Italian, Luxembourgish, and the list is growing everyday. Unfortunately, we have not been able to find any Thermian language software.

Arcade game or "edutainment"...

If your child enjoys arcade-action games, several excellent programs combine the drill or learning features with a fun game. This combination of entertainment and education is called "edutainment." Just remember my rule of thumb, look for programs with at least a 50/50 ratio of education to fun. This mean about half the time the child is drilling on important subject material and the other half of the time they are playing a game. (The drill programs mentioned above have at least an 80/20 ratio of education to fun.) Edutainment programs with at least a 50/50 ratio include the *Reader Rabbit*, *Math Blaster*, *Reading Blaster* and *Jumpstart* series. Their format consists of an arcade-style game interspersed with drills and various problems. Some of these types of programs are over-rated in their educational value; just take the claims of the publisher with a grain of salt. (See the article on *"But Mom, it's BOOOORING.")* On the other hand, kids who try *Lost Mind of Dr. Brain* love it. They think they are playing a game, but are actually challenging their math, word, logic, and thinking skills. Mary Pride gives it her highest rating, calling it "…a high-IQ adventure game." We love it too! *The Logical Journey of the Zoombinis* is a "game" as well, but children who are playing it are developing pre-algebraic and algebraic thinking skills without the use of numbers!

Other "must-have" software programs…

Most homeschooling families want their children spending more time learning about their Bible. Of all the Bible programs we've seen, *Bible Builder* outdoes them all. *Bible Builder* is a Bible-trivia style game that challenges both children and adults. We consider this a must-have for every family with an IBM-compatible computer. *Family Bible Challenge* is a new program we have seen that is as good as *Bible Builder*; its advantages are that is runs on both Windows and Macintosh computer and the ability to have it read the questions out-loud to the nonreaders in the family. It also has some additional Bible games as well as the "trivia" questions.

I also recommend every family investing in a Bible Study Software package. We recommend the *Online Bible* ("online" does not mean it runs through the Internet but "online" on your computer) for Windows or Macintosh. This is the best Bible package for the money. There are others out there: *QuickVerse* (Parsons Technology), *Logos* (Logos Research Systems), *WORDsearch* (NavPress), *PC Study Bible* (BibleSoft), and they are all excellent as well. For in-depth reviews of Bible research software, check out *Christian Computing Magazine* (www.ccmag.com), an excellent source for information on Bible programs and church management software.

Another must-have title is some sort of family finance/checkbook program. Our two picks are *Quicken* and *Microsoft Money*. Both are great and may even already be on your computer. I have used both and they are very similar in ease of use and quality. I am notoriously negligent in maintaining a checkbook and these programs have been real lifesavers. We recently opened a checking account at a new bank and needed to set up all the new transactions in *Microsoft Money*. I went to the bank's web site and was able to download (with a password of course) my transaction history right into the program on my computer—I did not need to enter every check or deposit! Quicken also offers online banking. Larry Burkett's organization, *Crown Financial Concepts* (www.cfcministry.org), publishes a great budgeting program called *Money Matters 2000*. To read an extensive review of *Money Matters 2000* vs. *Quicken*, check the *No Debt Living* web site: www.nodebtnews.com/articles.asp?ID=35 However, we have not seen *Money Matters 2000* ourselves.

Last but not least, *Kid Desk* is a program

for moms and dads designed to keep their computer safe from little hackers and not-so-little hackers, while making it easy for even nonreaders to run your programs. *Kid Desk* works by replacing the standard *Microsoft Windows* (or Macintosh) interface with a different, simpler, child-safe interface. Along with replacing the Windows desktop, it hides all the standard icons (little pictures) on the desktop as well as the start button, the menus and the entire task bar. What each child does see is his or her own customized, cartoon-style desk with only the icons of the programs that Mom and Dad want that child using. Different desktops can be created for each child in the family. Even 3-year-olds are able to recognize, choose and run their own programs without causing a disaster on your hard drive. The newest version, *Kid Desk Internet Safe*, also offers Internet protection. (Money-saving tip: You can download a *free* basic version of *Kid Desk* called *Kid Desk Lite* from the Edmark web site: www.edmark.com. What a deal! It can't get any better than a great product for free. You can even download other free programs. Go log on now. You can finish reading later!) Once set up, there is nothing that we know of that makes any computer easier to use for both you and your children!

QUICK TIPS BEFORE CHOOSING EDUCATIONAL SOFTWARE

When comparing prices, please, please, please remember that you almost always get what you pay for. More expensive software usually has more features, better sound, quality graphics, and significantly more content. There is almost always a good reason why one program is $29.99 and another "similar" program is $9.99. Remember, we live in a very capitalistic country. (And capitalism is a very good thing!) So always keep in mind one of the most basic laws of capitalism (in addition to the previously mentioned, "You get what you pay for." Or at least you hope you do!). Most marketing departments set the price of their products relative to how it compares with the competition. And they probably know more about the content and level of quality of their competition than you do. Consequently, if company A's software is priced at $9.99 and company B's software is $29.99 that should give you a hint as to what each company knows about the worth of the two programs.

As with most everything (except, of course, God's truths and principles) there are usually some exceptions to this whole you-get-what-you-pay-for thing. Sometimes you can buy software without all the fancy packaging. You buy the program in just the little plastic CD-holder case. (That case is called a "jewel case" We will be discussing this more later.) Buying software in this reduced, economy packaging can knock $10, $20, or even more off the price!

In addition to packaging differences, bear in mind that there are newer and older versions of many programs. Sometimes there are major differences between subsequent versions of the same program, and other times there are only minor differences. (See the article on "*Recycled Software*" for more detail because this is very important to understand and know about when you are shopping for software. The bottom line is if an older version is very similar to the latest version, there is no point in paying three times the price for the latest version. It may also be the case that you do not need all the fancy new 3-D graphics and bells-and-whistles of the latest release, if the previous version has all the functionality you need. (By now you have probably figured out that we think really cheap in our household. We have to with eight children!)

Still yet another factor to consider is the age of your computer. If your computer is older, you might be compelled to go with older versions of software anyway. For example, if the latest version of a particular program requires a minimum speed of 300 MHz, and your computer is only 166 MHz, then it won't work on your computer; however the previous release most likely would run on it. So in this situation, a "recycled" older version would actually suit your needs even better than the most recent release would.

Here are some tips for choosing between similar software programs:

• Check the age ranges. Program "A" might be $10 cheaper than program "B", but program "B" might cover twice the age range. This is especially important if you have multiple children taking advantage of different difficulty levels of the same program.

• Consider your child's learning style. Would he prefer a more visual interaction, audio stimulation or hands-on interface? Does the software narrate the material or require the child to read on his own? Most software teaches to all learning styles simultaneously, but some are very limited in its teaching style.

• Most programs have editing features that allow you to customize topics and difficulty.

• Consider your objectives:

Do you want to target a specific subject?

Do you want a comprehensive or integrated program that can teach a variety of subjects and skills?

Are you looking for a drill, tutorial, game, or a reference & research program?

• Last of all, this should go without saying, but it is important enough to remind everyone to check the system requirements of the software to make sure it runs on your computer.

QUESTION: WHAT IN THE WORLD DOES "J/C ONLY" MEAN?

Answer: J/C means Jewel Case, without the fancy cardboard box.

Question: So what's a Jewel Case?

Answer: A Jewel Case is the technical name for the plastic case that holds the CD when it isn't in the computer. You know, the little plastic case you keep telling your children to put the CD back into when they are done using the program.

Question: Why do the programs in the fancy cardboard boxes cost so much more?

Answer: It's called marketing and advertising.

Question: So why would I want to spend more to get a fancy cardboard box?

Answer: Either because it looks good sitting on your shelf or maybe because you want to contribute to the local landfill.

Question: Is that it? Is there anything else in those fancy cardboard boxes?

Answer: Yes. Air.

Question: Air?

Answer: Yes. Air. Usually these fancy boxes have absolutely nothing inside them except air, extra cardboard packaging, and probably a registration card for you to send in and get on 53 different mailing lists.

Question: What if I want to get on those 53 different mailing lists, but I only purchase the J/C version?

Answer: Well, most marketing departments have spent thousands of dollars researching this very problem and they usually come to some creative solution that enables you to fulfill that need to get your mailbox stuffed with junk mail on a regular basis.

Question: Is the program the same as the fancy box version?

Answer: Usually. Sometimes the J/C version will be the previous version, as opposed to the current release. If so, we try to mention that fact. But usually it is exactly same. In fact, some programs only come in J/C versions, and there is not any boxed version available.

Question: What about manuals?

Answer: Almost every CD contains "read me" text files or manual that can be read on the computer screen or printed out that have all the information needed to install, use, and troubleshoot the program. Also, most CDs contain a small manual inside the front cover of the CD jewel case. Some programs that require more information will come with the same full size manual as found in the box version.

Question: If J/C versions are such a great deal, why don't we see more of them in the stores?

Answer: Again, for the answer, we go to those brilliant college graduates in the marketing departments in skyscrapers somewhere, whose sole purpose in life is to convince, using any LEGAL means necessary (half truths, slick phrases, misconceptions, etc.), unsuspecting consumers to spend their hard-earned money on the contents of this fancy, attractive cardboard box. The fancy graphics (which usually look nothing like the chunky graphics YOU see on the computer screen) and promises of academic excellence are what they use to convince most unsuspecting, uninformed consumers to buy. You, on the other hand, are armed with the truth from *The Homeschool Advisor*! You will know what is really is inside those fancy boxes because we have spent our time and our money and have reviewed it for you. Which relates to our other goal here at *The Homeschool Advisor*: to save you money! J/C versions are always significantly cheaper. Also keep in mind that J/C versions often have limited availability, but on the brighter side, we are seeing better availability of J/C only type packaging than we used to see.

Again, all this brings us to a point that we have made before. In our humble opinion, based on our values, beliefs, and perspectives, much of the hype on many of those fancy boxes is so misleading as to be considered a lie. Now those statements on the fancy boxes may be true enough *LEGALLY* as to avoid lawsuits, but not necessarily accurate in the way we see things in the real world. Or as we have stated before, when a program says "teaches" it usually only "drills" what the child was taught somewhere else. Programs that say "covers a full year of..." or "for ages 12-15" do NOT mean that they are a comprehensive curriculum that covers everything for that time period, and you don't need anything else. Usually what it does mean is that it covers the same subject matter as would be appropriate for that range. This meaning it is probably too hard for the "typical" child younger than the year (or grade) range listed, and too easy for the "typical" child older than the year (or grade) range listed. Note that I put "typical" in quotes. What is "typical" does not mean "homeschooled." So when you are looking at the age range, factor in how your child compares academically to "public institutionalized" children of a similar age.

(Sorry for getting off on a tangent there. Now, back to our regularly scheduled Q & A.)

Question: What if the program is defective or I need technical support?

Answer: As far as defective CDs, our experience has been that nearly every CD that people have sent to us as "defective" turned out to work fine on our computers here and was not defective at all. So usually the fault is with the unique system configuration of their computer. But if the CD truly is defective, most companies will replace it either free or for a nominal fee. Nearly every educational software company that I know of offers free technical support for the products they manufacture. You may have to pay a long distance phone charge and be on hold for a while, but they will help you. On the other hand, software companies do go out of business (such as Sanctuary Woods did in 1999.) Although you can still find their titles on the market, don't bet on getting any technical support.

Chapter Three

HOW TO USE SOFTWARE IN YOUR HOMESCHOOL ...

TOP 11 WAYS TO UTILIZE A COMPUTER IN YOUR HOMESCHOOL!

1. A computer can motivate unmotivated learners.

If you change your children's attitude from "Do I have too?" into "May I?!" there will be a 180° change from "teacher burnout" into "learning fun." Our children see the computer as a reward and opportunity, not just one more workbook or curriculum that must be finished before they can do what they want to do. Usually what they want to do is get on the computer and use educational software! If your child finds a particular subject difficult or "boring", use a fun software program for drill and practice. For example, if your junior high student finds algebra to be real drudgery, use Edmark's *Astro Algebra* to motivate him in new ways. Want to sharpen your high schooler's logic and thinking skills? For introducing mathematical and algebraic concepts without numbers, try *The Logical*

Journey of the Zoombinis. Despite its strange name, this program will keep your preteens on their logic toes for hours! Also, try out Sierra Online's *Lost Mind of Dr. Brain*. Children (10 and up) who play this "game" are really sharpening their logic skills.

On the other hand, computer software can also give *motivated* students the tools and capacity to achieve their fullest potential. Almost all software programs cover at least two or three grade levels worth of material. A mathematically gifted child, for example, is not held back by a grade-level workbook but can cover the material in a math software program as quickly as he is willing and able. *NumberMaze Challenge* covers all basic whole-number math skills from pre-K counting up to 6th-grade, long division word problems. Children can then progress through the levels as they learn the material. In *Ultimate Word Attack*, the students can master new vocabulary as fast as they can work through the levels. Some kids are obsessed with geography and love the challenge of memorizing states, capitols, countries and more. *World Discovery Deluxe* gives these kids all the challenge they could ever want while teaching them geography skills.

2. A computer can reach all types of learning styles and special-needs students.

You can introduce concepts in new ways that appeal to all learning styles. A computer naturally supplies an audio, visual and hands-on interface that can teach to every type of learner. A computer is a powerful learning tool. A computer could also be the tool for your learning disabled child. It allows flexibility in choosing teaching methods that may be more effective. There are excellent writing programs that allow children with special needs to think and write far more fluently than might otherwise be possible. Handicapped children can also find the computer very empowering. Special equipment offers the opportunity to access the computer through elaborate switches, controls and keyboards. There is even a device to allow the user to control the computer through eye movements. Voice recognition software can allow your student to verbalize commands and input into the computer instead of typing the commands or using the mouse. New products are coming out all the time. (Check out the article *Tips for Your Special Kids*!)

3. A computer can prepare children for the job market!

Computer skills are essential to getting many jobs these days. Within five years, we feel that most job applicants will be required to show mastery of basic computer skills such as keyboarding and researching databases. Typing is taught as a regular course in many elementary schools these days. Our neighborhood school has kids learning typing as early as 3rd grade. *Mavis*

Beacon Teaches Typing and *Typing Instructor Deluxe* are wonderful computer tutorials that will teach typing to anyone old enough to read. Other programs are available for teaching other job skills. (See the article on *Top Ten Computer Skills of the Future.*)

4 A computer can give your little ones a head start.

Ever since I started homeschooling, one of the biggest challenges I and other homeschool moms have faced is "What do I do with the little ones while I teach the older ones?" Well, here's your answer! Get them started on a quality phonics software program or an early counting game! My four-year-old son is content to play learning games on the computer for an hour at a time—unassisted! Sometimes his two-year-old brother joins him. They are learning a great deal without Mom having to spend a lot of time in lesson preparation. Now my six-year-old is starting formal schooling (first grade) and he is breezing through his phonics and math workbooks because he played a lot of reading and math games when he was younger. (Tip: in the *Control Panel* of your computer, increase the font size on the screen to make it easier for little eyes.) However, make sure your little ones are not wasting time on the computer; our family limits time to one hour per child per day unless they are doing specific schoolwork activities. Also, have your preschoolers rotate their activities including their computer time. They should still spend time with crayons, play-doh, paints, and Lego's and get involved with natural playtime away from the computer.

5. A computer creates less mess.

A hidden benefit of the computer can be less mess. By having my little ones play their games on the computer, I reduce clutter in the home. Choosing an educational software program over a traditional educational board game is less messy because counting and sorting games on the computer don't have to be picked up, put away, and stored. My kids play puzzles and games on the computer and I don't have to nag them to pick up their mess, and we have yet to lose a single puzzle piece on any of our computer programs! I always recommend software for gift giving as well. Reduced mess is one of the best, hidden advantages to using the computer in your homeschool.

6. A computer can expand learning opportunities.

A computer can offer specialized tutoring and can teach subjects you wouldn't or couldn't teach otherwise: algebra, physics, chemistry, music, piano lessons, typing, computer programming, foreign and classical languages, art, animation, drawing and others! Software is available to teach, tutor and reinforce these subjects. With the advent of online courses, your student may be able to take all types of classes via the Internet from 2nd grade all the way up to college level!

Also, your children can experience, hear, see and do things they normally would never be able to do. For example, my 3-year-old has paved a road, installed a water heater, pumped gas, put out a fire, planted a field, made pretzels, and more, with just the *Busytown* program! My older children have suffered through a drought (*Go West! The Homesteader's Challenge*), heard a native speaker speak Chinese (*Rosetta Stone PowerPac*), designed a city (*SimCity 3000*), hunted buffalo (Oregon Trail 4), run a horse ranch (*SimFarm*), and performed an appendectomy (*Emergency Room Interactive*). (They didn't have to scrub up before surgery or even clean up afterwards!)

Another fun activity for our homeschool has been playing with the stock market. At a web site, www.marketocracy.com, you can get one million dollars in play money and buy and sell real stocks. My 10-year-old son has loved buying shares of Xerox, Mattel, and IBM. I have helped him somewhat but overall his picks did very well. That is, until the market collapsed. Then he learned some very valuable lessons about investing and economics.

The Internet has allowed students to go many places they never could have otherwise. Many museums offer online tours of all their exhibits. See the Mona Lisa anytime you want!

7. A computer can monitor skill proficiency.

When computers first became available for educational purposes, the first software was designed primarily for drill purposes. These programs were made up of simple software that would flash a word or equation on the screen and required the student to input an answer. As software evolved, drill programs became more sophisticated and now you can drill and test on things like math facts, phonics, spelling, typing, SAT preparation, and other skills and knowledge. Most current programs have editing features that allow you to customize for different ability levels and usually have record keeping maintaining a tally of right and wrong answers. Many programs have print utilities to allow printing of worksheets or readers to be used away from the computer, further maximizing the value of the program. *Math Blaster 6-9* can print out customized math worksheets to allow pencil and paper type testing. In addition, a computer is patient and repeats mundane tasks without complaining or tiring. As perfect as all parents want to be, the reality is that we still don't have endless patience or time like a computer does. Some programs can even adapt to the child's abilities. In *PhonicsTutor*, the program automatically re-tests all the missed words in the previous lesson, allowing the child to refine his spelling skills. The Learning Company has developed a new learning technology termed A.D.A.P.T., which pre-tests the child, customizes the learning activities and tailors them specifically to the child's abilities. When the child first uses the program, they take a quick test with a variety of relevant questions with variable difficulty levels. Based on how the child scores, the program starts at a particular spot determined specifically for that child. I predict you will see more of this type of programming technology in years to come.

8. The computer can encourage creativity in almost any child.

My children have made their own letters, pictures and illustrated booklets. They also enjoy writing out Bible verses and illustrating them with *Storybook Weaver Deluxe* on CD-ROM. Prior to introducing the computer to our homeschool, my daughters had great difficulty with writing assignments; now it is an activity of choice. A computer encourages creativity by giving children a tool that eliminates the tedium of such projects and enhances the learning and enjoyment. I first noticed this with my daughters and now

with my younger boys. My 10-year-old son begs to do his writing assignments on the computer rather than handwrite them. Boys seem to lag behind girls in handwriting skills until about age 11 or 12 and using a word processor on the computer can ease the frustration for both student and teacher. Kids also seem to be able to express themselves with writing on the computer at an earlier age. My 12-year-old daughter, who has great difficulty with writing and spelling, (but I love her anyway) sends detailed e-mails to her Grandpa almost every week. Grandpa loves it and doesn't mind all the goofy misspelled words and lack of punctuation. It's great practice for her, and builds their relationship.

Writing software offers many tools for effective writing. With spelling checks, children see errors right away rather than waiting for the teacher's red pen. However, children need to realize that spell checkers are not foolproof. For instance, they don't catch the word "too" when you meant to right "two." (Nor are spell checkers able *two* catch the word "*right*" when you meant to *right* "*write*"! Or is that *write* instead of *right*? I seem to have forgotten which is *right* is *write*! :)

Writing projects are easier to do on the computer. Projects can include writing newsletters, e-mails, journaling and more. These final products can used to accomplish the next important way to use a computer.

9. Using a computer in your homeschool can impress school officials, neighbors, and relatives who may question your ability and desire to give your child a quality education.

Unfortunately some people still think

homeschoolers live in log cabins out on the prairie without any modern conveniences! If they see you've invested in a computer and quality educational software, their opinion (for what it's worth) of you must escalate at least a little. You can mail Grandma those little books or stories and e-mail school reports and letters; you and your children can easily and quickly e-mail your congressman. By having a computer, you let the world know that you are taking your children's education seriously and are investing in their future.

In fact, we homeschoolers have the great advantage over the public schools of spending our money on what will benefit our students the most. We have no school board to impress, no PTA to argue with, no department head signatures to procure! We make the spending decisions as soon as the budget allows it. In addition, many technological resources go unused in schools because teachers have neither the time nor the training to use them. As homeschooling parents, we can invest that time as we see fit to help our kids use computers wisely. It has been also my experience that any homeschool with an older teen (especially a boy) has an in-house computer expert already!

10. Computers can increase cooperative activity.

Studies have shown that "the addition of computers and appropriate software to their [classroom] environment has had positive social consequences, including an increase in cooperative activity." Kids are interacting with each other as well as the computer! Here are some of their favorite programs to do together: *Oregon Trail*, *Spy Fox*, and *Dr. Brain*. My older children enjoy solving problems and tackling computer projects together. On the other hand, to discourage fights over the computer, we use a timer to track time spent by individual kids and limit them to a half-hour per child twice a day. Children who abuse this privilege lose their computer access for a whole week. Consequently, in addition to academics, the children are learning sharing, obedience and patience as well.

11. A computer in your homeschool can encourage investigation and research into other areas of interest.

One of the first functions of a computer was the storing of massive amounts of data and information. Now your homeschool can access dozens of different types of resources at little or no cost. Dictionaries, atlases, almanacs, Bibles, and encyclopedias on the computer can make unit study research a fun and educational adventure. For example, *World Book Encyclopedia* on CD-ROM offers a wealth of information at a fraction of the cost of a traditional set of encyclopedias and has built-in features to help design unit studies. Some educational programs create mysteries that the student must research using different sources in order to solve various puzzles or challenges. The Internet can be the source of a wealth of information but has its limitations. Web sites offer up-to-the-minute news reports, links to museums, access to almost any business, and avenues to the political realm. (See the section on the *Internet* for more information.)

USING SOFTWARE IN YOUR HOMESCHOOL

First, examine what you are learning right now in your homeschool. Unit Study on Anatomy? Literature based study of the Pioneers? Chemistry experiments? Egyptians and the Old Testament? Think of software choices when you are making curriculum purchases and creating lesson plans; and find software that will supplement, complement, and enhance your children's learning. Whatever you are studying there is most likely an excellent, high quality software program that can merge with your current learning path! Stop looking at software and thinking, "Will my kids like this, use this, and get something out of it?" Start thinking, "How can I integrate this into my lesson plans, curriculum or unit study?" However, don't use your computer like an overpriced video game. (See the section, *But Mom, it's BOOOORING!*) Read each software description carefully in the software review section and you will see my recommendations on the program's usefulness in different unit studies or curriculums.

If you want a complete, multimedia software solution to your homeschool needs, we recommend the following:

1. Choose a curriculum type or textbook based program such as *ALS* (listed under curriculum) as the skeleton of the curriculum.

2. Flesh it out with multimedia choices to fill in gaps, make it interesting, and bring in other learning opportunities.

For example, get *ALS World History* (4th-8th grade), D*orling Kindersley's History of the World, History Through Art*, and *Leonardo da Vinci*. All together you have an exciting, enriching, and engaging multi-grade curriculum, but with the *ALS* testing to hold the student accountable! (See our Unit Study Curriculum Packages for unit study ideas.)

Software should be used as a supplement to your schooling, not as an entire school curriculum. The computer is an assistant teacher, not a substitute teacher. If you are studying world geography, use *World Discovery Deluxe* as an introduction to familiarize your children with world geography. While introducing phonics, try playing *Reading Blaster Ages 4-6* for twenty minutes a day. Educational software works best with parental participation whereas the student is held accountable for their time spent on the computer. Use software to drill on skill proficiency and to periodically check progress. Use *Kid Works Deluxe* to write a story. Add this week's spelling list or science terms to *Spell It Deluxe* (Knowledge Adventure). Since this program has five separate activities, complete one activity each day of the week and have the program give the spelling test on Friday.

We do recognize that there are some software programs that can be successfully used in your homeschool as a core curriculum (such as *PhonicsTutor* or *Switched-On Schoolhouse*), but these are rare exceptions.

We also use computer time as a reward for completing regular daily assignments, but we limit time to one or two hours for older kids and an hour or less a day for younger ones. Don't use the computer like glorified worksheets; make sure some real give-and-take is happening while your child is sitting at the computer. If your child is just "guessing" to continue to play the "game", eliminate that game from his daily activities until you can monitor its use.

Take time to read the manual carefully to understand all the features, options and benefits of each program. Most programs have editing features that allow you to customize topics and the level of difficulty in order to teach a specific topic at a particular skill level or drill in a certain task. Also, they might have built-in record keeping which keeps a tally of right and wrong answers, giving you, the teacher, the ability to pinpoint weaknesses. Some programs, such as the *Reader Rabbit* series and *PhonicsTutor,* will even adapt automatically and re-quiz the child in the areas of mistakes. Many programs have great features that you will only discover by reading the manual. Taking these steps will give you an edge in customizing the program to your children's individual needs. Furthermore, reading the manual will help you get the greatest value out of your investment (and to figure out how to turn off that annoying background music).

To get the best results of all, talk with other homeschooling moms that use computers in their homeschools. See what works for them. Some of my best ideas for using educational software came from other creative moms!

"But Mom, it's BOOOORING...!!!!!!!"

With all due respect to some of you homeschooling moms, something we hear too often is "Oh, my child will never use a piece of software that is not fun." To that I say, "Meat and potatoes, **Mom**! Meat and potatoes!"

One of the absolutely biggest mistakes you can make with your computer is to turn it into a game machine. Now, I could go

into an explanation of the dangers of most games, but I won't. Most of you already understand that. There is another, more subtle danger that I would like to address: Twinkies. Yes, Twinkies.

"Twinkies?" you ask. "What in the world does that mean?!?"

I will elaborate.

As parents who love our children, why don't we allow our children a steady, unlimited supply of Twinkies, Ho-Ho, candy bars, pop (or "soda" if you are from other parts of the country!), and such? Well, why don't we? Is it because we are cruel, mean people? No. Is it because anything fun, enjoyable, or yummy must be evil and purged from our innocent, dear, sweet children? No? Well, then could it be because our children will drop dead of toxic poisons and radioactive Twinkie half-life particles (how long will those things last anyway)? No again. The greater damage to our children is not what these foods do to their bodies, but due to what they will rob from our children's bodies. A child with a stomach full of junk has no interest in anything nutritious. Who of us would take our children to a buffet and allow them to go straight to the dessert bar to load up for their entire meal?

I realize that this all sounds a bit silly, but based on the vast number of moms I talk with, this example is all too real for too many families. A parent will call asking for help with a specific educational need. We will recommend a title that is on the boring side and the parent will tell us that her child will not use it. A program does not *have* to be boring to be good. But many of the best educational programs are somewhat boring. Unfortunately, some families can't utilize the computer as a serious study tool because the children are conditioned into the mentality that if it is on the computer it has to be fun or they won't use it.

Yuck!

If this attitude exists in your home, then I will give you this to think about: What is your response when your children say "yuck" to the meat and vegetables at the dinner table? Do you say, "That's ok, go ahead and have some dessert," in response to them? Or is your reply more along the lines of "That's ok, you just sit there until you get good and hungry enough to appreciate having a nutritious meal."

Let me put all this a little more directly. When your child says, "Math is boring, and spelling is stupid, so I'm not going to do it." What is your response? I can't imagine it's to apologize to them and offer to find a more fun alternative.

The Homeschooler's Software Guide likes meat & potatoes!

We don't homeschool our children for their entertainment value. We do it because it is right, and we want the best for them. So we urge you to take a similar approach with your educational software. Many of our top recommended titles are not what our own children define as fun or ask to work on in their free time. We know that. It is okay for software to be fun, but we try to focus on software primarily for its academic value, not its entertainment value. Just remember this is *your* homeschool and you decide what and how your children will learn. If you decide that they should do a *PhonicsTutor* lesson everyday (like I do), then they should do it. If your children fuss or whine about it, then we are talking about a discipline issue, and you have a much bigger problem than what software to use. Take a step back and work on obedience in your home, because you will always have prob-

lems if your child says "no" when you ask him to do something he does not want to do. Ask other homeschool moms for discipline tips, or talk to your pastor. If and when you find software that fits with your lesson plans, use it. Your children will be the benefactors. And, please, pass the carrots.

The Search

In your endeavor to choose the finest educational materials for your homeschool, we know you search high and low for them. We also searched high and low for the finest educational software available. These programs may not be the most fun or the fanciest; they are chosen first and foremost for their educational value and wholesome content.

Other software companies, resources, and reviewers do not follow this above policy. Their attitude is, if it is fun or if it will sell, we will carry it or recommend it. Let me quote from one of the foremost software magazines on the market: "Even the most educationally sound program can't succeed in teaching if your child won't use it. For this reason, programs need an element of fun to help motivate kids. It's the difference between software kids may be using at school under close supervision and the software they use at home, where they can be doing so many other things. So along with humor and plentiful animated surprise to click on, familiar, friendly characters work best for younger kids. Older children like contemporary themes."

They say vs. we say

What is this magazine telling you? In the secular world, what is fun and what sells, overrules what is actually best. Don't get caught up in that same trap. Find the best for what your homeschool needs are and go with it. Don't worry what is or isn't on the latest best-seller list of software.

Think about all this for a moment longer. One of the most important factors in that magazine's software recommendation is the FUN factor: will it entertain kids, and will they use it on their own? They forget one crucial element of education: discipline. If you do not have discipline in the execution of your homeschool, all is for naught. No one will learn and every day will be chaos. This leads back to the fact that most educational software programs are not designed for homeschoolers. They are designed for kids who are at school all day and whose parents just want something to keep the kids busy, that isn't something totally brain-dead, like the general mindlessness of most Nintendo games.

Seymour Papert (the designer of *LOGO*, a programming language for children) in his book *The Connected Family* says this: "Actually the educational software industry does know best about something, but about something other than the best ways to learn mathematics. It has excellent knowledge about what can be most easily sold to parents." Top-selling programs are not designed for homeschoolers, and you will not see many "top-sellers" listed in our top ten. For example, one secular reviewer was not too impressed with *NumberMaze Challenge*, calling it "too didactic." Hmmm, I says to myself, what does didactic mean? I looked it up in my trusty dictionary.

di·dac·tic (d-dktk)
also **di·dac·ti·cal** (-t-kl). *adj.*

1. Intended to instruct.
2. Morally instructive.
3. Inclined to teach or moralize excessively.

Another dictionary said

Didactic: meaning to teach or instruct.

Hello? That's the whole point of educational software!!!!!! That's where Mom comes in. If you assign it, they will do it if you have discipline and accountability in your homeschool.

We say

When we review software, we know what homeschoolers want. We are homeschoolers too, and we desire to use only the best software available. We review most of the software you see in the stores in addition to software primarily marketed for schools only. We then base our recommendations on the criteria listed in our section *Computers, Software and the Occult*. If a software program meets your homeschooling objectives, you should include it in your lesson plans— your children for success regardless of its "FUN" factor! Do not turn your computer into an entertainment center; both your child's mind and time are far too valuable. Carefully read the descriptions in the software sections and choose software based on its learning potential, not its edutainment potential! Save the "games" for gifts and "afterschool" time! (However, Parents, if you do *your* homework right, you can find highly educational software like the *Logical Journey of the Zoombinis* that your children will think are games. Then you both win!)

Unit study combinations

Here are some ideas on how to combine software programs into a UNIT STUDY curriculum.

The following multimedia software packages provide a multisensory, comprehensive resource for your homeschool.

Science

•Natural Science

Recommended ages: 7-14
Amazing Animals
I Love Science
Encyclopedia of Nature 2.0
ALS Science II-VII

•Human Anatomy

Recommended ages: 9-14
My Amazing Human Body
ADAM: The Inside Story
Emergency Room Interactive
Dole 5 A Day
9-Month Miracle

•Mechanical Science

Recommended ages: 9-14
The Way Things Work 3.0
ALS Science VI
Invention Studio
Widget Workshop

•Physical Science

Recommended ages: 9-14
ALS Science VII-IX
ZAP!
Encyclopedia of Science 2.0

•Space and the Universe

Recommended ages: 9-14
Compton's Learning: Astronomy
Encyclopedia of Space and the Universe
Library of the Universe

History and Geography

•Ancient History

Recommended ages: 9-16
Imagination Express: Pyramids
Nile: Passage to Egypt
Exploring Ancient Cities

•General World History

Recommended ages 9-16
Imagination Express: Castle
Eyewitness History of the World 2.0
ALS World History

•General American History

Recommended ages 9-16
Imagination Express: Time Trip
SkyTrip America
What's the Big Idea Ben Franklin?
ALS US History

•Westward Ho!
American History 1600-1800

Recommended ages 9-16
Imagination Express: Time Trip
Oregon Trail 4

•Geography

Recommended ages 7-16
ALS World & US Geography
World Discovery Deluxe
My First Amazing World Explorer 2.0

General Subjects

•Toddler

Recommended ages: 2-5
Busytown 2000
Big Job
Sammy's Science House
Reader Rabbit Toddler

•Pre-K/Kindergarten

Recommended ages: 4-6
Reader Rabbit Math 4-6
Millie and Bailey Kindergarten
Jumpstart Kindergarten
Magic Applehouse

•Music Appreciation

Recommended ages: 6-12
Making Music
Music Ace 1 & 2
Piano Discovery

•Art Appreciation

Recommended ages: 9-14
Artrageous!
History Through Art
Leonardo da Vinci

•College World Prep

Recommended ages: 10-17
Any ACT or SAT prep program
Typing Instructor Deluxe
Cruncher 2.0

•Work World Prep

Recommended ages: 10-17
SimFarm
Cruncher 2.0
Typing Instructor Deluxe

Why study a foreign language?

As Christians, we are instructed to go to the very ends of the earth with the gospel. In the past, the language barrier was one of the biggest obstacles to preaching the gospel to all people groups. If we are to be a missionary to any particular country, being able to speak the native language is a pre-requisite to any degree of success. Now with computer technology, learning a foreign language or translating the Bible has never been easier.

Many languages are available on CD-ROM, and more are coming out everyday. In addition, foreign-language training will help with Bible translations all over the world. Many experts suggest Latin be studied when young to lay a groundwork for later foreign language instruction and better vocabulary. One good way to practice your new language is to find an e-mail pal in another country. Kids can connect up with e-mail pals (safely) at www.epals.com.

Tips for your special kids

I can understand the frustration in finding good materials to teach learning disabled or special needs children. Computers can offer a whole new learning environment for special needs children. I have done a lot of checking around for what works best for special-needs children and have come up with these tips for choosing software:

• Keep it straightforward and uncluttered.

• Find software that speaks and supplies strong reinforcement with both auditory and visual cues.

• Look for software that requires little or no reading for your delayed readers. Many programs now provide narration for many portions of the content. However, don't coddle the reluctant reader by giving them too easy of software.

• Find software that requires continuous and frequent responses from the child. I recommend 15 to 20-second maximum intervals. However, if the child is required to do things too quickly to "survive" or win, he may get frustrated. There is a delicate balance required here. Finding the right programs with the best pace for your child will take some hunting and experimenting, there is no easy science to it. Where possible, get recommendations from other parents with similar special needs children. However, don't forget the old adage that if it works for them it doesn't guarantee it will work for you.

• Look for software where the responses mean something. Most software has a multitude of clickable spots that initiate some animation or activity, but all too often, these animations have very little to do with the content. For example, the child will click on the flowers and the flowers will bloom and sing. These types of distractions are a hindrance, not a learning opportunity, for LD and ADD children. In this case, it is better to have the flowers count themselves or demonstrate a concept.

• Look at the child's strengths instead of weaknesses when you choose software. If the child is really good at math or creative thinking, but a poor reader, get a program like *Widget Workshop*. The child is challenged by the thinking required and is motivated to read the instructions out of sheer necessity to play the game. Furthermore, start at the child's current ability level. For example, a severely delayed child may be challenged merely by the cause and effect of most computer games. You may have to work with them at first by placing your

hand over his on the mouse and guiding his movements.

• Do whatever you need to do to make the computer accessible for your special needs child. There is software and hardware available to allow even a totally paralyzed person run a computer using only eye movement! They are also working on devices that allow one to do simple computer commands by thoughts only. Switches, touch-screens, optical readers and more are designed for every kind of physical and mental disability. Contact some of the companies below for more information. Access the control panel and re-size the font to make the letters on the screen even bigger. You are also able to modify the mouse characteristics as well, making it easier for kids to track and manipulate the cursor and mouse movements. Most word processors allow you to customize the font and background colors. LD kids seem to prefer blue letters on a yellow background. Using a talking word processor can be a lifesaver for the auditory learner.

• Check out a small software company called Scientific Learning (www.scientificlearning.com). They have created specialized software for children who have Central Auditory Processing disorder. Their software works like "mental aerobics" designed to strengthen weak connections in those parts of the brain that support language skills. Scientific Learning's software is very expensive but they may be able to help you find a local educational institution that has it available.

• Lastly, zero in on the child's "ability age." If his mental age is only five years old, get software designed for five-year-olds! He will love it. I have personally seen this "ability age" approach to be highly successful with children of various levels intelligence limitations, from mild to severe. If you use this approach when choosing software, you will be far more likely to choose wisely.

"Ability age" factors aside, some software just lends itself better than others to the special needs of special children. Some of the software below—*PhonicsTutor*, to name one—has been very successful in helping special children develop speaking and reading skills.

Based on the above criteria, I suggest the following titles:

- *PhonicsTutor*
- *Logical Journey of the Zoombinis*
- (Anything that Edmark makes)

Millie's Math House, Sammy's Science House, Bailey's Book House, Trudy's Time and Place House

- *Switched-On Schoolhouse*
- *Let's Go Read*
- *Earobics*
- *World Discovery Deluxe*
- *NumberMaze Challenge*
- *Reading Mansion*
- *Typing Instructor Deluxe*
- *SimCity or SimFarm*

Further descriptions of these programs are in the Software Review section later in this book.

Resources For Special Needs Kids

Books and Periodicals:

• *Choosing and Using Curriculum For Your Special Child*

By Joyce Herzog,

This extremely well researched guide will help you choose homeschool curriculum for your special child. Joyce is a unique lady with a real heart for special kids. She has spent many years working with them.

Her only focus is helping Christian homeschoolers. Joyce has also been a keynote speaker at many homeschool conventions. She has other resources for special needs children as well. Highly recommended!

Street price $12
Greenleaf Press
3761 Hwy 109
North Lebanon, TN 37087
800-311-1508
www.greenleafpress.com

• *Computer Resources for People with Disabilities*

By Alliance For Technology Access
Hunter House Inc., Publishers
PO Box 2914
Alameda, CA 94501-0914
415-455-4575
www.ataccess.com

• *NATHHAN Newsletter*

National Association of Challenged Homeschoolers

This organization is dedicated to helping Christian homeschoolers who have handicaps. Topics covered include Down's Syndrome, blindness, ADD, ADHD, autism, deafness, and more. A lot of practical Biblical advice and resources. I highly recommend their newsletter.

$25 donation/year for 4 issues of their newsletter and membership

NATHAN
5383 Alpine Rd. S.E.
Olalla, WA 98359
206-857-4257
www.nathhan.com

Companies and Organizations:

• Don Johnston, Inc.

This company is dedicated to developing software and tools designed for special needs kids. Whether the condition is blindness, ADD, paralysis, etc., they provide a solution to enable kids to access the computer. Order their catalog for more information.

26799 Commerce Drive
Volo, IL 60073
847-526-0749
www.donjohnston.com

• Edmark Corporation

PO Box 97021
Redmond, WA 98073-9721
800-362-2890
www.edmark.com

• Alliance for Technology Access.

This association provides opportunities for people with disabilities to have access to the type of technology that meets their needs. It is a network of community-based resource centers dedicated to providing information and support services to children and adults with disabilities, and increasing their use of standard and assistive technologies. Centers can be found all across the country. Contact them to find the one nearest you.

www.ataccess.org
Phone: (415) 455-4575
Fax: (415) 455-0654

• IntelliTools, Inc.

1720 Corporate Circle
Petaluma, CA 94954
800-899-6687 (USA and Canada)
Phone: (707) 773-2000
Fax: (707) 773-2001
www.intellitools.com

•Sunburst Communications

101 Castleton Street
Pleasantville, NY 10570-3498
(800) 431-1934, 914-747-3310
www.sunburst.com

THE 3 R'S & THE 3 C'S

Most people think of the 3 R's when thinking of the educational basics required for any kind of academic or general success in life. We feel you need to add 3 "C's" to those 3 R's. The three "C's" stand for "Character, Communication, and Common Sense." Without these three additional qualities, your child could have all the software and curriculum in the world and still be a failure in life. In my homeschool convention workshops, I exhort parents to realize they could spend tons of money out in the exhibit hall and still not prepare their child for the real world.

Character.

The most important of the three "C's" is "Character." A child can be the smartest kid in your homeschool group but if he or she has no character, that child will not be able to serve the Lord. As a parent, building character in our children is probably the hardest thing we will do. If a child has the qualities of honesty, integrity, diligence, perseverance, and kindness, he or she will be a success in almost any endeavor. Make Character the number one priority in your home and homeschool and God will bless your efforts.

Communication

Second in importance is Communication. The ability to speak and write well is another key to success in any career. Make writing and speaking a significant part of your homeschool curriculum. For example, join a speech and debate club. Homeschoolers are competing all over the country for the chance to attend the *Homeschool Legal Defense Association's* National Debate Tournament held in June every year. Also,

use your computer for research and writing. There are great software programs for writing effectively.

Common Sense

Last but not least, Common Sense is necessary. Show me a "well-educated" person who can't think logically or analytically, and I will show you a fool. We've all met more than one before. Knowledge and information without the ability to analyze them properly is pretty useless. Of course, wisdom is the most important "thinking skill" one can possess. However, analysis & logic is nearly as important as wisdom and good computer programs can assist in teaching these skills very well.

Every homeschooling family should have logic and thinking skills added as an actual subject in their curriculum. Additionally, every family needs at least one good thinking skill computer program. There are a lot of them out there, but most are usually junk, full of occult, and/or just an excuse to play an arcade action game.

For pre-teens, we think that the *Logical Journey of The Zoombinis* is one of the best logic and thinking skills programs. Based on what other homeschooling mothers say, those who already own it agree. Also, the *Thinkin' Things* series is excellent but different than the *Zoombinis*.

For teenagers, some of the better ones are *Yoiks!*, *Pit Droids*, or any of the *Dr. Brains*. Please note: we feel that the fourth title of the *Dr. Brain* series, *Time Warp of Dr. Brain*, contains too much arcade action and evolutionary themes for our taste.

For older teen, or extra-bright younger teens who need a challenge, consider *Myst* by The Learning Company. Both require much thinking (they're hard), much time to solve, and have no arcade action.

These are just a few of the thinking skills programs we recommend. Check out the software reviews section for other titles.

THE TEN MOST IMPORTANT COMPUTER SKILLS
(or)
"HOW TO USE YOUR COMPUTER TO PREPARE FOR THE JOB MARKET"

The following are the top ten most important computer skills your older child should develop to ensure success and better employability in any industry's job market.

Yes, computer programming is a valuable skill, which is great for those people who can learn it. However, like plumbing, auto mechanics, and medicine, not everyone needs to become an expert to use the plumbing, drive a car, or keep healthy. Similarly, one does not need to build, program, or design computers to use one as a tool.

For your younger children, *The Magic Applehouse* (no real magic!) will introduce some fundamental computer skills as well as some marketing, business and sales concepts.

This list is not in order of how much these skills are worth in income. They are listed in order of necessity, priority and the likelihood of using them on a job or in real life.

1. Understanding your computer.

Know how to install, uninstall, run and configure software programs on your Mac or PC. Know what kind of system you have: RAM, memory, hard drive, display, processor, etc. A computer is not a refrigerator! Not just your teens should learn these things, but Mom and Dad should too. Believe me, time spent learning at least the basics of your computer will pay off. A *USA Today* survey indicated that 41% of computer users consider their computer knowledge and ability was self-taught. See the section: *Top Ten Tips on Frustration Free Computing*.

2. Proficiency in typing.

Everyone should learn touch-typing by age fifteen. Not only will most colleges require this skill, most non-minimum wage jobs will as well. We recommend either *Typing Instructor Deluxe* or *Mavis Beacon Teaches Typing* to learn typing skills.

3. Ability to use a word processor and a desktop publishing program.

If a person is going to use a computer for just about anything, it will involve word processing as part of the job; whether it is a short memo or producing *The Homeschooler's Software Guide*! Have your teens practice with the software already on your computer, e.g., *Microsoft Works, Microsoft Word, WordPerfect* or *Microsoft Home Publishing*.

4. Ability to use a spreadsheet.

We, along with nearly every businessman, corporate executive, and computer expert that we have spoken with, feel that ability to use a spreadsheet is probably the most neglected computer skill. This skill is a great asset and can aid in being successful anywhere in business or corporate America. In fact it is amazing just how much spreadsheets can be used in so many other areas of life as well. To help prepare your child to enter the future work force of any field involving any type of computer use, we strongly urge you to purchase *The Cruncher 2.0* to teach spreadsheets. In fact, anyone who owns a computer should learn to use a spreadsheet.

5. Ability to use and make a database.

a. Database population: which is inputting and retrieving of information. Know how to write a database query that gives you just the important information you need, while leaving the nonessential material behind.

b. Database creation: Know how to set up a database and decide what type of information goes into it. We recommend taking an actual course in database creation and use. This skill is somewhat difficult to learn and apply on your own.

One of the most common databases used is CRM or Customer Relationship Management software. This type of database manages all the information pertaining to a company's client: addresses, names, contacts, phone numbers, personal information, buying behavior, and more. As crazy as it sounds, in the past, each department within a company would maintain their own contact list. Each of these individual databases would be in various stages of accessibility, portability, development, completeness and currency. Now companies are working to combine all these databases into one huge package, accessible to all in the company. So if marketing gets new information about a client or customer, it is entered into the database. Then other departments, such as customer service, will have access to it. This makes the company far more responsive to the customer's needs. Workers understanding the development, programming, and implementation of CRM software are in high demand today, commanding top salaries.

6. Creating multimedia

Some colleges, high schools and employers request all reports to be in the form of a multimedia presentation. If you want the ability to create your own multimedia presentations, *HyperStudio* is the best program to get and is what most schools and teachers use. Most Windows 98 computers come with *Microsoft PowerPoint*; which is the choice of corporate America. Project idea: Have your teen prepare multimedia reports on the family's unit studies including art, photos, video clips, written reports and more. Create or "burn" your own CD-ROM on a CD recorder and create a multimedia "portfolio" of your school year!

7. Hyperliteracy.

Hyperliteracy is the ability to thoroughly understand and use computer resources, hyperbooks and hyperdocuments. These are online resources such as text, graphics, videos, graphs, animations and sound clips. Soon many resources and even textbooks will come on CD-ROM or DVD. Why? A CD offers the ability to have massive amounts of information available and accessible at a very low production cost. Reprints and updates of CD-ROMs cost less than a dollar to mass-produce and are much easier and cheaper than books to distribute. By the time your children get to college, they may be handed a CD-ROM rather than a printed textbook, course schedule, assignments and syllabus. Everything will be on the CD-ROM: reading and writing assignments, quizzes, and exams. Student work will be e-mailed in rather than hand-delivered.

Even more important is the ability to use the Internet in an effective manner. Just because you can access and use a search engine does not mean you can come up with reliable and relevant information.

8. Networking.

"Networking" or hooking up two or more computers together so that they can "talk" to each other and share printers and other peripherals is a major undertaking in businesses all over the world. Any computer savvy employee who can network will have instant job security. Resource: "*Networking for Dummies.*"

9. Programming.

Programming is designing the programs and applications that run on computers. If you or your children are seriously interested in computer programming and the logic and theory behind it, I recommend getting *MicroWorlds Pro* for Windows. This highly specialized program provides tools for drawing, creating melodies, writing and programming in the computer language Logo. Another option is *Learn to Program BASIC* by Interplay. This tutorial is designed for students twelve and up to learn BASIC, one of the most fundamental programming languages and is great for beginners. If you have a student who is serious about programming, encourage him. Computer engineering is the fastest growing occupation of the future with an anticipated 100% growth in jobs.

According to my brother-in-law, a regional vice president at Monster.com, the most sought after programming skills are Java, C++, and Unix. Monster.com is major corporate recruiting firm.

10. Creating web pages and sites.

Although not all of us will be required to create web sites, this is still a very crucial skill of the future. If you have been on the web for any amount of time, you know that every corporation and organization will have a presence on the web eventually. Even some religious organizations that shunned the web as an uncensored demon spawned from hell now see the value of having their own web sites. The web is the yellow pages and library of the future. For beginning web page creation for the young ones, I recommend *Net Explorations: Web Workshop*. For more advanced web page/site creation, there are some other very easy to use programs available. I recommend Microsoft's *FrontPage* or *Claris Home Page*. To publish commercial quality web sites from scratch, one needs to develop proficiency in JAVA and HTML. JAVA is a programming code that allows you to create programs and animations that can run on any computer system. If you have an older teen who wants to make big bucks in the computer world, have him (or her) learn HTLP or JAVA immediately. I recommend getting the JAVA developer kit at http://java.sun.com and the books *Java for Dummies* by Aaron E. Walsh and/or *Java Programming For Dummies* by Donald and David Koosis (both published by IDG Books Worldwide, Inc.). HTML is HyperText Markup Language, i.e. the language of the web. *HTML for Dummies* by Ed Tittel and Steve James (published by IDG Books Worldwide, Inc.) is a good resource. To learn about HTML online, check out these web sites: http://www.cwru.edu/help/introHTML/toc.html or http://web.canlink.com/webdesign/. (Keep in mind these are secular resources not written from a Christian perspective.) Before your student gets online, read my tips on Internet use and censorship in the *Internet* section.

Chapter 4

USING YOUR COMPUTER

TOP TEN TIPS FOR FRUSTRATION FREE COMPUTING

(Actually, there are eleven but "ten" sounds better!)

1. Read the box.

Before you buy or order software, make sure you know exactly what kind of computer you have. Check the side of the software box to find the system requirements to know if it will run on your computer. If it says Pentium II, do not expect it to run well or at all on your Pentium I or your 486. If you don't even know what "do you have a Pentium I or II?" means, then you need to read your computer manual again or get *Windows 98 For Dummies* or *Windows Me For Dummies*. If you have a Mac, don't worry about a "486", just get *Macs For Dummies*.

2. Read the manual and/or "read me" file before you install and after you install!

A "read me" file is found on the CD-ROM and is often a *simple text* (words only) document that will give you further information on installation and use. Some programs don't even have a manual and expect you to read the "read me" file for all the questions you may have.

If the program is still not running smoothly, do NOT call the business that sold you the program. Your local computer mega-store does not maintain on-staff, technical support personnel that can troubleshoot every nuance and glitch of every software package they sell. Your best bet is to call the publisher of the software. Somewhere either on the outside of the box or inside is always some number to call for technical support. If you can't find it, check the *Appendix of Software Publishers* at the back of this book. If you are lucky it is a toll free number; if you are very lucky, you don't have wait on hold for hours to get help. Generally, we have found that most companies have very good technical support people and are able to help anyone. However, don't be surprised if you end up in "tech-support-hell." (See the technical support section in chapter eleven.)

After the program is running, read the manual again to find out about the program's features and benefits. Many programs have powerful customizing features that allow you to configure the software to meet very specific homeschool needs and objectives, but you will never know about them unless you read the manual.

3. Practice safe (virus-free) computing.

Never accept disks from others without first running a virus check. Never download programs from the Internet or online service or e-mail unless it is from a trusted source or checked for viruses. My brother sent an e-mail to my dad with an attachment, *Happy99.exe*. My brother had opened it, seen a cute fireworks display and sent it on to friends and family, who then also opened it. When my brother went to turn on his computer the next day, he found that the entire hard drive was trashed- everything was GONE. He immediately contacted all his friends and family to warn them but it was too late for my dad. He had already opened the e-mail and his hard drive crashed too. He ended up taking his computer into the shop for a re-install of the entire hard drive. Almost everything e-mailed to you is safe, but all it takes is one nasty virus to destroy everything. Therefore, be overly cautious and beware!

4. Backup, backup, backup!

The two big backing up mottos at my house are, "Back up early and back up often," and, "If it is worth backing up once, it is worth backing up twice."

Whatever documents you produce on your computer should be backed up regularly. If you have *Quicken* and use it to keep your checkbook records on, back it up every time you work on it. There are several ways to back up your files: on a diskette, on an external hard drive, or a "Zip" drive. A diskette is one of those little 3.5" disks that programs used to come on before CD-ROMs. You know, like those AOL diskettes that used to come free in just about everything? Follow your operating system manual's instructions on how to do this. You can also plug in an extra hard drive and back up your critical files and/or your entire operating system. An extra hard drive is a lot cheaper than it used to be. If you figure less than $0.01 per megabyte, a thirty-gigabyte hard drive is now under $100. I really like the new Zip drives; they're inexpensive and easy to use. The one time you do not back-up will be the one time you needed to! Believe me, I speak from experience!

Now I know that I said the scope of this book was not going to be "How to *use* a computer," but this backing-up issue is so important that it deserves some more coverage. You might think that backing up is something that only businesses and organizations need to do. However, most families usually have important documents that need to be backed up also. If you maintain your checkbook on the computer (which you should do because it is quicker and easier,) at the least you should back up every time you reconcile your monthly statement. Additionally, it is wise to save a different backup of each individual month's reconciliation. Hopefully you will never need it, but, hey, that's why you back up. You just never know.

Now that you've backed up this important information (like Great Grandma's top secret recipe for the world's best chocolate brownies), an equally important consideration is where to store these valuable bits and bytes. I have two simple tips for you. The quickest, and probably easiest, way to back up files is just to e-mail them to someone (even yourself). Then they sit out there in cyberspace until you need them. They could also download it to their computer, wherever that may be. Secondly, if you put the file on a floppy disk, you can send the backup with Dad to work to keep in his desk, locker, or whatever. If you are going to go through the effort of a back-up, don't let your backup be at risk to the very same dangers that could require you to need a back-up: fire, flood, tornado (your basic "Acts of God"), theft, or whatever.

5. Protect your computer from big and little hackers—use a desktop protection program.

In our experience, unsupervised children who explore unprotected computers are the biggest cause of computer failure. These innocent little children do not break the computer's "hard" ware; they mess up the "soft" ware. (Personal note: our 2-year-old once pushed the monitor off the desktop and right off onto the floor. It still works 4 years later!) You may think your child is not likely to mess up your software, but we have heard too many horror stories from parents who thought the very same thing. Just to be on the safe side, please install a desktop protection utility program and put your computer on a stable surface.

To protect you computer from getting messed up, we recommend *Kid Desk* or *Homeschool Desk*. These programs work by replacing the standard Windows desktop interface with a new one. The new desktop allows easy access to the authorized pro-

grams while restricting access to all non-authorized software. It also protects the computer's operating system from getting messed up. Think of these types of protection programs like insurance for the integrity of your computer's software. You don't need it until you need it, but once you've needed it, it is too late to get it. Sort of like closing the door after the cows have left the barn.

6. Monitor online time and costs.

Do not allow your child to be online unsupervised. Make sure you know the hourly charges for your online service (if any) and any access charges if you are dialing long distance to hook up to your online provider. (See *Internet* section for more information.)

7. Clean out your hard drive regularly.

If you find your hard drive getting full, clean out any unused files or programs. If you have Windows, you have a built-in file remover in the Control Panel. Just click Add/Remove Program. It makes it easy to delete folders without losing critical data. If you use the Internet a lot, make sure you clean out the temporary Internet files regularly. Back in your Control Panel, click on Internet Options. Then click on the tab that says "General," followed by clicking on "Delete files" under Temporary Internet Files.

8. Learn about your computer.

One of the greatest misconceptions we encounter is people's tendency to think of their computer as an appliance, like a refrigerator. You plug it in, you use it, and you ignore it as it does your bidding. A computer is not a refrigerator. A computer requires continuous maintenance and upkeep. It is imperative that you learn all you can about your computer to minimize frustration and maximize its potential. We recommend getting a book or two for starters. Among our favorites are the Dummies series. For PC owners, start with *Windows 98 for Dummies;* if there is a particular application you use often, such as Microsoft Word, get *Microsoft Word For Dummies*. For the Mac lovers out there, invest in *Macs For Dummies*. The Dummies series is not really for "dummies" just for us non-technically minded people who need an explanation or instruction in plain English, assuming we know nothing to begin with. I have a whole stack of "Dummies" books next to my computer.

Our research shows that free unlimited toll-free technical support (the help you get from the company who built your computer) is fast becoming a thing of the past. With more computers in homes of those with less tech-savvy, tech support resources are stretching computer companies' budgets to the limit. (One company that still offers 24/7 toll free tech support is Dell Computer Corporation. That's why I spent a little more and bought three computers from Dell. I have been very satisfied with my purchases.) Other companies are forced to charge up to $2 a minute to help you with your PC woes. Because of this, we recommend you take the time and effort to learn more about your computer so as not to rely on tech support people. Some families are blessed with a teen that is very computer savvy. You might also be able to find a computer "nerd" at church and supply them with free pizza and pop to get their help.

9. Buy a kitchen timer to regulate your children's time.

This is the easiest, cheapest and best way to eliminate fights about who gets the computer next. Let a "neutral" object like a timer be the policeman, and you will have few complaints about taking turns. I recommend 30-minute increments starting with the oldest child, and one hour per day per child.

10. Don't become addicted!

Needless to say, anything that becomes more important than the Lord, His Word and your family has become an idol in your life. Be careful that your computer is only a tool—not a god.

11. Teach your children these basic computer skills:

(Obviously, you will need to learn these yourself first!)

- How to point, double click, and navigate within kids programs
- How to turn on/shut down the computer properly
- How to use your desktop protection program, e.g. *Kid Desk, Homeschool Desk* or *At Ease*.
- How to open and quit a program, how to name and save their games, written files, or artwork.
- How to adjust the volume, use the microphone, restart the system.
- How to install software.
- How to backup onto a floppy disk.

TIPS TO KEEP YOUR COMPUTER RUNNING SMOOTHLY

• **Computer rule number one in our house: No food or drinks anywhere near the computer under any circumstance!**

• **Keep all magnets away from your computer and monitor!**

This includes all speakers that are not specifically designed for use with computers. Regular computer-style speakers are okay. But the magnetic fields from non-computer speakers of any kind will damage your monitor and your computer's hard drive memory if they within about a foot. On a related note, and for the same reason, unless your speakers have a special kind of shielding (like computer speakers have) they will also damage your TV screen if placed too close to the TV. The electro-magnetic field of the speaker magnets produces a really cool psychedelic rainbow effect on computer monitors and TV screen. Depending on proximity of the speakers and the strength of the magnets, this effect has the potential to be permanent. Whereas this effect tends to be somewhat beautiful, no one wants the computer monitor or TV to look as if it is suffering the electronic equivalent of doing some very serious hallucinogenic drugs! Lastly, don't let your child put magnets on or near the screen of your monitor; this will also produce some cool rainbow colors. Check your monitor's controls—usually right on the front of the monitor itself. There may be a button marked "De-gauss" or similar. Push this button to eliminate these rainbow blemishes. Otherwise, these imperfections will proba-

bly go away with time. You may think this is very unlikely to happen. Well, it has happened at least twice at our house.

• **Make a mess somewhere else!**

Pencil shavings, glue sticks, crayons, paper clips, etc. belong somewhere other than by the computer.

• **Handle CD-ROMS with care.**

CD-ROMS can take a fair amount of abuse based on my experience; however, too many scratches will disable the program. If you have trouble running a program that used to run fine, wash the CD very carefully. I wet the CD with some warm water, place a drop of dish soap on the shiny side and very gently rub the whole CD with my finger for 10-20 seconds. Then, while rinsing with warm water, I continue to rub the soap residue off for another 10-20 seconds. After a final rinse (without rubbing, and checking to make sure all the soap film is off) I shake off excess water and pat dry; do not rub. This procedure gets most CDs running again at our house; even the one that got coated with peanut butter. (Don't even ask.)

• **Get a good surge protector.**

Here are some things to consider: for starters, although most surge protectors take on the style of a power strip, most power strips are NOT surge protectors. So why a surge protector, and why do you need one? A powerful spike in electricity can "fry" your computer, and your TV, and your stereo, and almost anything else electrical. Lightning is the most well known source of power spikes. Spikes in power can also come from various things like failures in equipment along the power grid or even the operation of motors within your own home. The only way to protect against this type of damage is to plug your equipment into a surge protector and then plug the surge protector into the electrical socket. The surge protector works similarly to an electrical fuse in reverse. If and when a spike of electricity higher than acceptable limits hits it, it cuts off the power before the spike can hit your equipment. We have heard from a number of homeschool families who have had their computers ruined by a lightning spike, making it a very realistic risk. The risk is higher where lightening storms are more frequent, e.g. Florida. When shopping for a surge protector, look for one that has the backing of some kind of warranty against failure. Some come with guarantees for replacement of electronic equipment up to $5,000, $10,000 or more if it fails and an electrical spike damages the equipment. When you buy a surge protector with a warranty, that is one purchase you will really want to make sure that you send in the registration card! We also suggest you buy a surge protector that also has phone line surge protection as well. This will protect the computer from a spike coming in through the modem connected to the phone line.

• Place the computer on a very large, sturdy surface such a big heavy desk.

Just like an old, antique record player (you remember using one as a child, don't you?) it is very bad for the computer to be wiggled and jiggled while it is turned on. Contrary to what you might suspect, I think that most "computer desks" are insufficient in real work use. In actuality they tend not to have the layout for computers. For one thing, they tend not to be quite as sturdy as you would like for real world usage (2.7 children leaning and wiggling on it while watching one more child on the computer.) Another common shortcoming is that they

rarely seem to be deep enough. What I actually like best and would recommend is a large, old fashioned teacher's desk or a big, old metal office desk that seem to weigh half a ton. Now those are both sturdy and deep!

• Never turn the computer off without properly shutting it down. Learn the correct way to shut down the computer safely.

• Learn what to do when the computer freezes up.

With Windows 95 or 98 machines, you would want to press the ctrl, alt, and del buttons simultaneously. This will allow you to quit the offending program. If this does not tame the computer, press those three buttons (called the three-finger salute) again to force a restart of your computer.

• Never plug in or unplug mice, keyboards, printers or any other peripheral devices while the computer is on.

Always shut down the computer first! This won't damage the computer but may mess up your operating software. Some laptops allow you to "hot-swap" peripherals without shutting down, but most desktop-type computers do not.

• Again, we repeat this last tip, one of the most important yet most neglected: Back up early and back up often!!! I would add to this, if it is worth backing up, it should probably be backed up twice.

FAQ'S

As we travel around the country to homeschool conventions and talk to thousands of parents on the phone, there are always some 'Frequently Asked Questions' (FAQ). Here are some FAQ's and our responses, along with some recommendations by well-known homeschool reviewers.

Q   Is there something that will do everything on the computer?

A   See the article on Computerized Curriculum.

Q   What about *HomeQuest*?

A: (Note: Years ago, we had a lot more questions about *HomeQuest* than we do now. I can only assume that few are selling it anymore. But I did find one web site still promoting it and wanted to warn anyone who may consider buying the *HomeQuest* package.)

Cathy Duffy's book, *The Christian Home Educator's Curriculum Manual*, says this about *HomeQuest*: "History and geography are only offered from about 4th grade level and up. These areas should be definitely supplemented. Lessons vary in form of presentation, but typically, students read through instructional material, practice answering questions (e.g. multiple choice or fill in the blank), then take a test on that material, with the test closely resembling the practice material and format. 1000 hours of instruction. While it appears to be comprehensive, parents must understand that children cannot learn only through these programs. They require interaction to learn to read well, discuss course content, ask questions, explore topics not covered in the curriculum and cover other aspects of learning that cannot be handled by the computer. *HomeQuest* suffers from the same limitations as do many workbooks. Many skills are taught as isolated bits of information and it is expected that somehow they will come together into a coherent whole. While such exercises can be useful, they cannot adequately serve as a complete curriculum on their own. Recognizing such limitations, HomeQuest has tried to address one aspect of this limitation by building in extensive writing assignments through out the program. Students are given essay assignments where they actually type essays into the computer, but the evaluation must be done by the parent." You, the parent, are still required to be a facilitator of the child's learning.

Mary Pride says this in her magazine *Practical Homeschooling*: "Missing [in *HomeQuest*] are history, geography, grammar... and high school science. Graphics are jagged 16-color just-barely-VGA. Sound is nothing to write home about...Animation is primitive." We would expect that at some point (if it hasn't happened already) they would upgrade the quality of the graphics, but we have no knowledge of current plans.

I should mention that the new *ALS* (Advantage Learning Systems) curriculum does include grammar, history and geography but the original HomeQuest does not.

Here at *The Homeschooler's Software Guide*, we give our humble opinion: Even the *HomeQuest* company itself recommends only 1.5 hours of computer work per day with 1-2 hours of noncomputer activity. Given that there are 1000 hours of coursework in the entire K-12 curriculum, a student should only take about 2 years to finish all the work (K-12) if they take no time off for summer. That is a lot of money on ancient software that the child should be able to complete in 2-3 years!

If you love *HomeQuest* and/or sell it,

please don't send me nasty letters. Do not think I am criticizing it only because I am biased. You misunderstand our mission and business. If it were worth the money and I thought homeschoolers should buy it, it would be in our recommended list! However, it is rare when we talk to a homeschooler (who doesn't also sell *HomeQuest*) who is glad they bought *HomeQuest*. But on the other hand, we hear from many who regret it. One father sent me an e-mail saying this: "Our experience with *HomeQuest*…has been very negative… we regret each penny we paid and each minute that we lost in this learning experience."

In summary, our recommendations are:

• Basic, barebones: *ALS* titles with multimedia CDs to flesh it out. See our unit study packages on page 54.

• *Smartworks Gradeschool* offers some very good lessons for grades 2-5. See CURRICULUM reviews on page 192.

• More in-depth secular material: *Cornerstone* (Grades 3-8) or *SkillsBank 4* (Grades 6-12.) Call 1-800-825-4420 to order either series directly from The Learning Company.

• Complete Christian curriculum: Alpha Omega's *Switched-On Schoolhouse*. These are the *LifePacs* on CD-ROM. Available for Windows for grades 3-12. Their street price runs about $65 per subject per grade or $260 for single grade level consisting of Math, English, Science, History and Geography, and Bible.

Q Do the science programs have evolution in them?

A Since all the science programs come from secular sources (Except for Alpha Omega's *Switched-On Schoolhouse*) you will find a small amount of evolutionary material. It is usually in the form of the universe "is billions and billions" of years old. We try to screen out the programs that have a preponderance of evolutionary theory in them and we mention any obvious evolutionary material in the description of each science title.

Q What about those CD's the Amway people sell?

A Those titles are from the Zane or ZCI Publishing Company. All of the titles in that series are very good; some are excellent. Some of the science titles have too much evolutionary material for our tastes. We reviewed the titles that we like best and that fit with Christian homeschooling objectives. If you are going to use a lot of these CD's, I highly recommend getting a book called *Christian Home Learning Guides* by Marshall Foster and Ron Ball. (Street price $44.) This book is an excellent study companion to all of the Zane titles. As the book itself says, "The goal of this book is twofold: It is designed to (1) give the student a providential timeline of Christian history that highlights the people and events that have shaped our world from ancient times to the present, and (2) offer them instruction and encouragement needed to face the next century." Keep in mind that although the book itself is from a Christian viewpoint, the Zane CDs are secular. Also keep in mind that the scope of the book is limited to only the Zane CDs.

Chapter 5

USING THE INTERNET

USING THE INTERNET IN YOUR HOMESCHOOL

It's overrated.

It's uncensored.

It's a potentially significant time waster.

However, it can be a wonderful tool to...

• Research libraries, museum and universities to find information, book titles, and resources. I found extensive lists of books on my topics of interest at web sites like Amazon.com. Then I trotted off to the library to find them! I have also surfed to the library's web site to search its card catalog and reserve books. You do not have to be on the Internet to dial up most libraries.

• Access reference material such as dictionaries, thesauruses, fact books, maps, and various measurement tables. You can find articles and newspaper stories for electronic clipping but sometimes you need to pay extra for that service. As your children (and you) do research on the web, help them

learn how to critically analyze sources of information. Check these guidelines for critical analysis from *Failure to Connect* by Jane Healy:

Who provided this information? Why?

Is someone trying to sell us a product or a point of view?

How is the source coded (e.g., ".com" = commercial; ".gov" = government; ".edu" = educational institution, ".org" = nonprofit organization, ".mil" = military, etc.)? How might this influence our evaluation of its accuracy? Can we assume that everything from an educational institution, for example, is necessarily true and accurate? How about from a government source?

What possible biases may be detected here (e.g., an organization dedicated to environmental protection or a business selling a product)?

If quotes or data are provided, are they appropriately referenced?

How can we find other information with which to compare and evaluate accuracy (e.g., call sources, check authorized print sources)?

Does this information represent theory or evidence? What is the difference between these terms? How can we distinguish one from another? (Even undergraduate university students in the United States have difficulty with this question.)

Why might some sources be more accurate than others (e.g., many professional journals are "vetted" or reviewed by experts before publication)?

How do the visuals influence the way we receive this information? Is emotion a part of the design? Are sound effects intended to influence our thinking?

Do the visuals and the text convey the same message?

As a side note to these criteria, we can't help but add our own. But a tiny bit of background first. We debated together in high school before we started dating. These are four of the most important lessons we learned in debate:

You can find a "so-called" expert to "prove" almost any point or idea no matter how insane. The list of such examples is so ludicrous that I won't even start.

Statistics lie

Liars use statistics

If you really want to learn the truth about a subject, research it yourself.

(Sidenote: I know all this goes off on a tangent from the focus of this Guide, so just think of is as an extra freebie that we threw in at no extra charge. Yes, there *is* more than just this one in here!)

• Talk to experts and famous people! If you have a child who is a spider fanatic, find a spider expert online.

• Keep in touch with relatives, missionaries, politicians (if you dare!) Our church regularly receives e-mail from missionaries all over the world to keep us posted on prayer and praise requests.

• Contact companies directly—save time and money! By accessing their web site, you can zero in on the info you need without waiting on hold or playing phone tag. I found the Fisher-Price web site, e-mailed them my request and got a new copy of instructions for my safety gate. My father got a huge discount by booking airline tickets at the company's web site and I saved almost $200 by making my car rental reservation online. Contact online tech support and get help fast! This past year I did a lot of my homeschool supply buying right on the Internet. Most of your favorite homeschool suppliers have online shopping at their web site 24-hours-a-day, 7-days-a-week! Order a new Saxon math book at 2 AM; they won't care!

• Keep up with last minute news and happenings around the world: e.g. your support group, your church, your state organization, the homeschooling world, Home School Legal Defense, Focus on the Family and more. On election night, I could access up-to-the-minute electoral votes and state-by-state votes. When they called Florida for Al Gore, I could hardly believe it. The up-to-the-minute vote tallies for the state of Florida showed George W. Bush ahead by a large margin. I knew something was fishy! (George W. said, "If Al Gore invented the Internet, why does every Internet address start with a 'W'!") Most of the well-known Christian organizations now have web sites with information available 24 hours a day.

• Create a web site for your organization. I made a web site for both my homeschool support group and my church. I use *Microsoft Front Page* to build web sites. It was easy! The sites aren't fancy but they do the job!

• Search job sites and look for a new job or career. E-mail your resume electronically to companies and look mighty cyber-savvy! Great web sites for job hunting include www.monster.com or www.hotjobs.com.

• See videos of special events, e.g. Mars landing, news events and more. Many live events are now broadcast via the web.

• Take online courses. Online courses for second grade and up are becoming more and more available every day. (Recommended resource: *Prentice Hall Directory of Online Education Resources* by Vicki Smith Bigham and George Bigham— A very big book with an abundance of information.)

The world of the Internet is so vast, I recommend getting a book or two to give you some web sites to start with. Let other people do the research for you! Yes, there is a certain thrill of finding a web site by sheer exploration, but busy parents can't afford to spend hours online surfing the web.

Recommended resource:

Practical Homeschooling published by Home Life/Bill and Mary Pride.

This magazine has an entire section dedicated solely to the pursuit of helping homeschoolers find and use computer resources. It covers a vast array of subjects in each issue, including online courses, editorials, online services, computer books, shareware, programming, web sites, software and hardware reviews, PC and Mac Tips and Tricks, computer news, and more. I highly recommend subscribing. The subscription price will pay for itself in helping you choose computer resources wisely. Call 800-346-6322 and tell them Tammy and Dan Kihlstadius sent you!

Web sites for kids to explore:

* FBI web site for kids: www.fbi.gov./kids/kids.htm

* NASA star charts: www.nasa.gov

* Audubon bird information: www.birdsource.cornell.edu/cfw

* Earthquake information: www.geology.usgs.gov/quake.shtml

* Web site collection of the American Library Association for kids: www.ala.org/parentspage/greatsites

*Amazon Interactive: a web site about the Amazon with online games and activities: www.eduweb.com/amazon.html

*Anne Frank: www.annefrank.com

*Bill Nye the Science guy: www.nye-labs.kcts.org

* Crayola; includes games and activities and an online tour of a crayon factory: www.crayola.com

* Exploratorium; science museum and experiments online: www.exploratorium.edu

* Franklin Institute Science Museum: www.sln.fi.edu/tfi/welcome.html

* Magic School Bus: www.scholastic.com/MagicSchoolBus

* Search engines for kids: www.searchopolis.com or www.ajkids.com

* World Flag Database; flag and country information on every country: www.flags.net

* US Postal Service for kids: www.usps.gov/kids/welcome.htm

TOP TEN TIPS FOR FRUSTRATION FREE ONLINE TIME

1. Never allow children on the web unsupervised.

Older children (15+) you trust may be allowed online with you nearby. Place the computer in a public place in the home and instruct the child in family rules of Internet use. I recommend not allowing a child to keep a computer in their bedroom. Or a TV or phone for that matter.

2. Keep your privacy.

Never give out your credit card, address, name or phone number to anyone on the Internet or online service and tell your children to do the same. The exception: some online companies and internet browser software now have secure encryption systems in place to handle safe credit card transactions. Only deal with reputable companies and when in doubt, call or mail in your order instead. Only use a credit card, never send a money order, check debit card, or personal check. If the company acts fraudulently, you will not have any recourse unless you use a credit card.

3. Someone is watching.

Remember, whenever you are surfing, your screen name and activities are recorded at these web sites, leaving you open for junk e-mailers to e-mail you.

4. Know where you are going.

It is best to only travel to web sites at which you are confident of what you will see when you get there. This is especially important if you are online with a child. One story I read involved group of 4th graders who were "surfing" the web unsupervised and decided to do a simple, innocent search on their favorite stuffed bear Pooh. What they stumbled on was a wicked parody of Pooh, showing a grisly tale of drug abuse, mass murder and the beloved Pooh wielding a bloody ax. Also, be careful going to generic web sites like www.whitehouse.gov. If you type in www.whitehouse.com instead, you pull up a porn site. Personal note: I have spent a lot of time "surfing" the web lately and have NEVER encountered an offensive web site. However, I regularly get in my e-mail invitations to "click here" for live cyber-sex 24-hours-a-day; consequently, adult supervision is recommended for e-mail reading, especially if you get a lot of junk e-mail like I do. You may get very little or a lot, depending on who has your e-mail address. Professional spammers lurk in chat rooms and forums – even homeschool chat rooms and forums – collecting email address. See above #3.

5. Consider using blocking software.

While it is not 100% perfect, it does offer some protection. I have read good reviews of the programs *CyberPatrol* from The Learning Company and *SurfWatch* from SurfWatch Software, but I have not used them myself. One thing I am sure of is that no screening software is foolproof and you are the one ultimately responsible for what passes through those little eyes and ears. Another side effect of screening software is it can be too restrictive. One parent said his software didn't allow his kids to visit many of the web sites he approved of, e.g.

Microsoft's web site. Another option is to choose an ISP that screens sites on its end. Bill Gothard's organization *Institute in Basic Life Principles* (IBLP) has set up a web site (www.characterlink.net) to offer only screened access to the Internet and a family friendly ISP. IBLP has very restrictive filtering; they have to personally review and approve web sites for access. A somewhat less restrictive but Christian ISP is *American Family Online.* (www.afo.net 662.840.6464) When you access the Internet through these types of ISP's, you are completely blocked from offensive sites and there is no way around it.

6. Don't become addicted.

Needless to say, anything that becomes more important than the Lord, His Word and your family has become an idol in your life. Be careful that your computer is only a tool, not a god.

7. Beware of viruses.

Never accept disks from others without running a virus check. Never download programs from the Internet, online service or e-mail unless they are from a trusted source or checked for viruses. One horror story I read about was someone getting a "free" screen saver in his or her e-mail. They loaded it and ran it. While it was running, it pirated information about this person's online account and password; and then uploaded this information to the sender of the "free" e-mail. Soon afterwards this nasty guy started using this person's online account!

8. Don't download every file you see. Hard drives do fill up eventually.

9. Don't forward e-mails to others blindlessly.

Someone had forwarded an e-mail to me about an article at *The Onion* web site claiming J.K Rowling, the author of the *Harry Potter* series, was an evil Satanist. Since I don't like Harry Potter, I had no trouble believing this. I wanted to forward it to all my e-mail friends to warn them as well, but I wanted to confirm this info first. I went to *The Onion's* web site (www.theonion.com) to read the article. Sure enough, it was a very derogatory web article about Rowling. They quoted a *London Times* interview of Rowling where she says that Jesus was a loser and her books were leading children into Satanism. So I checked the *London Times* (on the Internet) to read this interview myself. There was no interview in the *London Times.* I went back to *The Onion* and read some of their other articles. I started laughing—*The Onion* is just a satirical, fictional parody of the real news!! This information about Rowling was completely BOGUS. Like everything else, be careful what you read and believe on the 'net! (Note: Some of the material at *The Onion* is not suitable for Christians.)

10. Be careful of what you say and maintain your Christian witness.

Many people lurk in chat rooms and folders and notice Christians behaving un-Christian-like. Once you post a "flame" or obnoxious statement, you can never take it back. Some message boards do allow you to edit your post but be careful anyway.

11. Learn about the Internet.

If you feel like a real "newbie" to the online world, get yourself a book to get you started. (Newbie: someone who is clueless to online etiquette, terminology and methods.)

Bottom Line:

In all truthfulness, the Internet is a lot safer than most public places these days. While strangers may approach your children in public places, it is very unlikely you will receive unsolicited interruptions online. Weirdos will not come looking for you unless you hang out where weirdos hang out.

Chapter Six

More Important than Computers or Software

THE FINAL ANALYSIS: THE BEST WE CAN SUGGEST FOR YOU

The ultimate goal of *The Homeschooler's Software Guide* is to further equip you with the tools to better prepare your children for success. In the search for the best of the best, we kept your children's success as one of the primary focuses.

Their success is a noble goal in and of itself, but we would never want to imply that you can't find something even better out there, that isn't a software program, to teach you children. We know there are some things that are better. Of all the possibilities that exist, we would like to recommend to you the one thing (outside of the Bible and attending a Christ-centered Church) that our family has found will do far more good than any software we could offer you. It is the one thing that would have the greatest benefit, not just in your homeschool, but also for your own life, as well as your children's lives.

At some time in our lives, each of us has heard or read some message that has motivated us to greater achievement or to make changes to better our lives. Of all those things you have read or heard that initially motivated you, how much of a lasting change had it actually made in your life a year later? So often we hear or read a great message that we want to embrace in our life, but a year later we often can't even remember more than a trace of it! Yes, there are those messages we absorb that have a lasting change in our life, but those are few and far between. And those tend to change only a small portion of one's life. Rarely does one hear a message or read something that has a positive, major impact in changing one's life forever.

My search, others' searches

(A personal testimony from Dan, the father of the Kihlstadius family)

I was 21 years old, living alone, and contemplating my future. Being convicted by the Holy Spirit, I realized my need to come to terms with the truths of the Bible and what place God should have in my life. In my search to learn more about Jesus Christ and the Bible, I attended a seminar that was recommended to me by my new pastor and by a Christian whose faith and walk with the Lord I highly respected. The first night I attended, it changed my life forever. The seminar that I attended is called "*Institute in Basic Life Principles.*" (Previously known as "*Institute in Basic Youth Conflicts*") It teaches seven key principles that affect everyone's life. I have seen more lives changed for the better from this seminar than any other seminar or book that I know of (outside of the Bible itself). On the subject of the Bible, nothing that I have ever seen even comes close to making the Bible real and more relevant to everyday life than this seminar. This seminar travels around the country every year and is offered in most major cities, and many smaller cities about once a year.

I learned many things at that first seminar in 1982 that have forever changed my life for the better. I would like to share just a couple with you.

One of the things I learned that made the biggest impact the rest of my life was about priorities: mine versus God's. With this new understanding, I looked back on my life and realized how very, very wrong all my priorities had been. Primarily, I wanted what I wanted, with no regard as to what God wanted in my life; what I wanted was physical gratification, emotional gratification, and money.

Another part of this was that all my priorities for looking for in a potential wife were wrong. Through the things that I learned, I purposed to accept that one person that God's wanted me to marry, instead of trying to find that someone who met all my personal, carnal standards. God knew that person was Tammy. Up until this time, however, I was too blinded by my carnal desires and priorities to see that. (Praise God that He gave Tammy the grace to stick

with me through my previous spiritual blindness!) Less than a year after that first seminar, we got married. And when I said "I do" I was able to say it having a peace in my heart and knowing that God had, in his sovereign wisdom, pre-selected Tammy for me, before I ever met her.

But like with every Christian's walk, God had only started working in my life. And I knew it. Having seen the value and importance of this seminar in my own life, one of the first things I wanted to do with Tammy, as husband and wife, was get her to this seminar too. Within a month we drove 1000 miles just so that we could attend it together, and within one month of that, we drove 400 miles to attend the "sequel" known as the *Advanced Seminar*.

By this point (less than a year after attending my first *Institute in Basic Life Principles* seminar) I had already made many major changes in my life, all for the better, but I still had so far to go (and still do.) One of those still needed changes was in the area of my plans for my family: NONE. I didn't want any children. I wanted my family to be "Tammy and me" and that was it! Obviously, I still had a lot more to learn about my (selfish, self-serving) priorities versus God's.

It was during that Advanced Seminar when I learned about God's purposes and priorities with children and for families. I learned for the first time that children were actually a blessing from God. What a concept! I had no idea! All my life, I had viewed children more as a curse, if anything. Certainly, they were a major hindrance and inconvenience. Previous to this, I had told Tammy that maybe we would have children in 5 years after we were married. I had lied. (Yes, God still had a lot of work left to do in me!) I was hoping I would be able to eventually convince Tammy to share my perspective on not having children. Well, I walked out of that session a VERY convicted man. We discussed what we had just heard and we could not deny the truths of God's word. We agreed that we would commit to following His way in this area of our life. That very night, the birth control pills went in the garbage forever. Sometimes we let the Holy Spirit work faster than others! Our first child was born about a year later. Praise God for His mercy and patience with our stubborn, selfish ways!

Now, I won't say that I never struggled with that decision since then. I have struggled with it. Over the years I have not been as faithful to this principle as God would desire me to be, especially when we had 5 children, all under the age of 7. But by faith, and faith alone, we now have 8 children, 16 years old and younger. When our last child was just a few weeks old we were already looking forward to when we can have our next!

There are so many other things I could share with you about the wonderful things God has done in our lives through what we have learned through the teachings of the *Institute of Basic Life Principles* and its materials. Since then we have met many other Godly families who all share similar testimonies—stories of the wondrous, life-changing things that have happened in their own lives from things they have learned from the Seminar and applied to their lives.

It is not the seminar itself that I want to give glory to. And it is not the Seminar that makes the changes. The Seminar is only a conduit, not the source, of the changing power. The power comes from hearing and applying God's truths and principles that come out of the Bible. This Seminar is sim-

ply the absolute best, clearest presentation of these principles I have ever seen or heard from one source.

What I would like to leave you with the most is this thought:
If this is the only thing you get out of this Guide (assuming here that you are already a Christian) if we can convince you and your family to attend this seminar, it will do more good for your whole family, than using any of our recommended software programs. A lot of this software is really good, but of all the things we could recommend for you, this seminar would be our first choice. It is the best thing we have ever experienced and learned from, and obviously, we can't recommend it highly enough.

We receive no money for promoting this seminar, and have no interest or connections, financially or otherwise, in its operation. If we can do anything to help you train your children for true success, and to better your own life, it would be to invite you to this seminar. If you contact us more than two months in advance of your local seminar, we can give you details on preregistration discounts! If you've ever attended the seminar before, you can re-attend at anytime for free! And we would encourage you to attend again if you haven't done so recently. There is a lot of new material, and much of the previous material has been updated, refined, and reworked for even better clarity and explanation. Also, at some cities they have added a "Children's Institute" for ages 6-12. Our children love it!

As I also referred to, there is also an *Advanced Seminar* for "Alumni" of the Basic. If you found the *Basic Seminar* helpful, you'll love this one. As with the *Basic Seminar*, if you register at least two months before your local seminar, you can get pre-registration discounts.

For more information, contact us, your local IBLP office (if you have one) or call the national headquarters at (630) 323-9800. You can also check out their web site at www.iblp.org. The page to register for a seminar nearest to your city is www.iblp.com/seminars/register/register.html.

Section II

Reviews

Tammy's Top Ten Picks!

1. (Find the right Bible program(s) for your family's age range.)
2. PhonicsTutor
3. NumberMaze Challenge
4. Quarter Mile Math
5. Logical Journey of the Zoombinis
6. Typing Instructor Deluxe or Mavis Beacon Teaches Typing
7. World Discovery Deluxe
8. World Book Encyclopedia Deluxe
9. Math Teacher
10. Excel High School

While you are perusing the hundreds of titles listed and recommended in this Guide, keep in mind we do not recommend you buy all of them. Listed above are the absolute essential software programs every homeschool should own. (Depending on the ages of your children.) Before you buy any other titles, make sure you own all of the top ten titles. Then peruse all the subjects and descriptions listed and buy software according to your family's interests and needs. Spend money on software that will meet a need in your homeschool and you will be happy with your investment.

Where to find all this good stuff!

(Especially the hard-to-find ones!)

When you are ready to purchase any of the titles listed in this Guide, check the Appendix of Software Resellers listed in the back. The companies listed are all owned and run by Christian homeschool families.

Please try *The Home Computer Market* first. (www.homecomputermarket.com) They try to have all my top ten titles in stock at all times. They usually have most of the other titles in stock or can sometimes special order them for you. They offer competitive pricing, phone or online ordering and top-notch service.

If you cannot find a particular title from a reseller, your next best bet is to call the company directly. See the Appendix of Software Publishers for their phone number and web site. Most offer online ordering as well.

About the Homeschooler's Software Planning Grid on the next pages

On the next two pages is a software planning "grid" that lists our top 80 or so titles organized by age and subject area. Use this grid of our top recommendations in each subject area for your curriculum planning.

THE HOMESCHOOLER'S SOFTWARE GUIDE: Software Curriculum Planning Grid

AGES ->	3	4	5	6	7	8	9	10	11	12	13	14	15	16	17 & UP

SUBJECT:

ALPHABET or PHONICS
- LETS GO READ 1 (ages 4–5)
- PHONICS TUTOR (ages 6–8)
- WORD MUNCHERS DELUXE (ages 8–11)

READING
- READING BLASTER 4-6 & 5-7 (ages 4–7)
- LETS GO READ 2 (ages 5–7)
- PHONICS TUTOR (ages 7–8)
- READING MANSION (ages 6–9)
- BIBLE BUILDER (ages 9–10)
- ULTIMATE SPEED READER (ages 12–15)

WRITING
- IMAGINATION EXPRESS or STORYBOOK WEAVER DELUXE (ages 6–12)
- ULTIMATE WRITING & CREATIVITY CENTER (ages 6–12)
- HYPERSTUDIO (ages 13–16)
- STUDENT WRITING CENTER (ages 13–15)

VOCABULARY
- WORD BLASTER (ages 9–11)
- WORDSMART (ages 13–14)
- ULTIMATE WORD ATTACK (ages 13–15)

SPELLING
- SPELLING BLASTER (ages 8–10)
- PHONICS TUTOR (ages 9–12)
- SPELL IT DELUXE (ages 10–13)

GRAMMAR
- ALS GRAMMAR (ages 11–13)
- GRAMMAR KEY (ages 12–13)
- SWITCHED ON SCHOOLHOUSE LANGUAGE ARTS (ages 11–15)

MATH
- MILLIE'S MATHHOUSE (ages 5–6)
- MATHBLASTER 4-6 (ages 4–6)
- READER RABBIT MATH 4-6 (ages 4–6)
- AXEL'S WHIRLED MATH (ages 7–8)
- NUMBERMAZE CHALLENGE (ages 7–9)
- MINDTWISTER MATH (ages 8–9)
- DECIMAL AND FRACTION MAZE (ages 9–11)
- QUARTERMILE MATH (ages 11–13)
- SWITCHED ON SCHOOLHOUSE MATH (ages 10–13)
- MATHTEACHER (ages 14–15)
- ASTRO ALGEBRA (ages 14)
- MATHBLASTER ALGEBRA (ages 14)

LOGIC & THINKING SKILLS
- PUTT PUTT SERIES (ages 5–6)
- SAMMY'S SCIENCE HOUSE (ages 5–6)
- READER RABBIT THINKING GAMES (ages 6–7)
- THINKING' THINGS GALACTIC BRAIN BENDERS (ages 9–12)
- LOGICAL JOURNEY OF THE ZOOMBINIS (ages 9–11)
- DR. BRAIN SERIES (ages 12–14)
- SIMCITY or SIMFARM (ages 12–13)

HISTORY
- MY FIRST AMAZING HISTORY EXPLORER (ages 5–9)
- OREGON TRAIL VERSION 3 OR HIGHER (ages 9–11)
- SWITCHED ON SCHOOLHOUSE (ages 10–12)
- HISTORY OF THE WORLD 2.0 (ages 13–15)
- ALS WORLD or US HISTORY (ages 13–15)

AGES ->	3	4	5	6	7	8	9	10	11	12	13	14	15	16	17 & UP

AGES -> 3 4 5 6 7 8 9 10 11 12 13 14 15 16 17 & UP

SUBJECT:

GEOGRAPHY
- TRUDY'S TIME AND PLACE
- MY FIRST AMAZING WORLD EXPLORER 2.0
- ALS WORLD or US GEOGRAPHY
- GEOSAFARI GEOGRAPHY
- WORLD DISCOVERY DELUXE

FOREIGN LANGUAGE
- KIDS SPEAK 10 IN 1 LANGUAGE
- ROSETTA STONE
- ARTES LATINAE
- LEARN SPANISH/FRENCH YOUR WAY

SCIENCE
- SAMMY'S SCIENCE HOUSE
- MY FIRST AMAZING SCIENCE EXPLORER
- SPACE ACADEMY GX-1
- EYEWITNESS ENCYCLOPEDIA OF NATURE 2.0
- GEOSAFARI SCIENCE
- INTEL PLAY: QX3 COMPUTER MICROSCOPE
- SWITCHED ON SCHOOLHOUSE SCIENCE
- MY AMAZING HUMAN BODY
- EYEWITNESS ENCYCLOPEDIA of SCIENCE 2.0
- A.D.A.M. or 9 MONTH MIRACLE (anatomy)

INTEGRATED
- JUMPSTART SERIES
- EXCEL SERIES
- KAPLAN SAT/ACT/PSAT
- HIGH SCHOOL ADVANTAGE

CURRICULUM
- SWITCHED ON SCHOOLHOUSE
- ADVANCED LEARNING SYSTEMS (ALS)
- ROBINSON CURRICULUM (for reference & research)

COLLEGE PREP & LIFE SKILLS
- MAGIC APPLEHOUSE (no magic in program)
- MAVIS BEACON TEACHES TYPING or TYPING INSTRUCTOR DELUXE
- QUICKEN
- THE CRUNCHER 2.0

BIBLE
- PLAY & LEARN BIBLE STORIES
- BIBLE BUILDER and/or FAMILY BIBLE CHALLENGE
- PATHWAYS THROUGH JERUSALEM
- PC MEMLOK
- ON LINE BIBLE
- LIFE OF CHRIST

OTHER MUST HAVE TITLES
- MUSIC ACE 1 & 2
- KID DESK OR HOMESCHOOL DESK

AGES -> 3 4 5 6 7 8 9 10 11 12 13 14 15 16 17 & UP

HOW TO USE THIS REVIEW SECTION

Example: Explanation:

Reader Rabbit Reading 1   ←→   Program Title

The Learning Company   ←→   **The company that publishes it**

Ages 4-6   Street price $18   ←→   **Age range & typical price on the title.**

Please note: The age ranges listed does NOT indicate the longevity of the material but rather the age appropriateness of the material. The longevity of each program will vary with each child's ability to master the material and the depth of the actual content. Each program varies significantly in its depth and we suggest you read each description carefully to understand fully the scope and sequence of each program.

Subject(s): Alphabet   ←→   **Subject matter**

Important: The subjects listed are not necessarily all inclusive for the age ranges. Very few programs can provide 100% of a subject area for any given age range.

Skills needed: mouse   ←→   **Prerequisite skills needed to use the program**

System Req.:WIN 95/98: 486SX33/8MB ←→   **What you need on your IBM Compatible computer to run the software.**

MAC: 040/8MB System 7.1   ←→   **What you need on your Macintosh computer to run the software.**

SYSTEM REQUIREMENTS EXPLAINED:

Numbers and systems listed are minimums. Please read all system requirements carefully!

PI   = **Pentium I or 586**
PII   = **Pentium II or 686**
PIII = **Pentium III or 786**
PMac = **Power Macintosh**

Standard MUST HAVE hardware requirements and specifications assumed but not listed with each title include:

- Hard Drive space available. Some CD-ROM programs require up to 20 MB.
- 4X CD-ROM or higher
- Windows 3.1, 95 or higher NOTE: ALL WIN 98 PROGRAMS WILL RUN ON WINDOWS Me
- Mac System 7.5 or higher
- 256+ colors
- SoundBlaster compatible 16 bit sound card and speakers (Not applicable to a Mac)
- Mouse

If there is a "+" after a specification given, then more is recommended. If more than standard hardware requirements are required, (listed above) they are listed as well. WINDOWS LISTED FIRST, THEN MAC IF AVAILABLE.

Chapter Seven

Software Reviews

GENERAL USE

Easy Plan
JCT Products
ALL AGES   Typical Street Price: $25
Skills needed: mouse
System Req: WIN 3.1/95/98 486/8MB
This homeschool lesson planner designed by a homeschool dad is basic but easy to use and effective. Track lesson plans, grades and assignments for all your students.

Homeschool Desk
JCT Products
ALL AGES   Typical Street Price: $25
Skills needed: mouse
System Req: WIN 3.1/95/98 486/8MB
This program is very similar to *Kid Desk* but more basic in format. Created by a homeschool dad, this desktop protection program sets up a screen whereby kids can only click on icons for programs you choose. *Homeschool Desk* takes a little more time to set up than *Kid Desk* because you have to select and set up one program at a time whereas in *Kid Desk*, you can select more than one program at a time. Otherwise, it's very basic and easy. Highly recommended.

Homeschool Safety Browser
JCT Products
ALL AGES   Typical Street Price: $30
Skills needed: mouse
System Req: WIN 3.1/95/98 486/8MB
This Internet-blocking software is designed as a browser that resides on your computer that can only access pre-viewed and approved homeschool and educational web sites. Multitudes of Internet choices are available from science to math, they are all safe for your homeschool child, and you can't go anywhere else on the 'net. Designed by a Christian homeschool dad, the sites are previewed by he and his family for suitability for Christian homeschoolers.

Kid Desk Internet Safe (Win 95/98 only)
Kid Desk Family Edition (Win 3.1/Win95/Win 98 or Mac)
Edmark
ALL AGES   Typical Street Price: $29
Skills needed: mouse
System Req: WIN 3.1/95/98 486/8MB
MAC: 040/8MB
Kid Desk gives children control over all the computer programs that you choose for them, without putting the rest of your programs and hard disk at risk. The *Internet Safe* edition also offers the ability to screen out objectionable

web sites. This program is especially wonderful for stopping little ones who want to "explore" around your hard drive (and inadvertently do damage in the process) With simple mouse clicks even our 2 and 3-year-old children can start their own programs by themselves — and without the need for supervision. No reading or computer skills needed once set up. *Kid Desk* is an excellent, inexpensive and easier to use alternative to Windows and/or DOS. It is even better and safer that the standard Mac desktop. *Kid Desk* creates icons on a cute little "desktop" customized for each child. *Kid Desk* allows you to smoothly run Windows, CD-ROM and DOS programs from the same desktop without leaving *Kid Desk*. You get none of the bugs of trying to run DOS programs out of Windows. If we can only recommend two programs, it would be this and *Bible Builder*. It is also useful for those teenagers who are getting into things, changing things and/or installing programs you don't want on your computer. Lots of moms have told us they prefer *Kid Desk* as their desktop choice for their own children. To save money, check out Edmark's web site and download *Kid Desk Lite*, a FREE basic version of *Kid Desk* (Win 95 or 98 only) that offers the basic hard drive protection everyone MUST have. www.edmark.com This program is one of Mary Pride's top picks. Note: as of this writing, Kid Desk Internet Safe is not available. You may still find it in bargain bins. Snatch it up if you see it.

The Magic Applehouse
McGraw Hill
Ages 5-10   Typical Street Price: $34
Subject(s): business, sales, computer use
Skills needed: mouse, reading
System Req: WIN 3.1/95/98 486/8MB
MAC: 040/8MB
This program is designed to teach a multitude of computer and business skills to children. *The Magic Applehouse* contains a collection of 14 multilevel activities centered on running a business of selling apples. Skills learned include: computer basics, use of *Tab* and *Shift* keys, resizing windows, following a sequence of

actions, cutting and pasting, spreadsheet basics, and more. Activities are carefully structured as to maximize learning and content. Highly recommended for any family wanting their children to be totally comfortable in using the computer as a powerful business tool. Note: No magic in program, only in the title name.

PRESCHOOL

"How early can a child use a computer?"

We have found most children are able to use a mouse proficiently at about 2.5. My 6th child Philip was a very precocious 22-month-old when he was able to navigate most toddler-ware. His favorites at that age were: *Early Math, Busytown, Sammy's Science House,* and *Fun in Toyland.* He could maneuver the mouse very deftly long before he could use the toilet. The following are programs designed for the beginner and youngest computer user in the family. Most do not teach a specific subject — if you are looking for a specific subject, look under that listing in the planning guide. Most of these "toddler-ware" programs are designed to stimulate thinking, creativity and get them started on the computer. The hidden advantage is they will be learning a great deal without you having to prepare elaborate "lesson plans." (And nothing to pick up or put away.)

Adventures of Elmo in Grouchland
The Learning Company
Ages 3-5   Street price $19
Subject(s): thinking
Skills needed: mouse
System Req: WIN 95/98/Me PI/90/16MB
MAC: N/A
After my four year old watched this movie about 6 times in a row, he was excited to try out this new program. Although not packed with educational value, it still was a lot of fun. The child guides Elmo from Sesame Street to Grouchland in search of his beloved blanket. Elmo is always pleasant and kind but he learns he has been selfish with his blanket. My son loved the goofy things you could do in Grouchland like make sardine and stinky cheese ice cream at the Bad Humor Ice Cream cart, dump messy stuff on cars and more. If you have an Elmo fan at your house, this is great gift.

A to Zap
School Zone
Ages 3-5   Typical Street Price: $28
Skills needed: mouse
System Req: WIN 3.1/95/98 486/8MB
MAC: 040/5MB
A to Zap is a collection of pre-reading/early learning activities centered on the letters of the alphabet. Absolutely no phonics; just fun and colorful activities involving music, shapes, animals, cars, x-rays, and more. Learn letter names, cause and effect, understand that letters make words, matching words and pictures. Keeps little ones busy.

Big Job!
Discovery Channel Multimedia
Ages 2-7   Typical Street Price: $19
Skills needed: mouse
System Req: WIN 3.1/95/98 486/8MB
MAC: 040/8MB
Sorry, moms, this is not a potty training program. (Don't I wish.) This is now the new favorite program at my house for my little boys. Three of our boys are ages 3-7 and they love this. 12 activities including building roads, driving rescue or construction vehicles, creating farms, constructing buildings, putting out fires and more. All the tools are here. No dangerous equipment or liability insurance needed for your budding engineers to take the helm and be construction workers. Many games offer a wide variety of activities and a range of challenges. One time the CD was lost and I had to open a new box to quell the pending riot. "Where is *Big Job*? Can't we play *Big Job*?" Recommended use: Excellent choice for GIFT.

Note: IF you can't find *Big Job*, Fisher Price *Big Action Construction* is an excellent alternative. See review below.

Busytown 2000

Simon and Schuster
Ages 2-5   Typical Street Price: $19
Skills needed: mouse
System Req: WIN 3.1/95/98 586/1MB
MAC: PMac/8MB.

This is one of the best pre-reader programs available. 12 engaging, entertaining and educational activities designed to teach about community workers. Our little ones find the Richard Scarry art and characters irresistible. With *Busytown*, your child can install a water heater, pave a road, pump gas, play doctor and more. Although this is an older program, my kids still play this often. The music, sound and graphics are simply delightful. This is one of Mary Pride's top picks. Highly recommended for every family with pre-readers. Nice feature: Can turn off music with function keys if you find music annoying.

Blue's Clues
Treasure Hunt Adventure

Humongous Entertainment
Ages 3-6   Typical Street Price: $19
Skills needed: mouse, following instructions
Subjects: logic, memory
System Req: WIN95/98: PI/16MB
MAC: PMac/80 MHz/16MB

This great new software program is based on the popular *Nickelodeon* TV show, *Blue's Clues*. *Blue's Clues* is one of the few programs I let my preschoolers watch regularly. No *Sesame Street, Barney* or *Teletubbies* at my house. I like the show because it's calm, peaceful and interactive. The kind and polite host, Steve Burns, gets the kids involved with the activities on the show by speaking directly to the camera continually. Blue is his dog and Blue leaves three clues (blue paw prints) around the house to help Steve guess what Blue wants, does, is thinking of, etc. So the kids "help" Steve find the clues and decipher their meaning. In the *Blue's Clues* software

programs, the graphics are so good it seems like you are interacting directly with the TV show itself. In this program they are off on a treasure hunt. Kids help Steve and Blue explore the house, park and school looking for clues. They are searching for the *Land of Great Discovery* and along the way they help others by recycling trash, rake leaves, and more. Kids need to remember details along the way to successfully complete the game and they are challenged to be attentive to find all the clues. Kids love Blue and playing this game and it offers all-around thinking skills for your preschoolers.

Blue's Birthday Adventure

Humongous Entertainment
Ages 3-6   Typical Street Price: $14
Skills needed: mouse, following instructions
Subjects: logic, memory
System Req: WIN95/98: PI/16MB
MAC: PMac/80 MHz/16MB

This great new software program is based on the popular *Nickelodeon* TV show, *Blue's Clues*. *Blue's Clues* is one of the few programs I let my preschoolers watch regularly. No *Sesame Street, Barney* or *Teletubbies* at my house. I like the show because it's calm, peaceful and interactive. The kind and polite host, Steve Burns, gets the kids involved with the activities on the show by speaking directly to the camera continually. Blue is his dog and Blue leaves three clues (blue paw prints) around the house to help Steve guess what Blue wants, does, is thinking of, etc. So the kids help Steve find the clues and decipher their meaning. In the *Blue's Clues* software programs, the graphics are so good it seems like you are interacting directly with the TV show itself. In this *Blue's Clues* software adventure, Steve and Blue are off on a scavenger hunt to find all the supplies needed for Blue's birthday party. There are four separate adventures and parents can set the difficulty level. With nine different activities within the adventures, there is a lot to keep kids involved and thinking. These activities are memory and logic type games like matching, puzzles and designing party favors. My kids, who are big Blue and Steve fans, loved this *Blue's Clues* program the most.

Curious George ABC Adventure

Houghton Mifflin Interactive
Ages 3-6   Typical Street Price: $18
Subject(s): Alphabet, listening, vocabulary
Skills needed: mouse
System Req: WIN 3.1/95/98
486SX33/8MB (12MB for Win95)
040/8MB System 7.1

Curious George takes your child through six engaging activities designed to help your child learn and practice their ABC's. In *Postcard Caper*, you help George match letters to pictures. At the bakery and the airfield, George plays letter-matching games. In *I Spy*, the child must find an object at the zoo that begins with a certain letter. Use the mouse to roam the zoo, searching. When the cursor passes over objects, they are highlighted and labeled with text and audio. When you find the right objects, they can be printed out and collected to make your own *Curious George ABC* scrapbook. Some record keeping tells parents how long child remains on task and how far the child has progressed. Recommended use: Parent directed practice in activities that the child needs practice or for open-ended play for little ones. Caution: Curious George does get into some mischief by only being curious but tries to put things right.

Curious George Early Learning Adventure

Houghton Mifflin Interactive
Ages: 3-5   Street price $28
Subject(s): early learning activities: patterns, shapes, letters
Skills needed: mouse
System Req: WIN 3.1/95/98 486/8MB
MAC: 030/8MB

This program is called Early Learning, but it is more like early arcade. I like the games; they are perfect for this age group, but they don't teach much. If you're looking for an arcade action game for your little ones that isn't too mindless, this is a fun choice. Recommended use: gift for the young Curious George fan.

Elmo's Preschool Deluxe

Learning Company
Ages 2.5-5   Street price $19
Skills needed: mouse
System Req: 486/4+MB

If your children like Elmo, they will love this program. Elmo introduces and teaches early preschool skills such as letters, numbers, colors, shapes and music through 15 different activities. Elmo is patient and kind and never gets "negative" about incorrect answers. The teaching is well done and the interface pleasant (if you like Elmo.) Does not have any other interactive Sesame Street characters or the politically correct garbage Sesame Street normally endorses. Strengths: Kindness, sharing, good phonics.

Fisher Price: Big Action Construction

Learning Company
Ages 5-up   Street price $19
Subject(s): logic, fun
Skills needed: reading, mouse
System Req: WIN 95/98:
486/66MHz/16MB
MAC: PMac/16MB

If you can't find *Big Job*, this is a great second choice. As in *Big Job*, kids get to work heavy machinery in this program as well. Smashing rocks with wrecking balls, playing with dynamite, building roads and buildings and more keeps those boys busy and happy. My kids loved playing this program and they really liked the lunch break time where they made sandwiches out of silly ingredients like bricks, cookies and other items. The program offers the chance to do all kinds of construction tasks and the graphics and sound are great. Not tons of education (career guidance?) but truckloads of fun.

Fisher Price: Great Adventures Castle

Learning Company
Ages 5-up   Street price $19
Subject(s): logic, fun
Skills needed: reading, mouse
System Req: WIN 3.1/95/98 486/8MB
MAC: 040/8MB

My kids really enjoyed this fun castle program where they had to find and recruit 7 knights to storm the castle and save the king. A lot of thinking activities but not a great deal of education makes this program a playtime gift only- not for school. Some counting and reading. Can build your own castle. Caution: One of the knights has magic-like powers- he is invisible.

Fisher Price: Great Adventures Pirate Ship

Learning Company
Ages 5-up   Street price $19
Subject(s): logic, fun
Skills needed: reading, mouse
System Req: WIN 3.1/95/98 486/8MB
MAC: 040/8MB

Kids love running this pirate ship with all the wacky activities. Shooting chickens out of the cannon was my kids' favorite activity. Young swashbucklers have a splash exploring eight play areas in search of the missing pieces of the mysterious treasure map. Along the way they'll meet a crew of fellow buccaneers, play ocean and pirate games and sing along with hilarious pirate tunes. Put all the pieces together and they'll find the long-lost passage to Pirate Island, where golden treasure awaits. Ten different maps let kids chart a new adventure in every game. These pirates do not rape, pillage and burn. Nothing objectionable — just not much learning.

Freddi Fish: The Case of the Missing Kelp Seeds

Humongous
Ages 3-8   Street price $19
Skills needed: moderate mouse skills, memory/thinking
System Req: WIN 3.1/95/98 486SX33/8MB
MAC: 040(25Mhz)/8MB

Great, colorful adventure program for little ones. Guide friendly, helpful Freddi as she helps others during her quest to find clue to the location of the missing kelp seeds. Designed as an engaging scavenger hunt, you help Freddi find clues and tools to solve the mystery. A favorite of our children. Some good thinking skills, memory practice and a little bit of arcade action.

Freddi Fish 2: The Case of the Haunted Schoolhouse

Humongous
Ages 3-8   Street price $19
Skills needed: moderate mouse skills, memory/thinking
Subjects: logic, memory
System Req: WIN 3.1/95/98 486SX33/8MB
MAC: 040(25Mhz)/8MB

Someone is "haunting" the schoolhouse and is taking all the toys. Through teamwork and smart thinking, you must help Freddi create a trap. There is no real ghost- it is just a disgruntled fish who never got Christmas presents as a little guppy. A good message of forgiveness and restoration. Background music can be turned off.

Freddi Fish 3:
The Case of the Stolen Conch Shell

Humongous

Ages 3-8   Street price $19

Skills needed: moderate mouse skills, memory/thinking

Subjects: logic, memory

System Req: WIN 3.1/95/98

486SX33/8MB

MAC: 040(25Mhz)/8MB

The Great Conch Shell is missing and Freddi Fish is on the case. Just like the other *Freddi Fish* programs, each screen is beautifully rendered graphics and the characters are interesting and fun. The suspect is Luther's Uncle Benny but the two amateur sleuths are sure he is innocent. So off they go to prove his innocence. Along the way, Freddi and Luther play lots of great games, collect clues and meet some friends. One activity entails creating music on an undersea organ, another finding items along the way, exploring undersea ruins, and floating on a raft to recover a lost monkey. This *Freddi Fish* is a little harder than the first two and is probably best enjoyed by the 5-8 age group.

Freddi Fish 4:
The Case of Hogfish Rustlers of Briny Gulch

Humongous

Ages 3-8   Street price $19

Skills needed: moderate mouse skills, memory/thinking

Subjects: logic, memory

System Req: WIN 3.1/95/98 PI/90/16MB

MAC: PMac/80/16B

Every Freddi Fish adventure is new and different and my kids can't wait to solve each mystery. In this program, someone has stolen ("rustled" in cowboy talk) cousin Calico's hogfish herd and Freddi and her buddy Luther must collect the clues and solve the puzzle of who stole the hogfish and where they are now. Similar to the *Putt Putt* series, Freddi and Luther must help out others to procure the items necessary to catch the rustlers. They must get items the others need to trade for the items Freddi and Luther need. Attention to detail and others' needs and a good memory are essential to success in this program. Every time the child plays the game is different because items are hidden in new places and a different character is the culprit. With the Wild West theme and many colorful fun characters, this game is very appealing to the young and the old.

Learning in Toyland

Learning Company

Ages 2-6   Street price $14

Subjects: shapes, sizes, making things

Skills needed: mouse

System Req: WIN 3.1/95/98

486SX33/8MB

MAC: 030(25MHz)/8MB

Music: Not offensive to me, but can be turned off.

Learning in Toyland is a favorite of my 4-year-old boy. Fun activities include baking and decorating cookies, building and painting things in the workshop (toys, trains, cars, more) designing wild contraptions in the garage. Simple interface with wholesome activities give this program a wide appeal. If you got a little one who loves trains (like I do), he/she will find this program especially fun. You get to drive the train around Toyland. Activities reinforce following directions, problem solving, numbers, shapes, patterns and more.

Let's Explore the Airport with Buzzy

Humongous

AGES 3-7   Street price $19

Skills needed: mouse

System Req: WIN 3.1/95/98 486/8MB

MAC: 030/8MB

Buzzy the knowledge bug takes you on a behind the scenes tour of the airport. Also has some additional activities including airport trivia questions, "Find It" detective game, and "What Is It?" a picture and word matching game. Includes a narrated mini-encyclopedia about airports so even non-readers can explore and learn.

My kids' favorite part: sorting luggage in a high-paced arcade game. Has a lot of information built into the program. Recommended use: Supplement transportation unit study for the little ones.

Let's Explore the Farm with Buzzy

Humongous
AGES 3-7   Street price $19
Skills needed: mouse
System Req: WIN 3.1/95/98 486/8MB
MAC: 030/8MB

Buzzy the knowledge bug takes you on a tour of a farm. Learn about the animals, and how things happen on the farm. Includes a narrated mini-encyclopedia about farms so even non-readers can explore and learn. Has a lot of information and fun games built into the program. Recommended use: Supplement animal unit study for the little ones.

Let's Explore the Jungle with Buzzy

Humongous
AGES 3-7   Street price $19
Skills needed: mouse
System Req: WIN 3.1/95/98 486/8MB
MAC: 030/8MB

Buzzy takes you to the jungle. Covers such topics as plants, animals, habitats, and such. Includes a narrated mini-encyclopedia about jungles so even non-readers can explore and learn. Has a lot of information and games built into the program. Recommended use: Supplement animal unit study for the little ones.

Junior Field Trip Collection: Let's Explore Jungle, Farm, and Airport in one box

Humongous
Ages 2-7   Street price $24
Skills needed: mouse
System Req: WIN 3.1/95/98 486/8MB
MAC: 040/8MB

This bundle is a great buy if you can find it. Includes all three Let's Explore titles.

Play and Learn Children's Bible Stories

See review under *Bible*.

Putt-Putt Enters the Race

Humongous
Ages 4-7   Street price $19
Skills needed: mouse, following directions
System Req: WIN 3.1/95/98 PI/90/16MB
MAC: Pmac/90/16MB

Putt Putt is getting ready for the big race, the Cartown 500 and needs some supplies. So off he goes in search of new tires, hubcaps and more. Along the way he meets some fun and wacky characters who are willing to help Putt Putt if he helps them. For example, Putt Putt needs a shovel to dig up the hubcaps and Betsy Bulldozer just happens to have a shovel. However, she will only trade it for a milkshake so Putt Putt is off to find a milkshake. As always, Putt Putt is kind, helpful and courteous and he always perseveres. To complete Putt Putt's mission, the child has to map the whole town in his head, remember where items are, be attentive to details and needs, and logically progress through acquiring the items he needs. One of the best *Putt Putts* titles according to my kids.

Putt-Putt Joins The Parade
Putt-Putt Goes To The Moon
Fatty Bear's Birthday Surprise

Humongous
Ages 2-7   Street price $25 for
                  the bundle
Skills needed: mouse, following directions
System Req: WIN 3.1/95/98 486/8MB
MAC: 040/8MB

Putt-Putt is very popular at our house and my 2 and 5 year olds especially love these interactive adventures. These highly interactive, fun programs for the little ones will keep them learning and busy for hours. The goal of each *Putt Putt* program is a scavenger hunt-like game. Putt Putt must find objects and complete tasks to fulfill the objective of the game. To play successfully, the child must possess a good memory and an eye for detail. In *Putt Putt Joins the Parade*, Putt Putt must prepare his car for the big parade. To pay for a car wash, he must travel around Cartown doing odd jobs (lawn mowing and delivering groceries) for money. He also collects decorative items like a balloon, a new paint job and a pet. In *Putt Putt Goes to the Moon*, Putt Putt is accidentally "blasted" to the moon in a freak fireworks factory accident. On the moon he must collect pieces to build a spaceship to get home. He even meets the Apollo moon buggy that was left behind long ago. The moon buggy was very lonely and Putt Putt cheers him up with his happy and cheerful friendship. Graphics, sound and play are all enjoyable and engaging. These are older Putt Putt titles but they are still great fun. Note: younger children (2-4) need help to play this game successfully. My little children still like to play it even if they don't do it right. One option we have utilized is to pair an older preschooler (5 or 6) with his younger sibling. This three in one bundle also contains *Fatty Bear's Birthday Surprise* which similar to Putt Putt's scavenger hunt theme but with different characters. Fatty Bear must procure all the items to make a birthday cake and prepare a birthday party for his owner, a sweet little girl. While she sleeps, Fatty Bear must sneak around the house to prepare for the party before she wakes up. Fatty Bear is also a favorite of our children.

Putt-Putt Joins the Circus

Humongous

Ages 4-7   Street price $19

Skills needed: mouse, following directions

System Req: WIN 95/98: PI/90/16MB

MAC: Pmac/90/16MB

Putt-Putt is an adorable, polite little car who is always helping out others. This time he has to help the ringmaster get the circus ready for the really big show tonight. To accomplish this he must recover items needed for the five acts. For example, he must find and recover the safety net to help the Flying Porkowskis (yes, they're pigs)

complete their daredevil trapeze act. Putt Putt lends his cheerful assistance to many different colorful characters to help them find their lost items. Bette Bandwagon needs help setting her organ pipes from the lowest to highest notes and Philippe the Flea needs a new tent for his troop. All these rescue operations require a great deal of patience, good memory and logic to accomplish. One of my favorite things about the *Putt Putt* series is that Putt Putt is always cheerful, courteous and helpful. Something I like to see in my own kids. My kids love playing *Putt Putt* and can hardly wait for the next one to come out. Sometimes they play together to maximize the brainpower and this builds cooperation. Fortunately for me, games can be saved so they can leave to eat or do chores. Caution: Magician does tricks in one part of game. Recommended use: afterschool playtime or gift.

Putt-Putt Saves The Zoo

Humongous

Ages 2-7   Street price $15

Skills needed: mouse, following directions

System Req: WIN 3.1/95/98 486/8MB

MAC: 040/8MB

Putt-Putt is very popular at our house and my 2 year old especially loves these interactive adventures. These highly interactive, fun programs for the little ones will keep them learning and busy for hours. The goal of each *Putt Putt* program is a scavenger hunt like game. Putt Putt must find objects and complete tasks to fulfill the objective of the game. To play successfully, the child must possess a good memory and an attentive eye to detail. Graphics, sound and play are all enjoyable and engaging. The goal is to rescue all the baby animals. Note: younger children (2-4) need help to play this game successfully. My little children still like to play it even if they don't do it right. One option we have utilized is to pair an older preschooler (5 or 6) with his younger sibling. One of the better thinking skills programs for non-readers.

Reader Rabbit Playtime for Baby and Toddler

Learning Company
Ages 1.5-3   Street price $29
Skills needed: ABSOLUTELY NONE
System Req: WIN 3.1/95/98 586/8MB
MAC: PMac/8MB

This new program from The Learning Company is now my favorite program for beginners. Designed for even the most inexperienced toddler, this program offers 20 simple, sweet activities to introduce your child to using the mouse, click and effect, and enjoying the computer. Includes songs with hand motions, matching baby animals to their mothers, animal matching game, creating melodies, counting animals in bubbles by passing the mouse over the bubble, passing the flashlight cursor over a dark woods to expose animals in the dark making their cute animal noises and completing puzzles with geometric shapes. This program was so sweet it made my teeth hurt! You can even personalize the program with the child's name. It's best features are the animal themes that appeal to little children, and the fact that the child need not click on anything to make the games work. All you need to do is move the mouse. Highly recommended for first software for your little ones. Use it as "lapware" by placing the child in your lap and playing the activities together. Great gift too.

Rescue Heroes: Hurricane Havoc

Fisher Price/The Learning Company
Ages 4-7   Street price $19
Skills needed: mouse, following directions
System Req: WIN 3.1/95/98
486/66/16MB
MAC: PMac/16MB

It is with some reluctance I add this title to our top 200. Although it great fun for kids and offers some excellent learning opportunities, it has this annoying rock beat (the box calls it "exciting music score") throughout the whole game play. And, there is no way to turn it off sans turning the volume completely off. However, you need the sound on to hear the myriad of instructions you get to rescue hurricane victims. And since this hurricane is serious business, there are lots of people (and animals) in need of your help. My boys loved playing this game and working all the realistic controls. By using a jackhammer, you clear out blocked roads. Fly a rescue helicopter to put out fires, ride a motorcycle to the disaster area to complete your rescue mission. My boys also enjoyed printing out rescue gear like badges, helmets and watches. (Watch that printing though — cost adds up quick.) Five different activities let kids try their hand at being a rescue hero. Fun afterschool activity.

Sammy's Science House

Edmark
Ages 2-7   Street price $19
Subject(s): elem. science, thinking skills.
Skills needed: mouse, following directions
System Req: WIN 3.1/95/98 486/8MB
MAC: 040/8MB

From the makers of *Kid Desk* comes a great science program for little children. This program offers sorting, classifying, weather, sequencing events, animal study, and building things in the workshop with a fun and easy interface. Especially designed for non-readers to learn essential early science skills. Also doubles as an excellent early thinking skills activity. My 3 and 4-yea-olds love Sammy. Even though we have had Sammy for 5 years now, my younger kids still enjoy playing it. Although this is an older program due for a major upgrade, it is still a favorite at our house. Since we have eight kids, we always have a new little one re-discovering Millie's, Bailey's, and Sammy's. A true software classic.

Stanley's Sticker Stories

See review under Writing & Publishing

Tonka Search and Rescue

Hasbro

Ages: 3-6   Street price $19

Subject(s):

Skills needed: mouse

System Req: WIN 3.1/95/98 486/8MB

MAC: 040/8MB

Got a budding fireman or paramedic? Or just a kid who loves emergency vehicles? Then get this program! Choose one of 22 vehicles and learn how to use it. Then choose a mission if you dare! Will you rescue animals from an earthquake at the zoo, put out a fire at the boat docks, or a rescue victims from a flood disaster? Use a helicopter to save people and animals, control cranes, drive dump trucks, fire engines, bulldozers or speedboats. Once you complete a mission, you can print out a certificate, license plates, or newspaper articles detailing your heroism. Kid enjoyed using all the cool vehicles and played the game over and over. Usually the game was the same each time but the kids played anyway.

Trudy's Time And Place House

Edmark

Ages: 4-7   Street price $19

Subject(s): maps, clocks, simple geography

Skills needed: mouse, parental help to get started

System Req: WIN 3.1/95/98 486/8MB

MAC: 030/8MB

Part of the excellent and popular Edmark House series, Trudy's uses sound and 3D animation to teach analog and digital clock skills, map development and reading, relative and cardinal directions, early geography skills and more. In Explore the Globe game, you can travel the world searching for special places. This program has a great deal of material and depth and is most suited for 5-7 year olds despite the box saying 3-6 years old.

Zurk's Learning Safari

Soleil

Ages: 3-6   Street price $24

Skills needed: mouse

System Req: 486/4MB

MAC: 030/4MB

Excellent early learning program with many skill areas covered such as Math (counting, matching, concepts) Science (animals and their environment) Literacy (letter recognition, reading, listening and vocabulary.) and others (logic, problem solving, art, music) Strengths: lots of very interesting animal games.

PHONICS

Most phonics and learn-to-read programs on the market today are pathetic. They only teach letter names, and associated item, e.g. "'a' is for apple" and sight-reading. Letter sounds are glossed over, pronounced incorrectly or virtually omitted. One well-known example of this is R*eader Rabbit's Interactive Reading Journey*. Although I feel this is a good program, it never teaches the letter sounds in its entire 40 lessons. We have researched and tested many phonics programs. We have seen the good, the bad and the ugly. (And believe me, we've seen a lot of "ugly"!) Some of our selections here may not be the fanciest, the funniest or the coolest but they are best for intensive phonics instruction. If you are choosing a phonics computer program to augment or supplement your learn-to-read curriculum, we recommend *PhonicsTutor* (Win95 or Mac only) as your first choice for school-time instruction and one or two phonics games for after-school practice. Choose *Color Phonics* for your auditory learner if you need focused attention on hearing and discriminating the letter sounds.

Alphabet Express
School Zone Interactive
Ages: 2-5   Street price $34
Subject(s): alphabet, phonics, dot-to-dot, matching
Skills needed: mouse
System Req: WIN 3.1/95/98 486/8MB
MAC: 030/8MB

This is a really cute program. Take the *Alphabet Express* (chooo chooo.) to a world filled with letters, animals and sounds. My 4-year-old who loves trains, loves to drive the train to a new letter section full of activities to learn more about that letter. Each of the 26 activities is designed to teach upper and lower case, beginning sounds, ABC dot to dots and more. Also included are mazes to test your audio discrimination of letter sounds and coloring pages that you can print out. This program has a wide variety of activities and learning comes in a fun way.

Bailey's Book House
Edmark
Ages: 3-6   Street price $19
Subject(s): alphabet, phonics, dot-to-dot, matching
Skills needed: mouse
System Req: WIN 3.1/95/98 486/8MB
MAC: 030/8MB

Brings 6 beginner-reader-type activities to a pre-reader level. Alphabetizing, simple three-letter words, phonics, rhymes, simple prepositions, create stories and greeting cards. My young ones enjoy creating simple greeting cards and birthday invitations. Although this is an older program due for a major upgrade, it is still a favorite at our house. Since we have eight kids, we always have a new little one re-discovering *Millie's*, *Bailey's*, and *Sammy's*. Same colorful interface and quality sound and speech as *Millie's Math House*.

Blue's ABC Time Activities

Humongous Entertainment
Ages 3-6   Typical Street Price: $14
Skills needed: mouse, following instructions
Subjects: letter recognition, rhyming words
System Req: WIN95/98: PI/16MB
MAC: PMac/80 MHz/16MB

This great new software program is based on the popular Nickelodeon TV show, Blue's Clues. Blue's Clues is one of the few programs I let my preschoolers watch regularly. No Sesame Street, Barney or Teletubbies at my house. I like the show because it's calm, peaceful and interactive. The host, Steve Burns, gets the kids involved with the activities on the show by speaking directly to the camera continually. Blue is his dog and Blue leaves three clues (blue paw prints) around the house to help Steve guess what Blue wants, does, is thinking of, etc. So the kids help Steve find the clues and decipher their meaning. In the Blue's Clues software programs, the graphics are so good it seems like you are interacting directly with the TV show itself. In ABC time, the child practices letter recognition and rhyming words. This program is not quite as good as the other Blue's programs we have reviewed but still is fun and educational. Blue needs to collect words for his word book and the child must match rhyming words and letters to pictures in different activities. Some of the matching was challenging because the child did not know what letter the picture was representing. Is it a cap or a hat? It would be helpful to the child if he passed the cursor over the picture, the program would speak the name of the item. Kids like the graphics and sounds but the activities would be more productive if mom or an older sibling helped out.

Color Phonics

Alpha Omega Publications
Ages 3-6   Street price $39
Subject(s): alphabet, phonics, reading
Skills needed: mouse
System Req: WIN 3.1/95/98 486/8MB
MAC: N/A

Color Phonics is a Christian phonics program

from the makers of *Bible Builder* and the *Rev-up* series. This package contains five CD's covering all the letter sounds and blends. Visual reinforcement of mouth and lip movements for each sound is its best feature. I highly recommend this program for your learners who need additional auditory discrimination practice. It drills over and over on listening to each sound and matching it to a word or picture. Includes some nice Bible and character themed storybooks. However, this program lacks in reading and spelling practice and *PhonicsTutor* is your best bet for teaching spelling and reading with practice and testing.

Earobics Pro Plus Step 1

Cognitive Concepts
Ages 5-7   Street price $59
Subject(s): phonics,
Skills needed: reading, mouse
System Req: WIN 3.1/95/98
486DX33/8MB
MAC: 030/8MB

Six interactive games with over 300 levels of play, for developmental ages 4-7. Accommodates 3 users. Features include systematically teaching the critical phonological awareness, auditory processing and phonics skills required for learning to read and spell. *Earobics* has beginning, intermediate and advanced starting levels and includes adaptive training and tracks progress. The program is best used for special needs children who have trouble with auditory processing problems. However, *PhonicsTutor* offers more content for the money.

Reader Rabbit's
Interactive Reading Journey 1

Learning Company
Ages 3-6   Street price $49
Subject(s): alphabet, reading
Skills needed: mouse
System Req: WIN 3.1/95/98 486/8MB
MAC: 030/8MB

This is a wonderful, comprehensive multimedia supplement to beginning reading. This CD has

40 lessons each focusing on a letter and its sound. You cannot proceed to the next lesson without completing the prior lesson. Each lesson has the child learn the letter, then play some phonics games and then read two 20-page stories. Lots of music and spoken instruction, amusing and friendly characters invite the child to continue playing and learning. Children enjoy playing this engaging program and seem to pick up a lot of reading skills. Includes 40 little storybooks to practice reading ala Bob Books but not as phonetically controlled. Progress tracker keeps track of skills mastered and levels covered. Note: Contains only small amount of phonics. Although I feel this is a good program, it never teaches the letter sounds in its entire 40 lessons. Only use along with an intensive phonics curriculum as this is primarily a reading drill and practice for children who either already know their phonics or are practicing reading.

JumpStart Kindergarten Phonics

Knowledge Adventure

Ages 4-7   Street price $19

Skills needed: moderate mouse skills, reading readiness

Subject(s): phonics, blending, reading

System Req: WIN 3.1/95/98 PI/16MB
MAC: PMac/16MB

Music: Some mild rock

Twelve activities to practice phonics and reading. Activities include identifying letters, sounds, upper and lower case, rhymes, and spelling. Provides excellent record keeping. Recommended use: all around fun phonics games.

Let's Go Read 1:
An Island Adventure

Edmark

Ages 4-6   Street price $19

Subject(s): alphabet, phonics, reading, spelling

Skills needed: mouse

System Req: WIN95: PI/90/16MB
MAC: 040/8MB

In our last edition of *The Homeschoolers*

Software Guide, I recommended *Alphabet Blocks* as my top pick for early phonics games. Now that this program is no longer available, *Let's Go Read* is now my top pick. This engaging but effective program starts with Robby the raccoon finding a sign on his tree. Robby can't read it and embarks on a journey to an island to learn his letters and sounds. Each letter is presented in a 20-minute sequence of activities stressing that one letter. Once the student has mastered the letter, the program goes on to the next letter. The activities are similar to a workbook in nature: sorting words, building sentences, reading stories, completing puzzles and more. Includes over 175 fun learning lessons and 12 original, progressively leveled, interactive, printable reading books. The most fascinating feature of this program is its speech recognition technology. It comes with a microphone and some of the activities require the child to speak the letter sound or word into the mike. A few people have trouble getting this feature to work properly but it can be turned off and not used. This does not affect the effectiveness of the rest of the program. Although these activities are not very arcade-like exciting, they are really effective. Recommended use: excellent supplement to any phonics curriculum.

Let's Go Read 2:
An Ocean Adventure

Edmark

Ages 5-7   Street price $19

Subject(s): alphabet, phonics, reading, spelling

Skills needed: some phonics

System Req: WIN95: PI/90/16MB
MAC: 040/8MB

As the sequel to *Island Adventure*, the content of this program picks up where Island leaves off. Focusing on blends, long and short vowels, and digraphs, these lessons methodically cycle through each phonetic sound. Bookworm has lost some books in the Ocean when her Bookmobile crashes and the activities focus on recovering those books. The activities are similar to a workbook in nature: sorting words, building sentences, reading stories, completing puzzles and more. Includes over 175 fun learning lessons and 12 original, progressively leveled, interactive, printable reading books. The most fascinating feature of this program is its speech recognition technology. It comes with a microphone and some of the activities require the child to speak the letter sound or word into the mike. A few people have trouble getting this feature to work properly but it can be turned off and not used. This does not affect the effectiveness of the rest of the program. Although these activities are not very arcade-like exciting, they are really effective. Features include record-keeping, voice recognition, the ability to jump to any lesson, and parental controls. Recommended use: excellent supplement to any phonics curriculum.

PhonicsTutor

4:20 Communications
PhonicsTutor CD-ROM $100
PhonicsTutor Teacher's Manual $49
PhonicsTutor Student Workbook $34
PhonicsTutor Student Reader $34
Ages 4-9+   Street price $100
Subject(s): alphabet, phonics, reading, spelling
Skills needed: mouse
System Req: WIN95/98: 486/8MB
MAC: 030/8MB

In a sentence, *PhonicsTutor* is by far the best and most complete phonics, reading and spelling curriculum for the computer that I have ever seen. In fact, as a true curriculum, I believe *PhonicsTutor* qualifies as the only complete computerized curriculum for any of the three individual subjects. *PhonicsTutor* is especially superior because it combines all three of these essential subjects into one comprehensive program. (I will explain the significance of this unique feature in a moment when I discuss the spelling aspect of *PhonicsTutor*.)

In addition to the CD, 4:20 Communications produces some excellent supplemental material in the *PhonicsTutor Student Workbook*, *PhonicsTutor Teacher's Manual*, and

PhonicsTutor Student Reader. The manual (250 pages) shows screen shots from every lesson, breaking the lesson down and offering teacher tips and activities to supplement the CD. The workbook (200 pages) offers simple but practical exercises to practice reading comprehension, spelling and grammar. It is designed to start after lesson 30 on the CD. The reader (200 pages) offers word lists, a moderate amount of enjoyable reading selections and teacher guides. Combined together these elements are nearly a complete first through third grade language arts curriculum. The only thing I would add would be a bunch of books to read!

Not only do we love *PhonicsTutor*, schoolteachers as well have endorsed PhonicsTutor as a great "learn-to-read" system. Read what one teacher had to say about this effective and comprehensive program:

This program is so intense on phonics that we use it as a differential diagnosis of a reading disability. If a student cannot gain in phonemic awareness through this program, they never will. I would go so far as to say the program "retrains" the brain. We are completely sold on the program. We have seen nothing better in our 28 years in education. And it's cheap. I compared similar programs from big publishers, and they can't even come close in quality and price.

(Jack O' Brien, Isanti Elementary School, Isanti, MN.)

Before I continue, let me stress these next two key points that are relevant to the vast majority of educational software: Most software programs which say they "teach" really only drill in one form or another on knowledge gained from other sources. They may also simply present the material in an informational way with maybe some kind of "memory regurgitation" type of quiz. Keep these points in mind as you read the following review.

Phonics: *PhonicsTutor* combines the spelling-family approach with Orton-Gillingham phonograms. The phonetic parts of each word can be examined and heard as often as necessary while the student studies a word list. Lesson 129 pre-

PHONICS

sents all 80 phonograms in the program with all of their common sounds. In our experience, most so-called phonics programs on the market today only drill initial consonants and short vowel sounds; or even worse, they dwell on the "a is for apple" type theme and never go into the actual sounds the letters or combinations of letters make. This method is an inaccurate approach to phonics and may even be detrimental to decoding more difficult words as your child's skills progress. The better programs I see have an excellent start, but fall short because they lack completeness. What they do, they may do well, but they leave much out that is necessary to teach more than just the basics. Of the ones we have seen, *Color Phonics* comes in at a distant second place as the closest to PhonicsTutor for completeness in phonics. Color Phonics is good for teaching and practicing auditory discrimination of sounds (as is *PhonicsTutor*), and has better graphics. However, *Color Phonics* was not designed to fully cover reading or spelling.

Reading: *PhonicsTutor* teaches all words phonetically, without pictures or other clues, so that your child learns to decode what is to be read. Many reading programs teach only sight-reading and never deal with sounding out letters and words. This sight-reading approach is called "whole language" and focuses on the child "memorizing" words by sight only and gaining clues on the word and its meaning from the words around it. Whole language has proven to be a dismal failure in teaching children to read. This also impedes the development of a child's decoding skills.

Spelling: In *PhonicsTutor* a student spells/types each word twice, once phonetically in the phonics drill and once in a regular spelling bee type test. All phonograms and spelling rules are taught before the student spells them. There are several wonderful spelling drill programs out there, such as *Spell-It Deluxe*. But their shortcoming is found in the key word "drill." These types of programs assume that someone is doing the actual "teaching" of the words found in the lists. These programs tend to essentially require

the student to parrot what they already know—not actually "teach" anything new. Either a child needs to be excellent at memorizing or he or she needs to be taught the phonics rules for the spelling patterns that go into the formation of a word. Which would you prefer for your child?

The user interface of *PhonicsTutor* is very clean, straightforward, non-cluttered and non-distracting. To put it in the simplest terms, initially it appears to be just electronic flashcards. No colorful graphics, animation or cute and smiling animal characters. For some, this plain, no non-sense approach interface may be a drawback. However, it will be a strength for many other users. Some children cannot focus on the educational content of a program when the game elements seem more fun. And just try to use the typical, cute, early elementary phonics program to teach a "soon-to-be-a-man" 12-year-old boy who is struggling with long vowels and vowel blends. Not a chance!

How it works: Before words are quizzed, each lesson presents a word group that has some similar feature, or is a review of words that have already been taught (emphasis on the word "taught"). Each word is highlighted as it is spoken. This is what I will refer to as the "presentation screen." At the beginning of each lesson, every word in that lesson is introduced. *PhonicsTutor* will pronounce each of the individual sounds contained in the word, highlighting each letter or group of letters that make a single sound, such as "ph" in phonics, as it says each sound. This manner of presentation is extremely helpful to a child being introduced to the subject of phonics. *PhonicsTutor* is one of the very few programs we have ever seen that introduces words this way. And none of the others have as large or as broad of a word list.

After all the words in the lesson are presented, the program gives your child a chance to review any of the words again. If they do a single mouse click on a word, the program will again highlight each letter(s) as it says each sound in that word. If they double-click on a word, the program will do the same thing, plus say the whole word at the end. Then, when all the words in that lesson are presented and, if need be, studied, the actual drills begin.

The next activity is a phonics-based word construction drill of all the words that were on the presentation screen. In the early lessons, the word lists are intentionally kept very short. They get quite long in the later lessons, making it possible for *PhonicsTutor* to cover over 3,500 words in the 130 lessons. There are over 10,000 individual interactive screens. It is this style of drill and testing that really sets *PhonicsTutor* apart from most other programs. Buying using this combination of investigation and word construction, the program works to actually teach the child the phonetic components of each word. The program says the word and then begins repeating (slowly) the first sound in the word. It will repeat this sound until your child correctly types in the phonogram (either an individual letter or as a combination of letters) that makes that individual sound in the word. On the screen are boxes, one for each phonogram. For example: It will say the word "phonics" and repeat the /f/ sound until he or she correctly types in "ph" on the keyboard. Typing the letter "f" will not work. There are no annoying beeps or negative reinforcement when a child makes a mistake. Instead, the program generates a highly detailed report of errors for Mom to track a student's progress. When the letter(s) for that sound are typed correctly, then the next sound is spoken. (Good place to mention that this uses actual recordings of real human voices—nothing computer generated or manipulated to sound cute.) At the end of all the words in a word list, the program will have your child review any words in which they made a mistake by having him repeat the drill for each word that was done incorrectly.

The next section is the reading drill -- very basic. A group of words, both from the current word list plus additional similar words, are seen on the screen. The computer then says a word, and the student is to point to that word (with the mouse) and click on it. Again, any errors will be reviewed at the end of the list.

I call the next set of drills the "pronunciation

screen". For all other drills, the program "knows" if the student gets the answer right or wrong either through what keys the student typed on the keyboard, or through the words clicked on with the mouse. However, in the pronunciation drill your child is on the honor system unless a parent or older sibling is watching over his shoulder. Your child will see a word on the screen. They are to read and say the word out loud. Then they click on the word with the mouse and the program will say the word correctly. If your child said the word like the *PhonicsTutor* program did, they are to click the "yes" button on the screen; but if they said it wrong, they are supposed to click the "no" button. And. of course, at the end of all the words, they will review any words with incorrect answers.

The last activity for a particular lesson is the "spelling bee drill." This is also done in a straightforward manner. The program speaks the word and the student is required to type it into blank spaces on the screen (and it will keep repeating it until done correctly).

PhonicsTutor goes through each set of screens (Presentation, Phonics, Reading and Spelling) for all 130 lessons, except the last two.

An additional feature of *PhonicsTutor* is the "?" button. At any point in the program, if your child is unsure what to do or what the correct answer is, he can click on the "?" button. *PhonicsTutor* will speak aloud with directions and/or part of the answer. For example, in the phonics drill, the "?" button repeats the phonogram and tells them the letters that are used to spell the word. In the spelling drill, the word is repeated and only the phonograms are said.

Put as briefly as possible, each *PhonicsTutor* lesson presents a common word group, breaking down each word by the individual phonograms and then saying the word. It then gives a phonics drill, a reading drill and a pronunciation drill for each word in the lesson. And lastly, at the end of each lesson it gives a spelling-bee-type drill for every word in the list as a final test to verify you child's actual learning and retention of the material presented.

If all this weren't enough, integrated into the lessons, are over 600 sentences that the student is required to type in "dictation" mode, with proper capitalization and punctuation. (At no extra charge.)

Phonics Workout

Poor Richard's Publishing
Ages 4-8   Street price $10
Subject(s): phonics, reading
Skills needed: mouse
System Req: WIN N/A MAC: 020/4MB

This text-based flash card phonics program drills on hundreds of three letter words. Hands-on creation of words by using the keyboard reinforce retention of reading skills. Place letters in order, hear the sounds and see how the word is formed phonetically. Developed by software developer with a learning disability, for children with learning disabilities (but usable by any child). If you have a Mac, I highly recommend picking up this nice litle program. This program is "shareware." You can download it for free. If you like it and want to keep it, you send in a check.
(www.ldresources.com/tools/shareware.html)

Reading Blaster Ages 4-6

Knowledge Adventure
Ages 6-9   Street price $19
Subject(s): phonics, reading
Skills needed: Some phonics, beginning reading
System Req: WIN 98/95 P90/32MB
MAC: PMAC/32MB

A.K.A. *Reading Blaster Kindergarten*
My son Philip (age 6) has not only enjoyed this new *Reading Blaster*, he actually got a lot of phonics and reading practice while he played. The activities take place under the sea while the Blaster Pals search for undersea treasures. To find the treasures, the child must first play five different letter games successfully to gain access to a maze. The treasures are hidden in the maze and kids love chasing through mazes. Features include a sticker maker, multiple difficulty levels, 450 vocabulary words (300 are printable),

pen-pal writing tools, eight read-along story-books and a progress tracker. Games cover such skills as phonics, opposites, categorization, rhyming, upper and lowercase letters, and spelling. The graphics and sound are well designed and really keep kids playing and learning. Highly recommended for your 5 or 6 year old to practice reading. NOTE: When you buy *Reading Blaster 4-6*, make sure you are getting the newest version (1999 or later) not the old 1995/1996 version; they are completely different. The older one has magic in it.

Reading Blaster Ages 5-7

Knowledge Adventure
Ages 6-9   Street price $19
Subject(s): phonics, reading
Skills needed: Some phonics, beginning reading
System Req: WIN 98/95 P90/32MB
MAC: PMAC/32MB

A.K.A. Reading Blaster First Grade or Reading Blaster Ages 6-7
The Blaster Pals head to the *Planet of Lost Things* to recover lost objects and your job is to complete five different multilevel activities to get them back. The activities stress reading comprehension, thinking and spelling skills. If kids finish the activities successfully, they get to play some exciting and fun arcade-action games. Over at the *Treasure Room*, kids can access even more fun activities including a mini-word processor and storybooks and word-search worksheets they can read or print out. Other features include record-keeping, great graphics and sound, and printable progress charts. Very easy to use, this program is great for practicing first grade reading skills.

Reading Blaster Ages 7-8

Knowledge Adventure
A.K.A. Reading Blaster Second Grade, Reading Blaster Ages 6-8, or Spelling Blaster See review under *Spelling*.

Rev-Up For Reading

Alpha Omega Publications
Ages 3-6   Street price $12
Subject(s): phonics, reading
System Req: 486SX25/8MB

One of the very few Christian educational titles available; provides fun, step by step lessons and games in letters and their sounds. Revver the mouse is your teacher. Good phonics, sound, graphics and music to reinforce your phonics lessons.

Reader Rabbit's Reading 1

Learning Company
Ages 3-6   Street price $19
Subject(s): alphabet, phonics, matching
Skills needed: mouse
System Req: WIN 3.1/95/98 486/8MB
MAC: 030/8MB

This is the classic, original *Reader Rabbit* updated for the new millennium. This is the same *Reader Rabbit* I had for my oldest daughter almost 10 years ago. Anna practiced beginning reading skills with *Reader Rabbit* and it was then that I saw the true potential of computer-assisted training. *Reader* Rabbit teaches beginning letter sounds, short vowel sounds, and 200 three-letter words like cat, fun, log, etc. Four different activities: a matching/concentration like game, a "fill in the letter" to spell the word game, pick the word that matches two of the letters on the target word to complete a train, a sorting game to identify a letter and its placement in a word. CD-ROM version enhanced with clear spoken instructions and better graphics and sound. This program is a perfect beginning reading game. Includes the ADAPT technology which enables the software to pre-test the child and configure the activities and questions based on the child's ability.

Reader Rabbit's Learn to Read With Phonics

Learning Company
Ages 3-6   Street price $19
Subject(s): reading, phonics, matching
Skills needed: mouse
System Req: WIN 3.1/95/98 486/8MB
MAC: 040/8MB

Includes *Reader Rabbit Reading 1* and *Interactive Reading Journey 1*. This new bundle contains two classic but updated programs but at an excellent price. See individual reviews of each title for more information.

Reader Rabbit's I Can Read With Phonics

Learning Company
Ages 5-8   Street price $19
Subject(s): reading, phonics, writing, alphabetizing
Skills needed: mouse
System Req: WIN 3.1/95/98 486/8MB
MAC: 030/8MB

Includes *Reader Rabbit Reading 2* and *Interactive Reading Journey 2*. This is also a new bundle at a great price. See individual reviews of each title for more information. Caution: *Interactive Reading Journey 2* has magician who does real looking magic tricks-not just sleight of hand.

Read, Write, And Type

Learning Company
Ages 5-8   Street price $20
Subject(s): alphabet, phonics, touch-typing
Skills needed: mouse
System Req: WIN 3.1/95/98 486/8MB
MAC: 030/8MB

Our top pick for a structured game for ages 5-8 for practicing phonics, reading, and typing skills. (We prefer it to the *Reader Rabbits*) However, it is difficult to find. The Learning Company still sells the school version to schools for about $60 and this may the only place you may still find it. The school version does provide some lesson plans, two copies of the CD

PHONICS

and teacher helps and is a good value. In the program, the 200-lesson adventure introduces each of the "Storytellers" (letters) and their sounds, where they are on the keyboard and how they come together to make words. Vexor, the virus, steals the letters off the keyboard and you must play 3 typing/phonics games to get them back: a flashcard style sound/picture association game, a keyboarding activity in which you type a pattern (e.g. FA FA FA FA), and a word game where pressing a letter makes a story about a letter. Along the bottom of the screen you see a "keyboard" with friendly talking hands showing where your fingers go. One mom who uses *The Writing Road to Reading* said *Read, Write and Type* works well with the WRTR curriculum. Note: Vexor the virus, an innocuous evil green blob steals the letters off the keyboard. Not actually scary, he's just the mean "bad guy".

Richard Scarry's Best Reading Program Ever

Simon and Schuster
Ages 3-6   Street price $19
Subject(s): alphabet
Skills needed: mouse
System Req: WIN 3.1/95/98 486/8MB
MAC: 030/8MB

New Richard Scarry/Busytown type program. Cute and fun but not a lot of true phonics. Most of the activities involve matching letter to letter or picture to letter. The graphics are not as good as the *Busytown* but a die hard Richard Scarry fan would be content with it. The music is the cheery *Busytown* tunes, cannot be turned off, and is mostly in the transitions. I only recommend this if you have a little one who can't get enough Richard Scarry in their diet.

Word Munchers Deluxe

Learning Company
Ages 6-12   Street price $10
Subject(s): language skills
Skills needed: mouse
System Req: WIN 3.1/95/98 486/8MB
MAC: 030/8MB

A.K.A. Leap Ahead Reading
Like the previous original version of *Word Munchers*, this is a fun and inexpensive Pacman like game that drills on vowel blends. Excellent reinforcement for any phonics program. Can customize difficulty levels for any age. Has super grammar and vocabulary drills as well. Find all the right words that match the target description (noun, verb, predicate, preposition, etc.). Also has some object categorizing drills that even a non-reader can play. Caution: some of the cartoon scenes between game grids are a bit slapstick-violent (think Wylie Coyote vs. Road Runner) in a cartoonish way. You can click and the program skips right past them. An older program but you can find it as recycled software (*Leap Ahead Reading*) or in a bundle (*Elementary Edge Grades 4-5*). Highly recommended.

READING

If your child is having difficulty reading, read the phonics tips above. If they need help with their comprehension, remember these tips:

• For better reading comprehension, the best treatment is more reading practice.

• For reading practice, we recommend a computer game that is fun but requires reading to play it. Some excellent choices are: *Dr. Brain, SimFarm, SimCity, Carmen Sandiego, Bible Builder, Operation Neptune,* any *Dorling Kindersley* program that fits their interest.

Arthur's Reading Games

Learning Company
Ages 4-6   Street price $19
Skills needed: none
Subject(s): reading, letters, phonics
System Req: WIN 95/98: P90/8MB
MAC: 040/8MB

With fun activities with the popular Arthur character, this program gives some nice reading practice to your kindergarteners and your first graders. Although in the format of a storybook, this program has some built-in activities to practice matching words to pictures, combining pictures to make sentences, and a board game to practice matching a word to a picture. Plenty of hints are given so even young non-readers can play the game. The program is primarily a storybook but is an enjoyable way to practice some reading skills using whole language clues. No real phonics are covered. Kids who enjoy the Arthur series would enjoy this CD a great deal.

Reader Rabbit's Interactive Reading Journey 2

Learning Company
Ages 3-6   Street price $19
Subject(s): alphabet, reading
Skills needed: mouse
System Req: WIN 3.1/95/98 486/8MB
MAC: 030/8MB

Interactive Reading Journey 2 picks up where *Journey 1* leaves off. This is a wonderful, comprehensive multimedia supplement to beginning reading. This CD has 40 lessons each focusing on a letter and its sound. You cannot proceed to the next lesson without completing the prior lesson. Includes 40 little storybooks to practice reading ala Bob Books but not as phonetically controlled. Note: Contains only small amount of phonics. Although I feel this is a good program, it never teaches the letter sounds in its entire 40 lessons. Only use along with an intensive phonics curriculum as this is primarily a reading drill and practice for children who either already know their phonics or are practicing reading. Caution: Has a magician who does real magic tricks.

PhonicsTutor

See review under **Phonics**.

Reading Galaxy

Learning Company
Ages: 9-14   Street price $9
Subject(s): reading comprehension, literature
Skills needed: reading
System Req: WIN 3.1/95/98: 486/8MB
MAC: 030/8MB

To encourage reading and appreciation of famous children's literature, this program pits plagiarizing aliens against your child. Each alien claims to have written a classic and by reading passages, your child proves the alien did not write the book. Several activities with in this wacky intergalactic game show involve answering questions about the story to reveal illustrations, unscramble pictures, complete crossword

READING

puzzles, and more. This program requires lots of reading to be successful and is good reading practice. Caution: Most of the books used are good. A few may not be on your recommended reading list. Recommended use: Goes well with Sonlight or any literature based curriculum.

Read, Write, and Type

See review under phonics.

Reader Rabbit Reading 2

Learning Company
Ages 5-8   Street price $29
Subject(s): alphabet, phonics, alphabetizing, matching
Skills needed: mouse
System Req: WIN 3.1/95/98 486/8MB
MAC: 030/8MB

Reader Rabbit Reading 2 includes four games in one that teaches alphabetizing, early reading, and word recognition. Drills for alphabetizing, letter blends, long and short vowels, compound words, phonics, and rhymes. Colorful and fun and includes spoken instructions. An older program but still a favorite of our children.

Reading Blaster Ages 6-9

Knowledge Adventure
Ages 6-9   Street price $19
Subject(s): phonics, reading
Skills needed: Some phonics, beginning reading
System Req: 486SX66/8MB
MAC: 040/12MB System 7.1

A.K.A. Reading Blaster 2000 or Reading Blaster Third Grade.

Outrageous space games on the "intergalactic reading network" designed to give advanced phonics and reading practice. Games include: making your own commercial, shooting letters on meteors, concentration game in which you match letters and sounds. The 5 games drill skills in identifying parts of speech, silent letters, compound words; recognizing synonyms, antonyms, and words that rhyme; phonics and reading. Caution: in the game Adventure

Stories, one of the stories features a Casper like ghost. Recommended use: supervised drill in specific activities. This is an excellent choice for those children past the "*Reader Rabbit*" beginning reading programs and need more work on reading comprehension and other more advanced reading skills.

Reading Mansion

Ideal Instructional Fair
Ages 4-10   Street price $24
Subject(s): alphabet, phonics, grammar, matching
System Req: WIN 3.1/95/98 P90/16MB
MAC: 040/16MB

You travel through a maze in a house collecting a list of objects. To pass from room to room you must answer talking phonics or reading questions. Has adjustable skill levels beginning with pre-reader letter recognition and matching pictures and letters. Upper levels even have some grammar drills with arranging sentence parts in the right order, recognizing complete sentences and true or false statements. Not a lot of fancy entertainment but solid drill and practice without rushing the child to compete in an arcade game. The child is able to answer questions at their own pace working towards the goal of finding all the objects on the list. Excellent value. 300+ levels with thousands of drills. Built in record keeping to monitor student's progress. The program has is a great customizing feature. I wish more programs had similar user-customizable options as the Great Wave products do. This really is something that is worth getting the manual out and reading about so that you can fully customize the features, options, and content of the program to your family's needs and usage. Highly recommended.

Ultimate Speed Reader
Knowledge Adventure
Ages 10-up   Street price $29
Subject(s): speed reading techniques
Skills needed: reading
System Req: WIN 3.1/95/98 486/8MB
MAC: 030/8MB

If you desire to increase you or your child's reading comprehension and speed, this is the program to get. This streamlined program is designed to test your current ability and get you started on some structured lesson and testing to bring up your speed and comprehension. Contains tons of reading choices plus the ability to add your own reading selections–the Bible is my first recommendation. We use this with our older children to prepare for test taking.

AUTHORING, WRITING AND PUBLISHING

Writing effectively, accurately and creatively is an essential skill. Many parents ask us if their child should begin or master typing before they are allowed to write on the computer. I suggest that you start typing when ever if fits best into the curriculum or at least by 4th grade. A younger child does not need to know how to type in order to use a word processor or storybook program. When a child barely able to read begins to put letters together to make words, their writing skills are on par with their typing skills; the words and sentences unfold slowly, letter by letter. I have found that even the most anti-pencil and paper writing child will write SOMETHING and maybe even write a lot, when given writing software they love to use. I have seen it over and over with my own children. We recommend starting even your non-readers with a storybook writing program to get them started in a lifelong habit of creative and expository writing. Then you may want the child moving up to an actual kid-sized word processor. Here are some age related tips to choosing the best writing software. Caution: Almost every writing program I have seen has a few story starter ideas that are not edifying. Also, a few have some pictures that are magic/occult in nature. Read the titles' specific description below to get more info about each title.

Ages 4-8

For storybook and fictional writing, a good place to start is *Storybook Weaver Deluxe*. For my non-readers, our school activity entails an assignment of creating the scene then dictating a story to the teacher or older student. We type it in for them, print it out, and the child has their own story to show and tell with. If you prefer a more structured "school" look with a manuscript font on primary lined paper, Kid Works Deluxe (A.K.A. *Writing Blaster*) is the best choice for an actual "my first word processor."

Ages 6-12:

Once the child is reading some and has more sophisticated reports and writing assignments, choose *Ultimate Writing and Creativity Center*, an actual beginner's word processor (journals, reports, poems, essays). For storybooks, continue on with *Storybook Weaver Deluxe* or choose an Imagination Express (historical fiction or unit study reports or stories) that fits your study plan. (See different topics below) *Imagination Express* offers a more mature feel and higher quality graphics than *Storybook Weaver* but fewer images. *Imagination Express* also has the ability to animate

some images in your story, e.g. make a horse and wagon clip-clop down the road.

Ages 13-16:

To bridge the gap between kid-sized word processors (above) and the adult word processors (*MS Word* or *WordPerfect*), you may want to have your child use *The Student Writing Center* for their writing assignments in these junior and senior high years. It gives them many powerful yet easy to use features and functions. For multimedia creations, try the *Multimedia Workshop*. On the other hand, if your older child is very computer savvy, try them out on your own word processor or multimedia presentation software such as *Hyperstudio*, *Microsoft Word* or *PowerPoint*. For the real die-hard computer junkie, try publishing your own web page.

Other printing needs:

If you are looking for a printing program that makes cards, banners, resumes and the like, my recommendation is either *Print Shop*, *PrintMaster* or *Print Artist*. Choose whichever fits your computer specifications. Both are excellent.

Amazing Writing Machine

The Learning Company
AGES 7-12   Street price $15
Subject(s): drawing, painting, creativity, writing, storytelling
Skills needed: mouse, parental help to get started
System Req: WIN 3.1/95/98 486/8MB
MAC: 030/8MB

The Amazing Writing Machine is a creative writing program offering a kid-sized word processor to make illustrated books, journal entries, (my children keep a daily journal with ease) essays, poems, or letters. Some of the story-starters are a bit rude or weird. It's like a *Kid Pix* combined with a word processor.

American Girls Premier 2nd Edition

Learning Company
Ages: 8-16   Street price $19
Subject(s): elements of a theater production, language and creativity
Skills needed: reading
System Req: WIN 95/98: P90/16MB
MAC: PMac/16MB

Places everyone! Quiet on the Set! Curtain! Have children who want to write, produce, direct and create stage plays for their favorite American Girl characters? This is just the program for them. Developed in cooperation with *The Children's Theatre Company* of Minneapolis, this program is designed to give your budding playwrights all the tools to create stage plays. Choose from 110 background sets, 48 actors who can walk and perform a variety of actions, sound effects and music, 4 types of lighting, 300 props and more to set up scenes, cued actions and drama. The characters will speak the dialog you type in and their voices can be varied in pitch, volume and speed of delivery. The overall setting is different American Girl history periods but can lend itself to many different stories, dramas, comedies, even Bible scripts. Recommended use: Excellent for theater literature, e.g. Shakespeare unit studies.

Hyperstudio

Knowledge Adventure
Ages: 8-up   Street price $50
Subject(s): multimedia authoring
Skills needed: reading
System Req: WIN 95/98: P90/16MB
MAC: PMac/16MB

Although most homeschoolers would never use a program like *Hyperstudio*, I wanted to include it because it is quite popular with the public school teachers for creating lesson presentations and for students to create multimedia reports. *Hyperstudio* is a full featured but easy to use multimedia authoring program designed to allow students to create multimedia reports and presentations. It is similar to *Microsoft's PowerPoint*. Features built-in include 1,400 graphics, 290 sound clips, 195 animations, and 30 movies. You can create multiple pages incorporating all these multimedia elements and create a presentation that is appealing to all learning styles. You can import graphics, sounds, etc from other sources such as your own digital camera. Also, you can email the final product to others and they can play back your presentation without having to own *Hyperstudio* software. Great for sending a multimedia, singing Christmas card to Grandma.

Imagination Express

Edmark
Ages: 5-12   Street price $25-$40
Subject(s): creativity, writing, storytelling
Skills needed: mouse, parental help to get started
System Req: WIN 3.1/95/98 486/8MB
MAC: 030/8MB

Imagination Express is a program of tools to create electronic books and printed books. Use backgrounds, character and object stickers, animations, music, sounds and more. Design multimedia storybooks where the horses rear and whinny or the birds fly and squawk. You can even add 30 seconds of your own recorded narration per page. Very similar to *Storybook Weaver* but pictures are crisper, richer in color and detail but less in number. Choose which

"Destination" suits your unit study or child's interests. Excellent choice for unit studies. Write historical fiction or a report based on a topic drawn from your lesson plans. Each destination has its own fact book with handy facts and information about each topic, further fueling your child's imagination and motivation in the writing process. *Pyramids* and *Time Trip* come in school editions only (higher price) but contain some excellent lesson plan ideas. In the future, Edmark may combine multiple titles together as a bundle. Destinations include: *Neighborhood* (real life, today items and resources), *Rain Forest* (jungle animals and scenes), *Oceans* (marine life and ecosystems themes), *Pyramids* (Egyptian times), *Time Trip* (pilgrims, colonists, American revolution and more; 1600 to present), *Castle* (Medieval times. Caution: A few pictures in the *Castle* destination are not suitable for Christian use-wizards and such. Advise your child to use discernment. Our girls really enjoy creating king and queen stories without putting in any of the occult images.) This program is usually only found in a school version. This "teacher's edition" offers lesson plans and optional activities plus two copies of the program. Buy this edition and share the 2nd CD with another homeschool family. The license agreement allows two "school rooms" to use the package.

Kid Works Deluxe a.k.a. Writing Blaster

Knowledge Adventure
AGES 4-9   Street price $14
Skills taught: child's first word processor
Skills needed: mouse, parental help to get started
System Req: WIN 3.1/95/98 486/8MB
MAC: 040/8MB

Kid Works Deluxe allows children to write & illustrate their own stories in a fun and painless manner. Allows true children's level "multimedia" electronic stories (computer voice reads it, or may be printed out, with printer). Our children love spending hours writing and drawing with *Kid Works*. Recommended use: For little ones just starting to write-especially those frustrated by late developing handwriting skills. Choose this program for K and 1st graders who need the structure of primary lined paper and the manuscript/ball and stick font on screen.

Multimedia Workshop

Knowledge Adventure
Ages: 12-up   Street price $14
Subject(s): multimedia project creation
Skills needed: mouse, reading, basic computer skills
System Req: WIN 3.1/95/98 486/8MB
MAC: 040/8MB

Designed to give beginners a start in multimedia creation, this program is packed with desktop publishing, paint, and video capabilities. *The Multimedia Workshop* has 3 programs in one. *The Video Workshop* allows you to create videos by choosing from a variety of backgrounds and patterns, and then add movie clips, pictures, or text. Next, lay out the scenes with music, sound effects or your own-recorded narration on the easy-to-use story grid. Included are 17 cool transition effects such as dissolves and wipes. *The Writing Workshop* offers an easy to use word processor with powerful desktop publishing capabilities and built-in templates for creating great-looking newsletters, magazines, and greeting cards. You can easily import graphics and photos from the built-in image libraries or other sources. Then crop and resize images right in your document. Also includes a spell-checker, a thesaurus, and a speech tool that will read aloud anything you write. *The Paint Workshop* allows you to create illustrations or customize photographs and clip art quickly and easily. With a huge assortment of cool paint tools like a pencil, paint roller, brushes, and spray tool, there's limit to your creative genius. And anything created in the *The Paint Workshop* can be imported into the *The Writing Workshop* or the *The Video Workshop*. The multimedia libraries include 300 photos, 600 pieces of clip art, 100 movie clips, 220 sound effects and 40 music clips. This program provides a lot of powerful tools for a small price. Younger kids (ages 8-12) can use this program if you provide help.

Otherwise, choose *Kid Pix Studio* for the elementary age group.

Net Explorations: Web Workshop
Sunburst
Ages 9-up   Street price $28
Subject(s): web page creation
Skills needed: mouse, reading, basic computer skills
System Req: WIN 3.1/95/98 486/8MB
MAC: 040/8MB

If you got children who want to create their own presence on the Internet, this basic program is the place to start. Includes easy to use paint tools, hyperlinks, background images, and clip art for the creation of your own web page. Includes some lesson ideas for school use. We consider this a very important computer skill and this can give your students a head start. However, the power of this basic program is limited. If you're thinking your students will need more powerful web design tools, choose *Microsoft FrontPage*. That is what I use and find it very easy as well but it has more power if I need it.

Rev Up For Writing
Alpha Omega Publications
Ages: 5-8   Street price $12
Subject(s): handwriting
Skills needed: mouse, parental help to get started
System Req: WIN 3.1/95/98 486/8MB

Handwriting on the computer. With Revver the mouse coaching the child, engaging graphics and sound make this a fun way to learn writing your letters. This classic ball and stick method is presented step-by-step on screen with the child using the mouse to build each letter with the appropriate shapes, like a puzzle. You can print out worksheets to practice the old fashioned way.

Stanley's Sticker Stories
Edmark
Ages: 3-6   Street price $19
Subject(s): storytelling, creativity and writing
Skills needed: advanced mouse, parent help in getting started.
System Req: WIN 3.1/95/98
486SX25/8MB
MAC: 030/8MB

Think of this as *Imagination Express* for little children using the Edmark "house" characters *Millie, Bailey, Sammy, Trudy* and *Stanley*. The child chooses a background (30 to choose from) then applies stickers (pictures of objects) to their scene. Most of the 300 stickers are animated and "smart' in that they resize in proportion to its placement in the scene. This program gives you a lot of features including on screen help, text in a variety of fonts and colors, the ability to add narration, and the ability to print out your stories. Recommended use: Story writing to go along with their time spent playing with the "*House*" characters. Writing math, science or reading stories. Younger children will need help getting started.

StartWrite
Idea Maker Inc.
Ages: 5-12   Street price $40
Subject(s): handwriting
Skills needed: mouse, parental help to get started
System Req: WIN 3.1/95/98 486/8MB
MAC: 030/8MB

This handwriting/reading program is very popular with teachers and homeschoolers. It allows you to create worksheets for handwriting, spelling, and phonics at any age level. Includes three different handwriting fonts: Manuscript (Zaner-bloser), Italic (Getty-Dubay) and Modern Manuscript (D'Nealian). You can customize the guide-lines, and dash, dot or solid fonts with arrow strokes. A 100,000-word spell checker keeps spelling accurate and clip art is included for making coloring sheets.

Storybook Weaver Deluxe 2.0

Learning Company
Ages: 5-12   Street price $19
Subject(s): creativity, writing, storytelling
Skills needed: mouse, parental help to get started
System Req: WIN 3.1/95/98 486/8MB
MAC: 040/8MB

To write a story, choose from dozens of background, e.g. desert, mountain, ocean, outer space, etc. Then choose the foreground, e.g. lake, grass, road, etc. Also choose night, day, evening, dusk, etc. Now the fun part. Choose the items for your story. With over 1600 images to choose from, any child will have no lack of creativity to create imaginative stories. Images include: animal, people, furniture, vehicles, plants and other objects. Add colors and sounds and you will have a multimedia storybook to impress friends and family. Reads story back to you and checks your spelling. This or the *Imagination Express* is the program to buy if you have an unmotivated writer. *Storybook Weaver* is our children's #1 pick for making stories. Caution: Has some magical, imaginary, and alien still-life pictures. We tell our children not to use those pictures when making stories. This latest version, 2.0, has improved graphics, voice record/playback, and the ability to copy and paste scanned images.

The Student Writing Center

Learning Company
AGES 10-Adult   Street price $25
WIN 3.1/95/98 $29
Subject(s): upper elem. and high school level word processor
Skills needed: reading
System Req: WIN 3.1/95/98
486SX33/8MB
MAC: 040/8MB

Excellent, easy to use, yet full of features for students to write, design, edit, and publish first-rate reports, letters, stories, and newsletters. Great for adult use too. Gives you the tools to add borders, 2 column, 3 column formats, headlines, clip art, different fonts and type sizes.

This is the word processor our children use. Includes a great deal of clip art as well. However, it is difficult to find. Currently it is available in the *Elementary Edge Grades 4-5* bundle. The Learning Company still sells the school version to schools for about $70 and this may the only place you may still find it. The school version does provide some lesson plans, two copies of the CD and teacher helps and is a good value.

Top Secret Decoder

Houghton Mifflin Interactive
Ages: 8-14   Street price $28
Subject(s): language, writing, logic
Skills needed: reading
System Req: WIN 3.1/95/98
486SX33/8MB
MAC: 040/8MB

Are your children like mine in that they love playing spy and detective, solving mysteries and catching the bad guy? This program helps you create and use your own spy language. Choose from dozens of encoding tools that automatically turn simple messages into complex codes that will stump your brainiest friends. *Top Secret Decoder is* loaded with code making techniques and tools, wacky sound effects and spectacular printed pieces. Included is a Decoder Challenge Game.

The Ultimate Writing & Creativity Center

Learning Company
Ages: 6-12   Street price $29
Subject(s): Writing reports
Skills needed: reading
System Req: WIN 3.1/95/98 486/8MB
MAC: 030/8MB

This pint-sized word processor has a lot of the "big kid's" tools. With a spell checker, dictionary, thesaurus, clip art, animations, sounds, drawing tools, and read-to-me feature this program has a lot of easy to use tools to help elementary age children write some great reports. With a little help from the over 1000 report idea generators, your child should be able to find something intriguing to research and write about. While drafting, students can choose templates that automatically format their words as a school report, newsletter, sign, storybook, or journal. This program is more full featured than *Kid Works Deluxe* but similar in presentation. Choose *Kid Works Deluxe* instead only if you want a writing format that has primary lines like "first grade' theme paper. Hard to find program but The Learning Company still sells the school version to schools for about $50 and this may the only place you may still find it. The school version does provide some lesson plans, two copies of the CD and teacher helps and is a good value. Note: I did not look at every report idea (1000) but every one I did look at was suitable for Christian homeschooling.

Recommended use: Everyday journal writing or general unit study reports; especially good for the one page a day writing recommendation for *Robinson Curriculum*.

PROGRAMMING

Learn to Program BASIC

Interplay
Ages: 6-12   Street price $29
Subject(s): Writing reports
Skills needed: reading
System Req: WIN 3.1/95/98 486/16MB
MAC: 040/16MB

Although the rock music and cool characters don't really appeal to me, the fundamentals of this program make it a must have for that student who wants to learn to program computers while still in Junior or Senior High. Twenty-six lessons cover basic BASIC (a programming language) concepts like while/send loops, if/then statements, go sub-routines, and Boolean expressions. The program is very well designed in that it breaks down complicated programming theory into manageable chunks, gives lots of hands-on practice and examples, and uses real fun arcade games to demonstrate concepts.

Microworlds Pro

Logo Computer Systems Inc.
Ages: 6-up   Street price $99
Subject(s): logic, memory
Skills needed: following instructions, reading, following instructions
System Req: WIN 95/98/NT/2000:
486DX/66MHz/8+MB
MAC: PMac/16MB

Looking for a program that allows even young children to learn computer programming and logic? *Microworlds Pro* gives kids the tools to design simple programs, simulations, mathematical models, video games, multimedia presentations, and visualize programming fundamentals using a programming language called LOGO. This program is very powerful and very educational, not just a game. Seymour Papert, a highly respected expert on child learning and development, designed it. He wanted to create a computer program that was a better alternative to the mindless games most kids play on their computers. He wanted to empower children with the tools to create and learn on their own rather than stifling their natural creativity and genius with closed-ended edutainment programs. In the beginner mode, the programming is as simple as directing a turtle to navigate across the screen in a specified manner. For example, the child programs the turtle to walk three spaces up, two spaces left, three spaces down, and then two spaces right to create a rectangle. Harder levels have the turtle doing more elaborate moves, creating special projects and adding sound or music to your creations. Although this program is expensive, it is very powerful and allows children to get the feel of real programming. Highly recommended. Great for your unit study on computers and programming.

My Make Believe Castle

Logos Computer Systems
Ages 5-7   Street price $35
Subject(s): logic, programming
Skills needed: mouse
System Req: WIN 3.1/95/98
486DX33/8MB
MAC: 040/8MB

I have never recommend this program before because it contains some magical characters. However, it is excellent for teaching young children the concepts of programming. The activity takes place in a castle, dungeon or forest scene. You choose characters and items from a palette and then place them into the scene. You "program" each character to do a certain movement and/or say something at a certain time and then it happens. For example, you direct the knights on horses walk across the courtyard and then jump over the river. My 6-year-old son has played this for several years and enjoys setting up medieval type scenes over and over again, laughing at their antics. It is a great introduction to programming concepts.

TYPING

Many parents ask us if their child should begin or master typing before allowing them to write on the computer. I suggest that you start typing whenever if fits best into the curriculum around 3rd or 4th grade. A younger child does not need to know how to type to use a word processor or storybook program. Hunting and pecking as a keyboarding technique is consistent with a child's reading, writing and spelling at this stage in their development. When a barely reading child begins to put letters together to make words, their writing skills are on par with their typing skills; the words and sentences unfold slowly, letter by letter. In other words, plans for text unfold letter by letter not word by word as needed for touch-typing. Read each typing program description below carefully to zero in on the best program for your family.

Jumpstart Typing

Knowledge Adventure
Ages 7-10   Street price $19
Subject(s): beginning typing
Skills needed: reading, mouse
System Req: WIN 3.1/95/98
486DX33/8MB
MAC: 040/8MB

This program takes you to the Olympics to learn the fundamentals of typing in 30 different arcade-style games. Some of the games include foosball, snowboarding, skateboarding, and wall climbing. The faster you type, the better you do at the games. My only objection to this game is that my kids seemed to just focus on the arcade aspect and did not care about accuracy in their typing. They just typed as fast as they could and hoped they win. Perhaps more discipline and structure in using this program would be productive but just be forewarned. Regardless of this objection, this program was fun to practice typing with.

Mavis Beacon Teaches Typing Deluxe V. 11.0

Learning Company
Ages: 8-up   Street price $39
Skills needed: mouse, reading
System Req: WIN 95/98: P166/32MB (v. 11.0) MAC: 040/16MB (v. 9.0)

Excellent typing tutor for all ages. This usually gets the highest rating wherever typing programs are reviewed. Mavis tests your skill level and sets up lessons designed to increase your speed. Gives clear and concise instruction on hand position and body posture. Along the bottom of the screen you see a keyboard with shadow hands showing the proper posture and movement. My daughter found it helpful but sometimes she found it distracting; "Sort of like subtitles in a foreign movie." She also liked the videos that demonstrated typing techniques. Includes eight interactive games to challenge your skills. You can customize your typing selection topic; choose from fiction, folklore, poetry, history, and science. You can even import your own text content. I recommend Bible verses! Mavis even analyzes your typing when you use other software programs! (Windows version only.) Highly recommended. One of Mary Pride's top picks. Access www.mavisbeacon.com for additional lesson content and typing tips. Note: the version number on Mavis changes about once a year. Going with the earlier version (one step back) will save you some money ($39 vs. $19) and you usually will not miss much in upgrades.

Type To Learn

Sunburst
Ages: 8-up   Street price $28
Skills needed: mouse, reading
System Req: WIN 3.1/95/98 486/8MB
MAC: 040/8MB

If you have a Mac and you don't like *Mavis Beacon*, *Type to Learn* is a good choice for you. A good solid typing tutor with 22 lessons and games that stress drill in things you can learn. For example, typing all the capitals of the states. Select either a primary or more advanced vocabulary. This program is automatically able to customize a lesson based on weaknesses that show up in the previous lessons. Millions of public school children have learned to type with this program. Good choice for elementary age children. Caution: Has a game that you name constellations- NOT astrology-just constellations.

Typing Instructor Deluxe 11.0

Individual Software
Ages: 8-up   Street price $28
Skills needed: Reading
System Req: WIN 95/98/Me/2000/ PI/133/32MB

Music: choose from a variety of music styles *Typing Instructor Deluxe* is somewhat different than Mavis in format but just as effective in teaching typing and keyboarding. Some reviewers like *Typing Instructor* better than Mavis. Very user friendly. This program seems better suited to younger students and kids like using it. The students can set their own level, goal wpm, and pace. The scene opens to an airport where you can watch videos about how to improve your typing. Then you can go on to the lessons customized to your abilities and goals. Has a travel/airport theme with virtual reality games (climb a mountain or zap garbage) to practice your wpm skills. You can also choose what kind of music plays while you type. Choose from over 250 best selling books, short stories and articles to practice typing with. Program provides detailed records of speed and accuracy and has 10 key training, timed tests, record keeping, and automatic customization.

TYPING

Recommended use: Full fledged typing course. Note: in one of the games, you are in a pyramid shooting a sphinx headed characters and mummies. Right now you can order version 10 for only $4.99 while supplies last at the company's web site. (www.individualsoftware.com) Older versions of this program (1996) do not have this game. Sometimes you can find this older version in bargain bins in packaging called *Blast. Typing.*

Typing Tutor 10.0
Simon & Schuster
Ages: 8-up   Street price $28
Skills needed: Reading
System Req: WIN 95/98 PI/90/16+MB
MAC PMAC/32MB

Music: choose from a variety of music styles *Typing Tutor* is another excellent typing program, designed for the older student. Starting with a pretest, the program gives solid lessons tutoring the child in both speed and accuracy. The customizable lessons also give you practice in typing in different environments such as e-mail, bulletin boards, chat rooms, and electonic order forms. Choose your background music and type of text you wish to type from. Music selections range from rap, disco, jazz, country to classical. Typing selection topics include cooking, history and politics, sports and music, horror (Shelley's Frankenstein), business (job hunting, resumes, business letters), health, and more. Included are eight games, record keeping and progress reports.

SPELLING

Do you want a program that will teach phonics/spelling rules or only offer them drill and practice in weekly spelling lists? For spelling rules, we recommend PhonicsTutor. It actually teaching spelling and the phonics rules behind various spelling words. On the other hand, if you want drilling in spelling words, our top pick and other homeschoolers' favorite is *Spell it Deluxe*. It offers the features, customization and value that homeschoolers need.

PhonicsTutor
See review under **Phonics**.

Spelling Blaster
Knowledge Adventure
Ages 6-12   Street price $19
Subject(s): spelling
Skills needed: reading, mouse
System Req: WIN 3.1/95/98 486/8MB
MAC: 040/8MB

This title is also known as Reading Blaster Ages 7-8 or Reading Blaster Second Grade. By the time you read this, this program may have even another name. Once again, Knowledge Adventure recycles another piece of software. However, this is still a great program for spelling practice. With over 1700 words built-in, elementary students have plenty to practice with. Five games offer arcade-like practice with the goal of catching the culprit- a "mumbler" who has stolen a treasured book. Completing each activity gives the student another clue to help deduce his true identity. Kids love playing the games and spelling practice time is maximized with these cleverly designed games. One drawback: you can add word lists to the spelling practice but the program does not speak the new words very well. My top pick for spelling is still *Spell It Deluxe* but if you are looking for a program with more arcade-action and fun for your elementary kids, *Spelling Blaster* is a great choice.

Spell It Deluxe

Knowledge Adventure
Ages: 6-14   Street price $19
Subject(s): spelling
Skills needed: some reading
System Req: WIN 3.1/95/98 486/8MB
MAC: 040/8MB

This is still the spelling program of choice for thousands of homeschoolers. Master up to 3600 commonly misspelled words in over 200 word lists at 6 difficulty levels. Has 5 different spelling game type drills (you can use a different one each day of the week) and "spelling bee" type testing. Games include a fill-in-the-blank sentence completion, crossword puzzle, shoot a "snake" at the correctly spelled word, find the misspelled word in a sentence and edit it, and reinforce spelling rules and patterns. Can personalize it by adding your own spelling lists or download additional lists from the Internet. *Every homeschool should own Spell it Deluxe.* Note: When you install *Spell It Deluxe*, choose the run from CD option to provide recorded human speech for the spelling words included with the program. Currently available in *Davidson's Learning Center Series: Spelling and Grammar.*

Super Solvers: Spellbound

Learning Company
Ages: 7-10   Street price $14
Subject(s): spelling
Skills needed: some reading
System Req: WIN 3.1/95/98 486/4MB
MAC: 030/8MB

An older program you can sometimes find in a bargain bin or recycled under a new name. Four fun games (Crossword, Flash Card, Word Search, and Spelling Bee) that teach spelling in a fun and painless manner. Use built-in word lists (Over 1000 words.) or modify to drill students with your own customized word lists (Add up to 2000 words.) Will verbally quiz child with 1000 spoken words built into the program. It also may reappear as recycled software or in a bundle; e.g. *Elementary Edge Grades 2-3.* Recommended for the early elementary ages. Kids really enjoy playing this game for hours on end and really do sharpen their spelling skills. Although this is a good spelling drill program, we feel that *Spell It Deluxe* is the best choice for homeschooling.

Switched-On Schoolhouse Language Arts

Alpha Omega Publications
Grades 3rd, 4th, 5th, 6th, 7th, 8th, 9th, 10th, 11th, or 12th.
Street price $67 per subject per grade
Subject(s): full language arts course (includes spelling)

A complete Christian Bible-based curriculum. This full language arts course includes spelling, grammar, vocabulary, and writing. See description under *Curriculum* for more detailed description.

SPELLING

GRAMMAR

Grammar Games

Knowledge Adventure
Ages: 8-12   Street price $14
Skills needed: 2nd grade reading level
System Req. WIN 3.1/95/98
486SX33/8MB
MAC: 030(25Mhz)/8MB

Very "environmentally correct" (save the rain forest). But if you can live with that, it has really good grammar drills. Four games to practice grammar include; Rain Forest Rescue- successfully detect sentence fragments and you can guide your helicopter to an endangered animal trapped by forest fire (Woe is me.) *Falling Fruit*- guide a Toucan to catch fruit with punctuation marks on the fruit to correctly punctuate a sentence, *Hidden Wonders*- word usage and verb/sentence agreement and *Jungle Gizmo*- plurals and possessives. This program has been discontinued but it may pop up as recycled software or in a bargain bin. Currently available in *Davidson's Learning Center Series: Spelling and Grammar.*

Grammar Key

Grammar Key Company
Ages: 9-adult   Street price $60
Subject(s): traditional grammar
Skills needed: reading, mouse
System Req: WIN 95/98: P90/16MB

Highly recommended by Mary Pride, Cathy Duffy, and the folks who make *PhonicsTutor*. Three levels: upper elementary, junior high, and high school-all in one program. Designed by a veteran public school teacher, the *Grammar Key* method of teaching grammar has been proven very effective in raising grammar test scores. Teaches from the approach of applying sentences to the grammar rules, instead of teaching grammar rules to the sentence. The format is similar to a workbook on the computer. Dry but very effective. Regular grade-level workbooks are also available for written exercises. Once

you complete the course, you will have covered all the grammar you need. Does not cover punctuation.

Reader Rabbit Reading 3

Learning Company
Ages: 7-10   Street price $15
Subject(s): sentence mechanics
Skills needed: mouse
System Req: WIN 3.1/95/98 486/8MB
MAC: 040/8MB

Reader Rabbit is back, this time as a junior reporter. An older program but it is effective and fun. Builds reading ability while improving writing, vocabulary, critical thinking skills and teaches proper sentence mechanics. Collect the "who, what, when, and where" of a story to create a newspaper article. Includes spoken instructions. Although this program has reading comprehension skills, it is primarily a grammar program. Hard to find but may pop up in a bargain bin or in a bundle.

Switched-On Schoolhouse Language Arts

Alpha Omega Publications
Grades 3rd, 4th, 5th, 6th, 7th, 8th, 9th, 10th, 11th, or 12th.
Street price $67 per subject per grade
Subject(s): Full Language Arts Course

A complete Christian Bible-based curriculum. This full language arts course includes spelling, grammar, vocabulary, and writing. See description under **Curriculum** for more detailed description.

Word Munchers Deluxe

See review under phonics.

VOCABULARY

Switched-On Schoolhouse Language Arts

Alpha Omega Publications
Grades 3rd, 4th, 5th, 6th, 7th, 8th, 9th, 10th, 11th, or 12th.
Street price $67 per subject per grade
Subject(s): Full Language Arts Course

A complete Christian Bible-based curriculum. This full language arts course includes spelling, grammar, vocabulary, and writing. See description under *Curriculum* for more detailed description.

Ultimate Word Attack

Knowledge Adventure
Ages: 8-adult   Street price $19
Subject(s): vocabulary with some spelling practice
Skills needed: 2nd grade reading level
System Req. WIN 3.1/95/98
486SX33+/8MB
MAC: 040/8MB System 7.1

Teaches new words and definitions as you build vocabulary and pronunciation skills essential to reading, writing and speaking. Five activities including a crossword puzzle (match words to definitions), arcade game where you shoot an object at one of four words that matches the definition displayed at the bottom of the screen. Other games include an arcade game where you guide the little word blaster guy to higher levels by jumping, running and munching the words that match the definition displayed, and a game where you match the correct word tile with the definition displayed. 3D interface is colorful, engaging and easy to master. Powerful tool for adapting to any curriculum you use; add your own word lists and definitions. Recommended use: Use to add your own word lists as you develop your lesson plans from other subjects, e.g. science, social studies etc. or systematically go through the 4000 words built into the program. I recommend assigning one activity (there are five) a day for a week and then test on Friday.

Word Blaster

Knowledge Adventure
Ages: 6-12   Street price $19
Subject(s): vocabulary with some spelling practice
Skills needed: 1st grade reading level
System Req. WIN 3.1/95/98
486SX33/8MB
MAC: 030(25Mhz)/8MB

Word Blaster is exactly the same as the program Ultimate Word Attack. (See above) However, the word lists have been edited to focus on the elementary age group. It contains 5 activities to practice associating the word with its definition, using it in context, and pronouncing it correctly. Powerful tool for adapting to any curriculum you use; add your own word lists and definitions. Recommended use: complete vocabulary curriculum or additional practice for unit study or traditional textbook vocabulary word lists from other subjects, e.g. science, social studies etc.

Word Munchers Deluxe

See review under phonics.

WordSmart

Smartek
Ages: see Level: Street price $39 each
level (A-J)
WordSmart Level A: reading level 4th to
10th grade
WordSmart Level B reading level 5th to
11th grade
WordSmart Level C: reading level 6th to
12th grade
WordSmart Level D: reading level 7th grade
to 1st year of college
WordSmart Level E: reading level 8th grade
to 2nd year of college
WordSmart Level F: reading level 9th grade
to 3rd year of college
WordSmart Level G: reading level 10th
grade to 4th year of college
WordSmart Level G: reading level 11th
grade to 4th year of college
WordSmart Level I: reading level 12th
grade to 4th year of college
WordSmart Level J: reading level 1st to 4th
year of college
Subject(s): vocabulary, spelling
Skills needed: basic reading
System Req. WIN 3.1/95/98
486SX33/8MB
MAC: 030(25Mhz)/8MB

MARY PRIDE'S top pick for vocabulary software: "*WordSmart* is by far the fanciest and
most educationally valuable vocabulary software on the market." Each CD-ROM covers
2000 definitions (200 primary, 1800 secondary)
and has 5000 pronunciations. (Please note: If
you cannot afford all the levels you need to
cover your needed reading level(s), then get
Word Blaster or *Ultimate Word Attack* as a
cheaper alternative) *WordSmart* also has some
spelling drills in it too (but we would not call it
a complete spelling program). Choose the
WordSmart level (A-J) that specifies the reading
level of the child using it (not the grade of the
child, but the reading ability grade level). Each
of those levels cover that grade and the 7 grades

above in vocabulary difficulty. For example,
level A is 4th grade through 12th grade. The
levels overlap on levels of difficulty but each
has a different world list. All 10 CD-ROMs
cover vocabulary up to Ph.D. difficulty (level J).
Highly recommended for vocabulary. Not sure
which level is right for you? Head to the
WordSmart web site at www.wordsmart.com
and take an on-line test to determine your level.

MATH & MONEY SKILLS

Decide if you want to focus on maximizing your child's speed drill and computational skills or their comprehension and the working of problems. For speed drill, we like *Quarter Mile Math*, *Mindtwister Math,* or the *Math Blasters.* For pure math practice and word problems, we highly recommend *NumberMaze Challenge.* For upper level math, choose the subject area; algebra, geometry, trig, etc., and choose any listed for supplemental tutorial and practice. The exception is the *Math Teacher*, which offers a complete tutorial in each subject, and it includes a teacher's manual. The *Switched-On Schoolhouse Math* is designed as a complete year long math course with no need to supplement. The *Math Advantage 2001* program could be used as an actual core curriculum, but you will need to supplement it with something for additional drill work.

(Also see titles listed under Curriculum.)

ELEMENTARY & JUNIOR HIGH MATH

Axel's Whirled Math

Ideal Instructional Fair
Ages 5-9   Street price $19
Skills needed: none
Subject(s): elementary math
System Req: WIN 95/98: P90/8MB
MAC: 040/8MB

From the makers of *World Discovery Deluxe* and *NumberMaze Challenge* (two of my favorite programs) comes a great new tutorial-based math program for ages 3-8. With built-in artificial intelligence, the software gently tests the student's ability and then presents the concepts and lessons based on that assessment. Animated characters guide the student through learning the concepts and playing the games. With over 1000 learning levels this could be used as major part of any early math curriculum. Keep in mind however, it is not designed for kids to just jump in and use on their own for fun. (*Math Blasters* are best for independent use.) Assigned time on the program and teacher supervision will result in the most benefits.

Blue's Clues 123 Time Activities

Humongous Entertainment
Ages 3-6   Typical Street Price: $19
Skills needed: mouse, following instructions
Subjects: early math
System Req: WIN95/98: PI/16MB
MAC: PMac/80 MHz/16MB

This great new software program is based on the popular Nickelodeon TV show, *Blue's Clues.* *Blue's Clues* is one of the few programs I let my preschoolers watch regularly. No Sesame Street, Barney or Teletubbies at my house. I like the show because it's calm, peaceful and interactive. The host, Steve Burns, gets the kids involved with the activities on the show by speaking directly to the camera continually. Blue is his dog and Blue leaves three clues (blue paw prints) around the house to help Steve guess what Blue wants, does, is thinking of, etc. So the kids help Steve find the clues and decipher their meaning. In the Blue's Clues software programs, the graphics are so good it seems like you are interacting directly with the TV show itself. In *123 Time Activities*, Steve and Blue are hosting a Backyard Fair and you play fair-type games to practice early math skills. Blue fans will love participating in the activities and a lot of learning goes on in these six well-designed activities. Skills covered include classifying and sequencing objects, measurement, counting, logical thinking, number recognition, early addition, subtraction, money skills and more. The difficulty level progresses as the child successfully plays the games. In one game, *Mother May I?*, (remember playing that one.?) the child learns counting by moving Blue and other characters across the finish line. After playing the games successfully, the child wins tickets to trade in for prizes at the prize tent. Program does not keep specific records on each child's progress but games can be saved. A fun way to practice math.

The Cruncher 2.0

Knowledge Adventure
Ages: 7-up   Street price $69 school edition
Subject(s): spreadsheet
Skills needed: basic reading
System Req. WIN95/98: Pentium/8MB
MAC: 040/8MB

Teaches how to use spreadsheets and graphs in everyday life. It computes, graphs, teaches and even talks. Tutorials take you step by step through setting up spreadsheet projects and understanding using numerical data in making decisions. Absolutely essential for any child looking for a career in business or "Corporate America." See the article on top ten computing skills. Note: this program is now only available in school version, a bundle, or a hard-to-find jewel case only. Currently you can find it in the *Excel Mathematics* bundle. The Learning Company also sells the school version to schools for about $70 and this may the only place you may still find it. The school version does provide some lesson plans, two copies of the CD and teacher helps. Highly recommended.

Decimal And Fraction Maze

Ideal Instructional Fair
Ages: 8+   Street price $19
Subject(s): decimals, fraction practice
Skills needed: basic reading
System Req. Comes on 3.5" disks. WIN 3.1/95/98 386SX33/4MB
MAC: 030(25Mhz)/4MB

Decimal and Fraction Maze is similar to *NumberMaze* (except no word problems) but covers place value, decimals and fractions instead of whole numbers. Will verbally ask math problems. Over 300 levels of difficulty, thousands of math drills starting with place value. There is a customizing option that is a great feature. I wish more programs had similar user customizable options as the Great Wave products do. This really is something that is worth getting the manual out and reading about so that you can fully customize the features, options, and content of the program to your family's needs and usage. Recommended.

Dollarville

Waypoint Software
Ages: 11-18   Street price $19
Subject(s): money, math
Skills needed: basic counting
System Req. WIN 95/98: PI/90/16MB
MAC: Pmac/16MB

Dollarville is a basic, well-designed program for teaching and reinforcing money skills. Skills covered include coin recognition, values and computation. Set in a western, cowboy setting, the scenery is average quality graphics but my kids always love cowboys so they did not mind. Not a lot of game feel but solid practice in money skills make this program good for school time practice. There are built-in quizzes with over 1000 game questions. Record keeping keeps track of student progress and videos demonstrate concepts.

Math Adventure

Smartek
Ages: 7-9   Street price $39
Subject(s): all of 3rd grade level math
Skills needed: basic math, reading
System Req: WIN 3.1/95/98 486/8MB
MAC: 030/8MB

This is similar to an animated textbook on computer. A teacher presents 140 typical 3rd grade math lessons including time and money, probability, measuring, fractions and decimals, addition, place values and regrouping, rounding, and geometry. Tutorials are included to explain the concepts along with tests and practice problems. Real-life games and activities reinforce the math concepts. For example, make sandwiches to visualize fractions, play basketball to practices addition and more. The "Let Me See" mode shows visual examples and working out of 100's math problems. Highly recommended by the developers of *PhonicsTutor*.

Math Blaster Ages 4-6

Knowledge Adventure
Ages 6-12   Street price $19
Subject(s): elementary math practice
Skills needed: mouse
System Req: WIN 95/98:
486/66MHz/16MB
Mac: 040/8MB

A.K.A *Math Blaster Kindergarten*
This past year or so, Knowledge Adventure came out with a whole slew of new *Math Blasters* for every early elementary grade. Almost all of them are excellent *and* wholesome. My kids really enjoy them and I find them very educational at the same time. This new *Blaster* covers Kindergarten math skills such as logic, counting, subtraction, and estimation, with a variety of unique math activities. The Blastership flies off to the planets each with an activity with built-in songs and additional games. Concepts are presented visually and very

effectively. Other features include record keeping, customization, great graphics and sound, easy navigation and lots of fun. Recommend use: supplement to Kindergarten math curriculum. *When you buy Math Blaster 4-6, make sure you are getting the newest version (1999) not the old 1995/1996 version; they are completely different.*

Math Blaster Ages 5-7

Knowledge Adventure
Ages 6-12   Street price $19
Subject(s): elementary math practice
Skills needed: mouse
System Req: WIN 95/98: PI/90/16+MB
Mac: PMac/32MB

A.K.A *Math Blaster First Grade*.
The Blaster Pals arrive at the Intergalactic Zoo to help care for the animals. Since these are unusual animals they need very special care. The Pals must measure out food, set clocks for bathing time, counting coins to buy food and practice skip-counting. Lots of fun and different activities packed with lots of math practice keeps kids doing math every minute they play this program. One feature homeschool moms will love is the ability to print customized worksheets to use away from the computer by multiple children. Other features include record keeping, customization, great graphics and sound, easy navigation and lots of fun. Recommend use: supplement to first grade math curriculum.

Math Blaster Ages 6-9

Knowledge Adventure
Ages 6-12   Street price $19
Subject(s): elementary math practice
Skills needed: mouse
System Req: WIN 95/98: P90/16MB
Mac: PMac/16MB

A.K.A. *Mega Math Blaster, Math Blaster Third Grade*.
This is the repackage of the same *Math Blaster* that has been around for about 20 years. Upgraded in 1998 to this current version, *Math Blaster* is one of the top selling programs in educational computing history but is not our

number one pick for math. However, if you are looking for a fun arcade style game that has a balance of 50/50 game/problems and lots of kid pleasin' appeal, *Math Blaster* is the one to get. With five different activities, three levels of play, six levels per subject, and entertaining, innovative 3-D friendly aliens, space and space-ship settings, this program is designed to give children lots of fun while they practice their math. Although the box says ages 6-9, it covers first through sixth grade math skills. Students or parents can edit levels and custom design the type of math problems to optimize game play value. My favorite feature is the ability to create customized worksheets. The program also comes with a 2nd CD containing a parent's guide filled with math tips and resources, plus the capability to customize sets of math problems for your students. Mary Pride's pick for fast drill of math facts. Recommended use: Math curriculum supplementation and/or GIFT.

Math Blaster Ages 6-8

Knowledge Adventure
Ages 6-12   Street price $19
Subject(s): elementary math practice
Skills needed: mouse
System Req: WIN 95/98: P90/16+MB
Mac: PMac/32MB
A.K.A Math Blaster Second Grade.
Set in a carnival, this *Math Blaster* stresses second grade level skills such as counting money, telling time, basic math facts, charts and bar graph interpretation, fractions, set theory, and skip-counting. In keeping with the carnival theme, kids place food orders by creating numbers with the correct place value of ones, tens, and hundreds, play arcade games, participate in a dunking contest and more. While practicing all these skills, the child is attempting to win the Intergalactic Grand Prize Trophy. To keep the child challenged, the levels automatically adjust to the child's skill level. Certificates can be printed to reward the child's progress through the levels. One feature homeschool moms will love is the ability to print customized worksheets to use by multiple children away from the computer. Other features include detailed record

keeping, customization, great graphics and sound, easy navigation and lots of fun. Recommend use: supplement to 2nd grade math curriculum.

Math Blaster Ages 7-9

Knowledge Adventure
Ages 7-9   Street price $19
Subject(s): elementary math practice
Skills needed: mouse
System Req: WIN 95/98: P90/16MB
Mac: PMac/16MB
A.K.A Math Blaster Fourth Grade or Math Blaster Ages 8-9.
A very challenging *Math Blaster*, this one focuses more on logic and thinking not just pure math facts. The child completes math activities to collect and reprogram mechanical bugs. These bugs are essential to catch a bad guy. Skills covered include addition, subtraction, measurement, fractions, multiplication and more. Includes logic and geometry activities. This program requires programming logic and some work to accomplish your mission. Some kids may find it too difficult but if you have a budding math genius, they may love the challenge.

Math Munchers Deluxe

Learning Company
Ages: 6-12   Street price $19
Subject(s): elementary math practice
Skills needed: basic math
System Req. WIN 3.1/95/98
486SX33/8MB
MAC: 030(25Mhz)/8MB
Fun graphics and sound with this Pac man like game to drill your math facts. Guide your muncher around a maze munching the correct equation that matches the target number shown above. Continual math computation is required to continue the game. Customize to drill specifically on any type of math problem you desire: whole numbers, fractions, decimals, and simple geometry. Caution: some of the cartoon scenes between game grids are a bit violent in a Road-Runner/Wylie Coyote-cartoonish way. You can

click and the program skips right past them. An older program but you can find it as recycled software or in a bundle. (Currently can be found in *Elementary Edge Grades 2-3.*) Highly recommended.

Mighty Math Series

A newer series released by Edmark to stimulate thinking, facilitate understanding, and motivate practice of math concepts. *Mighty Math* uses innovative and unique items and settings for virtual manipulatives. Choose a *Mighty Math* that contains the specific math topics you want to focus on. All are excellent and I highly recommend them for math concepts reinforcement and practice. Best used with the teacher right there, guiding the student through the lessons and examples.

Mighty Math K-2: Carnival Countdown and Zoo Zillions

Edmark

Ages: 4-7   Street price $39

Subject(s): math: money, story problems, number line, spatial awareness, multiplication, division.

Skills needed: intermediate mouse

System Req: WIN 3.1/95/98

486SX33/8MB

Mac: 030(25MHz)/8MB

Music: Not offensive to me but can be turned off.

Carnival Countdown

Set in an amusement park where children can play all sorts of virtual games and rides. In Carnival cars, children drive around colorful bumper cars that contain animals. Solve puzzles that require parking the right cars in the right area of the parking lot (Shhh. Don't tell the children they are finding out how Venn diagrams work.) Work with such imaginative manipulatives as bubbles, clowns, laughs, giggles and more. Contains both a child initiated "explore"

mode and a computer initiated "question and answer" mode where the computer asks the child to solve a problem or puzzle.

Zoo Zillions

This program covers the same age range as *Carnival Countdown* but covers somewhat different range of math skills. The setting is in a zoo with activities to visualize and practice math concepts. In the 3D geometry activity, you can design and play with 3D objects. Practice money skills by shopping at the "Gnu Ewe Boutique." Drive a train down a "number line" track to practice math and problem skills on a number line. Move fish in and out of a colorful fish tank to practice adding, subtracting, multiplying and dividing. Practice addition, subtraction and skip-counting as you navigate and travel a colorful jungle trail. All activities are designed to give the child a visual representation of math concepts and hands-on manipulatives to practice those concepts. Recommended use: Excellent supplement to any math curriculum. Best used with the parent or teacher.

Mighty Math Grades 3-6: Number Heroes and Calculating Crew

Edmark

Ages: 7-12   Street price $38

Subject(s): plane geometry, chance and probability, fractions and decimals, plus basic number operations, multiplication, division of whole numbers and decimals

Skills needed: basic math

System Req: WIN 3.1/95/98

486SX33/8MB

Mac: 030(25MHz)/8MB

Music: Not offensive to me but can be turned off.

Number Heroes

Using pleasantly warped heroes, this program is designed to give hands on solving of realistic math problems. Choose one of the four heroes to host a math activity. *Fraction Man* develops fraction visualization and calculations with on screen manipulatives represented by fireworks. Identify, add, subtract and multiply fractions to create a colorful fireworks display. The robot *Geobot* has you solve geometry puzzles using a virtual geoboard (rubber bands on a pegboard). In *Probability Machine* and *Quizzo*, the heroes have the student play quizzing games to visualize and solve probability and other math problems. The heroes have no real supernatural abilities but have courage, cleverness and motivation to solve problems. For example: putting an enormous cork in a volcano to stop it from overflowing and then spraying it with their handy freeze-ray gun.

Calculating Crew

This title provides more advanced level of math practice with multiplication and division of whole numbers and decimals, the properties of 2-D or 3-D shapes, and money transactions. Colorful characters utilize engaging graphics and virtual manipulatives to present math problems and concepts in 4 activities. Help *Captain Nick Knack* multiply and divide to deliver and distribute essential supplies on a far away planet. You must work out the problem on screen. Help super heroes buy needed supplies to save the city from disaster, e.g. freeze guns, corks, sponges, heat shields, etc. Accept payment and make change. Dive underwater and help *Wanda Wavelet* recover treasures by searching along a number line. Locate the correct place on the number line by estimating, rounding, adding, subtracting, and multiplying numbers from hundredths to thousands. Help *Dr. Gee* examine, design, and classify 2D and 3D objects. Excellent supplement to any math curriculum.

Mighty Math Cosmic Geometry

Edmark
Ages: 11-14   Street price $24
Subject(s): math: geometry
Skills needed: Saxon 6/5 or equivalent
System Req: WIN 3.1/95/98
486SX33/8MB
Mac: 030(25MHz)/8MB

Friendly polyhedral (many-sided) characters help you learn and experiment with 7th, 8th, and 9th grade level geometry topics. Covers such skill areas as problem solving, reasoning, attrib-

utes of shapes and solids, geometric constructions and transformations, 2D and 3D coordinated, length, perimeter, area and angles, surface area and volume, geometric terminology and notation, solving for unknowns, symmetry, mathematical elements of art. Uses hands-on, manipulative type games and puzzles to introduce and reinforce these concepts. Note: this is junior high geometry not senior high- no proofs presented. Recommended use: supplement Saxon 6/5 or 7/6 or equivalent on similar chapter topics.

Millie's Math House

Edmark
Ages: 2-5   Street price $19
Subject(s): early math
Skills needed: mouse
System Req: WIN 3.1/95/98 486/8MB
Mac: 030/8MB

Six colorful and engaging games to teach little ones sizes, shapes, counting and numbers. In "Build a Mouse House" you place shapes according to a blueprint to build different types of houses. Another activity has you placing the correct number of jellybeans on a cookie (I would've preferred chocolate chips.) In "Build a Bug"; you pick the number of and the type of facial feature to place on a caterpillar, e.g. 6 antennae or 5 eyes, to create a unique bug. Printing out custom-made bugs and coloring them is a favorite activity at our house. Excellent program to engage little ones in early math concepts. My 4 year old loves it and picks up a lot of math skills at the same time. Even though this is an older program, our family still enjoys it and uses it.

MindTwister Math

Edmark
Ages 7-10   Street price $19
Skills needed: reading, 1st grade math
Subject(s): math facts, rounding, measuring, telling time, counting money, probability
System Req: WIN 95/98: P90/8MB
Mac: 040/8MB

This new math quiz game gives lots of creative

math practice for second through fourth grades using a wide variety of word problems. The problems require practice with a wide variety of math skills in a fun, competitive manner. For example, the child needs to maneuver a submarine through a grid of numbers that match a particular math rule. Develops more advanced mathematical problem-solving skills such as visualization, deduction, sequencing, estimating and pattern recognition. Kids can compete against each other with the multi-player option. This program is great for multi-child use and everyday practice.

MoneyTown

Simon and Schuster

Ages: 5-9   Street price $18

Subject(s): money skills: making change, saving, money facts

Skills needed: mouse, reading

System Req: WIN 3.1/95/98 486/8MB

Mac: 030/8MB

Alas, the park is closed due to lack of funds and it's up to you to raise money to get it back in shape. (Great premise- they didn't raise taxes to pay for bigger fancier park.) Through 5 multi-level games, your child counts money, makes change, earns and saves up enough money to open the park. Includes a cash register activity to learn making change. Little nuggets of info come up as you play; "What does the phrase 'money burns a hole in your pocket' mean?" and others. Some of the game is arcade style and slightly addictive but overall the child does learn about money and how to handle it. Both girls and boys will enjoy the activities. This is an excellent but hard-to-find title.

NumberMaze Challenge

Ideal Instructional Fair/Great Wave Software

Ages 4-12   Street price $24

Subject(s): elementary math practice

Skills Needed: basic math, reading

System Req. WIN 3.1/95/98 486/8MB

Mac: 040/8MB

Child winds through 3–D maze doing math drills & solving word problems. As you go through the maze, you come to a door. To get through you must answer three math problems. The levels start out fairly easy with the child visually counting objects on the screen, 5 cars for instance (my younger children will put their fingers right on the computer screen to count them- and that's okay.) Then they press or click the "5". As the problems get harder, the child is required to work out each step of the problem on screen just like they would on paper. (They may need scratch paper to do some of the multiplying involved in solving long-division problems.) This program is particularly helpful for the child who hates to write out math problems or is so messy everything gets confusing.

This is one of very few math programs that has word problems. It will even speak the problems out loud. Nearly all our children taught themselves to count with the older 3.5" version of this game. Can be customized to drill on your choice of 350 different levels with thousands of practice problems starting at counting to five, through addition and subtraction, and going up to multiplication of four-digit numbers and six-digit division.

Program offers comprehensive, full coverage of all elementary level (K-6) whole number addition, subtraction, multiplication, and division skills. (See *Decimal and Fraction Maze* for coverage on decimals and fractions). This one has 3D graphics and is our #1 choice for whole number math drills and borrowing/carrying practice. When something better comes out we will let you know (and if you find a better one, let US know.).

Note: There are some other things you should know about *NumberMaze Challenge*. Our family was chosen as one of the test sites as *NumberMaze Challenge* was being developed. We were able to have some input into some of the features of the final product. One feature that we did not like was the magic performed by the owl. The people at Great Wave Software were sensitive to our concerns (as also shared by other homeschool families who had been chosen to test it out before release). As a result, they have included the ability to turn off the magical effects as one of the options in the CustomMaze file. If for any reason you need to contact the company (like sending in your registration card-which is something you should do...) PLEASE let them know your appreciation of their sensitivity to the needs and concerned of the homeschool market, and/or Christian families. If enough families show their thanks, it will help towards future consideration by the company for software for our families in the future. CustomMaze is a great feature. I wish more programs had similar user customizable options as the Great Wave products do. This really is something that is worth getting the manual out and reading about so that you can fully customize the features, options, and content of the program to your family's needs and usage.

One of my children's' favorite things to customize is the list of friends' names. They like to remove the old names and add the names of their friends, dolls, relatives and characters in favorite books. (You could even add pet names to make things even sillier.) The program then incorporates those names into the word problems. For example, one word problem may read like thus, "Anna gave 1,209 donuts to Dad. Bethany gave 2,366 more donuts to Dad. How many donuts does Dad now have?" My kids find this fun and enjoyable and it makes the game play far more personable. What makes the kids laugh harder is hearing the computer read these silly story problems aloud. Yes, this program will read the word problems aloud which is a great feature for the reluctant or delayed reader. This is also one of Mary Pride's top picks. Highly recommended.

Operation Neptune

The Learning Company
Ages 9-14   Street price $14
Subject(s): pre algebra practice
Skills Needed: basic math, reading
System Req. WIN 3.1/95/98 486/8MB
Mac: 030/8MB
Program combines undersea arcade action with math, logic and science problems. Although there is a lot of "game play" relative to actual math, the real world problem solving drills are great. Makes a great motivator (reward) for free-time computer use. A satellite carrying an alien substance has crashed into the sea and you must drive your submarine through underwater obstacles to find the pieces of the satellite. In between the underwater dodge-em game, you answer some excellent math problems involving science, graphs and charts, word problems and more. A perennial family favorite.

Quarter Mile Math series

Barnum Software
Ages 6-16   Street price $39 and up
Skills needed: counting
Subject(s): math facts, counting, keyboarding
System Req: WIN 95/98/2000/NT: 486/33MHz/16MB
Mac: 040/8MB

This popular series is now on CD for Windows with upgraded graphics and more options. Each unit in the series covers a variety of topics geared toward a specific age/grade range. The easiest topics cover basics like counting or adding up to 5 + 5. We use this often in our homeschool to drill on math facts and the kids really enjoy it. You start by signing in, choosing your topic (my third grader is working on the addition facts of "up to 10+10" topic) and then you choose whether you want to race horses or dragsters. Along the bottom of the screen you see a row of horses or cars with your racing horse or car on the far left. When you click "go", equations appear on the far lower right. You type in the answer and the next equation pops up. The faster you type in answers, the faster your horse or car goes. The first car or horse across the finish line, after doing about 10 equations (this is also adjustable), wins. The next time you race, you race against that time which is represented by one of the other cars or horses racing onscreen. Your horse (rider less) or dragster accelerates with each correct answer. Your competition in the other 5 lanes is exact replays of your own best 5 previous races.

Lanes scroll faster and faster as racers accelerate.

Very basic graphics and sound but very effective in motivating kids to practice their math. When I first saw this program (the DOS version), I thought my kids would never do it. Now that the Windows CD is on our computer, I am shocked! They like it. I never would've believed it if I have not seen it with my very own eyes. Nice feature: Some packages can even drill on letters and keyboarding. Mary Pride says, "The *Quarter Mile* series is the best math drill software we have ever seen...I cannot praise [it] too highly. This is the software the Pride kids use every day... One of our computers always has the *Quarter Mile* on it... The kids, one after another, come and use it during the day... It has worked wonderfully for us." There are several different packages. The cross-section package ($40) has a small sampling of all the other packages and covers 75 topics with 16,000 problems from beginning counting up to sixth grade math skills. The other packages focus on specific age ranges covering more topics but fewer grade levels. For example, there is a K-3 package ($40) covering 20,000 topics and a 4-7 package ($40) covering another 20,000 topics. There is also a package with all grade levels covering all 326 topics with 70,000 problems ($90). My suggestion, if the budget allows, is to buy the big package with all the topics. Especially if you have a broad range of ages of children.

Reader Rabbit Math 4-6 a.k.a Math Rabbit

Learning Company
Ages: 3-7   Street price $19
Subject(s): early elementary math practice
Skills needed: mouse
System Req. WIN 3.1/95/98:
486/66/16MB
Mac: 040/66/16MB

This old but now updated favorite contains four excellent math games to drill counting and early problem solving. Set at a carnival, the child plays arcade games to practice early math. Success earns you tickets, which you can redeem for typical midway prizes. As silly as it sounds, these "tickets" are highly motivating and kids love getting as many as possible. Can be customized to drill on chosen difficulty levels and type of problem. One of our top recommendations for this age group for practicing early adding and subtracting.

Reader Rabbit Math 6-9

Learning Company
Ages: 6-9   Street price $19
Subject(s): elementary math practice
Skills needed: mouse
System Req. WIN 3.1/95/98:
486/66/16MB
Mac: PMac/8MB

Reader Rabbit is back and he wants you to help him escape Pirate Island. After being stranded on the island, Reader Rabbit and you must collect pieces of the broken boat and outwit the pirates. As you attempt your rescue, you must play nine different math games. Skills covered include elementary geometry, clock reading, addition, subtraction, problem solving, equivalencies, place value and more. This is a fun way for kids to practice math and Reader Rabbit is a delightful companion. The skill level automatically increases as your ability increases. Other features include six different difficulty levels, ability to customize for individual students, and progress reports.

StickyBear's Math Splash

Optimum Resources
Ages: 5-10   Street price $24
Subject(s): math facts (addition, subtraction, multiplication, division.)
Skills needed: advanced mouse skills
System Req: WIN 3.1/95/98 486/8MB
Mac: 040/8MB

If aliens and spaceships aren't your style (*Math Blaster*), then check out lovable sweet *StickyBear*. Four interactive arcade-like games help your younger children practice his math facts. In one activity, *Rapid Fire*, the student quickly solves math equations to race a boat. Record keeping and customization make this and easy program to use during school time for supplementing regular course work.

Switched-On Schoolhouse Mathematics

Alpha Omega Publications
Grades 3rd, 4th, 5th, 6th, 7th, 8th, 9th, 10th, 11th, or 12th.
Street price $67 per subject per grade
Subject(s): Mathematics Course

A complete Christian Bible-based math curriculum. This is a full mathematics course. See description under **Curriculum** for a more detailed description.

Tabletop

The Learning Company
Ages: 6-16   Street price $100
Subject(s): data analysis and manipulation, logic
Skills needed: advanced mouse skills
System Req: WIN 3.1/95/98 486/8MB
Mac: 040/8MB

Tabletop is a school version only of a wonderful program that gives teachers the tools to teach data analysis. Includes a professional-quality database, kid-friendly graphics, onscreen manipulatives, curriculum activities, 50 challenge cards containing games and puzzles the students can solve using the software. By using cartoonish figures (some are the Zoombini characters from *The Logical Journey of the Zoombinis*), kid-friendly language and fun puzzles, kids learn seven methods of data analysis and manipulation. Most math curriculums don't cover these types of concepts adequately and the mastery of these concepts can help a child understand that the true power of a computer is analyzing data, not playing games.

ALGEBRA AND UPPER LEVEL MATH

Since there were about 8 different Algebra titles, I decided to have my 10th grade daughter try out all the curriculum-based Algebra programs and compare them. She is good at math and is about half way through *Saxon Algebra 2*. Her comments in the reviews will be in italics. Most of these algebra titles came in a bundle so the whole package is listed in this section. Also include in this section were other upper level titles such as Geometry.

Algebra Blaster a.k.a Algeblaster

Knowledge Adventure
Ages: 12-16   Street price $24
Subject(s): algebra
Skills needed: reading, Saxon 7/6
System Req. WIN 3.1/95/98 P90/8MB
Mac: 040/8MB

Contains a complete year of algebra in this excellent step-by-step tutorial. The student embarks on a space mission and uses algebra to solve the puzzles and problems. Guide a space ship through the galaxy solving algebra problems. Students also defend Planet Quadratica from alien invaders practicing and mastering graphing, equations, and translating word problems into algebraic equations. (However, this is not designed as an actual "all you need" curriculum.) Can be customized to drill on chosen difficulty levels and type of problem. Also packaged as *Davidson's Learning Center Series: Algebra*.

Astro Algebra

Edmark
Ages: 11-14   Street price $29
Subject(s): math: algebra
Skills needed: Saxon 7/6 or equivalent
System Req: WIN 3.1/95/98 P90/8MB
MAC: 040/8MB

This new algebra program from Edmark makes using Algebra in real life applications an outer space "blast." Two different modes give your student lots of algebra practice. In the "mission" mode, you the "captain" get an assignment to help some hapless alien. Using algebra you solve temperature conversions, x-y coordinates, slope equations and more. In the practice mode, you use the onscreen tools to explore and solve algebra problems. Offers basic tutorials and onscreen demonstrations of problem solving. Program's unique features offer virtual manipulatives to work out algebraic equations. Recommended use: Excellent practice for that student who hates to do algebra problems. Customizable topics offer the ability to zero in on specific areas your student needs practice on.

Boxer Introductory Algebra 2.0

Boxer Learning Inc.
Ages 13-18   Street price $49
Skills needed: reading, Saxon 7/6
Subject(s): Algebra II
System Req: WIN 3.1/95/98: P90/8MB

Although a good basic Algebra tutorial, it lacks some of the pizzazz and features of the other Algebra programs such as *Math Advantage, Excel Mathematics*, and *Princeton Review Algebra*. However, unlike these other programs just listed, *Boxer Algebra* allows you to actually work out the problems rather than just choose an answer from a multiple choice problem. This is a very important feature of accurate accountability of the student's abilities. That is: the ability to actually work out a problem, step-by-step, and get the right answer. My 10th grade daughter found the material "*dull but informative*." She added, "*The program includes a bookmark, a built-in calculator and hint button. It teaches well and has good feedback. The tests have you write in the correct answer and if you get any wrong, it shows you what your answer was and what the right answer was. Then the program tells you if there's anything you should review based on your incorrect answers.*"

Excel Mathematics

Knowledge Adventure
Ages 14-18   Street price $39
Skills needed: reading, jr. high
Subject(s): Algebra 1, Algebra 2, Geometry, Trigonometry, Pre-Calculus and Calculus.
System Req: WIN 95/98:
PI/133MHz/32MB
MAC: Pmac/100MHz/32MB

Excel Mathematics is a complete, self-contained software program that includes a basic mathematics curriculum. Teachers created the content. Lessons include short animated segments called 'Video Tutors' that demonstrate how math problems are solved. A handy 'pop-up' reference window conveniently displays math formulas and equations. My daughter reviewed the Algebra section and she says, "*You read the material which is presented in small chunks. You seem to go at a slower pace than other Algebra programs. Explanations are practical and short. When you take the tests, it does not show you which problems you got wrong or why. Tests are not timed and are multiple choice.*" The software also includes a complete version of *Advanced Placement Statistics*. While the lessons are rather dry and basic, the real value of the program is the extra CD-ROMS that come with: *Math Blaster Geometry* and *The Cruncher 2.0*. Caution: Also includes *Math Blaster Pre-Algebra*. It is very good but takes place in a creepy house with creepy characters.

ALGEBRA & UPPER LEVEL MATH

Geometry Blaster

Knowledge Adventure
Ages: 14-16   Street price $19
Subject(s): high school geometry
Skills needed: Saxon 7/6 or equivalent
System Req. WIN 3.1/95/98
486SX33/8MB
MAC: 030(25Mhz)/8MB

A.K.A Math Blaster: Geometry
Geometry Blaster is different than *Cosmic Geometry* in that it covers HIGH SCHOOL level geometry concepts. By using a space alien/multi-dimensional setting. *Geometry Blaster* gives practice in essential high school level geometry subject areas including: triangles, angles, Pythagorean theorem; properties of polygons and circles; coordinate and transformational geometry; proofs, theorems, and logic; perimeter, area and volume; similarity, ratio, and proportion. In this game you must travel through a 2D planet in search of hidden geometric puzzle pieces. Includes 50 animated video chalkboard lessons with step-by-step instructions and examples. Has an on-line textbook to teach and practice geometry. Best feature I liked: a drill in 2 column proofs required placing lines of a proof in the right order. A painless way to practice theory application. Note: The Evil Geometrons are not that "scary" but appear/disappear from the 4th dimension. Recommended use: Excellent supplement to a textbook: provides hands-on examples, practice problems and extra tutorial.

Geometry World

Cognitive Technologies
Ages: 10-15   Street price $40
Subject(s): geometry
Skills needed: reading, 5th grade math
System Req: WIN 95/98: PI/100/16MB
MAC: Pmac/16MB

24 excellent tutorials guide the student through some difficult geometry material such as triangles, area, volume and more. This isn't a flashy arcade game but just solid lessons in geometry and simulations demonstrating geometry concepts using tangram blocks, a geoboard or a Venn diagram. This is a great program for teaching or reinforcing a subject that a lot of homeschool moms may have trouble with.

Math Advantage 2001

Encore Software
Ages: 11-18   Street price $39
Subject(s): Pre-Algebra, Algebra I, Algebra II, Trigonometry, Pre-Calculus, Calculus and Statistics
Skills needed: Saxon 7/6 or equivalent
System Req. WIN 95/98: PI/90/16MB
MAC: Pmac/16MB

This all-inclusive, well-designed package of math topics offers a lot of tutoring for the buck. Covering topics including Pre-Algebra, Algebra I, Algebra II, Trigonometry, Pre-Calculus, Calculus and Statistics with interactive tutorials, lessons, and over 3000 problems, this program is a complete supplement to your upper level math subjects. The company is so sure you will like their product; they guarantee your satisfaction. Features include animated examples, practice exercises, games, quizzes, all lessons narrated, and detailed progress reports. A hint system, step-by-step problem solutions (for some problems), real-life examples of math applications are built-in to the program and are easily accessible. My 10th grade daughter says, *"After the tests and quizzes, you can click a "solutions" button to have the program show you the basics on how to do any incorrect problems correctly. The program reads the material aloud to you and includes a built-in calculator and dictionary. Also, if you get a practice problem wrong, it gives you a hint. The program covers more concepts at once than other Algebra programs."* Even includes a genius corner for the math whiz in the family. This is the best supplemental math program I have found for all around help in these tough high school subjects. One drawback: all questions are multiple choice- no chance to work out real problems and get an unknown answer. A good guesser can guess some questions right. If your student needs step-by-step help working out problems, I recommend *Math Teacher*. (See review below.) The best choice would be using both programs: *Math Advantage* for teaching and demonstrating concepts and *Math Teacher* for practicing problems.

Math Teacher

4:20 Communications
Ages: 13-18   Street price $119 each
Subjects: High School Math
System Req. WIN 3.1/95/98
486SX33/8MB
MAC: N/A

These are not games, or just drills, these are actual courses. *Math Teacher* can be your complete upper level math curriculum. *Math Teacher* has an expression parser not found in other computer-aided mathematics tutorials. Its benefits include: No pencil and paper. No multiple choice. The problem with most other math software curricula is that the questions come in the form of multiple choice. A good guesser could possibly fake his way through. Not so with *Math Teacher*. Each problem can worked out onscreen. Students type symbolic expressions in a free format style. *Math Teacher* analyzes each line and indicates whether it is correct or not. This analysis detects common mistakes and provides focused help. Process repeats until the answer is reached. The program perceives the proficiency of the student and generates problems accordingly. This is unlike ANY other math program. Other significant benefits of *Math Teacher*: A "Utility Toolkit" is able to create, customize and print problems (with/without answers) as homework or tests. A calculator designed to work with algebraic expressions. Rational expressions yield both rational and the approximate real result. Several levels of help: a Tutorial on each concept; Guidance of general instruction on how to begin or continue a problem, and Hints to solve the specific problem. When applicable, graphs and figures are provided. Also built into the program is the Lab: a place to experiment with algebra and graphing equations. Student scores are collected automatically. These unique features make *Math Teacher* the private-tutor of each student. Worst features of this program include basic graphics,

looks like a workbook on computer with no entertaining graphics or animations. However, this program is not designed to entertain but to teach math concepts in a powerful manner. Highly recommended.

Algebra 1

Algebraic Expressions 1: Operations, substitution, building expressions, factorization. *Area and Volume:* The metric system, calculation of area and volume. *Equations 1*: Equations and inequalities of the first degree. *Algebraic Expressions 2*: Special products, factorization, building equations, integer exponentiation

Algebra 2

Equations 2: Equations and inequalities of the second degree. *Equations 3:* Equations and systems with two variables. *Equations 4:* Quadratic systems, linear equations and systems with a parameter. *Sequences:* Explicit and recursive definitions, arithmetic and geometric progressions. *Word Problems 2:* First-degree problems dealing with geometrical shapes and uniform motion.

Word Problems and Probability

Word Problems 1: First-degree problems in percentages and numbers. *Word Problems 2:* First-degree problems dealing with geometrical shapes and uniform motion. *Probability 1:* Calculation of probabilities. *Probability 2:* Combinatorial, binomial and normal distribution.

Analytic Geometry and Trigonometry

Analytic Geometry 1: Points in the plane, the straight line, the circle. *Analytic Geometry 2:* The ellipse, the hyperbola, the parabola. *Trigonometry 1:* Definition of the trigonometric functions, solving triangles and shapes. *Trigonometry 2:* Extension of functions to R, identities and equations.

Calculus and Linear Programming

Integrals: Antiderivatives, calculation of area and volume. *Derivatives 1:* The notion of the derivative, investigating polynomial functions. *Derivatives 2:* Deriving and investigating elementary functions. *Linear Programming:* Inequalities and systems with two variables, solving problems.

Princeton Review: Math Library

The Learning Company
Ages: 14-up   Street price $19
Subject(s): algebra
System Req: WIN 3.1/95/98 486/8MB
MAC: 040/8MB

My 16-year-old daughter Anna's comments on the *Princeton Review: Algebra 1: Gives good information, tips on test taking, and tips on how to write out the problem properly. You can create your own problems to see how a concept works. Includes dictionary of terms, formulas and rules. Narrates much of the instructions, which is very helpful. Practice problems have visual helps, multiple-choice answers, good hints that make you think. I like this format of teaching.* The six CD package has a solid set of lessons, designed to teach high school algebra, geometry, calculus and trigonometry. While not fancy, this is a useful reference package with its easy to access index of terms, formulas and rules.

StudyWorks! Mathematics Deluxe

MathSoft
Ages: 14-up   Street price $39
Subject(s): pre-algebra, algebra 1 & 2
System Req: WIN 3.1/95/98 486/8MB
MAC: 040/8MB

I asked my daughter to check out this Math package as well as the others mentioned here. She gave it a big thumbs down. *"I do not like the format. This would not keep my attention. It was too complicated to work with and it made me frustrated. You needed to go online for tests and I did not like that."* She added that it did cover a lot of material and included a built-in calculator. However, there are better math products to spend your money on.

LOGIC

Brain Builder

National Academy for Child Development
Timberdoodl, distributor
System Req: Win 95/98, 586 90 MHz /16MB
Ages: 4-up   Street price $40
Subject(s): logic, thinking skills, memory
Skills needed: some reading helpful

This software, developed by the National Academy for Child Development, helps increase memory and problem-solving skills. *Timberdoodle* carries this product and here is a review courtesy of Deb Deffinbaugh of *Timberdoodle.*

Do you have a child that cannot remember what you just said to him, or what he just read? No? Then this software is not for you. What *Brain Builder* will do for the rest of us is to boost our family's ability to absorb and process information more quickly and easily, and all it takes is just ten to fifteen minutes per day. The level of difficulty is automatically set and adjusts to help anyone as long as he know his numbers and can navigate on a keyboard. *Brain Builder* helps to develop "sequentials processing: which determines how quickly and clearly we can grasp concepts with 3 or 5 or 7 components. With regular use you should see significant, lasting changes in auditory and visual sequential processing skills and short -term memory. Your child will have less need to reread information or hear it repeated.

There are three visual activities, three activities, and one intensity activity. The six core activities all involves seeing or hearing, and then recalling, a series of numbers. The core activities, if done too long, will get tedious. To maintain his eagerness we suggest that you have your child do only one lesson per day in each of the core activities. The intensity activity, on the other hand, is a blast, and one you may have to limit because of time, not tedium. The biggest negative to this program is the "Professor" whose encouraging words can quickly become a source of irritation. Especially when he says, "You are a real wiz!," an abbreviated form of wizard and not an approved compliment in our household. Thankfully the "Professor" can be turned off, and these annoyances go away.

Brain Builder was originally designed by NACD, the National Association for Child Development, as a tool to help children with leaning disabilities and attention problems, so it may not be a necessary addition to every home. However, you could be interested in knowing that the activities in *Brain Builder* have also proved themselves equally effective in accelerating learning and improving problem-solving abilities.

Review courtesy *Timberdoodle*, www.timberdoodle.com. See appendix of software resellers.

Castle of Dr. Brain

Knowledge Adventure
System Req: Win 95/98 PI 90 MHz/16MB
Ages: 10-up   Street price $10
Subject(s): logic, thinking skills, memory
Skills needed: some reading helpful
(Despite the title, this program contains no magic.) The player goes from room to room in Dr. Brain's castle to solve numerous brain teasers, logic puzzles, math problems, word puzzles, deductive reasoning games and more. They think they are playing a game—so don't tell them they are learning how to think logically and analytically. For teenagers and adults—we enjoyed it so much we stayed up until 2:30 AM the first time we tried it. Highly recommended. This program is only available in *Smartworks*

Grade School.

Chessmaster 8000:
Win 95/98, 586 90 MHz /16MB
Chessmaster 6000: Mac

The Learning Company
Ages: 10-up   Street price $40
Subject(s): logic, thinking skills
Skills needed: some reading helpful
This chess program is designed for the serious chess player building on a 27,000 game chess database with advanced query capabilities, interactive tutorials, opponents with the personalities of the grand masters, and 3D game boards. This program can provide any chess enthusiast with a challenging game at any level, anytime, and all the tools and tips to help improve even the worst of players. Although I am not a chess expert, every review and critique I read said that *Chessmaster* was the best for serious chess players. If you are a beginner, I recommend *Maurice Ashley Teaches Chess*, but if you are a die-hard chess player looking for serious training and challenge, get *Chessmaster*. Caution: the cover of the box has a wizard-looking guy but there are no wizards or magic in the game.

Dr. Brain Action/Reaction

Knowledge Adventure
Subject(s): logic, thinking skills
Skills needed: advanced mouse skills, reading
System Req: WIN95/98 PII/166+/32+MB
When I first saw this game, I thought for sure it was just another brainless arcade game. But the more I watched my kids play, the more I realized how much thinking was going on. The setting is a futuristic submarine and you are a scientist held prisoner who must break out and stop the evil villain from destroying the world. (Where have we heard that one before?) Using a 3D first per-

LOGIC

son perspective, you use the keyboard and the mouse to move through 22 levels with a total of 45 puzzle rooms solving puzzles. You see the world down the barrel of a gun (Don't worry, you shoot boxing gloves not lethal bullets.) and you have to defeat robots, open doors, flip switches and more. No bloodshed. You can save your games, jump to any level or play against other players over the Internet. This program is hard and if you let younger kids play, they will just experience the arcade action, not the real thinking behind the puzzles. Caution: the rock music is very annoying. You can turn it down but then you do not hear any of the other sound effects. You can access more Dr. Brain games online at www.drbrain.com.

Dr. Brain Thinking Games: MindVenture a.k.a IQ Adventure

Knowledge Adventure
Subject(s): logic, thinking skills
Skills needed: advanced mouse skills, reading
System Req: WIN95/98 P90/16MB

Unlike the older *Dr. Brains*, *MindVenture* is more like an arcade game than a series of brainteasers. *Dr. Brain* has transported you to a strange and dangerous planet and you have to wind through these many dangers to get off the planet. As he travels he can meet 10 different weird species, collect things like brain fruit to recharge his energy and green bugs that can defend him from hostile plants. The puzzles pop up and Dr. Brain must solve them as he goes. Puzzles cover such thinking skills as matching, sequencing, memory, patterns, spatial relations, and logic. Can turn off the music if you like.

Dr. Brain Thinking Games: Puzzleopolis a.k.a. Puzzle Madness

Knowledge Adventure
Subject(s): logic, thinking skills
Skills needed: advanced mouse skills, reading
System Req: WIN95/98 P90/16MB
MAC: PMac/8MB

This is the only new Dr. Brain that will run on a Mac; unfortunately it is not the best of the three. However, the seven puzzles are very clever but very hard to figure out. Dr. Brain has, oops, created an evil clone of himself and you need to solve the puzzles to stop him from destroying the town. Kids have to put together a maze of pipes in the Factory Fracas and adjust magnetic fields in Power Towers as they get a moving particle to hit a target. Another challenging game entails programming a robot.

DroidWorks

Lucas Learning
Ages: 10-up   Street price $24
Subject(s): logic, memory
Skills needed: reading, following instructions
System Req: WIN 95/98: PI/90/16MB
MAC: PMac/16MB

Although I have some philosophical disagreements with the spiritual nature of the Star Wars movie series, this program is pure logic, robots and programming. None of the "force" new age spiritualism here. The basic premise centers on building a droid in the Droid Workshop. You must design it specifically to accomplish one of 13 different missions. You combine up to 88 robotic parts, each with a specific design, function and unique characteristic. If you make your droid too heavy, it will need more batteries. In one mission, Fire When Ready, you must adjust the design of the robot and a catapult to enable the droid to be hurled across a vast chasm. You must account for mass, direction and trajectory to successfully complete the mission. By manipulating varying degrees of weights and shapes of droid parts, batteries, and other factors, you are challenged by some intense engineering and physics concepts. This is not a program for the easily frustrated child. With rich 3D graphics and robust musical score, this game has a top-flight video game feel to it. The puzzles are challenging but with a little coaching, most pre-teens and teens will love this well-designed game. Needs at least 81 MB of hard drive space.

Logical Journey of the Zoombinis Deluxe

The Learning Company
Ages: 6-14+   Street price $19
Subject(s): logic, algebra
Skills needed: advanced mouse skills, no reading required
System Req: WIN 3.1/95/98 486/8MB
MAC: 030/8MB

Zoombinis are strange but cute little characters who encounter 12 sets of puzzles and challenges as they journey in their trek in search of a new homeland. When I first saw the box for this one I thought, "Well it sure looks really interesting, but there is probably occult stuff in it and I can't imagine it living up to all its claims." I am happy to say that my children and I have enjoyed getting through most of it and we haven't seen anything occult yet. The box describes this as "advanced math thinking skills and logic". These are some of the "skills developed" also listed on the box: Algebraic thinking, data analysis, data sorting, set theory, graphing, logical reasoning, data organization, pattern finding, sequential logic, and attribute comparison. Now I nearly always take all software box descriptions with a grain of salt and assume that an

advertising specialist who borders on lying writes them. Well in this case, I was pretty impressed with the accuracy-and the most amazing part of it is that it introduces these concepts without using any numbers. It is all done through the variations of things like the *Zoombinis* physical features (long hair, short hair, pony tail, nose colors, eye shapes, etc.). We would best describe *Zoombinis* as looking like a type of blue Mr. Potato Head with changeable features. Some of the puzzles were even a challenge for me. Because of the excellent logical and analytical thinking skills this challenges and develops, it is one program that I will encourage my children to play as much as they want. Your children should be doing this one too. You can adjust the level of difficulty, choosing from not so easy, hard, very very hard and so very hard. Can also turn off background music but it isn't offensive to me. Highest recommendation. (I can't wait to see the sequel.) HINT: There are lots of good tips in the manual for getting though the different puzzles. The deluxe version is basically the same as the original.

Madeline Thinking Games Deluxe

The Learning Company
Ages: 5-9+   Street price $21
Subject(s): logic, memory, melody, simple words in French or Spanish
Skills needed: advanced mouse skills, following directions
System Req: WIN 3.1/95/98 486/8MB
MAC: 040/16MB

This package has two Madeline programs: *Madeline: Thinking Games* and *Madeline's European Adventures.* With gentle art and sweet music, *Madeline: Thinking Games* should please the Madeline fans in your home. In this game, children can go to Madeline's house and play 11 different

LOGIC

games in the house or garden. Spelling words, matching pictures, watching Madeline music videos, playing a piano keyboard and more will keep the child busy playing "thinking games" with sweet Madeline! *Madeline's European Adventures* is a great program and similar in style to *Thinking Games* but has a genie with a magic lamp as your host. Beware.

Lost Mind of Dr. Brain

The Learning Company
Ages: 10-up   Street price $14
Subject(s): logic, thinking skills
Skills needed: some reading helpful
System Req: WIN 3.1/95/98 486/8MB
MAC: 030/8MB

For brainteasers and logic puzzles, nothing beats *Dr. Brain*. Premise: *Dr. Brain* has transferred his "mind" into his lab rat and you must solve all the puzzles to restore his great brainpower before it's too late. With varying degrees of difficulty, this program contains 5 different activities including memory building, musical training, and 3D designing. For an addictive game that will build your child's thinking skills, this is our pick. Caution: When *Dr. Brain* reads his lab book in the introduction, it floats. Highly recommended.

Microworlds Pro

See review under PROGRAMMING.

Pit Droids

Lucas Learning
Ages: 10-up   Street price $24
Subject(s): logic, memory
Skills needed: following instructions
System Req: WIN 95/98: PI/90/16MB
MAC: PMac/16MB

Take robots, programming, logic and great graphics and sound and you get the visually engaging and educational *Pit Droids*. Your goal is to lead a group of robots (droids) through challenging obstacle courses and puzzles. Although I have some philosophical disagreements with the spiritual nature of the Star Wars movie series, this program is pure logic, robots and programming. None of the "force" new age spiritualism here. By using programming theory and logic, the child manipulates the robots by placing tiles to direct them through ever increasingly difficult puzzles. For example, a blue arrow makes blue droids turn a certain direction. Other tiles direct the droids to divide into columns and different directions. The puzzles get a little bit harder each time and the robots are cute and funny, so this program is very engaging, enjoyable and challenging. A tutorial mode is built into the program to offer readily available help for those tougher puzzles. This program offers lots of depth with over 300 puzzles and the ability to customize your own puzzles as well. As you complete the puzzles, you rack up points to access deeper levels of the game. *Pit Droids* is for the child that demands a rich and deep playing experience and doesn't shy away from something that just a little too hard.

Reader Rabbit's Thinking Adventures

The Learning Company
Ages: 4-6   Street price $24
Subject(s): logic, memory
Skills needed: following instructions
System Req: WIN 95/98: PI/90/16MB
MAC: PMac/16MB

Looking for a logic and thinking game for your preschoolers and kindergarteners? This fun, new game offers eight games designed to develop logic and thinking. Upon signing in, the child is given a pre-test to determine their current skill level and then the games are programmed to match the child's exact abilities. The program also has the fun ability to speak the child's name. Although my son Geremiah did not understand why I had to type in his name as Jeremiah to have the program to speak it correctly, he thought it great fun to hear Reader Rabbit say his name.

Thinkin' Things Toony the Loon's Lagoon a.k.a Thinkin' Things 1

Edmark

Ages: 4-8 Street Price $29

Subject(s): logic, memory, melody.

System Req: WIN 95/98: P90/16MB

MAC: 040/16MB

Skills needed: advanced mouse skills, following directions

Six activities designed to improve critical thinking skills, visual memory, creativity, comparing similar (but different) items, and pattern and sequence. All activities come with many levels of difficulty. As with all Edmark programs, this program has two modes: explore or Q&A. The child can investigate and experiment at their own pace and interest, or choose Q&A to have the program ask them questions. A.K.A. *Thinkin' Things 1*, now enhanced with better graphics and sound.

Thinkin' Things All Around Frippletown

Edmark

Ages: 5-9 Street price $29

Subject(s): logic, memory, melody

System Req: WIN 95/98: P90/16MB

MAC: 040/16MB

Skills needed: advanced mouse skills, following directions

Four unique environments designed to improve critical thinking skills, memory, creativity, comparing similar (but different)

items. All activities come with many levels of difficulty. 100's of puzzling problems to solve. The Fripples, small cute creatures, have run short on supplies. Use pattern recognition, logic, programming, deductive reasoning, map reading and more to solve the puzzles and help them. Design and develop recipes to make the cookies of your customer's dreams. Program ice skaters on the ice rink to create intricate patterns.

Thinkin' Things Galactic Brain Benders a.k.a Thinkin' Things 3

Edmark

Ages: 7-12 Street price $29

Subject(s): logic, memory, melody, programming

Skills needed: advanced mouse skills, reading, following directions

System Req: WIN 95/98: P90/16MB

MAC: 040/16MB

This group of activities is by far the best *Thinkin' Things* Collection so far. Aimed at older children, these activities stress stock-broker-like trading, a deductive and inductive reasoning game, 3D designing of experiment in physics concepts of motion, friction, and inertia, programming of movements of football players, marching bands, and cheerleaders on a football grid, and more all designed to improve critical thinking skills and deductive reasoning The thinking activities in this are different than in the Logical Journey, and it takes a different approach. We give this a high recommendation as well. A.K.A. *Thinkin' Things 3*, now enhanced with better graphics and sound.

LOGIC

Thinkin' Things 2

Edmark
Ages: 5-9   Street price $19
Subject(s): logic, memory, melody
System Req: WIN 3.1/95/98 486/8MB
MAC: 030/8MB
Skills needed: advanced mouse skills, following directions

Five activities designed to improve critical thinking skills, memory, creativity, and includes comparing similar (but different) items. All activities come with many levels of difficulty. There is a "concentration" game that uses both visual and sound cues for developing listening, observation, and memory skills.

Yoiks!

The Learning Company
Ages: 12-up   Street price $30
Subject(s): logic, memory, programming
System Req: WIN 95/98: P90/16MB
MAC: N/A

From the maker of our beloved *Logical Journey of the Zoombinis* comes a new brain bending game. In this cleverly designed program, kids need to extricate some nasty little bugs or "yoiks" who have messed up the inside of your computer. To do this, you must guide the bugs through 30 different grids or "puzzles." Each puzzle gets increasingly difficult as the game progresses. To get through each puzzle, you must examine each of the group of yoiks on the grid. On the grid are spots where the bugs are manipulated or changed. You set the bug on a course to get to the exit and as the bug passes over these spots, he changes or turns depending on his design. For example, a red yoik passing over a red arrow turns in the direction of that arrow. A blue yoik is unaffected by the red arrow. The spots are unchangeable; you must set the bug on a course to navigate through these spots to get to the exit. To complicate the challenge, the bugs usually have two characteristics; one is color and the other is a design such as spots or stripes. Some of the exits are only open to certain designed yoiks so negotiating all the spots and exits takes some thoughtful planning and execution; otherwise known as "programming." This program is great for developing programming strategies (step-by-step solutions called algorithms), reasoning skills and algebraic thinking. Includes a practice mode to help students figure out strategies without penalty. This is a very challenging program and not for every kid. Other reviewers gave a low rating because it was too hard for the average kid. But we know homeschoolers are above average and love a challenge. Highly recommended.

HISTORY

A Child's History of the World

Calvert School
Ages: 9-up   Street price $40
Subject(s): World history
Skills needed: reading
System Req: WIN 95/98: 486/8MB
MAC: N/A

Calvert has long been regarded as a top homeschool curriculum producer. Although not inherently Christian, their courses are wholesome, classic, and rigorous. Recently they have added some wonderful CD-ROMs to their course offerings. *A Child's History of the World* is a multimedia version of their very popular book of that title. Written long ago by Virgil M. Hillyer, this book and CD contain 91 stories covering the most famous stories of world history. The CD is broken into three sections or venues: timeline, geography, or the table of contents. You can access any of the stories through these venues. The first and last pages of the story are narrated by a kindly Mr. Hillyer, which makes some of the material accessible to even non-readers. The stories have about four or five screens and contain clickable spots within each one. Some of these clickables take you to additional information. Clicking on a word in red allows you to hear the word pronounced. Games and quizzes following the story help you test how much you remember. Although not real glitzy, this CD offers a lot of learning and will fit nicely into any elementary world history course or unit study.

Ancient Greece

Calvert School
Ages: 9-up   Street price $40
Subject(s): Ancient Greece history .
Skills needed: reading
System Req: WIN 95/98: 486/8MB
MAC: N/A

Calvert has long been regarded as a top homeschool curriculum producer. Although not inherently Christian, their courses are wholesome, classic, and rigorous. Recently they have added some wonderful CD-ROMs to their course offerings. *Ancient Greece* is one of the best of the bunch. Although not loaded with multimedia bells and whistles, this CD is full of detailed, colorful illustrations and animations. Built into the program are lessons covering the history and culture of ancient Greece. Each lesson presents you with questions to think about while you read the material. With narrated text and plenty of built in clickable links to more information (both on the CD and on the Internet). After the lesson the student can take a short quiz to test their knowledge. This CD is a great place to start if you want to study ancient history. A must-have if you are using the Classical Education method.

Carmen Sandiego's Great Chase through Time

Learning Company
AGES 9-UP   Street price $19
Subject(s): World History
Skills needed: reading
System Req: WIN 3.1/95/98: 486/66MHz/8MB
MAC: PMac/12MB

In this *Carmen Sandiego* title, you must chase criminals through world history by solving clues. This new upgrade to an old classic Carmen Sandiego is very well done. My kids really enjoyed solving the history clues to track down Carmen. Includes 18 historical adventures that emphasize technology, culture, government or exploration. Features 50 interesting individuals such as Ben Franklin, Queen Elizabeth I, Ludwig van Beethoven, and Sacajawea. Can access learning resources on the Internet. (I recommend parental supervision for Internet use.) Makes learning about history (and a little geography) fun and exciting. Highly recommended for a fun but educationally challenging history game.

Chronicle of the 20th Century

Dorling Kindersley
Ages 12-up   Street price $19
Subject(s): history: 1900 to present
Skills needed: reading, interest in subject
System Req: WIN 3.1/95/98 486/8MB
MAC: 030/8MB

This new title from Dorling Kindersley brings their wonderful multimedia presentation format to modern American history. Content is based on the news, events, and people that have happened since 1900. It's massive content includes 8000 articles, 1,000 news screens, 130 biographies, and 100 video clips. You can search the content to locate a particular subject, keyword or person. Check out the "on this day" feature to see what happened the day you were born. Has a trivia game to help you get into the material. Recommended use: Reference material or supplement to modern American history unit study. Caution: I did not look at every item in this CD-ROM so keep in mind, not everything that happened in the last 97 years is suitable for general audiences. What I saw was acceptable.

Exploring Ancient Cities

Sumeria
Ages: 9-up   Street price $40
Subject(s): Crete, Petra, Pompeii, Teotihuacan history
Skills needed: reading
System Req: WIN 3.1/95/98: 486/8MB
MAC: 040/8MB

In this rich and detailed history CD, you are given a choice of taking a grand tour of the four cities: Crete, Petra, Pompeii, or Teotihuacan or digging into the other components of the program. In the grand tour, you enjoy a narrated slideshow of the city. Also built into the program are beautiful and detailed timelines, video clips, photos, maps to zoom in on, and hyperlinked key words. Click on highlighted words and see a photograph about that word. You may also see slideshows on sculpture, painting and architecture. While not very interactive, this CD is full of information and beautiful photos. My daughter adds, "It has cool music. Sort of ancient sounding. Not rock-n-roll."

Eyewitness History of The World 2.0

Dorling Kindersley Multimedia
Ages: 10-up   Street price $28
Subject(s): timeline history
Skills needed: advanced mouse skills, reading
System Req: WIN 3.1/95/98 486/8MB
MAC: 030/8MB

This jam-packed CD ROM contains practically an entire history curriculum. With 70 animations, over 25 video sequences, 700 photos and illustrations, 150,000 words and 3 hours audio, this resource offers a multimedia timeline-based study of historical people, inventions, places, voyages, events and more. With a globe and a timeline, children are able to browse through over 400 different articles about the history of human civilization. Afterwards, test your knowledge of world history with a built in quiz feature. A great supplement to any unit study or curriculum. A history book may bore a lot of children, but these CD's from Dorling Kindersley make history a lot more interesting.

Geosafari History

Educational Insights
Ages 8-up   Street price $24
Subject(s): history
Skills needed: reading, mouse
System Req: WIN 3.1/95/98
486DX33/8MB (4X CD-ROM recommended) MAC: 030/8MB

This rich and detailed quiz game can offer lots of fun to learning History facts. The program speaks your name and quizzes you with animations, illustrations, videos, audio and diagrams on 15 different History topics including Currencies, Capitals, Flags, Great Inventions, Who Said That?, World War II, and more. Similar to the regular Geosafari electronic tabletop game in format but multimedia in delivery.

Go West!
The Homesteader's Challenge!

Steck-Vaughn
Ages 9-up   Street price $59
Skills needed: reading, basic math
Skills taught or reinforced: critical thinking, logic, planning, American History, agriculture, business
System Req: 486DX66+/8MB
MAC: 040/8MB

If you are familiar with the *Oregon Tail* series of programs, this is sort of like how an *"Oregon Trail Part 2"* would be. This program lets you pretend you are a pioneer homesteading in Kansas in the 1880's a la Little House on the Prairie. Buy land or get it free from the government (those were the days.) Learn when to plant crops. Raise

your family. Discover how to budget your money to survive winter. Raise farm animals. Secure water supplies. Save up your money to buy a house. Run a business in the small town. Become the mayor. My 11-year-old daughter now plays *Go West* instead of *Oregon Trail*. Can only be bought as school version at company's web site (www.steck-vaughn.com). Recommended use: Unit study supplementation. Excellent for Prairie Primer or Laura Ingalls unit study.

History Through Art
1450 AD to 1900 AD

Zane Publishing
Ages: 8-18   Street price $29
Subject(s): art, history
Skills needed: advanced mouse skills, following directions
System Req: WIN 3.1/95/98 486/8MB
MAC: 030/8MB

Just like the title implies, this 4-CD set covers history by looking at art in the time period of 1450AD-1900AD covering the Baroque, The Enlightenment, Romanticism and The Pre-Modern Era. This program is from Zane Publishing and is like a multimedia narrated slideshow on CD-ROM. Sit through the slideshow, which combines the visual and musical sequences illustrating the cultural era, presented. Musical excerpts from renowned compositions complement magnificent paintings, sculpture and architectural treasures and how they relate to historical events or, at any time, click on a highlighted word and go to the cross referenced glossary to research different topics, terms, people, etc. Has built in quizzes to test your knowledge. Recommended use: Excellent supplement to any curriculum or unit study covering these time periods.

HISTORY

History Through Art 800 BC-1450 AD
Zane Publishing
Ages: 8-18   Street price $29
Subject(s): art, history
Skills needed: advanced mouse skills, reading helpful but not required
System Req: WIN 3.1/95/98 486/8MB
MAC: 030/8MB

Just like the title implies, this 4-CD set covers history by looking at art in the time period of 800BC-1450AD covering Ancient Greek, Ancient Rome, The Middle Ages and the Renaissance. This program is from Zane Publishing and is like a multimedia narrated slideshow on CD-ROM. Sit through the slideshow in which combines the visual and musical sequences illustrating the cultural era presented. Musical excerpts from renowned compositions complement magnificent paintings, sculpture and architectural treasures and how they relate to historical events or, at any time, click on a highlighted word and go to the cross referenced glossary to research different topics, terms, people, etc. Each CD-ROM has a full screen enlargement of each work of art, 100+ questions with explanations.

Imagination Express: Time Trip
Edmark
Ages: 6-14   Street price $28
Subject(s): creative writing, history
Skills needed: reading
System Req: WIN 3.1/95/98 486/8MB
MAC: 030/8MB

Program of tools to create electronic or printed books. Use backgrounds, character and object stickers, animations, music, sounds and more. Very similar to *Storybook Weaver* but pictures are richer in detail although fewer in number. Story themes cover pilgrims, colonists, and more. Covers the time period of 1600 to present. Contains historical reference material as well. Great for creating fictional or non-fictional stories for American history unit studies. This is the school edition and includes two copies of the program, some helpful lesson plans and study ideas.

InventorLabs: Technology
Houghton Mifflin Interactive
Ages: 10-up   Street price $16
Subject(s): history, science history, science
Skills needed: Serious interest in subject, reading
System Req: 486SX33/8MB
MAC: 040/8MB

In *InventorLabs: Technology*, the student can explore the re-created laboratories of three of the world's most celebrated inventors — Edison, Watt, Bell. He or she can also examine and test their intriguing inventions. Review over 100 historic films, photographs and original recordings. Discover basic principles of electricity, optics, sound and light. Peruse inventors' patent drawings, scrapbooks and mementos. Recommended use: Unit study and/or curriculum supplementation.

InventorLabs: Transportation
Houghton Mifflin Interactive
Ages: 10-up   Street price $16
Subject(s): History, Science
Skills needed: Serious interest in subject, reading
System Req: 486SX33/8MB
MAC: 040/8MB

Explore the re-created laboratories of three of the world's most celebrated transportation inventors- the Wright brothers, Gottleib Daimler, George Stephenson. Examine and test their intriguing inventions. Review over 100 historic films, photographs and original recordings. Discover basic principles of 4-stroke engines, flight, and the world's first locomotive. Peruse inventors' patent draw-

ings, scrapbooks and mementos.
Recommended use: Unit study and/or curriculum supplementation.

Leonardo da Vinci
Forest Technology
Ages 12-up   Street price $34
Subject(s): science, art, history, reading comprehension
Skills needed: jr. high+ reading/interest level
System Req: WIN 3.1/95/98
486SX33/8MB
MAC: 040/8MB
This CD-ROM is a compilation of da Vinci's writings, works and life. It goes far beyond any textbook or book in giving the reader an engaging, exciting look at all this incredible man accomplished in his life. Includes a virtual museum tour of his works, a step-by-step tour of his experiments. This CD contains a "virtual" translation of his great work *Codex Leicester*. Which, by the way, he wrote *backwards*. I highly recommend this CD-ROM as a resource for any art, science or renaissance history unit study.

My First Amazing History Explorer
Dorling Kindersley
Ages 6-10   Street price $19
Subject(s): world history
Skills needed: reading, mouse
System Req: WIN 95/98:
486DX/66/16MB
MAC: PMac/8MB
A history professor is lost in time and your mission is to go back in time to rescue him. Children travel back to *The Industrial Age, The Roman Empire* and *Ancient Egypt* to find key historical artifacts. Along the way, kids play activities, take quizzes and are able to learn a great deal of history. Built into the program are 150 narrated pop-up screens with 2 hours of narration, multiple-choice quizzes and a glossary of terms to look up the answers. Kids are motivated to earn the stickers and learn the history along the way. This program is jam-packed with fun and history. Even though the box says 6-10, the child needs to be a reader to successfully complete the games.

The Oregon Trail 4th Edition
Learning Company
Ages: 9-up   Street price $38
Subject(s): US History with some geography
Skills needed: reading
System Req: WIN 95/98: P200/32MB
MAC: PMac/16MB
Oregon Trail 4 is an interactive virtual trail adventure. Discover the excitement and hardships of the westward movement. Relive two decades in history; blaze new trails west with incredible 3-D rendered towns and forts, digitized speech and video clips of dozens of interesting characters. You have more choices in routes plus dozens of new interactive scenarios. Highly recommended. Warning! You do NOT need to play the first *Oregon Trail* before you play this one. *The Oregon Trail 1, 2,* or *3* are simply older versions of the essentially the same game. *Oregon Trail 1* and *2* have lower quality graphics, less variations in play, and overall is just simply not as good as this newer version. If you see cheap versions of the *Oregon Trail* in stores at $15 or less, you can be sure it is the oldest version and not the newest version available. We recommend spending the extra money and getting the newest version of *Oregon Trail: Oregon Trail 4* if your computer can handle it. If you have an older computer, *The Oregon Trail 3rd Edition* is still a great program.

HISTORY

147

Survivors: Testimonies of the Holocaust

Knowledge Adventure
Ages: 12-up   Street price $30
Subject(s): WWII history with some geography
Skills needed: reading
System Req: WIN 95/98: P100/16MB
MAC: Pmac/100/16MB 6X CD-ROM

In *Survivors: Testimonies of the Holocaust*, four Holocaust survivors — Bert, Paula, Sol and Silvia — give their firsthand accounts of history's darkest hour. Over the course of approximately 80 minutes of videotaped testimony, the survivors' experiences are illustrated with archival photographs and film footage, and woven together with descriptive narration. The time period covered includes the pre- and post- WWII era. I asked my 16-year-old daughter to review this title for me and later we were discussing her notes she took while using this CD. "That Survivor CD was really interesting Mom," she said. My husband overheard her and his reaction was one of shock, "Why are you even wasting time on reviewing anything that has to do with that awful TV show? It should go straight in the trash." After I calmed him down, I explained that this CD was about true survivors – survivors of the holocaust. This CD is jam packed with moving accounts, videos, and photographs. My daughter says, "This CD is good for studying WWII history and has extensive information. It has video clips, timelines, and interactive maps of the personal stories of four people who survived the holocaust. I could go through this program for hours and there would still be more to see." Features include soft music, an Internet link, timelines, narration, and definitions. This is an awesome history experience come to life via multimedia. If you are doing or will be doing a unit study on WWII, I highly recommend getting this resource now. It may not be available when you need it.

Switched-On Schoolhouse History and Geography

Alpha Omega Publications
Grades 3rd, 4th, 5th, 6th, 7th, 8th, 9th, 10th, 11th, or 12th.
Street price $67 per subject per grade
Subject(s): history and geography course
This is an actual full Bible-based history and geography course. Choose from grades listed above. See full description under *Curriculum*.

What's the Big Idea, Ben Franklin?

Scholastic
Ages: 9-up   Street price $60
Subject(s): US History, biography of Ben Franklin
Skills needed: reading
System Req: WIN 95/98: 486/66MHz/16+MB
MAC: 040/16+MB

This great interactive program gives new meaning to making history come alive. By using narration, animations, and activities, the program draws the student into the life and times of Ben Franklin. On screen you see a Rubik-like cube with one side facing you. On this side are 9 facets, each accesses nine different chapters in Franklin's life: *Early Years, Apprenticeship, In Philadelphia, Early Ideas, Inventions and Innovations, Electricity, In London, Declaration of Independence,* and *Later Years.* The content focuses primarily on his scientific contributions with additional information about his political life. The activities test your knowledge in fun quizzes and short essay questions on the content. If you are doing a unit study on early American History, this is an excellent supplement.

Yukon Trail

Learning Company
Ages: 9-up   Street price $14
Subject(s): US History with some geography
Skills needed: reading
System Req: WIN 3.1/95/98 486/8MB
MAC: 030/8MB

Join the gold rush of 1897 in Alaska. Race against time and the elements as you make life or death choices. Very similar to the format of *Oregon Trail* but you shop for a sled and other appropriate cold weather supplies. My children have enjoyed reliving this part of American history but have learned to stay away from the crooked con men of Klondike. Caution: Optional poker and betting games. However, could be a good object lesson because you usually lose. Older program but you may be able to find it in a bargain bin or bundle.

GEOGRAPHY

What is the subject "Geography?"

A long time ago, Social Studies was called Geography. Geography is known as "the study of the earth and its features and of the distribution of life on the earth, including human life and the effects of human activity." We recommend you look at Geography as having two components: (1) maps and places, and (2) people. When we study maps, we learn the boundaries of continents and nations as well as the geographical features of the earth itself: rivers, lakes, oceans, etc. The study of people is just the study of different people groups and their cultures. If you are looking for a Geography program, keep in mind which of these two aspects of Geography you are trying to cover.

Africa Trail

Learning Company
Ages: 9-16   Street price $14
Subject(s): facts about Africa, decision making, reading maps, budget
Skills needed: basic math, reading
System Req: WIN 3.1/95/98 486/8MB
MAC: 040/8MB

Imagine *Oregon Trail*, only you have a bike instead of a wagon, you're in Africa instead of Missouri, and it's 1997 not 1897. That's the *Africa Trail*. With many of the same fun features as our favorite *Oregon Trail*, this program is designed to give an in-depth look at Africa as you travel on your bike with your friends. Encounter hardships such as heat, hunger, thirst, injury, and challenging terrain as you plot a course through some of the most interesting regions of Africa. You start at one of four points and choose from three companions including a physician, a biologist, or a professional adventurer. Just like the original *Oregon Trail*, you consume valuable resources such as food, money, health, bike parts, and morale as you make your day-to-day trek across Africa. You must plan well to avoid running out of these resources and being forced to abandon the trek. The hundred of photos and many video clips make it a very real adventure but the graphic quality is not as good as *Oregon Trail II*. Recommended use: Excellent supplement for Africa unit study or fun afterschool game for your biking fans. Older program but you may be able to find it in a bargain bin or bundle.

Carmen Sandiego Junior

Learning Company
Ages: 5-8   Street price $19
Subject(s): World geography
Skills needed: mouse
System Req: WIN 3.1/95/98:
386/33MHz/8MB
MAC: 030/8MB

This is Carmen Sandiego for the younger set. No reading required as you solve the puzzles by deciphering symbols representing people, places, and things. Not a lot of content but good wholesome fun for your younger ones who want to play the games big brother and sister are playing. Some learning of geography and cultures. My 7-year-old non-reader really enjoyed playing a "big kid's game."

Compton's 3D World Atlas Deluxe

The Learning Company
Ages 8-up   Street price $24
Subject(s): geography
Skills needed: reading, mouse
System Req: WIN 3.1/95/98
486DX33/8MB
MAC: 030/8MB

This easy-to-use multimedia world atlas offers a nearly inexhaustible depth-of-content with over 38,000 articles, facts about every country, 3D rotating globes, satellite photos, a complete set of US road maps, 20,000 photos, illustrations and narrated videos. This is a great resource to have on any homeschool bookshelf.

Geosafari Geography

Educational Insights
Ages 8-up   Street price $24
Subject(s): geography
Skills needed: reading, mouse
System Req: WIN 3.1/95/98
486DX33/8MB (4X CD-ROM recommended) MAC: 030/8MB

This rich and detailed quiz game can offer lots of fun drilling on Geography facts. The program speaks your name and quizzes you with animations, illustrations, videos, audio and diagrams on different topics including Currencies, Capitals, Flags and more. If you are looking for a fun multimedia quiz game, this is the one to get.

My First Amazing USA Explorer

Dorling Kindersley
Ages 6-10   Street price $19
Subject(s): USA history and geography
Skills needed: reading, mouse
System Req: WIN 95/98:
486DX/66/16MB
MAC: PMac/8MB

Dorling Kindersley has made some great programs in their *Explorer* series. All are packed with fun and educational value. The best part is they are specifically designed for the early elementary ages and cover significant amounts of history and geography. Not many programs out there for younger kids to learn these subjects. In *USA Explorer*, the child must deliver a package to Joe. Problem is, Joe travels all over the 50 states. Clues are given as to his whereabouts and as the child tracks Joe down; they visit dozens of fascinating places and landmarks. The program narrates bits of information about everywhere the child visits and he earns stickers of landmarks, characters or animals indigenous to that area. The ultimate goal is become an official *"USA Explorer."* This is achieved after finding Joe five times. The narration can be turned off if you wish your student to do the reading on his own but it is great for the younger student. Features include two levels of difficulty, extra games and activities and loads of fun while kids learn.

My First Amazing World Explorer 2.0

Dorling Kindersley
Ages 5-9   Street price $19
Subject(s): Geography, maps, our world
Skills needed: Advanced mouse skills, able to follow directions, beginning reading.
System Req: WIN 95/98:
486DX/66/16MB
MAC: PMac/8MB

Excellent beginning, introductory program designed to allow early elementary children to explore the world and it's people. Just like a real traveler, your child can visit all kinds of faraway places will earning stamps for their "passport." Animated maps with varying levels of play keep the child interested and learning about their world. Includes three different games to get your children traveling all over the world learning fascinating facts. Recommended use:

Unit study and/or Curriculum supplementation. Because this is such an in-depth program with many layers of playability, I suggest you work with your student on this one to get them going, another option would be pairing an older sibling with a younger one. This is my first pick for beginning geography.

Nile: Passage to Egypt

Discovery Channel
Ages 9-up   Street price $24
Subject(s): Egyptian and Nile history and geography
Skills needed: advanced reading and interest in subject
System Req: WIN 3.1/95/98 486/8MB
MAC: 030/8MB

Guide your own felucca (Egyptian boat) down the Nile River, starting in Uganda, Africa through the ancient kingdoms of Egypt. You can turn in all directions, North, West, East, and South. As you travel you can examine and investigate artifacts and landmarks. Includes five different games helping the student understand more about the region. This program has a great deal of depth and fascinating material including 351 narrated topics of several paragraphs each, an 89-word glossary, video clips, and photos. Caution: Some of the Egyptian idols talk when you complete the puzzle of putting them back together. Recommended use: Wonderful supplement to any Egyptian unit study, appropriate for all ages if the interest level is there!

Rescue Geo 1

Houghton Mifflin Interactive
Ages 6-12   Street price $60
Subject(s): US geography, history, maps
Skills needed: reading, mouse
System Req: WIN 3.1/95/98 486/8MB
MAC: 030/8MB
Viruses have invaded a super computer

called Geo 1 and your job is to eliminate the viruses by answering geography questions. Topics include: The World in Spatial Terms, Physical Systems, Human Systems, Environment and Society, Places and Regions, and The Uses of Geography. Hints are provided to help answer the questions and the program has information on map reading and history as well. This program is easy to use and offers lots of practice in elementary US Geography and related topics. Only available in the school edition.

SkyTrip America

Forest Technologies
Ages: 9-up   Street price $30
Subject(s): US History with some geography
Skills needed: reading
System Req: WIN 3.1/95/98 486/8MB
MAC: 030/8MB
This multimedia scavenger type game is designed to get the student to fly with different flying vehicles (balloon, hover jet or old-fashioned biplane) from coast to coast across the USA, from past to present, learning about the peoples and places of our country. Contains 360-degree views of 12 regions full of clickables, 249 narrated articles, 25 video clips and 100 photos. Recommended use: Excellent supplement for any elementary or junior high American History or Geography curriculum.

Switched-On Schoolhouse History and Geography

Alpha Omega Publications
Grades 3rd, 4th, 5th, 6th, 7th, 8th, 9th, 10th, 11th, or 12th.
Street price $67 per subject per grade
Subject(s): history and geography course
  This is an actual Bible-based full geography and history course. See full description under *Curriculum*.

Where in the USA is Carmen Sandiego Deluxe

Learning Company
Ages: 9-up   Street price $19
Subject(s): US geography
Skills needed: reading
System Req: WIN 3.1/95/98
486/66MHz/8MB
MAC: 040/20MHz/12MB
In this *Carmen Sandiego* title you chase *Carmen* and her henchmen criminals across the United States by solving clues. You get a clue such as "Carmen went to the Keystone state." Then you must research which state is the "Keystone" state. So you're off to Pennsylvania. Makes learning about geography fun and exciting. Children love to play it. Because of the detective aspect, it is a thinking skill/reason and deduction game as well. It requires some reading and researching to find the information in the online encyclopedia that is built into the program.

Where in the World is Carmen Sandiego Deluxe

Learning Company
Ages: 9-up   Street price $19
Subject(s): World geography
Skills needed: reading
System Req: WIN 3.1/95/98
486/66MHz/8MB
MAC: 040/20MHz/12MB
In this *Carmen Sandiego* title you chase

Carmen and her henchmen criminals around the world by solving clues. For example, *Carmen* escaped to a country that has lyre as its currency; you research the almanac, deduce which country that is and you hop on a plane to Italy to find her. Once you are in the country she is in, you hunt down clues pertaining to landmarks within the country. Has a 3D high tech look with all kinds of gizmos on screen to use in your search. Makes learning about world geography fun and exciting. New version has several new features including: 50 scrolling landscapes where you pan through beautifully painted locations rich with history, art, music, and over 200 animated characters. Take an *"Acme Good Guides"* tour to collect interesting facts for future cases. Get information for school assignments in Explore mode. This mode allows you to learn all the information in the program without playing the game. Children love to play it. Because of the detective aspect, it is a thinking skill/reason and deduction game as well. It requires some reading and researching to find the information in the *Special Carmen Sandiego Edition World Almanac* included or the on-line built in database filled with essays, spectacular color photos and video clips from National Geographic Society.

World Discovery Deluxe

Ideal Instructional Fair
Ages: 6-up   Street price $24
Subject(s): Maps and geography
Skills needed: mouse, some reading helpful
System Req: WIN 3.1/95/98 486/8MB
MAC: 030/8MB
Teaches world and US geography (countries, states, major cities, capitals, rivers, lakes, locations and more). Allows a parent to customize and adapt for your child's specific curriculum needs or topic. Great pro-

gram for school time. If you want the best map skill and drill program on the market, this is the one to get. It has the depth and flexibility to offer all ages of students instruction and practice learning all types of geographical features. Our 10-year-old enjoyed using the quiz to learn her states. Our top pick for map drill skills. Deluxe CD ROM version has great graphics (satellite image maps), and more options, activities, and maps. One 10th grader raised her geography grade from nearly failing to an A after a few weeks with *World Discovery Deluxe*. This is a must-have title for every homeschool!

World Walker Destination: Australia

Soleil Software
Ages: 9-13   Street price $34
Subject(s): science, geography
System Req: WIN 3.1/95/98 486/8MB
MAC: 030/8MB
You are the explorer of the on screen habitat of Australia. The flora and fauna native to the desert, the woodlands, or a swamp surround you. Sometimes it's rainy, sometimes dry. As you wander, you encounter riddles that invite you to learn more about Australia and its inhabitants and environments. There are games, animals and caves to explore. Recommended use: Excellent for an Australia unit study.

Zurk's Alaskan Trek

Soleil Software
Ages: 5-9   Street price $24
Subject(s): Alaskan ecosystems, math, science
Skills needed: some reading helpful
System Req: WIN 3.1/95/98 486/8MB
MAC: 040/8MB
Although not a flashy multimedia program, *Zurk's Alaskan Trek* offers a lot of learning in its activities. With five main activities,

this program provides exploration in Alaskan plants, animals, people and customs. Other activity areas include balancing weights and comparing them to different animal weights, a 36 animal field guide, two animation and writing projects, and scenes where you can have animals walk around in a scene coordinated by you. Recommended use: Excellent choice for Alaska unit study or parent directed activities. Otherwise, it may not get much use in your homeschool.

FOREIGN LANGUAGE

How to learn a foreign language.

It is true that very young children have the amazing ability to absorb foreign languages and even adopt perfect accents. There are several reasons for this. One, new and unusual vocalizations are easier for children at this age. And, children are less inhibited about trying these new sounds. Lastly, I believe their brains are still wired in the learn-the-language mode they were born with. My brother married a native Japanese woman who knew very little English. Both English and Japanese surround their two children 24 hours a day. My niece Sasha would switch back and forth between the two languages while she talked to her parents. She would use both in one sentence but she also knew they were two different languages. All this by age 5. Unfortunately most children don't have this opportunity to learn a foreign language. In our multicultural world, with families looking toward the mission field and with Spanish soon to be a major second language right here in the USA, a second language is a very valuable skill in more ways than one. Using your multimedia computer to expose your child while they are young can yield some major dividends down the road.

Language experts believe the best programs take the immersion approach to teaching a foreign language. What this entails in a CD-ROM game is no English is spoken after the introduction. Instead, video clips, engaging games, interactive exercises, and great graphics keep the student playing, learning and using the language. And, language experts say using the language is essential to acquiring it. With immersion-based software, students are in the middle of the language, associating words and phrases with real life objects and activities. Learning their new language just like they learned their first language from the day they were born. "You need between 500 and 800 words to get by in any language," said Robert Miller, CEO of a large foreign language software company. Joseph Mwantuali, assistant professor of French at a college says, "It's possible to learn a foreign language without a teacher," he says, "but it takes much longer. For best results, software should be use in conjunction with a class." For homeschoolers, one option is to find a native speaker in your community or church who would like to test your students speaking ability. Another option would be to contact a local Christian college and adopt a foreign student believer who needs a friendly family. And don't forget that many storybook CD's can be read in a foreign language to get more practice. Most software also has a record and playback feature so you can compare your language skills with a native. Although I am not a foreign language expert, rest assured these titles are the best available. We have researched and pre-screened these for high quality and wholesome content, relying on foreign language experts and experienced users of these products to narrow our recommendations to these titles.

All In One Language Fun

Syracuse Language Systems
Ages: 3-up   Street price $15
Subject(s): beginning foreign language
Skills needed: mouse
System Req: WIN 3.1/95/98 486/8MB
MAC: 030/8MB

In *All In One Language Fun*, a set of 27 games teaches over 200 spoken foreign words and phrases. Games include Bingo, Simon Says, Concentration, puzzles. You play the games by listening to the foreign word spoken and clicking on the corresponding picture; this quiz, correct and test method is used in all of the 27 games in multiple levels of difficulty. It is an excellent program for the little beginners and for those who would be otherwise intimidated by a foreign language. Many have multiple levels of difficulty. Easy for even a non-reader to pick up a foreign language. Even the youngest ones can do the activities in English. Not sure which language to start with? Not a problem, because all five languages (Spanish, French, German, English, and Japanese) are all on the same disk.

FOREIGN LANGUAGE

Artes Latinae

Level I

Level II

Bolchazy-Carducci Publishers

Ages: 10-up   Street price $212 CD only

$270 complete package

Subject(s): Full Latin course

Skills needed: mouse, reading

System Req: WIN 3.1/95/98 486/8MB

MAC: N/A

After hearing Mary Pride rave about this foreign language program for years, I finally acquired a copy to review. And then I put it to a real test. I gave it to my 10th grade daughter who has had absolutely no Latin training whatsoever and told her it was now part of her homeschool curriculum. She has used the Level I CD for the past seven months. Her feedback has been very educational. She says it makes learning Latin effortless, enjoyable and painless. She has learned so much in such a short time; I can only give this program my highest recommendation. The company says much younger students can use the program as well but I haven't tried it on my younger kids. My opinion is that younger kids (8-up) could use it if they had enough self-discipline to keep them going since it is a completely self-taught program. There is absolutely nothing objectionable in this program although a few of the Latin sayings refer to "the gods." Although this is a very expensive program, you will not be disappointed. The Level I CD covers over one year worth of high school Latin; Level II covers the 2nd year. Also keep in mind that multiple children can use the program, reducing per student costs. The program is very simple in its interface; basically step-by-step flash cards with human voice instruction. Content is broken down into little bites called "frames." There are three voices using two types of pronunciations to choose from: Restored Classical and Italian/Ecclesiastical. Each Latin term or concept is introduced, then practiced, and then tested. You will need to use the test booklet, reference notebook and graded readers (comes with the full package) to fully round out the course with written work.

Easy Language
25 World Languages

IMSI

Ages: 12-up   Street price $35

Subject(s): multi-languages

Skills needed: reading

System Req: WIN 95/98: 486/16MB

MAC: N/A

This basic program offers a lot of languages for the money. Twenty-five different languages to be exact. One great feature of this program is the ability to help you learn any of these languages even if your native language is not English but one of these other twenty-five languages. For example, a German-speaking person can choose to learn Thai or vice versa. Although the program offers only 1000 basic words in every language, the flexibility to learn any of these languages offers a lot of versatility and value. Included with the program is a microphone, dictionary and built-in quizzes. My 16-year-old daughter used this program as well and had these comments: "The voice is a little choppy but has good pronunciation and covers a lot of good information. You can change the language you want to learn at any time. The program can read everything to you or you can click individual pictures to learn. It also has a built-in section on grammar which is a definite plus." The languages included are *Arabic, Czech, Chinese, Danish, Dutch, English, French, German, Greek, Hebrew, Hungarian, Indonesian, Italian, Japanese, Korean,*

Polish, Portuguese, Romanian, Russian, Spanish, Swedish, Tagalog, Thai, Turkish, and Zulu. This program offers such a quick and easy way to pick up basic conversational terms in so many languages, I recommend having it on your shelf. You never know when you may need to say "Hello" in Swedish.

Foreign Language Advantage 2001

Encore Software
Ages: 12-up   Street price $40
Subject(s): Spanish, French, German
Skills needed: reading
System Req: WIN 3.1/95/98 486/8MB

This set of five CD's seems to offer the greatest amount of foreign language instruction for the money. Lessons cover all the material and they include tests and quizzes to test your knowledge, games and exercises to practice the material, and hints for proper pronunciation. My 16-year-old daughter comments, "This five CD set seems the most complex. It has good tests and good games for practicing." Also includes a translator that can convert an English document into any of the included languages. Good for the more advanced student, this package includes Italian, Spanish, French, German, Portuguese or Japanese. They are mostly older versions of the Transparent Language titles: see the *Language Now* review.

Greek Tutor or Hebrew Tutor

Learning Company/ Parsons Technology
Ages: 12-up   Street price $50
                per language
Subject(s): Hebrew, Greek
Skills needed: reading
System Req: WIN 3.1/95/98 486/8MB

As the name suggests, these are tutorials designed to teach about one year of college Biblical Hebrew or Greek. The program is divided into four sections: learn, drill, exercise, and review. Features include audio pronunciations, clear instruction, and lots of practice exercises to reinforce the learning. You'll hear the pronunciations of letters and words as you see them to learn Hebrew by sight and sound. The program takes you step-by-step from learning the alphabet all the way to translating and reading the Book of Ruth for yourself. Either program will serve as a great supplement to a regular language course or as a stand-alone curriculum. They can give children or adults the tools to read the Bible in its original languages. Highly recommended.

Instant Immersion Spanish

TOPICS Entertainment (formerly CounterTop Software)
Ages: 6-10   Street price $30
Subject(s): Spanish
Skills needed: reading
System Req: WIN 95/98: 486/16MB
MAC: N/A

This four CD set offers a lot of content for the money. Two of the CD's offer sequential lessons in beginning Spanish (*Talk Now. Spanish, World Talk Spanish*) and multiple users can use the program. My daughter used the program and had these comments, "The program is bright and inviting, fairly self-explanatory, and covers a lot of information. The voice is a bit choppy which makes it difficult for a beginner. Features include the ability to record and playback your own voice and print out information, and has volume control, built-in quizzes, narration of written material, a good dictionary, effective games for practice and no annoying music. Also includes an awesome Spanish mystery game (*Who is Oscar Lake?*) for advanced Spanish speaker." The other two CD's are a dictionary (*Webster's*

New World Five Language Talking Dictionary) and the Oscar Lake game. The Oscar Lake game is a whodunit mystery where no one speaks English and you must interpret the language and the clues to solve the mystery. This is a top-selling program and carries a money-back guarantee. The program is also available in French, German, Italian and English. Note: this company makes lots of educational software. While not super glitzy, they are full of information. I have not seen anything objectionable in their material but did not have time to review them all.

Jumpstart Spanish

Knowledge Adventure
Ages 5-10   Street price $19
Subject(s): beginning Spanish
Skills needed: reading, mouse
System Req: WIN 3.1/95/98
486DX33/8MB
MAC: 040/8MB

Although I usually recommend *All In One Language Fun* or *Smart Start* for beginning Spanish, this program has some fun activities as well. The student plays games and along the way learns 200 Spanish (or English) vocabulary words. In one game, students match animals, toys, body parts, and furniture. With 10 activities, there is a lot of variety. Most activities entail exploring objects and their names or checking your ability through a test activity. After five correct solutions, the student gets a star and then they can turn five stars to get a fish or accessory for their fish tank. Kids seem to enjoy this reward and loved collecting fish.

Kids! Spanish

Knowledge Adventure
Ages: 6-10   Street price $30
Subject(s): Spanish
Skills needed: reading
System Req: WIN 3.1/95/98 486/8MB
MAC: 040/8MB

Just like the other Syracuse language programs, you won't hear any English spoken in this immersion method based program. All instructions are in Spanish and this helps the child pick up the language in an almost effortless manner. Cartoonish and colorful monsters guide the child through learning Spanish in dozens of vocabulary games such as Bingo and Connect the Dots. Features include the ability to record and playback your voice to check your pronunciation. The program is very easy to use and offers lots of different ways for elementary kids to practice Spanish. Recommended use: Elementary Spanish.

KidSpeak 10-in-1 Language Learning

Transparent Language Systems
Ages: 6-up   Street price $24
Subject(s): Spanish, French, German, Italian, Japanese, Indonesian, Korean, Hebrew, Mandarin Chinese, Portuguese
Skills needed: reading helpful but not required
System Req: WIN 95/98: 486/8MB
MAC: 040/8MB

My seven-year-old dived right into this game and then came running up to me and exclaimed, "Do you know what seven is? It's 'zeiben'" I figured he must be doing German but he didn't know for sure. This three CD set is jam-packed with language learning fun. With 40 multi-level games and songs, this interactive program introduces the child to over 700 words in each language. As the program starts, you choose which language you want to learn. You meet a cartoon friend who speaks the new language and is ready to teach you too. Easy-to-understand icons and menus help even the young child navigate and make this program child-friendly. Using the immersion method, very little English is used to teach words and phrases for such basic concepts as greetings, animals, colors, parts of the body, numbers, letters and more. Songs and games make the learning fun. The animations are a bit long but kids seem to like them. No record-keeping. This program offers a lot of value for the money. Highly recommended. Caution: In one section, characters appeared and disappeared with a puff of smoke.

Learn To Speak 8.0 series

Learning Company
Ages: 12-up   Street price $79
                per language
Subject(s): foreign language: German, Spanish, French, English
Skills needed: reading, some language experience
System Req: WIN 3.1/95/98 486/8MB
MAC: 040/8MB

Learn to Speak provides the student with about one year+ of high school or college level beginning language instruction. Each title provides 30-36 beginning and intermediate language chapters with over one hundred lessons covering everyday vocabulary, pronunciation, comprehension, grammar, reading, and writing with lots of drill and practice using games and exercises. Speech-recognition technology (Windows version only) evaluates students' pronunciation and rates their accents on a sliding scale (native————+————tourist). Video and audio recordings of native speakers help students improve comprehension in a real life conversational context. Multimedia exercis-

es and a 400-page textbook/workbook build students' grammar skills. The lessons cover such topics as money, transportation, hotels, and shopping. I recommend starting the student out in *All In One* or *Rosetta Stone* to get a feel for the language. Choose from Spanish, French, Japanese, German or English.

Rosetta Stone PowerPAC

Fairfield Technologies
Ages: 7-up   Street price $48
Subject(s): foreign language
Skills needed: reading
System Req: WIN 3.1/95/98 486/8MB
MAC: 030/8MB

We've read nothing but great reviews about this program. This program uses an immersion method of teaching comprehension of the language by flashing pictures and hearing the appropriate foreign word or phrase. The student then clicks on the correct picture. It is similar in methodology to *All in One* but covers a lot more material and is more structured. It is excellent for the middle elementary ages to start with learning a language. With six languages on the same CD each containing 22 "chapters" taken from the full program of about 90 chapters for each of Spanish, French, German, Italian, Russian, Chinese and Japanese, this program is packed with content. This is the same software use by NASA to train astronauts for the MIR space station project. Additional levels available for each language (90 chapters) cost $195 for each level. Both levels together are equivalent to about 2 years of foreign language study. Languages available in full length courses include: Vietnamese, Japanese, Spanish, Latin, French, Polish, Hindi, Korean, Dutch, German, Danish, Thai, Arabic, Hebrew, Swahili, Indonesian, Turkish, Chinese (Mandarin), Russian, Welsh, Portuguese,

FOREIGN LANGUAGE

Italian, Luxembourgish.

Practice Makes Perfect Spanish or Practice Makes Perfect French

Learning Company
Ages: 12-up   Street price $30
                  per language
Subject(s): foreign language
Skills needed: reading, some language experience
System Req: WIN 3.1/95/98 486/8MB
MAC: 040/8MB

This is only the pronunciation practice portion of the *Learn to Speak* series. Includes 2300 words with pictures and native speakers teaching pronunciation. Has record and playback technology. (Windows only) Shows videos and animations showing proper tongue and mouth movements.

Language Now!

Transparent Language
Ages: 12-up   Street price $50
                  per language
Subject(s): foreign language
Skills needed: reading
System Req: WIN 3.1/95/98 486/8MB
MAC: 030/8MB

Takes the frustration out of foreign language learning by giving your student interesting stories to read, videos to watch, and fun, challenging games to play (Vocabulous, Unscramble, and Plug-n-Play). By placing the cursor on any text, you can instantly see the full meaning of words, sentences, grammar and more. Learn over 16000 words. The style of this program is rigorous and the student should have some language instruction prior to this course. I recommend starting the student out in *All In One* or *Rosetta Stone* to get a feel for the language before you start *Transparent Language*. Results are guaranteed by the publisher. Highly recommended by every reviewer of foreign language software. Choose from Spanish, German, Italian, Japanese, Russian, Dutch, Arabic, Portuguese, Chinese or French. Company guarantees their product. Their web site (www.transparent.com) offers online foreign language games and quizzes that any student can play.

Learn Spanish Your Way or Learn French Your Way

Knowledge Adventure
Ages: 14-up   Street price $59
                  per language
Subject(s): foreign language
Skills needed: reading, some experience with the language
System Req: WIN 95/98/2000: PI/166/64MB
MAC: N/A

From the makers of *SmartStart/TriplePlay* comes a full-featured course for those who have mastered *SmartStart/TriplePlay*. This is a multimedia immersion program designed to put the student right into real life situations. On screen you see comic strip like story lines and you choose options that a tourist may choose: should you take a bus or a taxi? You communicate the directions in the target language via mouse or orally by speaking into the microphone (included free) and the computer interprets the dialog. Your conversation can be oral only or you can see the text on screen. English translation to help you along is available with a click of the mouse. Includes workbook, music CD, and conversational audio CD for language practice on the go. Caution: Some cartoon bar scenes where you are offered alcohol. That gives you the opportunity to refuse graciously. Recommended use: high school level course; requires some previous experience with the language.

Smart Start series
a.k.a Triple Play Plus

Knowledge Adventure

Ages: 8-up   Street price $20
                    per language

Subject(s): foreign language

Skills needed: reading

System Req: WIN 3.1/95/98 486/8MB

MAC: N/A

A beginner program with foreign language games designed for the older child. A younger child could handle this material if they have mastered the *All In One* (A.I.O) Language Fun. The method is similar to A.I.O. in that there is no translation given-this is called immersion. Mary Pride says, "This challenging and absorbing set of games covers a huge variety of vocabulary categories." You choose from six categories: food, places, people, transportation, home, office or number activities; each having three levels of difficulty. Within each level there are plenty of games to choose from. Teaches approximately 1000 words and phrases. Good choice for an informal introduction into the language. Record and playback feature allows you to compare your pronunciation with that of native speakers. You can access the *Smart Start* web site where you'll find quizzes to check your progress, the Cultural Cafe to discover a great French film or a new recipe to try out, plus language FAQs and cultural links. (Use at your risk. I have not checked the entire site.) Includes free microphone. Choose from French, German, Italian, or Spanish.

SCIENCE

Amazing Animals

Dorling Kindersley

Ages: 4-9   Street price $24

Subject(s): Animals

Skills needed: mouse, reading helpful but not required

System Req: WIN 3.1/95/98 486/8MB

MAC: 040/8MB

This activity pack contains an interactive CD-ROM, animal books, Creepy Crawlies Sticker Sheets, bird mobile and more. With animal games and activities, an interactive resource center packed with photos, graphics and sounds, this program is a must for the child who loves animals. Even my little children love looking up animals, particularly snakes and spiders. (Mom's comment-ugh.)

Big Science Carnival

Grolier Interactive

Ages: 9-12   Street price $50

Subject(s): physics

Skills needed: mouse, reading

System Req: WIN 3.1/95/98 486/8MB

MAC: 030/8MB

This wacky comic book adventure features the same little Bumptz from *Bumptz Science Carnival*. Your mission, should you decide to accept it, is to guide the Bumptz out of the basement, where they are trapped, to the studio where their damaged spaceship is. To accomplish this you must solve a series of difficulties including; traversing open spaces, climbing stairs, pulling companions out of pies, and more. These problems are actually scientific in nature. In each case, a simple machine will do the trick. The child must experiment with concepts of force, mass, balance, and energy to devise a solution. This program also includes about 20 experiments for off computer time. Recommended use: The science topics in this program matches up pretty well with the topics covered in 4th and 5th grade science curriculums: simple machines, principles of force, friction, energy, harmonic motion and static equilibrium. This program only comes in a school version, which includes lesson plans and additional activities.

Bumptz Science Carnival

Grolier Interactive
Ages: 6-12   Street price $50
Subject(s): science: force, energy, friction, harmonic motion
Skills needed: mouse, reading helpful but not required
System Req: WIN 3.1/95/98 486/8MB
MAC: 030/8MB

You control little *Bumptz*, little bubble like characters, on their rides at the carnival. Apply fans, magnets, friction and other objects in over 200 animated puzzles to make the Bumptz go into the right hole. This program teaches physics concepts of light buoyancy and magnetism to even the youngest in your family. Even a construction kit to let children create their own science puzzles. Includes 12 animated shorts about how science works and 20 hands on experiments children can do at home. Great fun! This program only comes in a school version, which includes lesson plans and additional activities.

Asimov's Library Of The Universe

Zane Publishing
Ages: 8-up   Street price $34
Subject(s): astronomy
Skills needed: reading helpful but not required
System Req: WIN 3.1/95/98 486/8MB
MAC: 030/8MB

A lot of material for the money these six CD-ROMs from Zane publishing cover Astronomy, The Inner Planets, The Outer Planets, The Solar System, Space Exploration, and The Universe. Isaac Asimov guides you on an educational exploration of the cosmos with 255 minutes of multimedia, narrated slideshow. You can view, full screen, and print more than 2,400 space images. Includes 600 interactive questions on the material and an extensive glossary of terms with hot links from the material to the glossary. The material mentions some space evolution theory.

Connie and Bonnie's Birthday Blastoff

Active Arts
Ages: 6-12   Street price $30
Subject(s): astronomy
Skills needed: reading, mouse
System Req: WIN 3.1/95/98 486DX33/8+MB
MAC: 040/16MB

Twins Connie and Bonnie accidentally receive an invitation to a birthday celebration on Pluto. On their way there, they learn about the sun, moon and other planets. A lot of information is packed into this interactive story and some of it is a little advanced for most elementary kids but they learn some along the way. Features include colorful charts, dozens of science-fair winning projects, a complete paint program, and fun riddles to test the user's reading comprehension and retention. Story pages feature multiple hot spots that, when clicked, reveal facts about our solar system- space travel, the planets and other space phenomenon. The student is presented the information in various ways, from animated demonstrations, narrated vignettes, to actual NASA videos.

Critical Mass

Forest Technology
Ages 12-up   Street price $24
Science, history, reading comprehension
Skills needed: jr. high+ reading/interest level
System Req: WIN 3.1/95/98
486SX33/8MB
MAC: 040/8MB

Discover the extraordinary science and people behind a pivotal event in world history-the building and testing of the first atomic bomb. This program is designed to give you a comprehensive, multimedia and interactive immersion into the people, events and science of this profound achievement. Browse through extensive collections of multidimensional timelines, interviews, documents, video clips, biographies, reference material and more. Recommended use: This is an outstanding resource for a unit study on scientists, 20th century or W.W.II. Caution: includes a few early rock and roll recordings.

Dole 5-A-Day Adventures

Dole Food Company
Ages: 12-up   Street price $FREE
Subject(s): nutrition
Skills needed: mouse, reading helpful but not required
System Req: WIN 3.1/95/98 486/8MB
MAC: 030/8MB

This fun CD teaches kids about good nutrition with games and activities. Just mail a letter to the company on "school" letterhead and order it! Make your own letterhead on your computer, write a letter and mention that you are a homeschooler and they will send it out. You can't beat the price!

Earth Quest

Dorling Kindersley
Ages: 10-up   Street price $29
Subject(s): science, earth science, and geology
Skills needed: reading+
System Req: WIN 95/98: P133/24MB 8X CD-ROM PMac 100/32MB 8X CD-ROM

Rocks, volcanoes and lava always fascinate my kids. If your kids wonder how mountains are made or how earthquakes happen, this is the CD to get. In this CD, you walk into a virtual 3D museum filled with earth science exhibits and a collection of minerals from the Smithsonian. As you browse the museum, you will find fascinating exhibits that pop up on the screen. You can browse different topics, take a multiple-choice quiz on a variety of topics, or play one of the fun games. One game was a favorite, *The Earth Builder* where the student unlocks each of the earth's 17 tectonic plates by answering three questions for each plate. This CD is very good at explaining difficult concepts behind the processes behind tidal waves, weather, tides, and earthquakes. Excellent for unit study.

Emergency Room Interactive 2

Legacy Interactive
Ages: 12-up   Street price $34
Subject(s): science, medicine, first aid, anatomy
Skills needed: reading+
System Req: WIN 95/98: P133/24MB 8X CD-ROM PMac 100/32MB 8X CD-ROM

Begin your medical career as a medical student and learn your way up to hospital chief of staff. When the patient arrives at the hospital, use the on screen tools to check for symptoms, examine wounds, and perform triage. Take patient histories, order tests, initial treatment procedures; you are THE doctor. Patients live or die because of your

SCIENCE

decisions. If someone dies, don't worry; simply move on to the next patient. There are no malpractice suits and no angry relatives. The program provides you with over 20 minutes of digital video, 500 voice-overs, 1,500 photo-real 3D graphics, 100 different cases, and a 6,000-word medical glossary. Also included are anatomical charts to make your life-saving decisions. By being in a virtual reality-like hospital and picking up instruments, you feel like a real doctor without having to go through 5 years of medical school. Note: Examinations of female patients are kept discrete by drape covering the private parts.

Eyewitness Encyclopedia of Nature 2.0

Dorling Kindersley
Ages: 5-up   Street price $29
Subject(s): Animals, insects, plants
Skills needed: mouse, reading helpful but not required
System Req: WIN 3.1/95/98 486/8MB MAC: 030/8MB

With 70 animations, over 50 video sequences, 850 photos and illustrations, 200,000 words and 3 hours clear, narrated audio, this easy-to-use resource is a must for the student who loves nature. This content-rich CD includes hundreds of illustrated articles on all the major animal groups, including sections on World Habitats, Climate, Microscopic Life, and Prehistoric Life. Layers of menus allow access to increasingly more details as the child's interest leads. Learn a lot or learn a little, depending on desire and maturity. Even my little children love looking up animals, particularly snakes and spiders. (Mom's comment-ugh.) Has built in quiz feature. Caution: Some references to environmental concerns and the age of the earth being "billions and billions" of years old.

Eyewitness Encyclopedia of Science 2.0

Dorling Kindersley
Ages: 12-up   Street price $29
Subject(s): mathematics, physics, chemistry, biology
Skills needed: mouse, reading helpful but not required
System Req: WIN 3.1/95/98 486/8MB MAC: 030/8MB

One of the best multimedia presentations of comprehensive scientific and technological subjects covering four main subject areas: Mathematics, Physics, Chemistry, and Life Science. Includes more than 1,000 new in-depth articles an additional 750,000 words over the old version for a total of 900,000 words. Scores of screens let you explore fast developing areas of science such a particle physics, chaos theory, and gene technology. Interactive features include an *Encyclopedia Navigator*, improved search capabilities, 3.5 hours of audio, 800 full color photos and illustrations, 3D models of molecules and chemical compounds, 40 videos and 80 specially created animations, a fully featured *Quiz Master*, and a link to the *Eyewitness Science Online* site on the World Wide Web. (Use this link at your own discretion; I have not checked it out myself.) Also includes material on famous scientists. (Caution: Darwin is included and praised for his great works.) This CD is great resource to illustrate and bring science to life. Very popular.

Eyewitness Encyclopedia of Space and the Universe

Dorling Kindersley
Ages: 12-up   Street price $29
Subject(s): space exploration, astronomy
Skills needed: mouse, reading helpful but not required
System Req: WIN 3.1/95/98
486DX33/4+MB
MAC: 030/8MB

Once again, DK has produced an excellent multimedia resource for your homeschool. This CD-ROM is jam packed with 28 video sequences, 60+ color animations, 2 hours of audio, more than 400 full color photos and illustrations, 200+ key articles, and hundreds of Data Boxes and Fact Files. (Data boxes and Fact Files are multimedia's equivalent of a sound bite — nuggets of info with every topic.) Includes multiple tools to explore Space and the Universe. In "The Universe", fly through virtual 3D tours of the planets Mars and Venus, fly by stars and galaxies, and examine space phenomena such as white dwarfs, supernovas, and Black Holes. Check the "Who's who" database to learn all about famous people in the history of space exploration and study. Head over to "Star Dome" to observe the night sky from anywhere on earth from any point in time. What did the sky look like the night you were born? Research the history of astronomy to learn how we came to understand the universe today. Play interactive space games like landing a lunar module- or launch a rocket into space. Read the "Technical Manual" to find out how astronauts are trained and how the space program is run. If your children long to go where no man has gone before, this CD-ROM will get them there, if only in their dreams.

Geosafari Animals

Educational Insights
Ages: 6-up   Street price $24
Subject(s): science: facts about animals
Skills needed: reading, mouse
System Req: WIN 3.1/95/98
486DX33/8MB
MAC: 030/8MB

Children and animal lovers will love this new quiz game from Geosafari. With games designed to stress real analysis of information. By using many different types of questions, categories and games, players get their animal IQ tested to the limit. Includes pictures, videos, sound clips, 250-entry printable glossary and printable awards for perfect scores. You can play alone or against their friends. Recommended use: Animal unit studies or gift for the animal lover in your family.

Geosafari Science

Educational Insights
Ages 8-up   Street price $24
Subject(s): science
Skills needed: reading, mouse
System Req: WIN 3.1/95/98
486DX33/8MB
MAC: 030/8MB

This rich and detailed quiz game can offer lots of fun drilling on science facts. The program speaks your name and quizzes you with animations, illustrations, videos, audio and diagrams on different topics including Great Inventions, Who Said That, Anatomy, The Bee, Weather, Insect Defenses, and more.

SCIENCE

I Can Be A Dino Finder

Educational Insights
Ages 6-12   Street price $25
Skills needed: reading
Subject(s): archaeology
System Req: WIN 3.1/95/98
486/66MHZ/8+MB
MAC: 040/40MHz/8+MB

If your kids are like mine, they love dinosaurs. Nothing is more fascinating to children than these great reptiles that roamed the earth. In this program kids get to be fossil hunters and discover dinosaur bones all over the world. Once you arrive at a dig, you choose the appropriate tool such as a jackhammer, pick ax, or brush and excavate your bones. After digging up all the bones, your task now is to assemble them in a drag and drop puzzle-like activity. Games are included to teach more about dinosaurs and famous paleontologists. There are over 50 different sets of dinosaur bones to find and assemble and lots of built-in learning. Of course, there are the references to dinosaur bones being billions of years old and such but older kids can be taught the truth about dinosaurs and still enjoy learning about specific dinosaur characteristics.

I Can Be An Animal Doctor

Educational Insights
Ages 6-12   Street price $25
Skills needed: reading
Subject(s): pet medicine, veterinary science
System Req: WIN 3.1/95/98
486/66MHZ/8+MB
MAC: 040/40MHz/8+MB

This is a great program for your budding animal lover/vet-to-be. The scene opens up to a field office that has detailed and interesting information on animals and veterinary medicine. The vet-to-be is then on to one of four habitats: forest, desert, savannah, or farm. Once there, they find an animal in need of medical care. After transporting the animal to the field office, the vet-to-be will use the tools and instruments to assess the health of the animal. After checking heart rate, weight and temperature, the child will access other diagnostic tests such as x-rays, tissue samples and more. A built-in "computer" aids in the diagnosis and suggests treatment(s) to follow. Also includes six educational games. Playing doctor has never been more fun and educational. With 26 animals with changing ailments, this program is fun to play over and over again.

I Hate Love Science

Dorling Kindersley
Ages 7-11   Street price $19
Skills needed: reading
Subject(s): science: physics, biology, matter
System Req: WIN 95/98: P90/16MB
MAC: PMac/16MB

This interactive science program lacks game pizzazz but makes up for it in depth of content. With over 100 experiments built into the program, teachers or parents can use this in any elementary science curriculum as a supplement. Chemistry is experienced in Al's Kitchen with experiments in chemistry concepts and materials. Two other labs give the student experiments in physics and biology. No other program gives elementary students a chance to try out so many experiments and learn from them. Recommended use: elementary science curriculum supplement.

Intel Play:
QX3 Computer Microscope
Learning Company
Ages 8-up   Street price $100
Skills needed: reading
Subject(s): mouse skills, keyboard, logic
System Req: WIN 98: P90/16MB
MAC: N/A

This easy-to-use microscope plugs into your computer (USB port) and allows your children to zoom in close on all the tiny things we all like to study: bugs, skin, pond water, and more. Using the latest digital imagery technology, this versatile microscope comes with software that captures the images so they can be manipulated. Magnify things at 10X, 60X and 200X. Includes paint tools to allow students to label, combine, distort, and manipulate images. You can also import images in JPEG, BMP or Photo CD formats. Export images in JPEG, BMP, or AVI formats. The unit is removable from its stand for handheld mode to go mobile (while tethered to the computer). Take the images and make a slide show for a science project. Import a picture into a written report. Print images as posters, reports or even stickers. The possibilities are endless. My kids had great fun taking a sequence of pictures of little Lego guys and creating a "cartoon" slideshow. My daughter just received stitches and the boys went crazy over magnified pictures of that. (You have to understand that my kids are extremely hands-on when it comes to body parts and science studies. After my last baby was born, the first thing my boys did was don doctor gloves and poke around at the placenta.) Whenever your kids want to examine something that would otherwise be invisible to the naked eye, pull the microscope out and have a teachable moment. This microscope is a great addition to any homeschool and well worth the money.

Invention Studio
Forest Technologies
Ages 9-up   Street price $29
Subject(s): Science, reading comprehension
Skills needed: reading
System Req: WIN 3.1/95/98
486SX33/8MB
MAC: 040/8MB

If you've got a budding engineer in the house who is desperate to create, design, and built some gadget, this is the program to get. Invention studio gives your engineer all the tools and instructions to develop, designing and testing inventions. The user manual describes the seven essential steps, with a detail explanation of each. The steps are: finding a problem, writing notes in a journal detailing its development, doing research on the problem, creating a design, building it in either the Garage or the spaceship-like Gadgetorium, and testing it. Build vehicles, aircraft, mousetrap mazes and more. Included is a patent office to patent your ideas along with information on how crucial patents and copyrights are to inventors. The program has great 3–D graphics and realistic sound but it is a bit tricky to get started and understand all the functions of the program but any brainy, computer savvy homeschooled kid should have no problem. This program has the added advantage in giving children a chance at understanding the process in solving real life problems. That is: defining a problem, developing a plan of action, seeing that plan through to completion. Included are one-minute videos of the history of inventions and inventors. This offers great mental exercise. Recommended use: Supplement to invention or science unit study or great Christmas gift.

SCIENCE

Kid Science with Philip Gebhardt

Arc Media

Ages 6-12   Street price $12

Subject(s): elementary science experiments

Skills needed: reading

System Req: WIN 3.1/95/98: 386/4MB
MAC: 030/4MB

Mr. Gebhardt is a science teacher who likes to do experiments. This CD contains 12 basic experiments. Each experiment includes onscreen and printable instructions, and a short video of Mr. Gebhardt presenting the experiment. The experiments are simple, easy for kids to do, and used materials you generally find around the house. They include experiments on how to make water sticky, making a great paper airplane, building a sundial, how to tune in to distant radio stations, and more. Also included were explanations of the concepts presented. A cheap supplement to your elementary science curriculum.

LEGO MINDSTORMS Series

Lego Mindstorms

Ages 9-up   Street price $150+

Subject(s): programming, logic, science, engineering

Skills needed: reading

System Req: WIN 95/98:
PI/166/16MB/Serial Port MAC: N/A

We did not shell out the money to personally review these titles but wanted to let you know about them. Every review we have read about these programming titles has raved about them. They sound like a great deal of fun as well as a great deal of educational value. The programs are based on making robots with Lego's and programming them. Caution: Some are based on the Star Wars movie. Some of the sets come with a built-in microprocessor (thus eliminating the need for a computer) and allows children to design, build and program a real working droid (robot). Perfect gift for that budding engineer.

Magic School Bus Series

Microsoft/Scholastic

Ages 6-10   Street price $30

Skills needed: reading

Subject(s): mouse skills, reading

System Req: WIN 95/98/NT: P133/16MB
MAC: Sys 8.1+ Pmac233/32MB

If you can get past the fact that the school bus is "magic", this series offers a lot of fun and learning opportunity. The bus isn't really magic as in a "spell-casting" sort of way but has amazing abilities to shrink, fly, and do other incredible feats. The driver of the bus is a wacky teacher named Ms. Frizzle and her goal in life is to make learning fun for her students. Most of the topics are science based and offer games and activities to learn about the topic. While the games were entertaining enough to keep kids busy, the depth of content was shallow. Younger elementary kids will get the most benefit; older kids will find the information tedious and juvenile. My 12-year-old daughter, the in-house bug expert, enjoyed the *Magic School Bus Explores Bugs* but claimed she learned nothing new.

Multimedia Horses

Educational Insights

Ages: 5-up   Street price $29

Subject(s): Science, nature

Skills needed: Gotta love horses.

System Req: WIN 3.1/95/98 386/4+MB
MAC: 020/4+MB System 6.07

Outstanding professional photography, video, audio, articles make this CD-ROM a real treasure for those children who love horses. Explore 101 different breeds each with their own video, full screen and fact page listing temperament, size, maintenance, etc. Includes a quiz game, horse sounds, a geographic listing. Even investigate the cost of owning a horse and calculate the budget for different breeds. Recommended use: Excellent supplement to horse unit study or gift to the horse lover in your family.

My Amazing Human Body

Dorling Kindersley
Ages: 5-9   Street price $19
Subject(s): human anatomy
Skills needed: reading helpful
System Req: WIN 3.1/95/98 486/8MB
MAC: 040/8MB

Seemore Skinless, friendly skeleton, invites you to learn all about the human body. This amusing (not scary) host takes the child on a delightful tour of the human body from a child's perspective. If you are looking for an anatomy program for your elementary kids, this is the one to get. With games and activities, Seemore makes learning about the body fun. Four engaging and educational activities help teach about how our organs, skeletons and skeletons work. Seemore teaches about each of these body parts (35 in all) and how they work. Included are multiple-choice questions, a build-the-body activity, a "Day in the Life" where you choose the events in the skeleton's day (running, eating, walking, etc.) and watch how the day goes. A built-in journal allows kids to record important events like "When I was a baby," and what their favorite food is, their height and weight. An indepth information section allows kids to dig deeper into the subject of anatomy. Although I did not look at every bit of the info, I saw nothing objectionable such as safe sex psychobabble.

My First Amazing Science Explorer

Dorling Kindersley
Ages: 5-9   Street price $19
Subject(s): elementary science
Skills needed: reading helpful
System Req: WIN 3.1/95/98 486/8MB
MAC: 040/8MB

The challenge in this great science program is to become a full-fledged Science Explorer. To do this the child must earn eight Explorer Prizes, collect 24 stickers for the Science Workbook and find 72 badges for the Science School. Quite a challenge. This program does not have much in hands-on science activities but it does have a lot of information. And by exploring all the informational screens and quiz activities, kids learn enough to earn their stickers and badges. There are four different locations where kids can access games and activities: a city, a kitchen, a countryside and workshop. In these areas, you find science related to the areas. Other features include printable experiments and worksheets (great for homeschool.), great graphics and sound, and the ability to save your game. This program is a great supplement to elementary science curriculum.

Nine Month Miracle

ADAM Interactive
Ages: 4-up   Street price $29
Subject(s): reference, anatomy
Skills needed: mouse
System Req: WIN 3.1/95/98 486/8MB
MAC 030/8MB

This in-depth look at pregnancy and birth gives pro-life it's best ammo ever. It's the best pro-life message we've seen/heard outside of a pulpit (and without any Bible references-just presenting the FACTS are enough.) Close-ups and animations of the fetus alive and kicking within the womb and details of the pregnancy recognizing the

SCIENCE

LIFE that exists within the expectant mother give a radical perspective on life beginning at conception. Has a kid's section that explains in easy to understand, discrete terms, what is happening in mommy's tummy. Like *A.D.A.M.*, has a "modesty" setting to lock out conception details. Caution: Expectant father portrayed somewhat disrespectfully as somewhat of an airhead. But our family really likes it (even Dad). A must have for any family expecting a new addition, or with older daughters interested in raising a family someday.

Nine Worlds

Educational Insights
Ages: 9-up   Street price $24
Subject(s): solar system
Skills needed: reading
System Req: WIN 3.1/95/98 486/8MB
MAC: 040/8MB

Patrick Stewart (Star Trek: Next Generation) narrates this multimedia tour through our solar system. Animations, videos, artists' renditions, photos, and narrated text make this trip very enjoyable and informative. The information is divided into three main areas: *Planets, Resource Explorer*, and *Mankind's View*. Guided tours to each of the nine planets can be found in the first area with information-packed narrated animations and vacation planners to help you decide what to pack should you decide to visit a distant planet. In the Resource Planner you will find quizzes, databases of information and more. This resource section is great for teaching and offers a way to do extensive research. In Mankind's View, you can research the history and future of space exploration and astronomy. Based on a timeline, this section offers units on Galileo, the Apollo space program, and more. Great artwork and music accompany this information making it an enjoyable learning experi-

ence.

Operation: Frog Deluxe

Scholastic
Ages: 9-up   Street price $50
Subject(s): frog dissection
Skills needed: reading
System Req: WIN 3.1/95/98 486/8MB
MAC: 030/8MB

This virtual frog lab software offers your student the chance to dissect a frog right on your computer. Includes teacher's manual with pre-lab activities and lesson plans. This software is easily used over and over by multiple children and offers an entire dissection course studying all systems of the frog's body: mouth, reproduction, digestive, respiratory, circulatory, and skeletal systems.

Operation: Weather Disaster

Forest Technologies
Ages: 9-up   Street price $39
Subject(s): weather, earth science
Skills needed: reading
System Req: WIN 3.1/95/98 486/8MB
MAC: 030/8MB

Looking for a good science game that makes your children learn, investigate and apply weather science principles? In *Operation: Weather Disaster*, you help the Team Xtreme locate the Team leader Stratus, defeat the (slightly) Evil Weather and restore normal weather all by learning and applying weather and science knowledge. (With a few arcade action games thrown in to make it interesting.) You must use logic, thinking and weather information in the on-line weather database to play the game successfully. Very fun adventure simulation game that children love to play. Recommended use: Excellent supplement for weather unit studies or a GIFT for the game player in your family.

Pinball Science

Dorling Kindersley
Ages: 9-up   Street price $19
Subject(s): physics: force, magnetism, gravity
Skills needed: reading, some astronomy
System Req: WIN 95/98: PI/100/16MB
MAC: N/A

All kids love pinball and this program turns pinball games into pure science. Questions pop up and the student answer queries concerning friction, levers, magnetism, force, and gravity. If the student does not the answers, they can research the on screen inventor's journal to learn about physics concepts. Correct answers are rewarded with a new part to build a pinball machine, such as a spring, flippers, levers or rockets. Once the machine is fully assembled, the students get to play pinball with a machine they built themselves. Since kids love to play the game, they are highly motivated to continue researching and answering questions. The built-in quizzes have three levels of difficulty, presenting harder material as the child progresses. The graphics and sound are very realistic and the balance of education and fun is excellent.
Recommended use: Excellent gift or supplement to Jr. High physical science.

Prairie Explorer

Ideal Instructional Fair
Ages: 8-13   Street price $29
Subject(s): science, prairie ecosystems
Skills needed: reading
System Req: WIN 95/98: 486/8MB
MAC: 040/8MB

If your kids are studying or reading about Laura Ingalls Wilder, you need this program. Designed as a multimedia resource all about the prairie life circa 1800, this program is full of fascinating and educational material. Included are activities to learn how the prairie ecosystem works: including clas-sifying plants, constructing food webs, identifying animals and their habitats and more. Pictures are not photos but artists' drawings. (Photos would have been a good addition.) While this CD lacks in glitz, it makes up for it in sheer educational value. Lots of learning here (text and pictures); it is a good addition to any pioneer or westward curriculum. The school edition for $10 more offers lesson plans and reproducible worksheets.

Red Shift 3 a.k.a
Compton's Learning Astronomy

Learning Company
Ages: 9-up   Street price $29
Subject(s): astronomy
Skills needed: reading, some astronomy
System Req: WIN 95/98: PI/100/16MB
MAC: N/A

If you know a serious astronomy buff or student, this is the program to get. Powerful and packed with information, this program is designed to be a reference tool for the intermediate or serious astronomer. Includes the ability to take tours through space to observe space phenomena, see a virtual planetarium show, links to online info, virtual reality simulations and animated 3D models. Database includes 1000's of vivid photos, Hipparcos & Tycho star catalogs, detailed planetary maps, Sky Diary, and Penguin's Dictionary of Astronomy. Although complex to use, serious students will be rewarded for their diligent use of this program. Note: Includes various theories on the origin of the universe including the Big Bang Theory.

SCIENCE

Science Blaster Jr.

Knowledge Adventure
Ages: 4-7   Street price $29
Subject(s): elementary science
Skills needed: mouse
System Req: WIN 3.1/95/98 486/8MB
MAC: 030/8MB

The Blaster Pals take their spaceship on a science trek, introducing your child to early science concepts: weather, light, magnetism, colors, states of matter and more. Seven multilevel activities let children explore and experiment learning by trial and error...true scientific exploration. Usually only available as a school edition. Recommended use: I don't recommend a formal science curriculum for these ages and this program can fill in for a hands-on science for the kindergarten/first grade curriculum.

Science Sleuths

Learning Company
Ages: 7-12   Street price $N/A
Subject(s): elementary science, scientific methods
Skills needed: mouse, reading
System Req: WIN 3.1/95/98 486/8MB
MAC: 030/8MB

Solve different real world science mysteries by using tools, graphs, articles, and tables and conducting experiments. Graphics are very realistic and the program helps you along in your research and deduction. *Science I* has the *Mysteries of the Blob* and the *Exploding Lawn Mower*; *Science II* has the Mysteries of the *Biogene Picnic* and the *Traffic Accident*. You do not need to do I before you do II; they are independent of each other. Now only available in *Princeton Review: Middle School Edge*.

SimPark

Electronic Arts/Maxis
Ages: 8-up   Street price $19
Subject(s): science: biology, ecosystems
System Req: WIN 3.1/95/98 486/8MB
MAC-n/a

If you have an animal lover, or a child who wants to be a park ranger or zookeeper, this is a great program for them. You start with an empty space and you add birds, mammals, plants, reptiles and more to create a balanced ecosystem- at least that is your goal-balance. Put too many mice in and they will overrun the park. Put too many carnivores in and they will eat everybody else. (Hmm...I wonder if *that's* politically correct.) Don't plant enough of the right plants and the herbivores will starve. (No ordering out for veggie pizza here.) The seasons change right on the screen, the animals wander around, it snows, hawks fly overhead in search of prey, the sounds are real. With 9 North American climate zones as settings and 132 plant and animals species, you can build just a little neighborhood park, an expanse of national park or anything in between. Plenty of onscreen help, park management reports, and a friendly ranger to comment on your progress keep you on top of the health of your personal ecosystem. Recommended use: afterschool fun, excellent gift.

SimSafari

Electronic Arts/Maxis
Ages: 8-up   Street price $19
Subject(s): science: biology, ecosystems
System Req: WIN 3.1/95/98 486/8MB
MAC-040/8MB

If you have an animal lover, or a child who wants to be a park ranger or zookeeper, this is a great program for them. You start with an empty space and you add birds, mammals, plants, and reptiles and build a safari park and tourist camp. Your first goal is eco-logical balance at least that is your goal-balance. Put too many mice in and they will overrun the park. Put too many carnivores in and they will eat everybody. (Hmm...I wonder if *that's* politically correct.) Don't plant enough of the right plants and the herbivores will starve. (No ordering out for veggie pizza here.) The season change right on the screen, the animals wander around, it snows, hawks fly overhead in search of prey, the sounds are real. Your second goal is to make income for the park by building a tourist campground and concessions. Plenty of onscreen help, park management reports, and a friendly ranger to comment on your progress keep you on top of the health of your personal ecosystem. Recommended use: afterschool fun, excellent GIFT.

Space Academy GX-1

Edmark

Ages 7-12   Street price $29

Subject(s): astronomy, science, planets

Skills needed: mouse, reading

System Req: WIN 95/98: PI/90/16MB
MAC PMac/16MB

Virtual manipulatives allow students to learn about the solar system in this excellent program. Movable diagrams, tables of information, and hands on simulators offers the student the chance to change and observe variable outcomes to different experiments. The program has four different learning areas; three of which offer activities that can be used in open-ended exploratory fashion or in question and answer mode. These two modes are standard in most Edmark programs, making them excellent for students to use on their own or for teachers to use to reinforce a concept. Children can use data from animated diagrams and tables to answer space questions at the *Planetary Data Center*. Simulator controls such as the

Earth/Sun/Moon Simulator let children explore the relationships between the Earth and Moon; giving them the opportunity to actually watch orbits and movement. Children can learn about orbit, trajectory, and velocity as they navigate spacecraft and embark upon missions to far-off planets in the *Gravity Pilot Trainer*. But first they will need to read up on the planets to make sure the outgoing mission teams carry the appropriate materials and supplies. Other skills covered include: principles of inertia, Newton's Laws of Motion, ballistic and orbital trajectories, earth's rotation and tilt and its effect on seasons. Since this program comes only in the Teacher's Edition, the package comes with lesson plans and reproducibles. Features include built-in tutoring when a child makes repeated errors, and great hands-on learning. If you are doing a unit study on the solar system in the elementary grades, this program is a must have and a valuable addition to your learning library.

StudyWorks! Science Deluxe

MathSoft

Ages: 14-up   Street price $39

Subject(s): earth science, biology, chemistry, physics and astronomy.

System Req: WIN 3.1/95/98 486/8MB
MAC: 040/8MB

This package contains a great deal of information but suffers from a rather dull interface. My daughter refused to review it any further after about 30 minutes of use. "There is no point in purchasing this program because of the great emphasis on evolution in it. I feel no further reviewing is necessary because this program goes against the Bible." She was right, there was a lot of evolution in the program. I suggest you avoid this title.

SCIENCE

Super Solvers: Mission Think

Learning Company
Ages 7-12   Street price $14
Subject(s): mechanical science
Skills needed: mouse, reading
System Req: WIN 3.1/95/98 486/8MB
MAC: 030/8MB

More fun than education, this program intersperses science and mechanics (physics) puzzles with lots of fun arcade action. You must run around inside a warehouse dodging bad guys collecting parts to build a flying machine. To get around you must answer simple physics and mechanics questions. Once you get the parts, you put it together in the most air dynamically way and race against the Master of Mischief. My children enjoy it and they learn a little science each time they play. Note: this program follows my 80/20 rule: 80% of the time you are playing a arcade game, 20% of the time you are solving some good physics puzzles. Recommended use: Gift or after-school reward. This is an older program but usually you can find it in a bargain bin, in a bundle (*Elementary Edge Grades 2-3*) or on the Internet.

Switched-On Schoolhouse Science

Alpha Omega Publications
Grades 3rd, 4th, 5th, 6th, 7th, 8th, 9th, 10th, 11th, or 12th.
Street price $67 per subject per grade
Subject(s): Full Science course
A complete Christian Bible-based curriculum. See full description under Curriculum for more details.

Ultimate Human Body 2.0

Dorling Kindersley
Ages: 12-up
Subject(s): anatomy, reference
Skills needed: mouse, reading
System Req: WIN 95/98: P90/8MB
MAC PMac/8MB

Ultimate Human Body is similar to *A.D.A.M.* (a little more advanced and detailed) but not as entertaining. However, with over 100,000 words of text, 170 animations, 1030 full color illustrations, 25 new video sequences, 1500 sounds, 745 screens and pop-ups, this comprehensive anatomy program has wonderful depth and multimedia adventure. Vivid and detailed videos and animations demonstrate bodily functions while games and quizzes help teach the material. Includes a 360-degree view of the skeleton, which allows detailed examination of the human structure. Includes a link to the Body Online web sited for more information. Choose *Ultimate Human Body* over *A.D.A.M.* if you have older children (12-up) who want more detail in their study of the human body. Caution: Unlike *A.D.A.M.*, *Ultimate* does NOT have a modesty setting to lock out the reproductive chapters.

Virtual Labs: Electricity

Edmark
Ages 10-up   Street price $80
Subject(s): electricity
Skills needed: mouse, reading
System Req: WIN 95/98: PI/90/16MB
MAC: PMac/8MB

This program is only available in the school version but is well worth the price if you need help teaching the difficult concept of electricity. The package comes with 2 CD's so you can share with another homeschool family and 40 reproducible lab sheets. Features include onscreen labs and a built-in "Sci-Clopedia" of electricity information. The lab activities generally entail building electrical models such as a doorbell. The student can also freely build contraptions that run on electricity as well. The program gives excellent hands-on activities for any student who is fascinated by electricity and how to make things that run on electricity. The tutorials are well designed and will help students understand even the most complex concepts about electricity. This program is similar to the program *ZAP!* but without the cartoon, game-like feel. If you don't need the classroom and lab emphasis, *ZAP!* would be a better choice.

Virtual Labs: Light

Edmark
Ages 12-up   Street price $80
Subject(s): light
Skills needed: mouse, reading
System Req: WIN 95/98: PI/90/16MB
MAC: PMac/8MB

In science, light is one of the most hard-to-understand concepts. This program gives you tools to explain light and how it behaves in a very visual and understandable manner. You get a virtual workspace supplied with different filters, lenses, mirrors, colored lasers and light targets. You can manipulate any of these items to play with light and lasers or you can work on any of the 42 built-in lab experiments that are included in the teacher's manual. Just like *Virtual Labs: Electricity,* this program is only available in the school version with two copies of the CD-ROM. If the lessons or labs stump your student, they can access the onscreen "Sci-Clopedia." Great program for any science curriculum grade five or higher.

Virtual Physics: Escape from Braindeath

Cubic Science
Ages 11-15   Street price $35
Subject(s): science: light, sound, mass, electricity
Skills needed: 6th grade science
System Req: WIN 3.1/95/98 PI/75/12MB
MAC: 040/12MB

Virtual Physics opens with a scene that looks like a clip from the "X-Files". A spaceship lands somewhere in "Downtown, USA" and a lone figure is abducted. The user has become a 'guest' of the alien 'Spring-horns'. They have traveled to earth to determine the worthiness of the human race to join their empire. As their prime subject, the student is encouraged to "fill (his or her) brain". This is done by performing exercises and experiments, viewing tutorials and videos, and undertaking practice problems designed to solidify and review newly acquired knowledge. However, the abductee needs to escape and needs to find a key to the escape pod on the spaceship. To earn pieces of the key, the child must complete each of the 22 lessons in the program. As the child completes the lessons and answers the questions, they learn about waves, electricity, mirrors, lenses, clock and more. Although the material is hard, it's presented in an interesting and easy-to-under-

SCIENCE

stand way and covers a lot of material.

Volcanoes! Life on the Edge

Forest Technology
Ages: 10-up   Street price $24
Subject(s): science, history
Skills needed: reading helpful but not required
System Req: WIN 3.1/95/98 486/8MB
MAC: 040/8MB

This CD is a multimedia expose' of the history of volcanoes and volcano research. With dozens of video clips, study of and interviews with volcanologists, and a searchable glossary, this is a fascinating, engaging look at many volcanoes all over the world, the science of volcanoes and significant eruptions of the past e.g. Pompeii. Includes more than one hundred detailed articles featuring text, photographs, animations, and audio commentary. Caution: Includes some material about people who worship volcanoes and their beliefs. Recommended use: Perfect for geology or volcano unit study or course.

The Way Things Work 3.0

Dorling Kindersley
Ages: 6-up   Street price $29
Subject(s): mechanical science, inventions
Skills needed: mouse, reading helpful but not required
System Req: WIN 3.1/95/98 486/8MB
MAC: 030/8MB

This multimedia version of the popular book, *The Way Things Work*, contains 70,000 words, 1,000 illustrations, 1,500 screens and pop-ups, 300 animations, 60+ minutes of audio, 20 short movies, instant cross-references to other subjects. The program is broken down into sections that are cross-referenced: *Inventions, Inventors, Principles of Science* and *Timeline*. Also includes visual demonstrations of inventions and principles of science, timelines, inven-

tors, more. You are able to visually understand the mechanics and insides of many everyday objects by watching videos and animations. For example, see how holograms or video cameras work. Also, explore how the same scientific principle is behind more than one invention. This is one the children will love and use for hours. Recommended use: GIFT.

Widget Workshop

Electronic Arts
Ages: 6-12   Street price $28
Subject(s): science
Skills needed: reading helpful but not required
System Req: WIN 3.1/95/98 486/8MB
MAC: 030/8MB

This CD is a virtual software workshop with hundreds of objects that can be put together in unlimited ways. Simulating objects, parts, and such, they can do projects you would never let them try in the real world. Conduct generally scientifically accurate experiments with light, sound, time, mathematics, logic, cause and effect, gravity, random numbers and more. Widget Workshop is similar to Even More Incredible Machine in concept but more complex in its execution. Designed to stretch your student's science and math thinking and creativity, this game gives you the tools to construct inventions, solve pre-built puzzles and experiment with hands on science tools. Think of it kind of like a cross between the board game "Mouse Trap" and an erector set. Very challenging. Great for that child who always wants to put things together, take things apart, make things, or experiment.

ZAP!

Edmark
Ages: 6-12   Street price $28
Subject(s): science
Skills needed: reading helpful but not required
System Req: WIN 3.1/95/98 486/8MB
MAC: 040/8MB

Almost any kid would love to play with lasers but alas; most homeschool budgets can't afford real lasers and tools to experiment with those lasers. With this program from Edmark, students can play with lasers, light rays, sound waves and electrical gadgets. No mess, no expensive equipment. Realistic hands-on labs give teachers and students the chance to see how light rays react and how electricity can be manipulated. Built-in lessons present problems in easy-to-follow format, starting with easy material and concepts and working in bite-sized pieces to more difficult concepts. After successfully completing the labs, the student is rewarded with the components to build a concert complete with music, light and lasers. The student can go through the directed lessons or just play with the components in freeform play. Also includes a built-in database of 260 science articles. If you have a child who likes to build electronic gadgets (or take them apart), this is great program for learning and fun.

REFERENCE AND RESEARCH

A.D.A.M.: The Inside Story 1997

ADAM Interactive
Ages: 4-up   Street price $24
Subject(s): anatomy
Skills needed: reading helpful but not required
System Req: WIN 3.1/95/98 486/8MB
MAC: 040/8MB

Mary Pride's #1 pick for anatomy. This CD is a wonderful, fun, fascinating and discrete interactive multimedia journey through the human body and all its functions. Contains animated discussions and explanations on body functions such as: what happens when you sneeze, when a bee stings you, when you choke on something, and more. Has an excellent modesty option (the only anatomy program I know of that does) where you can lock out the chapter on reproduction with a password. ADAM Interactive offers Jr. High and Sr. High Packages with lesson plans designed as a complete anatomy course. Note: there is a section on breast cancer that shows an extensive drawing of breast tissue and the lymphatic system. Highly recommended by many of our customers as well as our own children.

Compton's 3D World Atlas

See review under *Geography*.

Compton's 2000 Interactive Encyclopedia

Learning Company
Ages: 10-up   Street price $40
Subject(s): reference
Skills needed: reading helpful but not required
System Req: WIN 3.1/95/98 PII/16MB

Compton's 2000 Interactive Encyclopedia is a top-rated CD-ROM encyclopedia. Perfect for all that unit study research. Please note: this is the *Deluxe* version, not the lesser content *Standard* version. The *Deluxe* version has more material that would be of interest to a homeschooling family. There is a cheaper *"Standard"* version available, but it does not have all the features a home-schooling family wants that are in the *"Deluxe"* version. This version includes 360-degree panoramic views and online activities from the San Francisco children's science museum. Also covers a review of the major events of the 20th century. Loaded with material these CD's are packed with 40,000 articles, thousands of links to the Internet, 150 videos, animations and slide shows, and 16,000 photos. *Compton's* has more articles than *World Book* but they are not as in depth. Students will find easy to use tools for researching and writing reports. Compton's is not making any more encyclopedias after 2000.

Encarta 2001

Microsoft
Ages: 10-up   Street price $40
Subject(s): reference
Skills needed: reading
System Req: WIN 95: PII/16MB
MAC: N/A (of course - consider the source)

From a technological viewpoint, Encarta is a wonderful encyclopedia. However, it is just too anti-Christian and new age for us to recommend it. If you get one free with your computer go ahead and keep it, just be aware of this bias. We have this title listed as one of our "Software to Avoid" programs.

Grolier's 2001 Interactive Encyclopedia DELUXE

Grolier Interactive
Ages: 10-up   Street price $45
Subject(s): reference
Skills needed: reading helpful but not required
System Req: WIN 95/9/16MB
MAC 040/8MB

Grolier is a highly rated CD encyclopedia but not always the top-rated. It is very good and offers a Mac version, which other encyclopedias don't. Still great for all that unit study research. Featuring two jam-packed CD's, this easy-to-use program contains 38,000 articles, 177 videos, thousands of links to the Internet, 15,000 images, and a 250,000-word dictionary. Built into the program are an atlas, timeline and research helpers. Includes activities to help delve into the material one layer at a time. You can also access free content updates every month on the Internet. Please note: this is the Deluxe version, not the lesser content Standard version. The Deluxe version has more material that would be of interest to a homeschooling family. There is a cheaper "Standard" version available, but it does not have all the features a homeschooling family wants that are in the Deluxe version.

Library of the Future

Able-Soft
Ages: 8-up   Street price $19
Subject(s): literature
Skills needed: mouse, reading
System Req: WIN 3.1/95/98 486/8MB
MAC N/A

Imagine having a complete library on your computer. This CD-ROM contains the full text of over 5000 books, stories, plays, poems, children's classics, historical and religious documents, plus over one hour of audio readings and selected video clips. You name a classic piece of literature- it's on here. You would need an entire classroom full of shelves to store every book on this program, not to mention the time it would take to find a particular document on those shelves. Now you can hold this whole library in the palm of your hand, and access any document instantly with the click of a mouse. It includes great works such as *Moby Dick, Gulliver's Travels, the Declaration of Independence, Tale of Two Cities, Tom Sawyer* and more. Contains the Bible as well as other religious works such as the *Word of Buddha* and the *Egyptian Book of the Dead*. While I don't recommend reading these non-Christian works, be aware they are on this CD. You have to keep in mind that this is a library and should be used as such, with discernment and wisdom. The *Library of the Future* can be searched by key word, author, title or subject and has over 5000 works. In contrast, the *Robinson Curriculum* is pre-screened from a Christian perspective, but cannot be searched, costs a lot more and has only about 250 books. I suggest getting both. There is not much duplication.

My First Incredible Amazing Words & Pictures 2.0

Dorling Kindersley
Ages: 4-9   Street price $19
Subject(s): dictionary, vocabulary
Skills needed: mouse
System Req: WIN 3.1/95/98 486/8MB
MAC 040/8MB
Contains 17,000 words, 1,000 of which have definitions. The CD has 1,000 illustrations, 1,000 animations, four hours of audio, and 1,250 screens. This is the only chil-

dren's dictionary that will narrate the definitions-important for auditory learners. Has three games to learn about words. Recommended use: first vocabulary program. Also excellent for children with delayed speech or similar language handicaps. Caution: a witch flies across the screen in the opening sequence, also has "witch" as an entry. But then, most dictionaries do.

The Robinson Curriculum V2.0

See complete review under CURRICULUM in next section.

Worldbook Encyclopedia 2001

IBM Multimedia
Ages: 10-up   Street price $65 and up
Subject(s): reference
Skills needed: reading
System Req: WIN 95: PII/16MB
MAC: PMac/16 (Standard version only)
Please note: this is the *"Deluxe"* version, not the lesser content *"Standard"* version. The *"Deluxe"* version has more material that would be of interest to a homeschooling family. There is a cheaper *"Standard"* version available, but it does not have all the features a homeschooling family wants that are in the *"Deluxe"* version. The Mac version is only the *"Standard"* version. This popular encyclopedia has been converted to CD ROM by the IBM Corp. This is the best encyclopedia on CD-ROM in this price range in my opinion. With the entire contents of a set of $500 encyclopedias combined with multimedia, you have an impressive amount of information. This CD set includes 21,000 articles, thousands of links to the Internet, 160 videos, 700 sounds, charts, maps, and a handy pop-up tool kit with writing tools and a dictionary. Also, WB is written in a specific manner in which

REFERENCE AND RESEARCH

the word most commonly looked up by young readers have articles specifically written at about a 4th grade reading level. Major articles are designed to present simpler concepts and reading levels at the beginning of the article. These articles then build toward more sophisticated levels toward the end. Subsequently, a child looking up a topic will find material to match her reading level immediately. In addition, the search engine is easy to use. Lastly, there is a 3rd CD in the set that contains research and study outlines designed to help students do report writing and aid moms in unit study planning. Altogether this makes the encyclopedia a great resource for kids and by far the easiest. If you want more resource material, there is a *"Premier"* edition that also includes the *Merriam-Webster Reference Library, Information Please Almanac* and *Rand McNally New Millennium World Atlas Deluxe*. For the serious researcher, this is the one to get. Both editions can utilize IBM's voice recognition technology *ViaVoice*, which you must purchase separately. This technology allows all the written words be spoken aloud.

INTEGRATED (MULTI-SUBJECT TITLES)

Arthur's Kindergarten

Learning Company
Ages 2-3   Street price $19
Skills needed: none
Subject(s): early reading, phonics, counting, creativity, memory
System Req: WIN 95/98: P90/16MB
MAC: 040/16MB

Arthur's treehouse has been wrecked by a bad storm and he and his friends must earn money for new treehouse parts by doing odd jobs around the neighborhood. Your child helps Arthur and his friends and along the way they practice their phonics, counting, creativity and memory skills. Built-in features help adjust the program levels to the individual learner, progress tracking, smart help and personalized features.

Big Thinkers 1st Grade

Humongous Entertainment
Ages: 5-7
Subject(s): phonics, addition, spelling, subtraction, reading, money
Skills needed: mouse
System Req: WIN 3.1/95/98
486/33MHz/8MB
MAC 040/8MB

The new Big Thinkers multi-subject first grade from Humongous covers a lot of material in these 20 activities. Although this program is not as "fun" as *Jumpstart First Grade*, it has far more educational value. Activities cover phonics, addition, spelling, subtraction, reading, and money. Ben and Becky Brightly host the activities and use their bodies in clever ways to demonstrate concepts: Becky turns into a train or Ben turns into a crane to demonstrate fractions. Features include: ability to save games, automatically adjusts difficulty level, and well-designed games. Kids enjoyed collecting smart stars when successful. Highly recommended. Currently this title is in a combo pack, *World of Fun and Learning 1st Grade* ($20), combined with *Freddi Fish 2*; which makes it a great deal.

Big Thinkers Kindergarten

Humongous Entertainment
Ages: 4-6
Subject(s): phonics, early reading, math, thinking
Skills needed: mouse
System Req: WIN 3.1/95/98
486/33MHz/8MB
MAC 040/8MB

The new Big Thinkers multi-subject Kindergarten from Humongous covers a lot of material in these 13 activities. Although this program is not as "fun" as *Jumpstart Kindergarten*, it has far more educational value. Activities cover letter-sound association, time telling, word recognition, size estimation, counting, measurement, logic, addition and musical instruments. Ben and Becky Brightly host the activities and use their bodies in clever ways to demonstrate concepts: Ben's face turns into a clock or their arms stretch to conduct a counting activity for example. Features include: ability to save games, automatically adjusts difficulty level, and well-designed games. Kids enjoyed collecting smart stars when successful. Highly recommended. Currently this title is in a combo pack called *World of Fun and Learning Kindergarten* combined with *Putt Putt Saves the Zoo* ($20), which makes it a great deal.

Carmen Sandiego's ThinkQuick Challenge

Learning Company
AGES 9-UP   Street price $19
Subject(s): World History
Skills needed: reading
System Req: WIN 95/98: PI/90MHz/16MB
MAC: PMac/16MB

Carmen and her evil Knowbots are causing trouble by committing such fiendish crimes as stealing ABC order, radio waves and more. Your job is to travel to various spots on the globe and answer multiple choice quizzes in such diverse subjects as math, science, music, language arts, geography, and history. You can even set up the games to be played competitively by up to four players at once. It's a great way to brush up on facts and various subject area knowledge. One great feature: the ability to add your own questions. This would be fun for any homeschool family to create quizzes on any unit study they are involved in, make Bible quizzes, or even family history quizzes. Questions are not read aloud so proficient reading is required.

ClueFinders Series

The Learning Company
Ages: 8-12
Subject(s): all subjects
Skills needed: mouse, reading
System Req: WIN 95/98: PI/90/16MB
MAC PMac/8MB

This series of multi-subject includes lots of great learning activities. However, most of them have some borderline elements. They did not bother me much but I want parents to be aware of them. Elements include pagan-like statues, jungle tribe themes, crystals (they have no powers), evil villains. Kids love playing the games and they are very educational. Caution: *ClueFinders Reading Adventures Ages 9-12* has a sorceress and *ClueFinders 4th Grade Adventure* encounters ancient Egyptian "powers of destruction."

Dr. Seuss Kindergarten

Learning Company

Ages 2-3   Street price $19

Skills needed: mouse, following instructions

Subject(s): early reading, early math

System Req: WIN 95/98: P90/8MB

MAC: 040/8MB

Playing this program is like walking into a Dr. Seuss book. Back in Seussville, Gerald McGrew has built a brand new zoo. Your mission, should you decide to accept, is to successfully play math and reading games in order to procure eight sets of animals. Familiar characters and art highlight the scenes and delight Dr. Seuss fans. Find the Star-bellied Sneetches, the Barbaloots and Birthday pets to fill up the zoo and you win the game. To do this you must play measuring, rhyming, matching, alphabetical order, phonics, some sight-reading and other engaging games. Includes three different levels of difficulty, 50 Seussian characters and five original songs — all pleasant to listen to.

Elementary Edge Grades 2-3

Encore Software

Ages 9-11   Street price $39

Skills needed: reading

Subject(s): US History, World History, Geography

System Req: WIN 95/98: P133/132MB

This bundle of software contains some excellent software at a great price. Titles include: *Math Workshop Deluxe* (a great math program but caution: one puzzle in the puzzle activity has a vampire and another has a ghost rising out of a graveyard), *Exploration Station* (a nice but older science program), *SuperSolvers: Spellbound, Amazing Writing Machine, SuperSolvers:*

Mission Think, and *Word Munchers Deluxe*. See reviews under specific subject headings.

Elementary Edge Grades 4-5

Encore Software

Ages 9-11   Street price $39

Skills needed: reading

Subject(s): US History, World History, Geography

System Req: WIN 95/98: P133/132MB

This bundle of software contains some excellent software at a great price. Titles include: *Math Munchers Deluxe, The Way Things Work 1.0, Student Writing Center, Multimedia Spelling* (a great little spelling program similar to *SuperSolvers Spellbound.*), and *Where in Time is Carmen Sandiego*.

Excel High School

Knowledge Adventure

Ages 14-18   Street price $20

Skills needed: reading, jr. high

Subject(s): Algebra 1, Algebra 2, Geometry, Trigonometry, Pre-Calculus and Calculus, Life Science, Earth Science, Grammar, and Vocabulary.

System Req: WIN 95/98: PI/120MHz/8MB

MAC: PMac/100MHz/32MB

Excel High School is a complete, self-contained software program that includes over 300 lessons of a basic high school curriculum: Algebra 1, Algebra 2, Geometry, Trigonometry, Pre-Calculus and Calculus, Life Science, Earth Science, Grammar, and Vocabulary. Teachers have created the content. The math lessons include short animated segments called 'Video Tutors' that demonstrate how math problems are solved. A handy 'pop up' reference window conveniently displays math formulas and equations. The presentation is less student-friendly than High School Advantage but still offers a lot of lessons and learning. The main value of the program, in my opinion, is the extra titles you get: *Ultimate Word Attack, Multimedia Workshop, Geometry Blaster, Typing Tutor,* and *Ultimate Speed Reader* are worth the price alone. (See their reviews separately.) Given the exceptional value of this package, I highly recommend getting this program before it is no longer available. A must-have.

Also includes these additional titles *New Millennium Encyclopedia, Spanish for the Real World, French for the Real World.* Note: the Spanish and French Real World Titles are very good but have a fortuneteller in one scene.

Excel Middle School

Knowledge Adventure
Ages 12-15   Street price $20
Skills needed: reading, 6th grade
Subject(s): US History, World History, Geography, Ancient Civilizations, Pre-Algebra, Algebra, Life Science, Earth Science, Physical Science, Grammar, Reading Comprehension and Vocabulary.
System Req: WIN 95/98: P133/32MB
MAC: PMac/32MB

Excel Middle School is a complete, self-contained software program with over 330 lessons that cover a basic middle school curriculum: US History, World History, Geography, Ancient Civilizations, Pre-Algebra, Algebra, Life Science, Earth Science, Physical Science, Grammar, Reading Comprehension and Vocabulary. Teachers have created the content. Designed to make learning fun, the program contains 'Video Tutors', which are colorful animated 'mini movies' that demonstrate how math problems are solved. The presentation is less student-friendly than Middle School Advantage but still offers a lot of lessons and learning. The main value of the program, in my opinion, is the extra titles you get: *Ultimate Word Attack, Multimedia*

Workshop, Typing Tutor, and *Ultimate Speed Reader* are worth the price alone. (See their reviews separately.) Also includes these additional titles *New Millennium Encyclopedia, Spanish for the Real World, French for the Real World.* Given the exceptional value of this package, I highly recommend getting this program before it is no longer available. A must-have. Caution: the *Spanish* and *French Real World* titles are very good but have a fortuneteller in one scene. Also, *Math Blaster Pre-Algebra* is very good but takes place in a creepy house with creepy characters.

JumpStart series

Everybody asks me, what about the Jumpstarts? They are, actually, one of the best selling software series ever. In fact, many software companies are now copying the formula of having grade level, all subject, multi-activity software packages. For example, The Learning Company has now released *Reader Rabbit Toddler, Preschool,* and *Kindergarten*.

The *Jumpstarts'* popularity stems primarily from the fact that children love them. However, I feel the educational value is mediocre overall. Yes, they do give some good extra practice but remember, they (and most other software programs) are designed for children who are at school all day and their parents just want something to keep the children busy but is not totally mindless-e.g. *Nintendo*. Top selling programs are not designed for homeschoolers and you will not see many "top sellers" listed in our top ten. For example, one reviewer (who gave all the *JumpStart* near perfect ratings) was not too impressed with *NumberMaze Challenge*, calling it "too didactic." Hmmm, I say to myself, what does didactic mean?? I looked it up in my trusty dictionary: didactic: meaning to teach or instruct. Hello? Is there anybody in there? That's the whole point of educational software...... Sooo, back to the *JumpStarts*. Buy one, see if you like them. They are a few *Jumpstart* titles that feature some occult material. Check our **Software to Avoid** list first. (The company guarantees 100% satisfaction or your money back). Just send it back to them. My children love them but I recommend them for afterschool only.

JumpStart Toddler
Knowledge Adventure
Ages 2-3   Street price $19
Skills needed: none
Subject(s): mouse skills, keyboard, logic
System Req: WIN 95/98: P90/8MB
MAC: 040/8MB
Simple, enjoyable activities for your youngest computer user to help them learn mouse control and more. The main menu is an inviting child's bedroom where you can click around to find the hot spots, seven of which lead to activities. What makes it so good for toddlers is that any click or movement of the mouse leads to success. My two-year-old can do it by himself. My little ones still play this one often.

JumpStart Preschool
Knowledge Adventure
Ages 3-5   Street price $19
Skills needed: mouse skills, reading readiness
Subject(s): phonics, math, logic
System Req: WIN 95/98: P90/8MB
MAC: 040/8MB
Music: Some mild rock
Ten modules covering 20 educational areas with three levels of difficulty for your preschooler: dot-to-dot, numbers, letters, picture/sound matching activities, colors, shapes and more. This program has a more arcade fun-factor than *Millie's and Bailey's*

Preschool but less educational depth. Great graphics and sound make this a wonderful game for all-around afterschool practice of early learning skills.

JumpStart Kindergarten
Knowledge Adventure
Ages 4-6   Street price $19
Skills needed: mouse skills, reading readiness
Subject(s): math, science, English, logic, more
System Req: WIN 95/98: P90/8MB
MAC: 040/8MB
Music: Some mild rock
Fourteen learning modules with over 80 puzzle and game activities with traditional kindergarten subjects such as reading math and language arts. Activities cover such topics as drawing and coloring, letters (matching, letter sounds, upper/lower case), sorting by size, shape and color, telling time to the hour, alphabet order and sentence structure. Includes an excellent record-keeping feature for parents or teachers to keep tabs on the number of plays and percent correct. A favorite of my 4-year-old. Caution: Halloween characters in October calendar activity.

JumpStart First Grade
Knowledge Adventure
Ages 5-8   Street price $19
Skills needed: mouse skills, reading readiness
Subject(s): phonics, reading, math, more
System Req: WIN 95/98: P90/8MB
MAC: 040/8MB
Music: Some mild rock
Fun activities for first grade level; words-to-pictures games, telling time, painting, reading comprehension, geography, science, color mixing, measurement, grammar, money, letters, counting, addition, story books and more. This upgraded edition has

ten new activities for your first grader. He or she must earn three clues found in various classrooms. Once they have the clues, they gain access to one of six islands. On each of these islands is a treasure to be had. Activities are very well designed and fun. For example, kids get to learn units of measurement by following recipes. By using tablespoons, cups and other items, kids make yummy concoctions in the kitchen. Other kitchen duties include using fractions to make pizzas. Is your favorite pizza ? pepperoni or only ? pepperoni? Goofy ingredients like seaweed and anchovies can be added to these homemade pizzas to make the game even sillier. Other activities include playing with musical instruments, measuring out pocket change for the snack machine and playing math games. While not totally educational in time spent, this program offers afterschool fun with some skill-building as well. Kids love it.

JumpStart Second Grade

Knowledge Adventure
Ages 6-9   Street price $19
Skills needed: moderate mouse skills, reading
Subject(s): phonics, blending, reading
System Req: WIN 95/98: P90/8MB
MAC: 040/8MB
Music: Some mild rock

Twenty-two enjoyable activities to reinforce traditional second grade material including science, math, friendship, personal responsibility, music, and more. Arcade action games and puzzles help kids practice and fine-tune their spelling, math and logic skills. Caution: Still life pictures of werewolf and vampire on two milk caps in one game. Even includes an activity to learn Braille and American Sign Language. Activities have three adjustable levels of difficulty and parent-friendly progress reports.

This program is another fun one for after-school time and extra practice on essential skills.

JumpStart 3rd Grade

Knowledge Adventure
Ages 7-10   Street price $19
Skills needed: moderate mouse skills, reading
Subject(s): all curriculum areas
System Req: WIN 95/98: P90/8MB
MAC: 040/8MB
Music: Some mild rock

This is sort of like Dr. Brain for younger children. You must find clues in a mysterious mountain to find and capture 25 robots. These robots were sent back in time to change history by a bratty girl named Polly. By solving the clues you correct history and stop Polly's evil plans. Polly is arrogant and rude but not "wicked." Play games that test your knowledge, brainpower and skill in spelling, grammar, vocabulary, math, science, astronomy, history, geography, art and music. Compose folk and classical music. Create your own art. This is my favorite of all the Jumpstarts.

JumpStart 4th Grade

Knowledge Adventure
Ages 8-11   Street price $19
Skills needed: moderate mouse skills, reading
Subject(s): all curriculum areas
System Req: WIN 95/98: P90/8MB
MAC: 040/8MB
Music: Some mild rock

Please make sure you get the newest version of JumpStart 4th grade. The older version takes place on a haunted island. The new 4th grade version is wholesome but not that great. 5th or 3rd grade would be a better choice.

JumpStart 5th Grade

Knowledge Adventure

Ages 7-10   Street price $19

Skills needed: moderate mouse skills, 4th grade reading skills

Subject(s): all curriculum areas

System Req: WIN 3.1/95/98

486dx/66MHz/16MB

MAC: 040/25MHz/8MB

Some Jumpstarts are no more than dressed up arcade games, but *Jumpstart 5th Grade* is no brainless arcade game. Challenging but fun, this program features Jo Hammet, crack amateur girl detective. The evil Dr. X is planning to destroy the industrial sites in town and Jo must solve puzzles in order procure the necessary tools to stop the impending disaster. The puzzles are challenging; requiring research, quick thinking, logic and memory skills. Once you solve a puzzle you receive another clue to solve the case. This program is not easy and covers a broad range of subjects from art history to math. Don't get this for a child who gives up easily.

High School Advantage 2001

Encore Software

Ages 13-up   Street price $39

Skills needed: moderate mouse skills, reading

Subject(s): all curriculum areas

System Req: WIN 95/98: P90/8MB

MAC: 040/8MB

This bundle packs a lot of value for the money. With six CD's, High School Advantage offers some oldies but goodies software programs. *Cartopedia World Atlas, Super Tutor Composition, Eyewitness Encyclopedia of Science 1.0, Super Tutor Vocabulary, A+ French, Eyewitness History of the World 1.0* and *Compton's Encyclopedia 1999*. The tutorials offer exercises in vocabulary, composition, chemistry, physics, life sciences, algebra II, trigonometry, French, world history and geography. This is a great addition to any homeschool software library.

KidsTime Deluxe

Ideal Instructional Fair

Ages 5-10   Street price $20

Skills needed: moderate mouse skills, reading

Subject(s): all curriculum areas

System Req: WIN 3.1/95/98: 386/8MB

MAC: 020/4MB

This multi-subject program has five activities including *ABKey* (letter recognition and keyboard skills), *Dot-to-Dot, KidsNotes* (beginner music program, lets children create melodies too), *Story Writer* (Children create their own stories using icon type pictures and words), and *Match-It*. Mac and Windows versions offer lots of playability and value. In *Story Writer*, the computer reads the story to the child. Simple, basic graphics, but our younger children play it over and over again. Older program runs on almost any computer.

Millie's and Bailey's Preschool

Edmark

Ages: 3-5   Street price $19

Subject(s): science, math, reading, thinking skills

System Req: WIN 3.1/95/98 486/8MB

MAC: 040/8MB

About two years ago, Edmark took *Bailey's Book House, Millie's Math House* and *Sammy's Science House*, combined them into one huge program and then roughly chopped the whole thing in half age wise. The result was *Millie's and Bailey's Preschool* and *Millie's and Bailey's Kindergarten*. Both halves do not contain all the activities that each of the individual programs has. The preschool collection has a well-rounded set of eight math, reading and science games. One of my kids' favorites is using geometric shapes and a simple blueprint to make a "mouse house" complete with windows and doors. Other activities cover thinking skills as well. With multiple levels, the offer lots of playtime and fun. My kids play them over and over.

Millie's and Bailey's Kindergarten
Edmark
Ages: 4-6   Street price $19
Subject(s): science, math, reading, thinking skills
System Req: WIN 3.1/95/98 486/8MB
MAC: 040/8MB

Ten activities, all right on target for kindergartners, cover subjects like early reading, counting, science and math. Each activity is carefully designed, accommodating children with differing abilities by offering both "explore" and "question/answer" modes. One activity has children following blueprint patterns to build objects in a workshop. Another has children experimenting with the sequence of events by placing story frames in order. The program also has handy options that let adults control volume and printing. Adults will appreciate that they can control both sound and printing. This is a great package of learning activities. See also the descriptions of *Millie's and Bailey's Preschool, Millie's Math House, Bailey's Book House, Sammy's Science House.*

Princeton Review: High School Edge
The Learning Company
Ages: 14-up   Street price $39
Subject(s): science, algebra, English, history
System Req: WIN 3.1/95/98 486/8MB
MAC: 040/8MB

Includes: *Bodyworks 5.0, Practice Makes Perfect Spanish, Practice Makes Perfect French, Success Builder Geometry* and *Algebra, Princeton Review SAT 98*. See sep-

arate reviews of these titles.

My 16-year-old daughter Anna's comments on the *Success Builder Algebra*: *Gives good information, tips on test-taking, and tips on how to write out the problem properly. You can create your own problems to see how a concept works. Includes dictionary of terms, formulas and rules. Narrates much of the instructions, which is very helpful. Practice problems have visual helps, multiple-choice answers, good hints that make you think. I like this format of teaching.*

Princeton Review: Middle School Edge
The Learning Company
Ages: 11-14   Street price $39
Subject(s): science, math, English, history
System Req: WIN 3.1/95/98 486/8MB
MAC: 040/8MB

Contains an assortment of older programs: *Science Sleuths, Artrageous., Word Smart* (not the Smartek version, it's the *Princeton Review* vocabulary program), *Slam Dunk Typing,* and *Princeton Review Algebra Smart.* See separate reviews.

Reader Rabbit Kindergarten
The Learning Company
Ages 4-6   Street price $19
Skills needed: mouse, some reading
Subject(s): all curriculum areas
System Req: WIN 95/98: P90/8MB
MAC: 040/8MB

Includes the ADAPT technology which enables the software to pre-test the child and configure the activities and questions based on the child's ability. Maddie the mouse must get ready for summer camp by collecting all the appropriate gear: bug spray, a storybook, a rope, a pillow, etc. She must travel to four areas of the camp collecting these items. The four sections offer activities stressing such skills as counting, alphabet, shapes, early reading, adding and subtracting and more. Successful completion of all four activities allows Maddie and the other campers to experience a campfire, cookout and campout. Kids enjoyed the program and sharpened some skills along the way. Caution: At the campfire one of the stories is a "ghost" story but does not involve a real ghost – just someone pretending to be a ghost.

Reader Rabbit 1st Grade

The Learning Company
Ages 6-8   Street price $19
Skills needed: mouse, some reading
Subject(s): all curriculum areas
System Req: WIN 95/98: P90/8MB
MAC: 040/8MB

Reader Rabbit's hometown of Wordville is having its annual musical show and he needs to help the town prepare. Off he goes on a hunt through the four main areas of Wordville, searching for costumes, sets, props, scripts and musical instruments. Along the way kids count coins when purchasing clothes, practice spelling and word recognition for the scripts and put a calendar in order. Other features include a calendar maker, music maker, drawing activity, and rhythm game. The activities required more work than the Reader Rabbits in this series but the educational value is high and the game entertaining. Includes the ADAPT technology which enables the software to pre-test the child and configure the activities and questions based on the child's ability.

Reader Rabbit 2nd Grade

The Learning Company
Ages 7-9   Street price $19
Skills needed: mouse, some reading
Subject(s): all curriculum areas
System Req: WIN 95/98: P90/8MB
MAC: 040/8MB

Sam the Lion is in a castle looking for his buddy Reader Rabbit (RR). To find RR, he needs to complete dozens of short activities giving the child practice in basic 2nd grade material. These activities very good and kids enjoy the scavenger hunt like feel to the game. Skills covered include: plural words, math equations, verbs, nouns, writing, geometry, reading comprehension, music, and drawing. The activities are short so kids don't lose interest and are motivated to continue. If your kids love Reader Rabbit, they will really enjoy this game.

Includes the ADAPT technology which enables the software to pre-test the child and configure the activities and questions based on the child's ability.

Superman Activity Center

Knowledge Adventure
Ages 5-10   Street price $19
Subject(s): logic, creativity, problem solving
Skills needed: reading, mouse
System Req: WIN 3.1/95/98 486/8MB
MAC: 040/8MB

This fun little program is not loaded with educational value but has some nice activities. Remember, Superman is not magic but imaginary- his body is from another planet with less gravity. And he always fights for truth, justice, and the American way. Features include 13 fun activities, games and puzzles. One activity my kids particularly enjoyed was exploring the Daily Planet and creating their own newspapers with different articles they write themselves. If you have a Superman fan, this is a great gift.

Student Resource Advantage 2001

Encore Software

Ages 11-up   Street price $40

Skills needed: mouse, reading

Subject(s): all curriculum areas

System Req: WIN 95/98: P90/8MB

MAC: 040/8MB

Once again, Encore offers a lot of software values for the money. This six-CD set contains eight different programs to help any high school student. Included are *Mavis Beacon Teaches Typing 8.0, Getwise on the Web, Day Planner Pro, Webster's New World Dictionary and Thesaurus, Compton's Deluxe 3D World Atlas, Compton's Encyclopedia 1999, Student Writing and Research Center,* and *Computer Coach.* Although there are more current versions available for some of these titles, you can't find a better deal. Some of the titles are very hard to find anywhere else. See the various reviews under the individual title names. (We only reviewed *Mavis Beacon Teaches Typing, Compton's Deluxe 3D World Atlas, Compton's Encyclopedia,* and the *Student Writing and Research Center.)*

Geosafari Knowledge Pad: The Plato Collection

Educational Insights

Ages 8-up   Street price $25

Skills needed: reading

Subject(s): all subject areas

System Req: WIN 95/98: P90/16MB

MAC: PMac/16MB

This program from the makers of Geosafari just landed in our house the day before we finished this book. This program is packed with content. It is a first in a series and it contains 96 different quiz games. Our Planet, Animals, Man & Nature, Once Upon a Time, Art & Culture, Technology, Abstract (brainteasers) and Sport & Leisure. This is a great quiz game for the whole family, covering lots of material. Quizzes can be adapted to any curriculum. Kids learn as they play. Although the program required reading, most kids jumped right in. Note: some pop-culture questions. Good for school time learning!

CURRICULUM

Advanced Learning System

American Education Corporation

Ages 7-18   Street price $70 per unit

Skills needed: moderate mouse skills, reading

Subject(s): all curriculum areas

System Req: WIN 95/98: P90/8MB

MAC: 040/8MB

Although the presentation is rather dry and basic, this barebones curriculum offers some good practice and overview. The ALS curriculum is used in some Christian schools. Subjects covered are:

Social Studies (8 units covering US Geography and History, World Geography and History, Economics and Government from grade 4-12)

Language Usage (Nine units covering grades 1-12)

Grammar and Writing (Six units covering grades 1-9)

Reading (Nine units covering grades 1-12)

Vocabulary (Nine units covering grades 1-12)

Spelling (Seven units covering grades 1-7)

Math (Eight units covering grades 1-8)

High School Math (Ten units covering Pre-Algebra, Algebra I, Algebra II, Real World Math, Geometry, Trigonometry, Calculus in grades 7-12)

Science (Eight units covering grades 1-8)

High School Science (Five units covering Biology, Chemistry, Chemistry II, Earth and Space Science, and Physics).

Each unit covers about one year of material and contains about 40-60 lessons. The material is basic, just the bare essentials of core curriculum. The lesson format is fairly simple and is basically a workbook on computer. You read a few pages of material then answer a 10-question quiz. If you get the questions right, you get to play a game similar to Wheel of Fortune. Each lesson takes about 20 minutes. We have used this in our homeschool during times my kids needed to have some basic practice when mom can't teach. This curriculum is also excellent as a supplement and form of accountability to unit studies. Multiple children can use the software, making it an economical choice as well. One of the best features is the ability to add your own material and quiz questions.

Cornerstone

The Learning Company
Ages 8-14   Street price $249 per unit
Skills needed: moderate mouse skills, reading
Subject(s): math, English skills
System Req: WIN 95/98: P90/8MB
MAC: 040/8MB

While I did not review the entire series, *Cornerstone* appears to have some very good math and reading lessons for grades 3-8. Each subject series is broken into 3 units or levels (grades 3-4, 5-6, and 7-8). The Language Arts series covers 175 lessons in total. The topics include capitalization, punctuation, spelling and grammar. The Reading Comprehension series covers 112 lessons in total. The content of the reading material is taken from Cobblestone Magazine. The Reading Vocabulary series covers 140 lessons in total. The Mathematics series is broken into 3 levels (grades 3-4, 5-6, and 7-8) and covers 82 lessons in total. While the program is dated, 1996, it still has some decent graphics, color and sound. Teachers and home educators will appreciate the detailed record keeping

and tracking system. Lessons are good and take the child through each concept step-by-step. However, the price is quite high and the content falls short of a full-fledged year-long curriculum.

The Robinson Curriculum V2.0

Oregon Institute in Science and Medicine
Ages 7-21   Street price $195
Skills needed: moderate mouse skills, reading
Subject(s): all curriculum areas
System Req: WIN 95/98: P90/8MB
MAC: 040/8MB

Professor Robinson developed this curriculum to allow his 6 children to teach themselves when their mother suddenly died. The three components of his daily curriculum are: 2 hours of *Saxon Math* starting with *Saxon 5/4*. (*Saxon* is NOT included on the CDs in this set, it must be purchased separately.), 1 page of writing on any topic and then reading from good literature to fill in the rest of the 5-6 hour school day, 6 days a week, 10-11 months a year.

To fulfill the reading portion of the curriculum, you use this set of 22 CD's. They are encased in a handy but sturdy storage case, with rigid flip pages holding each CD. In this massive database, he compiled 120,000 pages of scanned in text from more than 250 carefully selected, very high quality books, selections from diaries, literature and other writings, the complete 30,000-page 1911 *Encyclopedia Britannica*, the complete 400,000 word 1913 *Noah Webster's Dictionary*, high school level science text books and answer keys, and more-both in print and out of print. The books are generally sequenced by grade level starting with first grade. Either print out each book or read on screen. Note: you cannot search on topics, keywords, or author- it is just one long list of books. The Dictionary and

Encyclopedia, however, have the entry words listed along side the text. Click on an entry and the program pops up that scanned in page. Each page in either the books or the reference material looks like a "picture" of the book, not like text in a word processor that you can copy, paste and edit.

What everyone wonders about is what you actually get on these CD's. Dr. Robinson has requested that the entire book list not be printed, as that is part of the program's value. However, here is a smattering of selections to give you an idea of what the *Robinson Curriculum* includes. Books: *McGuffey's Readers, Elsie books,* old *Bobbsey Twins, The Rover Boys, Swiss Family Robinson, The Jungle Book, Five Little Peppers, The Prince, Robinson Crusoe, Treasure Island, Pilgrim's Progress,* Tom Swift books, *The Wealth of Nations* and more. Authors: Shakespeare, Horatio Alger, Jr., Isaac Newton, George Washington, Winston Churchill, John Milton, Benjamin Franklin, Washington Irving, Samuel Langhorn Clemens, Jules Verne, David Crockett, James Fenimore Cooper and many more.

Technical stuff: How do you read all these? First, get lots of paper and ink for your ink jet printer. Then, be ready to spend some money. To print the entire 120,000 page collection would cost approximately $6,000 if you figure about 5¢ a page. If you have a laser printer, it can be closer to 1¢ a page. Second, start your printer. Keep in mind however, these books are to be printed and read over a 12-year period of time. Printing it yourself is cheaper than buying a book, and some of the titles are out of print so unless you find it at a used bookstore, being able to print these types of books to add to your own home library can be invaluable. There is a handy option to print the odd

pages first and then flip the stack of paper over and print the even numbered pages on the opposite side, cutting your printing costs substantially. I have printed out selections, punched three holes in them, and then placed them in a binder or folder to keep them nice for the next reader coming along.

Some additional features include vocabulary flash cards keyed to the books, phonics flash cards you print out to teach reading, and some multiple choice and essay based exams. Only about 45 of the books have corresponding exams. The questions on the exams are designed to make you think about what you have read, not just regurgitate the plot and main characters. I had fun reading the questions, as some are very un-politically correct. Example: A question from the *Five Little Peppers* asked how Mrs. Pepper supported herself and one of the answer choices was she had food stamps and welfare. Obviously this was not the correct answer. You must correct these exams yourself, somewhat negating the idea of a complete self-teaching program. However, correcting 42 exams over a course of 12 years doesn't sound too tough for this busy homeschool mom. For the college bound student, he includes about 5 science textbooks with answer keys; physics, chemistry, thermodynamics. Also included are an economics textbook, an un-politically correct but rational, scientifically based environment book and a "be ready for nuclear war" book. Keep in mind however, these are not interactive textbooks but are meant to be printed out and used the old fashioned way. No teacher's manuals are included.

Overall, the reading choices contain about 70% fictional literature, 10% autobiographies, 10% textbooks, and about 10% various other writings.

The CD's also contain the Robinson's story

CURRICULUM

and educational philosophy. He recommends no TV, no sugar, and no computer use until the child has completed *Saxon Calculus*. This too seems incongruous to the placement of this entire curriculum on CD-ROM.

I do use this in our homeschool on a fairly limited basis. However, I must stress the following points: Whereas I use this material, we sell it, and we recommend the CD ROM set; we use and sell it more as a reference and research library-not as a full "this is all you need" curriculum. Technically, you can use it that way, and we know some families who do, but most homeschooling families use it as a supplement to their existing curriculum. I personally recommend supplementing with some science and social studies materials for grades 1-8. In addition, Dr. Robinson claims the program has all the phonics and math flash cards you need to use and master to read and start *Saxon 5/4*. Personally and in my experience, I feel a great deal more teaching must take place before your child is reading proficiently and be able to start *Saxon 5/4*.

Best Features: A prescreened, ready to print library of exceptional literature and autobiographies.

Worst Features: Not enough testing and application of learned principles. You must trust that your child will learn enough spelling, grammar, writing skills, science, history, and geography all on their own from independent reading. Some homeschool moms love this type of freedom from structure but it would drive me crazy. Do not plan to use this set of CD-ROMs as a full-fledged curriculum unless you enjoy this type of schooling. However, I feel that any homeschool can greatly benefit from Dr. Robinson's educational ideas and this wonderful library of books. Future upgrades

could include more quizzes on reading material and perhaps more direction in the actual course of study. It wasn't clear to me what and when a child should be reading, and what and if any pre-requisite study was required before tackling any of the textbooks or more challenging reading selections.

SkillsBank 4

The Learning Company
Ages 13-18   Street price $249 per basic skill or $1245 for the six basic skill sets: Language, Reading, Mathematics—Basic and Intermediate, Writing, and Information Skills.
Skills needed: moderate mouse skills, reading
Subject(s): remedial math, English skills
System Req: WIN 3.1/95/98: 386+/8MB
MAC: 040/8MB

SkillsBank is completely computerized remedial high school courseware. Designed to help students catch up or complete essential high school course work, this program covers only the bare essentials of a high school equivalency program. Included are 300 self-paced lessons covering basic topics such as Language and Language Practice, Reading Comprehension, Mathematics—Basic and Intermediate, Computation Practice, Writing, and Information Skills. SkillsBank would be a good choice for parents who may want their previously public schooled teen to review basic concepts before beginning homeschooling.

Smartworks Grade School

Knowledge Adventure
Ages: 7-11   Street price $38
Subject(s): English, math, science
Skills needed: reading
System Req: 486SX33/8MB, 040/8MB
This collection of learning activities provides a "school room" of learning; 400 English lessons broken down into 4 grade

levels (approx. 100 per grade level) and then 3 subject areas per grade: Reading and Writing, Spelling, and Study Skills; 400 Math lessons broken down into 4 grade levels (approx. 100 per grade level) and then 3 subject areas per grade: numbers and calculators, measurements, and patterns and geometry; 400 science lessons broken down into 4 grade levels (approx. 100 per grade level) and then 3 subject areas per grade: earth (includes astronomy, earth systems, climate, pollution) Life (includes respiration/circulation, ecosystems, interdependency, mammals) and physical (includes chemical/matter, electromagnetism, light, energy transportation) Includes lessons on grammar, punctuation, proofreading, comprehension, vocabulary, and more. Each sub-subject has 8 lessons with each having about 4 paragraphs of material and 5 questions to test your retention. Each of the questions is drawn at random from a database of over 4,000 questions or exercises. Subsequently, each time you take a test, the quiz is a little bit different. Choose your own lesson, complete successfully, earn points and then you are allowed to play one of the dozen or so games. Some of the games are great (Castle of Dr. Brain) but some are a complete waste of time; a couple I recommend avoiding. (For example, *Yobi's Magic Spelling Tricks*.) I suggest monitoring your student's progress through this particular courseware. If you are doing a lot of unit study work, this is one way to assure that you aren't totally missing any key subject areas. Recommend use: unit study accountability or curriculum reinforcement.

Switched-On Schoolhouse

Alpha Omega Publications
Grades 3rd, 4th, 5th, 6th, 7th, 8th, 9th, 10th, 11th, or 12th.
Street price $67 per subject per grade or $285 for entire grade level
Subject(s): language arts, math, history and geography, science, Bible
Skills needed: reading.
System Req: WIN 95/98: PI/133/16MB

A complete Christian Bible-based curriculum, Alpha Omega's *Switched-On Schoolhouse* is LIFEPACS GOLD on CD-ROM. The Alpha Omega curriculum is designed as a textbook approach but broken down into ten bite-sized pieces called LIFEPACS. Each LIFEPAC contains all you need for complete instruction: text, exercises, projects, review questions and tests. The exercises contain various activities such as True/False questions, fill-in-the-blank, multiple choice, crossword puzzles, essay questions and others. The main advantages to using the LIFEPAC curriculum are: completely Bible-based, everything you need for one year of work in one package, completely self-paced, and very little teacher prep needed. The CD-ROM offers the valuable advantage to having this all on your computer. The computer also offers multimedia clips and animation, keeps all the records, grades all the tests, and even offers customization for the teacher/parent. As the teacher, you can control the grading curve, the mastery level, the rate of progress and more. When you set the mastery level, you determine the level of proficiency the student must exhibit before he or she can progress to the next level. The *Language Arts* covers grammar, spelling/vocabulary, literature and creative writing for each grade level. I highly recommend this curriculum for the beginner homeschooler or the harried (e.g. me) homeschooler. To a mom with

eight children, six being homeschooled, this
all-in-one, self-paced and self-instructional
program with automatic grading and scoring
offers a lot of teacher relief. New for 2001:
the ability to print out lessons, quizzes,
tests, answer keys, grade reports, spelling
lists, supply lists for science experiments,
solution keys for upper-grade math (this is
crucial for moms who don't, won't or cannot work out those complex algebra 2 equations – yuck.), and complete scope and
sequence. Call them for a demo CD at 800-
622-3070. You can also contact them online
at www.switched-onschoolhouse.com. You
can download a free math and language arts
placement test online as well.

Here is a chart of the scope and sequence.
You can find a more detailed scope and
sequence at Alpha Omega's web site
(www.switched-onschoolhouse.com).

Switched-On Schoolhouse Scope & Sequence Chart

	3	4	5	6	7	8	9	10	11	12
Bible	Introduction to the Bible	Christian Discipleship	Christian Basics	Bible Survey	Christian Basics II and Life of Christ	Practical Christianity and Church History	New Testament Survey	Old Testament Survey	Doctrine and Application	Essentials for Christian Service
Lang. Arts	Reading and Sentence Building	Word Study: Grammar Skills Composition	Literature Poetry Reports	Reading for a Purpose: Sentences and Poetry	Composition and Literature	Speaking and Writing Skills	Elements of Literature: Structure and Language	Literary Genres: Effective Writing	American Literature: Research and Reports	British Literature: Structure of Language and Poetry
Math	Symbols Multiples Fractions Addition Subtraction Carrying and Borrowing	Multiplication and Division Sequencing Rounding Estimation Charts and Graphs	Plane & Solid Shapes Perimeter Area Fractions Decimals & Probability	Multiplication & Division, Fractions & Decimals Lines Shapes and Formulas	Pre-Algebra Pre- Geometry	Pre-Algebra Pre- Geometry	Algebra I	Geometry	Algebra II	Trigonometry
History & Geo.	U.S. Communities	World Geography	History of the Western Hemisphere	World History and Culture	Social Science Survey	U.S. History	Civics and World Geography	World History	U.S. History	Government and Economics
Science	Plants and Animals	Changes in Matter Solar System & Planet Earth	Life Cycles: Balance in Nature	Plant & Animal Behavior Molecular Genetics and Chemical Structure	Earth Science	Physical Science I	Physical Science II	Biology	Chemistry	Physics

ART & MUSIC

Artrageous 2.0

Learning Company
Ages: 8-up   Street price $24
Subject(s): art theory, art technique, and art appreciation
Skills needed: reading helpful but not required
System Req: WIN 95/98: P90/8MB
MAC: 040/8MB

This interactive exploration of the world of art is a comprehensive, historical resource that makes learning about art FUN and EASY. Inside the program are five virtual 3D worlds that let you learn, investigate, and experiment with color, light, perspective, composition, and life of art. Within these worlds, you can examine the history, techniques, playing with and other attributes. Many works of art and artists are used within each topic to fully explain, in layman's terms, art theory, history, and technique. There are over 20 activities and games to play with the art to visually understand these concepts. The tone is traditional art theory with simple yet thorough explanations. There is a database of art information presented encyclopedia-like and an index of the paintings, activities, and painter biographies. The music is mostly pretty classical music with a few jazzy pieces thrown in. The introduction and exit has some rock music. I found the music in the main program to be a pleasant accompaniment overall. Recommended use: If you are interested in learning art theory, this is an excellent CD to own. Caution: There were dozens of paintings included on the CD; I looked at most of them. I saw three with nudity (e.g. *Creation of Adam* by Michelangelo) but they are within the context of the material presented. This program has been discontin-

ued but can still be found in some bundles of software. Currently it is in the package *Princeton Review: Middle School Edge.*

Classical Music

TOPICS Entertainment (formerly CounterTop Software)
Ages: 10-up   Street price $30
Subject(s): music
Skills needed: reading
System Req: WIN 95/98: 486/16MB
MAC: N/A

This five CD collection is full of information about great classical composers and their music. Two of the CDs are packed with information about Chopin and Mozart; another is The Hutchinson Encyclopedia of Music. All the CDs are full of music clips, photos, information, recommended music listening lists and more. Built into the program are quizzes, timelines and an extensive music glossary. This program can work as a high school music course. This package is a great resource for the classical music lover in the house.

Jumpstart Artist

Knowledge Adventure
Ages: 4-7   Street price $18
Subject(s): art, drawing, animation
Skills needed: reading helpful but not required

Children visit an art fair where they can access five enjoyable and educational art games. These activities are cleverly designed to teach even the youngest child about art concepts. Different games teach about light, form, antiquities, color, hue and many more concepts. In one activity, kids can make their own artwork and make them come to life. After completing an activity, kids can collect pieces of a carnival rides for the art fair. The onscreen guide offers 52 (one for each week) additional non-computer art activities making this program great to use as a full-fledged kindergarten or first grade art curriculum. Teacher suggestions include making potatoes prints, puppet shows, quilts, nature blocks and many more. Also included is a draw and paint area with all kinds of "virtual" messy kindergarten materials; paint, tissue paper, chalk, needle-point patterns and much more. Kids can draw and create almost anything in this creative program.

Kid Pix Deluxe 3rd Edition

Learning Company
Ages: 3-up   Street price $28
Subject(s): art, drawing, animation
Skills needed: reading helpful but not required

This completely revamped CD-ROM version of *Kid Pix* has LOTS more features. Includes text-to-speech, voice painting-paint colorful images using the tone and pitch of your voice, photo-editing, print posters, pictures, storybooks and comic books. Kid Pix is a wonderful painting and drawing program that gives the child dozens of tools to explore their creativity. Includes multimedia and animation tools. Excellent electronic substitute for paint, crayons, glue, construction paper, scissors, markers, and all those other messy "creativity" supplies. This new version is almost too much power for some kids. Packed with so many options and features, children are a bit overwhelmed at first. One reviewer referred to it as "Kid Pix on drugs." You may want to track down the older version of this program, *Kid Pix Studio Deluxe*. It will be easier to use and cheaper. This will captivate all ages for hours. Highly recommended. CAUTION: Has a few magical and alien still life pictures.

Making Music

Forest Technologies
Ages: 4-12   Street price $29
subject(s): music appreciation
Skills needed: mouse
System Req: WIN 3.1/95/98
486SX25/8MB
MAC: 030(25MHz)/8MB
Music: no rock unless you create it.

This program provides an exploratory composing space for children. Imagine an infinitely manipulatable (is that a word?) *Kid Pix* of music. Designed by composer, this program presents the components of music visually and aurally, so children can use all their senses in learning about music. Features include melody and rhythm maker; alter pitch and rhythm- hear how they sound separately and together; building blocks-transpose or change six simple tunes to learn about structure and repetition; flip book- combine three elements: melody, rhythm, and instrumentation from a musical flip book; games that can be played using the child's compositions.

Music Ace

Harmonic Vision
Ages: 8-up   Street price $40
Subject(s): music fundamentals, reading music, key signatures, pitch, etc.
Skills needed: reading
System Req: WIN 3.1/95/98 486/8MB
MAC: 030/8MB

A very thorough and engaging music tutorial designed to teach music fundamentals in a painless manner. Containing 24 tutorials or lessons, this program has musical games, singing and smiling notes, and a musical creation feature called the *Music Doodle Pad* (the *Music Doodle Pad* can be purchased separately). Topics covered include: staff & keyboard relationship, pitch identification, note reading, listening skills, sharps

ART & MUSIC

& flats, intro to key signature, keyboard basics, major scales, octaves, treble, bass & grand staff, whole & half steps. This program is one of Mary Pride's favorites and highly recommended by many reviewers. It is a complete beginning music curriculum.

Music Ace 2

Harmonic Vision

Ages: 8-up   Street price $40

Subject(s): music fundamentals, reading music, key signatures, pitch, etc.

Skills needed: reading

System Req: WIN 95/98: 486 66MHz/32MB

MAC: PMac/32MB

Music Ace 2 picks up where *Music Ace* leaves off. This program contains 24 engaging, self-paced lessons that accelerate development of fundamental music skills and music theory. Lessons cover: standard notation, tempo, comparing rhythms, rhythmic dictation, echoing, counting, quarter notes, eighth notes, rests, measures, all key signatures, hearing melodies, melodic contour, syncopation, half notes & ties, dotted quarter notes, sixteenth notes, rhythmic composition, time signature, major & minor scales, intro to intervals, three sounds per beat, 6/8 time, intro to harmony, ear training, composing melodies, distinguishing melodies & harmonies.

Musicware Piano

Musicware Inc

Ages: 9-up   Street price $78

Subject(s): music fundamentals, piano

Skills needed: reading

System Req: WIN 3.1/95/98 486/8MB

This piano tutorial is similar to *Piano Discovery* in scope but more straightforward and structured in approach. Some of the more serious piano teachers prefer its more serious, academic approach to teaching piano. Lesson screens offer a good balance of visual/aural/tactile activities with uncluttered screens, large words and notes, and attractive colors. Includes keyboard practice tips, glossary of music terms, immediate feedback and automatic review of un-mastered skills. Skills taught include learning the keyboard, positioning the hands, the concept of rhythm, music theory, notation, ear training, and sight-reading. Package includes software that covers approximately 1 year with about 250 lessons. You can purchase additional years of piano lessons for $79 each. I recommend this program over *Piano Discovery* for the more serious student.

Piano Discovery Version 3

(Formerly known as the MIRACLE PIANO TEACHING SYSTEM)

Jump Music

Ages 7-up   Street price $48

With MIDI keyboard $188 • Year 2 and 3 $48 each

Subject(s): piano

Skills needed: Reading helpful not essential if the teacher helps

System Req: WIN 3.1/95/98: PI/16MB

MAC: 040/16MB

A complete piano tutoring system designed by a concert pianist from Julliard School of Music. Artificial intelligence figures out which exercises you need to practice and which you have mastered. By the end of the course you will have completed one year of music lessons for just a fraction of the cost of regular music lessons. Skills taught include sight-reading, rhythm, chords and more. Includes 60 songs — no rock and roll — 900 individually narrated lessons, and 70 video demonstrations. You can buy it with a basic MIDI keyboard, but we recommend that you go out and get your own MIDI compatible keyboard. If you would like more specifics on the *Piano Discovery*, check out their web site at www.jumpmusic.com. You can download additional songs and lessons at this web site as well. You can also upgrade your version 2.0 for a fee. Note: You can use the *Piano Discovery* software with a *Miracle Piano* keyboard. Highly recommended for the younger student or less serious piano student. Note: As I write this, the publisher of *Piano Discovery* (Jump Music) has gone out of business. However, it is most likely that some other company will buy the rights to the *Piano Discovery* software and continue to distribute it.

Piano Discovery For Kids

Jump Music
Ages 5-10   Street price $48
Subject(s): piano
Skills needed: Reading helpful not essential
if the teacher helps
System Req: WIN 3.1/95/98 486/8MB
MAC: 040/8MB

This children's version of *Piano Discovery*, hosted by the Animaniacs, is similar in design and content but has a more kid friendly appeal. The curriculum is especially tailored to teach basic music theory concepts more slowly and with more interactive feedback. Artificial intelligence figures out which exercises you need to practice and which you have mastered. By the end of the course you will have completed one year of music lessons for just a fraction of the cost of regular music lessons. Skills taught include correct posture and hand position, sight-reading, rhythm, chords and more. Includes 33 songs- (one pop song and 4 Animaniacs' songs) 450 individually narrated lessons, and 70 video demonstrations. The PC version comes with a small keyboard overlay that goes right over your QWERTY keyboard, but we recommend

that you go out and get your own MIDI compatible keyboard. If you would like more specifics on the Piano Discovery, check out their web site at www.jumpmusic.com. Note: You can use the *Piano Discovery* software with a *Miracle Piano* keyboard. Note: As I write this, the publisher of *Piano Discovery* (Jump Music) has gone out of business. However, it is most likely that some other company will buy the rights to the *Piano Discovery* software and continue to distribute it.

ART & MUSIC

SIMULATIONS & GAMES

3-D Ultra Lionel Traintown

Knowledge Adventure

Ages 7-up   Street price $20

Skills needed: mouse

System Req: WIN 95/98:

PI/120MHz/16MB

MAC N/A

This new train simulation is a cross between SimCity 3000 and Incredible Machine in design and format. But in this program, you get to design and lay out train tracks, settings, and other details. The graphics and sounds are very realistic and detailed and a lot of fun to manipulate. Also include are 72 challenges in which you must guide a speeding train through a maze of switches, bridges, cars, and other obstacles so you can deliver Christmas presents, or just to keep traffic flowing. Kids have a blast playing the challenges but they don't realize they are practicing spatial skills, logic, thinking skills and programming concepts. This program is intuitive and easy to use and also has six levels of difficulty so younger and older kids can play. If you have a train fan, this is the program to get.

Babyz

Learning Company

Ages 5-up   Street price $19

Subject(s): logic, critical thinking, childcare

Skills needed: reading, mouse

System Req: WIN 95/98: PI/90/16MB

MAC: N/A

I don't know about your family but everyone in my family just absolutely loves babies. My kids couldn't wait for their new baby brother to be born. SO we just had to check out this virtual childcare program. Pick a baby, or two, or three, choose their clothes and then you take care of them. My kids loved taking care of all their virtual babies; rocking them when they were tired, feeding them when they were hungry, changing them when they were messy, etc. It was fun to hear them play the game because all you hear is cooing and gooing and little baby laughs and an occasional cry. You can set up the program as a screen saver as well. Then little babies float or crawl across your screen cooing and gooing. Just adorable. Sorry, I just love babies. If more of us loved babies as blessings from God, maybe there would be less abortion. Hmmm.

Backyard Baseball

Humongous Entertainment

Ages: 6-12

Subject(s): baseball, strategy

Skills needed: mouse, reading

System Req: WIN 95/98: P166/16MB

MAC PMac/133/16MB

In this kid-sized baseball simulation, kids get to choose their teams play a realistic game of baseball complete with crowd noise and outfield chatter. My kids really enjoyed playing this game even though they never play baseball in real life. Choose your players, strategy, batting order, positions, and colors. In this new 2001 edition, you can even choose one of 31 major league players such as Cal Ripken Jr. Features include the ability to choose pitches, when to swing and how hard. Although this program had only marginal educational value, it was a lot of fun and the young (and old) baseball enthusiasts in your home would love it as a gift. Humongous also makes *Backyard Soccer* and *Backyard Football*. Caution: some of the infield chatter can be a bit rude but you can turn it off.

Civilization II: Test of Time

Hasbro Interactive
Ages: 10-up
Subject(s): history, social studies, strategy
Skills needed: mouse, reading
System Req: WIN 95/98: PI/90/16MB

In this simulation game, players design a civilization and control it. They can choose a democracy or a dictatorship, negotiate with other countries, set tax rates, acquire technology, form a military, and conquer other countries. By utilizing military and political strategy, players try to gain control of the entire world. With realistic graphics and sound, this game is both fun and entertaining. There is a bit of violence when armies kill off each other but no gratuitous bloodshed. I recommend it for the older kids only (14+) because it was difficult for my younger kids and they really missed the point of the whole game. I have talked to other parents who say when their kids play this game and think the strategy through, they find the best way to play the game is to avoid war and seek peace. Features include a variety of settings (worlds) to choose from, trade and combat systems, a variety of tools to build villages, churches, and a military. Caution: In addition to the regular worlds (Europe, Greece, Mediterranean, Pacific) to choose from, there is science fiction (futuristic) worlds and fantasy (magical) worlds.

Kid Cad

Knowledge Adventure
Ages: 6-up   Street price $19
Subject(s): creativity
Skills needed: reading helpful but not required
System Req: WIN 95/98: P90/8MB
MAC: 040/8MB

Think of this as Lego's for your computer. Build your own 3-D houses (or any other structure you can imagine) complete with interiors, yards, furniture, and fixtures, decorations-even people, pets and plants. Pick your colors. Pick your materials. Pick where you want to live. But best of all, nothing to pick up (or step on.) Not "purely educational", but definitely pure fun. Hard to find.

Return of the Incredible Machine: Contraptions

Knowledge Adventure
Ages 7-up   Street price $30
Skills needed: mouse
System Req: WIN 95/98/2000: PI/90+/32+MB
MAC: SYS 8.5.1 PMac/8MB

This puzzle game challenges children to build Rube Goldberg-style contraptions by using gravity, heavy objects, mouse-wheel generators and other outrageous objects. The program opens with the option of either freeform building or choosing one of over 250 puzzles to solve. This new edition has added even more items and gadgets in the workshop. In contrast to older versions, this new version has more physics and mechanical engineering concepts built into the puzzles and 128 parts. Some of these parts include rockets, gears, batteries, light bulbs, alligators, candles, nitroglycerin, springs and more. Altogether the program gives kids the tools to create their own inventions or experiment with physics concepts. Best used for demonstrating mechanics and physics concepts during school time but you will catch your kids playing this one all on their own. Not wholly educational but a lot of wholesome fun. The older edition: *The Incredible Machine 3.0* is very good too.

SIMULATIONS & GAMES

SimCity 3000

Electronic Arts/Maxis
Ages 8-up   Street price $19
Subject(s): city planning
Skills needed: mouse, reading
System Req: WIN 95/98: PII/32MB
MAC: PMac/32MB

Design and build your own city; fight crime, control budgets, mass transit, etc. Even design your own landscape. Teaches child awareness of how government affects people's lives and choices. "You know Dad, you raise the taxes and the people move away." Too bad the real politicians can't figure that out. Even though children love this, it's still educational. This version has more elaborate features, more complex scenarios, more hands-on control, and better graphics (this one is in 3D.). Design your city with added features like highways, subways, rail lines, power plants (10 different types.), water, sewer, parks, zoos, stadiums, and more.

SimFarm

Electronic Arts/Maxis
Ages 4-up   Street price $15
Subject(s): farming
Skills needed: mouse, reading helpful to be a success
System Req: WIN 3.1/95/98 486/8MB
MAC: 030/8MB

Anyone with any interest in farming or business will love it — and even some that don't. All my children love to play it: from the 4 year old who builds a farm and then has a tornado go through it, to my 14 year old daughter who lives out a fantasy by running a horse farm. SimFarm is a realistic simulation of day-to-day details of farming. Design, lay out, and plant your own farm. Choose what crop you want to raise: wheat, strawberries, corn, more. Raise livestock. Deal with nature and all the factors of a

farm. Pay taxes and borrow money (if you dare.) How much fertilizer and pesticide is too little or too much? Should you sell now on the futures market or wait until harvest? Buy it and find out! Recommended use: GIFT, business simulation and/or practice, unit study supplement.

SimPark

See review under Science.

SimTower

Electronic Arts/Maxis
Ages 7-up   Street price $19
Subject(s): city planning
Skills needed: mouse, reading
System Req: WIN 3.1/95/98 486/8MB
MAC: 030/8MB

Another program in the tradition of SimCity This time you are the landlord and owner of a building. If you properly layout future expansion and you satisfy the tenants, you could be on your way to a skyscraper containing shops, restaurants, services, and apartments. We see the program's biggest pluses are things like planning, problem solving, deducing cause and effect, business skills, and just plain fun. Also a great real-life business simulation.

SimTown

Electronic Arts/Maxis
Ages 7-up   Street price $24
Subject(s): city planning
Skills needed: mouse, reading
System Req: WIN 3.1/95/98 486/8MB
MAC: 030/8MB

Another city-building program in the tradition of *SimCity*. This cute, cartoonish program is for younger children. Caution: one of the buildings you can place in your city is a haunted house, but program can be played without it. It just has some bats flying around and every once in a while, a ghost peeks out the window.

Spyfox in Dry Cereal

Humongous Entertainment
Ages 6-12   Street price $19
Subject(s): logic, critical thinking
Skills needed: reading, mouse
System Req: WIN 3.1/95/98 486/8MB
MAC: 040/8MB

All my children loved playing this game together. Not a lot of pure educational value but great fun. Spy Fox is a secret agent ala James Bond/Maxwell Smart. He is clever and debonair and is out to catch the head bad guy. This villain has stolen all the cows hence the lack of milk, which of course, causes dry cereal. The bad guy wants everyone to drink goat milk and his new slogan is "Goat milk?" The child must go from place to place looking for clues as to the whereabouts of all the cows in the world. Along the way, Spy Fox gets to use some really cool gadgets like a laser toothbrush and x-ray gum. If you are looking for a wholesome mystery game the whole family can play, Spy Fox is a great choice. My only caution: one time I saw Spy Fox tell a white lie to accomplish his mission. But then again, he is a spy. This would be a good chance to discuss if it is ever "right" to lie for a good purpose.

Spyfox in Some Assembly Required

Humongous Entertainment
Ages 5-10   Street price $19
Subject(s): logic, critical thinking
Skills needed: reading, mouse
System Req: WIN 3.1/95/98 486/8MB
MAC: 040/8MB

All my children loved playing this game together. Not a lot of pure educational value but great fun. Spy Fox is a secret agent ala James Bond/Maxwell Smart. He is clever and debonair and is out to stop an evil robot in this sequel to *Dry Cereal*. The robot's off switch is located at the World's Fair and Spy Fox must find it. Along the way he finds clues and uses more of these great gadgets. He meets unusual characters and the tone is very humorous and wacky. My kids also solved this one together and learned to work cooperatively. This *Spy Fox* was a little easier than the first, and both would be hard for a five year old. I recommend it for ages 6 and up. Fun gift for the whole family.

COLLEGE PREP & LIFE SKILLS

Driver's Ed '99

Sierra
Ages: 16-18   Street price $15
Subject(s): driver's education course
Skills needed: reading
System Req: WIN 95/98: PI/90/16MB

This program was a big hit at our house with the younger kids but its primary purpose is to be a full-fledged driving course for your high schooler. That's just what my 15-year-old daughter used it for. With 70 extensive lessons and thousands of real-life test questions, you'll learn driving preparation, defensive driving skills and traffic laws for all 50 states, plus the District of Columbia. After completing the lessons, you receive a virtual permit to drive through Virtual City. The driving can be done with a mouse and keyboard but a real-life steering wheel attachment for your PC is much more realistic and I recommend getting one. My daughter completed the course and went on to take a regular driver's ed course at a nearby high school (Yes, a public school. Oh, the horror of it.) She passed the course with the highest grade in the class, A+. The course itself is enough prep on its own to get most students to the permit-test taking phase but some students may need more instruction from a qualified instructor. (Check with your own state's laws.)

Princeton Review: Inside the PSAT/SAT 2000

Learning Company
Ages: 16-18   Street price $30
Subject(s): prep for SAT
Skills needed: finished 10th grade work
System Req: WIN 95/98: PI/16MB
MAC: PMac/16MB

Although not everyone will appreciate the irreverent and disrespectful tone in the opening scenes and the main menu, the content of this SAT prep course is excellent and mild mannered. Using live videos of young adults, this course presents tips, tricks and inside info on the SAT testing process and the traditional practice curriculum of vocabulary and math. Includes 4 full length, real life SAT tests to get a real feel for the test, diagnostics to pinpoint your weaknesses, and games to practice your speed and testing skill. I wish I had this program before I took the test. Caution: Intro and main menu features a shaved-headed girl smoking, then a teacher smoking and a student spray-painting a rude saying on a wall. He doesn't complete it and the next scene shows him scrubbing it off—he apparently gets caught.

Higher Score Guaranteed on the SAT/ACT/PSAT 2001

Encore Software/Kaplan
Ages: 16-18   Street price $30
Subject(s): prep for SAT/ACT/PSAT
Skills needed: finished 10th grade work
System Req: WIN 95/98: PI/90/16MB
MAC: PMac/24MB

This test preparation course is based on the long successful Kaplan teaching strategies. Once carried by Knowledge Adventure, Encore Software now distributes it. Pre-testing creates a customized learning package where the lessons and questions are tailored to eliminate your weaknesses and strengthen overall test-taking ability. Has built-in analysis of your performance by question type, topic, technique, and more. Teaches you test-taking strategies such as pacing yourself, when to guess, how to eliminate choices, etc. With five full-length SAT simulated tests and two full-length ACT simulated tests with over 2700 test questions, and four regular paper tests. Games are included to give some fun to the test practice and the program is well designed with a search engine, flash cards, and a print-and-study vocabulary list. This is the best SAT prep package I have seen. The deluxe edition has a third CD with college (*Newsweek Guide to Colleges*) and financial aid information (*Paying for School*). Although the format is highly explanatory and enjoyable, some of the music is annoying. Highly recommended.

BIBLE

Beginner's Bible Series

Baker Book House
AGES 3-8   Street price $12
Subject(s): Bible stories
Skills needed: mouse
System Req: WIN 95/98: PI/90/16MB
MAC: PMac/16MB
Noah's Ark Activity Center
Birth of Jesus Activity Center
The Story of Easter

Finally, some fun programs based on Christian themes. The *Activity Center* titles include many Bible-based activities including matching programs, jigsaw puzzles, sing-along songs, mazes, trivia questions, coloring pages and music. You can help Noah prepare for the flood or aid an angel preparing for the arrival of baby Jesus. The artwork is based on the *Beginner's Bible* series and kids love playing these interactive games with these family favorite characters.

BibleLand.com

Chariot Victor Publishing
AGES 6-up   Street price $12
Subject(s): Bible stories
Skills needed: mouse, reading
System Req: WIN 3.1/95/98: 486/16MB
MAC: 030/16MB

The characters of the Bible have now created their own Internet. In this interactive resource/game, all the famous people of the Bible have their own web site. Surf the holy virtual web while learning about each of your favorite people and places but never really go online. For example, type in Joseph. Go to his web site, read all about his life and times and then click on a link to Egypt or Pharoah or his father Jacob. Lots of info built into the program makes it easy for kids to learn a lot while having fun.

Gives kids a feel for how the Internet works without having to face the real Internet.

Bible Builder

Alpha Omega Publications
AGES 7-ADULT   Street price $12
Subject(s): Bible trivia, maps, memory verses
Skills needed: mouse, reading
System Req: DOS: 386/4MB (will run under WIN95/98)

If we can only sell you two programs, this is one of them (Kid Desk is the other). The best Bible trivia/Bible quiz program we've seen. Topics covered include Bible stories, Bible verses, Bible facts, teachings and parables of Jesus, Proverbs, "Name that Hymn" and more. This content-rich Bible program has six difficulty levels, 700+ Bible references, 50 animated Bible scenes, and 33 actual hymns. Can even select the version of Bible your family prefers: KJV, NIV, RSV or Living Bible. If your family enjoys the Bible, they will love this "game". This program is also good as a reading comprehension drill. If you would like to see a Macintosh version of this program, call the company at 602-438-2717 and let them know. They seem to have the attitude that there aren't enough Mac users out there who would buy it (reminds me of someone saying that the Bible only needs to be printed in English.) Maybe if enough of you call, they might get the message this should be made for the Mac as well.

Bible Library

Ages 12-up   Street price $29
Subject(s): Bible study
Skills needed: mouse
System Req: 486SX/8MB

This all-inconclusive Bible library includes 9 versions of the Bible, 2 language dictionaries, 3 word study books, 6 dictionaries and references, 2 commentaries, 1 hymn stories book, and 2500 sermon outlines.

Search globally for a word or phrase or search each work individually. This program makes a great Bible study tool.

Daniel and the Lion's Den

Learning Company
Ages 3-7   Street price $18
Subject(s): Bible story
Skills needed: mouse
System Req: 486SX/8MB
MAC: 030/8MB

An interactive story of Daniel in the *Living Books* style. Each page of the "book" has an array of animated surprises and original music. Fairly accurate. Living Bible type of storyline. Nice, Godly alternative to secular programs of a similar nature.

Family Bible Challenge

Chariot Victor
Ages 5-up   Street price $28
Subject(s): Bible trivia, maps, memory verses
Skills Needed: mouse
System Req. 486SX33/8MB
030(33Mhz)/8MB

Great new Bible "trivia" game where the trivia is not trivial. This program is designed to quiz in 6 different categories, including Old Testament, New Testament, places, objects and events, numbers or general. Three types of games: play against the computer or other players in a board game, or test your memory with the Memory Match-up Game. "Read-to-me" option allows even nonreaders to have questions and answers read to them by the computer as they follow along. Over 1000 Bible-based questions. A close runner-up to *Bible Builder* as our top Bible game pick.

Family Bible Collection

Encore Software
Ages: 10-up   Street price $35
Skills taught: Bible resource
Skills needed: reading
System Req: WIN 3.1/95/98:
486DX/50MHz/8MB
MAC: N/A

Package contains *Bible Builder, Children's Bible Stories, Bible Clip Art, The Bible Library, Jerusalem* (a basic program about Jerusalem and its history. But it is not as good as *Pathways Through Jerusalem.)* Great deal for the money.

Life of Christ

Discovery Software
Ages: 10-up   Street price $35
Skills taught: life of Christ
Skills needed: reading
System Req: WIN 3.1/95/98 486/8MB
MAC: 030/8MB

(This next review is courtesy of Neil MacQueen of Sunday School Software (www.sundaysoftware.com), an expert reviewer of Bible software.)

Discovery's *Life of Christ* CD has 40 multi-media lessons on the Life of Jesus from his birth to his resurrection. Each presentation is about 8 minutes long. They are very well done, ecumenical, and presented with older elementary and youth in mind. At the end of each lesson presentation, students (ages 9 to adult) are presented with a six question quizzes about what they just saw and heard. Answering 5 or 6 correctly rewards the student with an answer to question from their cluebook which they are trying to fill. Some cluebook answers can only be found while exploring the richly detailed 3-D MYST-like castle (*MYST is the most popular secular CD game in history*). Students search castle rooms for clues. Rooms can only be opened by answering questions about Christ's life

from the presentations. This CD blends great content and game play in a very creative way. As students progress through the lessons (in what ever order you choose) they are awarded certificates and parts of a combination code which when complete will allow them to unlock two mystery chests in Professor Newheart's study. Professor Newheart's study is the interactive menu screen from which students can elect to go into the 40 lessons, the castle, cluebook, a variety of books of the Bible games, and extra Bible trivia quizzes. The professor's filing cabinet can be opened revealing a variety of video clips, slides and narration of places in Israel.

- Lessons can be used in any order.
- The theology of the CD is straight down the middle.
- This is the first CD we've seen (and liked) that works like its own curriculum.
- Fun to play
- Tracks individual users and rewards them as they progress
- The program allows for multiple users.

Grades 3 through 12, young adults, and yes, even adults will enjoy playing through this program. *Life of Christ* was designed especially with young teens in mind, but can easily be stretched downward.

Note from the authors: If you buy this great program from Sunday School Software (www.sundaysoftware.com) they will include, at no extra charge, access to their 19 page free teaching outline, teaching tips and answers to all 60 clues (not provided by the manufacturer).

Online Bible

Ages 5-up   Street price $ (free.)
Subject(s): Bible study
Skills Needed: mouse
System Req. WIN 95/98 486DX/8MB
MAC 040/8MB

The *Online Bible* is a popular "Bible on computer" program. Includes the complete *King James Bible* text (and *ASV* and *RSV*), *Strong's* numbers, cross reference, Greek & Hebrew lexicon, *Treasury of Scripture Knowledge, Thompson Chain Reference, Matthew Henry's Commentary, Easton's Bible Dictionary*, cross reference, foreign translations, and much more. Has wonderful search function. Many consider the Macintosh version to be the best "Bible on computer" program available. You may download the *Online Bible Starter Package* free of charge from their web site (www.onlinebible.org). You can't find a better deal than that. If you want to order the CD so you have a copy of your own, it runs about $40. If you need additional translations, you need only call with your credit card and then unlock the additional translations right on the CD with an access code.

Pathways Through Jerusalem

Sunday School Software
Ages: 10-up   Street price $45
Skills taught: history of Jerusalem from the Old Testament to today
Skills needed: reading
System Req: WIN 3.1/95/98 486/8MB
MAC: 030/8MB

(This next review is courtesy of Neil MacQueen, an expert reviewer of Bible software.)

Pathways Through Jerusalem is generally acclaimed to be one of the best pieces of religious software ever produced. It was produced in Israel in late 1995 by a team of Israeli software developers for a New York based company named Future Vision. This entertaining 2-CD set contains over 1000 megabytes of terrific VIDEO, AUDIO, ANIMATION, and MUSIC, telling the story of Jerusalem from its founding by King David to modern times. Rich in historical, archaeological and biblical details. A marvelous script full of scholarly information and spiritual insights. Presented in an interactive, witty and often humorous style. Theologically speaking, *Pathways Through Jerusalem* is scholarly and modern without being *dry* about it. This program is being used in Sunday Schools and pastor's studies, adult Bible studies and at home. King David tells the story of his life and the founding of Jerusalem, and the building of the Temple. King Herod tells the story of the Roman period. Empress Helena, Dirk is a riotous English Crusader, Sultan Suleiman, Raphael, Tammar, Azziz and Daniella are your other guides. This program is far more than just a travelogue like other Jerusalem programs. Users have complete control over each pathway through a pop-up control panel that includes a pause button. Throughout each tour, travelers are presented with a number of interactive choices to make including: viewing scripture references, archaeological information, legends and related traditions (often animated), video clips, a searchable database and much more. Each of the nine pathways runs about 30 to 40 minutes in length WITHOUT the users taking the many sidetrips each pathway offers.

(Here is the authors' review.)

This encyclopedia like resource is designed to give you a multimedia, multiple (9) perspectives of the history and cultures of Jerusalem. For example, see the city through King David's eyes as he gives you a guided narrated tour, explaining how the city grew and changed while he was king, what each building and construction purpose was, and more. Find out what King Herod saw when he ruled, use the searchable index to learn more about a topic, check out the timeline to see the relationship between historical events. Caution: includes a Muslim view of the history of Jerusalem. I found this to be a valuable insight as to the future of Jerusalem as it pertains to God's plans, i.e. Revelations. Recommended use: Excellent supplement to Ancient History or Bible History unit study. If you buy it from Sunday School Software (www.sundaysoftware.com), get the teacher and tourist Guide for an additional $12. It is 40 pages and spiral bound for easy classroom use. In addition to a complete outline of all 9 pathways, the Guide contains commentary, devotions, questions, articles, worksheets and example strategies for teaching with *Pathways Through Jerusalem.* In fact, Sunday School Software is probably the only place you can find it. Highly recommended.

PC Memlok 2.1

Memlok

Ages 5-up   Street price $59

Subject(s): memory verses (choose from NIV, NAS, KJV, or NKJ).

Skills Needed: mouse

System Req. WIN 3.1/95/98

486SX33/8MB

A Bible verse memory program, *PC Memlok* was originally designed as a flashcard system (*Memlok*) and the creator made a good program even better by putting it on the computer. All you need for 12 years. 48 topics, 700 verses. This CD includes all the translations but you only pay for one (choose from NIV NAS KJV or NKJ). For an additional $19 each, you can unlock additional translations. (Only $15 if you

order on the Internet) If you own PC Memlok 1.0 version, you can upgrade for only $27. Automatic review system, tracks everyone's verses for life. Easy for everyone to do their own topics & verses. You can compare different translations of the same verse. Or you can print out onto Avery Business cards to carry in your pocket, wallet or purse. Includes a timer to spur you on or control "dawdling" child. *Personal Notes*: a pad to attach personal application/insights. *Practice Pad* to test yourself (you can correct as you go). Phrase-by-phrase learning capability. Flexible reviewing in case of sickness, vacations or choice. 550 quiz questions (Man Says, but God Says) Prepares you to deal scripturally with the world, the flesh and the devil. Color to aid your memory. Every church ought to own one copy of *PC Memlok*. Imagine. Every teacher has access to 550 full-page reproducible pictures for 550 verses for coloring and teaching pages. Print any picture on full page to reproduce for coloring with or without verse on it. *InstaLink* to Memlok website for updates. Scripture memory is the best thing you can have your kids doing every day. Memlok makes it easy! Highly recommended.

Play and Learn Children's Bible Stories

Chariot Victor

Ages 5-up   Street price $18

Subject(s): Bible stories, games, memory verses

Skills Needed: mouse

System Req. WIN 3.1/95/98

486SX33/8MB

MAC: 030(33Mhz)/8MB

Fifty animated Bible stories cover key Bible events at a level children can understand and enjoy. Includes three types of activities. Interactive Bible Stories: children can hear the story read, then click and find the hidden actions, facts, and background information. Storybook: offers children a choice of values — courage, wisdom, kindness — and brings up a Bible story teaching that lesson. Game room: entertaining and educational activities include electronic coloring pages, puzzles, mazes, matching card games- and even a music box which plays sing-along songs. "Read-to-me" option allows even nonreaders to have stories read to them by the computer as they follow along. Nice, Godly alternative to secular programs of a similar nature. This is by far the best "Bible Story" CD available.

Story of Creation

Learning Company
Ages 3-7   Street price $18
Skills needed: mouse
System Req: WIN 3.1/95/98 486SX/8MB 030/8MB

The Story of Creation is an interactive account of creation in the Living Books style. Each page of the "book" has an array of animated surprises and original music. Fairly accurate, Living Bible type of story line. Nice, Godly alternative to secular programs of a similar nature.

Switched-On Schoolhouse Bible

Alpha Omega Publications
Grades 3rd, 4th, 5th, 6th, 7th, 8th, 9th, 10th, 11th, or 12th.
Street price $67 per subject per grade
Subject(s): Language Arts, Math, Social Studies, Science, Bible
Skills needed: reading.
System Req: WIN 3.1/95/98 486DX66+/8MB

A Complete Christian Bible-based curriculum, Alpha Omega's *Switched-On Schoolhouse* is LIFEPACS on CD-ROM. The Alpha Omega curriculum is designed as a textbook approach but broken down into

ten bite-sized pieces called LIFEPACS. Mary Pride recommends the sixth grade Bible course as the best year in the Bible series. Each LIFEPAC contains all you need for complete instruction: text, exercises, projects, review questions and tests. For a complete review, see listing under *Curriculum*.

Section III

Computer Hardware

Chapter 8

HOW TO CHOOSE A COMPUTER
(...without losing your mind)

Before you go out and buy any computer, it is very important that you understand the terms. That way you can be assured that you are getting what you need.

LET'S START BY DEFINING A FEW TERMS (IN **PLAIN** ENGLISH)

CPU or Central Processing Unit: the actual computer chip (microprocessor) or "brain" of the computer. "Pentium" is the brand name of Intel's flagship processor. The importance of this part of the computer can be seen through the hundreds of millions of dollars that Intel has spent on advertising it. You won't see Seagate advertising their latest, greatest, and fastest hard drives on evening sitcoms like Intel does. But a computer does not require a Pentium processor to run. There are other processors too. AMD produces two processors that run all the same software that a Pentium runs, and depending on the configuration, some are even faster. The Athlon chips from AMD are the premium line and the Duron chip is for the economy line. A general rule of thumb when comparing computer processors is that bigger numbers usually mean newer, faster, and costlier. The fastest processors now available run at about 1000 MHz or 1 Giga Hertz. (As units of measurement a Giga is 1 billion and M or Mega is 1 million.) My first IBM-compatible, purchased in 1993, ran at 33 MHz and that was FAST then!

DOS: (also known as MS DOS) This is the name given to the original complicated and cryptic software that ran the earliest PCs. Some of its structure is still found at the core of the current Windows operating systems.

Dot pitch: A technical term describing the size of the tiny dots that make up the image on the computer screen. The size of the dot pitch affects how sharp or fuzzy the images will be. We recommend .29 or smaller (smaller is better).

Gigabyte, Gig. or GB: One thousand Megabytes (see "Megabyte" for more.)

GUI: Graphical User Interface (GUI): That means you see little pictures or symbols (known as "icons" in computer-speak) which represent programs or other information, instead of using the cryptic code names of files like DOS uses. Using icons allows you to be able to point at things and "click" on them to get them to work, instead of needing to remember and type in the cryptic DOS commands. For example, the icon representing a letter file or document may look like a loose-leaf piece of paper, a file containing multiple documents or programs looks like a little manila folder. On the Macintosh, the icon for the trash (where you throw unwanted items on your computer to erase them from memory) looks like a little trash can. The trash symbol on Microsoft Windows is called a politically correct "recycle bin." The computer screen itself is referred to as "the desktop" as if all these folders and documents were just lying on your desk, ready to be opened and used.

Hard Drive or Hard Disk: High-capacity data storage device, the "electronic garage" where you keep your programs and data when not in use. Capacity used to be measured in MB (megabytes). However, with the price of technology dropping so fast, hard drives are now measured in Gigabytes (1000 Megabytes). Program sizes vary dramatically, some programs are less than 1MB and others are over 600MB in size.

You could also think of the hard drive like your kitchen cabinets or closet where you store things. More on this shortly.

Internal RAM: The part of the computer that holds the active information or data being processed by the CPU. The CPU is the electronic "workshop." You could also think of the RAM as being like your kitchen countertops. This is where the work actually gets done.

Megabyte, Meg. or MB: One million bytes; a byte is a unit of data that can hold one character, like "A" or "1". The text from a 250-page book would take up about one MB of storage capacity.

MHz or Megahertz: The speed of the computer; the higher, the faster, the costlier. Anything over 400 MHz is usually sufficient for home use, with much software requiring far less to be able to run.

Monitor: The "T.V." screen part that displays everything. The computer sends information to it via a special cable.

Windows: an operating system or environment (the way you talk to the computer) for the PC that uses the "point to and click the button" GUI capabilities of the mouse, instead of DOS code commands.

WHAT KIND OF COMPUTER SHOULD I BUY?

When we discuss "kinds" of computers, we are not referring to brands of computers, but what type of system runs the programs on the computer. Of all the different types of computers, there are really only two types to consider for home use: Apple's Macintosh and the IBM type. The IBM types are also known as PCs, Wintel (Windows-Intel) or IBM-compatible clones. If you already own a PC type of computer, and you are satisfied with it, you will want to get another PC for your next computer. If you have never owned any computer before, or if you are extremely frustrated with operating your current PC, you might want to at least consider if a Macintosh would be better for you. This might be especially true if you feel a bit "computer-phobic." Please read the Macs vs. Windows section for more insights for determining which would be better for your family, based on your needs and your computer abilities. With that said, the next section will be primarily in the context of a PC, but much of it also applies to Macs as well.

Specific brand recommendations

Choosing from all the IBM/PC clones out there can be very confusing. Performance, configuration, and quality can vary greatly from manufacturer to manufacturer. Brands that have consistently ranked high for performance, reliability, and technical support are Compaq, Hewlett Packard (NOT to be confused with Packard Bell), IBM, and Dell. Gateway is also a fine computer for most home users. (Apple, which of course is not a traditional "PC", consistently rates one of the best in all categories). With different models coming and going, and different specials and promotions being run, it is impossible to recommend one specific brand as the best to buy. Over the last seven years, these brands have usually ranked high, and based on how the companies are run, they should continue to be safe choices in the future.

As for our family, the last three PCs we bought have been from Dell (plus one Macintosh from Apple) and we have been very pleased so far, especially with their extended hours for technical support. As of this writing, Dell offers toll-free 24-hours-a-day, 7-days-a-week free technical support; and barring totally unpredictable events, it is very likely to continue. Extended tech support hours are a very important feature for busy homeschooling families who are using their computer far longer then just standard "business hours." Before you buy ANY computer, you need to know what the manufacturer's technical support hours and policies are. You will also want to know how long the manufacturer's current support hours and policies will be in effect.

Another tip for buying your next computer: of all the people that you know, find the one person who knows the most about computers. Pick his brain for current recommendations. He is likely to know if there is any new, "must-have" computer technology. He is also likely to have a pretty good idea of what companies are currently building the best computers and which brands are having more problems. But beware of the geek (no offense to you computer nerds- you know who you are and we are humbled by your tech knowledge and skill - really!) who offers to build a computer for you. Although your new custom-built computer may run just fine, your buddy may not provide the technical support and warranty service mainstream computer companies can offer.

Computers to avoid

Before I get into more specifics on what to buy, it would be good to cover what NOT to buy. And, before I get into the issues of what computer hardware not to buy, there is a very critical software element that you want make sure that you avoid buying.

Picking the correct version of "Windows."

If you buy an "IBM-compatible PC" then it will come with some version of Microsoft Windows. Microsoft produces basically two versions. A consumer version and a business version.

As of this writing, the business version is Windows 2000. This version is NOT the upgrade from Windows 98, which is the upgrade of Windows 95, which is the upgrade from Windows 3.11. Now, you would think that if you go from naming a product after the year it was released (1995 and 1998) that when you release a new product called Windows 2000, naturally it would be the upgrade from the Windows 98 release. However, if you came to that natural, logical conclusion you would be wrong. Very wrong. That is because Windows 2000 is the upgrade from the version 4.0 of Windows NT. Windows NT is a high-end computer operating system that is more advanced, more memory hungry (both RAM and hard drive memory), and far less compatible with most of the software you want to run. Windows NT (and, hence Windows 2000) was designed strictly with business software in mind. Not games, not educational software, and not much of the software you will want to run in your homeschool.

Now, before you start thinking that it sounds pretty stupid not to work with so many different kinds of software, you need to understand what it WAS designed for. Hospitals will not be running games or phonics drill programs; a large financial institution could care less about flight simulations or multimedia encyclopedias. However, what both of them do demand is the highest level of stability possible and the ease of hooking up to networks, printers, and such. Their computing needs are far, far different then those of your family. If your computer crashes, it can be a royal pain, but not the kind of pain it can be for a hospital and its patients if their computer(s) crash.

You see, the real secret here to this whole computer hardware and software thing is compatibility. Computer compatibility is similar to pregnancy in that it either is or it isn't. Yes or no. Theoretically, if it is compatible it runs. If not compatible, then it's like trying to get light out of a burnt-out light bulb. Probably ain't going to happen. The hardware/software compatibility needs of corporate environments are far different than those of a family, so Microsoft has actually done a very good thing by developing two different types of operating systems to meet the needs of both.

"Why all the fuss?"

By now you might be wondering, why the need to go into all the detail about this? Why is this stuff so important to actually understand? Why not just say "Don't buy Windows 2000, buy Windows Me instead"? (Window Me stands for Windows Millennium Edition, which represents the year 2000 version of Windows 98, and which it WOULD have made more sense to call Windows 2000 instead of Windows Me; but they couldn't because they already called the year 2000 upgrade of version 4.0 of Windows NT 'Windows 2000.' So, since Windows 2000 was already taken by the upgrade of Windows NT, it would naturally make sense to call the year 2000 version of Windows 98 'Windows Me' wouldn't it?

Well, at least it made sense to all the college-educated wizards in the marketing departments who get paid the REALLY big, big bucks to make it clear to the rest of us. But, I digress too much on this.) ANYWAY, back to the question.

By the time you actually need to choose an operating system for your computer, it is very likely that both Windows 2000 and Windows Me will be no more. As of this writing, Microsoft has announced that yet again they are going to be consistently inconsistent. Microsoft has selected a name for the next release of Windows NT, to be released sometime (in theory) the second half of 2001. (I added "in theory" because based on some of Microsoft's track record of predicting release dates, a "second half of 2001" release date could end up being sometime in 2002.) And it won't be called Windows 2001 or Windows 01. Nope. In a move that is true to their inconsistent fashion, the marketing geniuses at Microsoft have been hard at work to come up with another confusing name for the upgrade version Windows 2000. It is called "Windows XP."

Now, I just know you are saying to yourself, "Why, of course, 'XP!' After all, when going from NT to 2000, it only makes sense to go back to a two letter name like 'XP.'" But, then you ask yourself, "Ah, just what exactly does 'XP' stand for, anyway?" In Microsoft's own words, as taken from their press release announcing the new name: "The XP name is short for 'experience,' symbolizing the rich and extended user experiences Windows and Office can offer by embracing Web services that span a broad range of devices." Isn't that sweet? Microsoft wants to help us all embrace the web. However, there are a few subtle points, which they don't really address. The new XP version is the upgrade from the NT ver-

sion previously targeted at businesses and computer professionals. Therefore XP kind of also stands for "eXPerienced users only need apply." Another factor that is actually far more relevant to you and your family's computing needs is the issue of compatibility with existing software. As just mentioned, most of the software (educational and home-use software) that you want to use on a home PC will not work with Windows NT or 2000. I doubt much will be different with Windows XP. So a strong word of caution before you buy any computer with Windows XP loaded on it. Make sure the software you will want to be using is compatible with the operating system of your next computer, before you buy the computer. Right now, we recommend sticking with Windows Me or Windows 98. There are users who may want to stick with Windows 98. For example, when I bought a new laptop in Fall 2000, I had a choice between Windows 98 or Windows Me pre-installed on the computer. I chose Windows 98 because I already had Windows 98 on my full-size desktop and I did not want to hassle with upgrading my "older" (purchased in January 2000) computer. I was also happy with Windows 98. So to ensure compatibility between the two computers, I got Windows 98.

And now, back to our regularly scheduled feature ... Computers to avoid.

Discount brands: Are they worth the savings?

As a general rule the answer is no. In years past, "no-name" brands of computers could potentially save you many hundreds of dollars, but this is no longer true. With prices down to a fraction of what they were a few years back, a 10 to 15% savings doesn't translate to very much actual dollar savings compared to what it used to be. We realize that you want to be frugal and a good steward of your resources, but in the long run you can't afford this type of savings.

The bottom-line if you buy a bargain brand? If you have no problems, then no problem. If you have a problem - well then, you may have a problem. Is that worth saving 10-15%? Keep reading for more.

There are a number of brands that are fine computers, and then there are those brands that are far more likely to be a nightmare. A general rule of thumb is that if you don't recognize the brand name, you probably want to avoid it. The brands with the greatest problems will vary from time to time. So how do you know? The best thing to do before you buy is to do a little research. Go to your local library and look through some of the PC magazines. What you want to be looking for are surveys, reports, and ratings of various models. The ratings usually cover rankings on overall customer support, service, satisfaction and/or reliability. Some reports will also give you the return rate of various brands. The best reports are the ones that do comprehensive rankings of all the brands at once. PC World magazine runs a wonderfully extensive article on these very topics once a year. Get that article first. Then go shopping.

What about those free or really inexpensive computers?

Often we see ads for computers at unbelievable prices, promising something for virtually nothing. But there is a catch. Sign up for three years of Internet service and get up to $400 off your computer purchase. We would recommend staying away from these so-called "deals." Most people we talked to regretted getting locked into a service agreement. If you try to cancel before the end of the term, substantial penalties may apply. If you are locked into an agreement, you cannot change your Internet service if you a) move b) get a new or second computer c) hate the service d) find a better, different, cheaper service e) don't want to spend $25/month for Internet service anymore or e) decide the Internet is not for your family altogether.

The "Grand-daddy" of discount brands

To give you an idea of just how important all this can be, consider the case of Packard Bell (again, not to be confused with Hewlett Packard which is a very good computer company). Packard Bell was incredibly notorious in the computer industry for consistently having some of the lowest prices, but also for having some of the lowest quality. Additionally, Packard Bell had one of the highest return rates in the industry and its technical support was rated as very poor. Virtually no one who knew anything about computers would ever buy a Packard Bell. Now, I realize that in computer years, these next quotes are like ancient history, but they really illustrate the point. Consider these quotes from PC World, Dec. 1995:

"It (Packard Bell) consistently gets negative ratings for service, with its customers among the least likely to return for a second system...Analysts also question the quality of Packard Bell PCs, saying they're less compatible and less reliable than those from competitors such as Compaq, Hewlett-Packard, and IBM."

"...in five consecutive Reliability and Service reports since June 1994 ... PC World readers rated Packard Bell's service as among the "worst" of all firms reported on. (And) reported one of the lowest levels of satisfaction with any company in our report."

So with all this bad press and bad reputation, who would actually buy a Packard Bell computer? Unsuspecting first-time computer buyers and people shopping for the cheapest and "best" deal they could find. It turns out they usually got more than they bargained for. Other inside information came out that Packard Bell was refurbishing returned computers and selling them as new. That's a big no-no in computer retail operations.

In previous personal experiences, whenever I spoke to people who were having problems with their computers or couldn't get a software program to run, I would ask them if their computer was a Packard Bell. Amazingly enough (but not very surprisingly) the answer often was "Yes," they owned a Packard Bell. Furthermore, they would often make a reference to the fact that they will never buy another one, no matter what kind of deal it is.

In other words, people who bought them tended to hate them, and they never made the same mistake twice. How many of those people do you think wished they had spent 10-15% more and bought a better brand?

Now, lest you think I am exaggerating the facts and the circumstances, consider the next fact. Eventually, Packard Bell ran out of first-time suckers, oops, I mean first-time computer buyers, and they went out of business.

It does go without saying, but I will say it anyway to stress the importance, that when you buy your next computer, you want to be buying a brand that will be in business for longer than you own the computer.

What about "homegrown" computers?

I will give you a warning regarding hometown "locally-built" PC companies.

Some can be wonderful but others are a nightmare. One homeschooling mom told me the following story:

She took her computer into the shop because it couldn't run a particular program that it should have been able to run (the computer specifications met all the criteria required by the software). After billing her $150, they reported to her that they could not get the program to run, nor could they figure out why it wouldn't run. Here's the scariest part: they are the ones who built the computer!

As I said, some locally built computers can be wonderful. They might offer absolutely superb technical support. However despite their best efforts, they simply do not have all the resources at their disposal, like a multi-billion dollar IBM or Dell Corporation has. The best engineering and development comes out of the larger companies. Just something to think about if you are considering buying a locally built computer.

One last thing on buying a locally built computer. There is nothing like the advice from a few computer people you might know who have bought computers built by the business you are looking at buying from. If the people you know really know computers well, and they are very happy with their locally built computer, then you probably will be happy too.

As we mentioned earlier, we also recommend staying away from "Joe's Home-Made Computers." He may be your pal or associate, but a PC owner must have easy access to competent and dependable technical support. You will call them often! If you decide to buy a PC, no matter which brand you buy, technical support is critical to successful computing.

WHAT EXACTLY IS RAM AND WHY DOES EVERYONE WANT MORE?

Now, I realize that for those of you (probably most reading this) who have been using a computer a while, you pretty much understand all this. On the other hand, I have spoke to many moms who have used their computer for years, but never fully comprehended it. Since these are such important terms and ideas to understand, I am going to be very simple here for the benefit of those who don't fully understand the concept of what hard drive and RAM memories are, how they work, and how they are different. (For the sake of clarity, I will refer to RAM as "RAM memory" even though RAM stands for Random Access Memory.)

If you don't quite understand the difference between RAM memory and hard drive memory, I'll explain it this way: RAM is like the computer's kitchen countertops (think workspace), and the hard drive is like its kitchen cupboards (think storage). MB (megabyte) is an electronic unit of measurement explaining how big they are.

Here is the scenario: You want to finish typing the letter you started last night. You find the icon that represents the letter that you saved and you "double-click" on it. This is your way of "telling" the computer that you want it to open up that letter. When you created the letter last night, you "saved" it, asking the computer to store it. This allowed you to turn off the computer, go to sleep, wake up, turn the computer back on, and find your letter stored in the permanent (hard drive) memory waiting for you whenever you are ready to finish it (or print it, erase it or whatever else).

Back to the 'opening up the letter' part. This is where the difference between RAM memory and hard drive memory comes in. Here is what happens when you double click on the icon of the letter: The computer takes a "copy" of the original letter that is stored on the hard drive. It then sends that copy into the RAM memory where the "brain" of the computer (the CPU) is able to make whatever changes you want to make to the letter. Putting all this another way…(in plain English). It makes a copy of the letter that is sitting in the cupboard and puts it on the kitchen countertop (the original stays in the cupboard). You then work with the letter on the countertop (RAM). The more RAM you have, the larger your electronic workspace in which to do projects. The type of computer chip (e.g. 486, Pentium) controls how fast the computer is able to do the computer's part of the work.

When you tell the computer to save all your additions to the letter, this is what it does: it makes a copy of the letter that is currently on the countertop and puts it in the cupboard for permanent storage. Unless you tell your computer to change the name of the letter (such as from "Letter to Grandma Kihlstadius" into a new name like "Letter to Grandma Knapp") the computer will replace the letter you started last night (which is currently stored in the hard drive) with the one you just finished. This is a very good thing if you want to keep all the additional things you added to the letter over the last hour. In fact, the best way to work on a document is to save every few minutes as you work. Most word processors now have an auto-save feature that saves your document every so often automatically. Now that a copy has been saved, it will be waiting there for you until you want to make more changes to it, or until you want to delete it from the computer because you just printed it out and mailed it off.

What I am about to explain next is a critical factor in the difference between the two types of memory. When you turn off your computer (or unplug it), everything stored in the cupboards (hard drive) is still there waiting for you the next time you turn it on, just like whatever is on a videotape will still be there if the VCR is turned off. Another similarity between the hard drive memory and a videotape is that even if the VCR is unplugged, or the video is ejected, everything recorded on the videotape will still be there the next time you go to play it.

On the other hand, RAM memory acts much more like the time and date of your VCR (or microwave oven). If you unplug your VCR, the time and date are gone along with all the programming to tape your favorite weekly shows. You have to reset it. As far as a computer, whatever is in the RAM memory is "temporary." Everything in the RAM memory is forever "gone" every time your quit the program you are running, or when the computer is turned off, unless it has been "saved" to the hard drive.

Think of it this way; you spend an hour writing a letter. You walk away from the computer, without having "saved" a copy of it to the hard drive (this in itself is a big mistake. Remember our old adage: "Save early and save often", even if just saving it to the hard drive.). While you are away from the computer, little 18-month-old Junior (or "Juniorette") comes up to your computer and plays with the on/off switch. "Oh what fun! See the monitor flash on and off!" Everything on the hard drive "should" be safe. However, whatever was only in the RAM memory (that 5-page letter you spent the last hour writing) is electronic history. Had you saved the letter, only what you had written since the last time you used the "Save" command would be gone.

Here is another way to think of it. It is as if when you turn off the lights in your kitchen, little robots with laser beams come in, take everything left on the countertop (whatever you didn't save by putting it in the cupboard) and vaporize it. Gone. Permanently erased.

As a general rule of thumb, just like your kitchen cupboards and countertops, you can never have too much space, and it is better to have too much than to have too little. Fortunately, most current computers sold today have plenty of both RAM and hard drive memory.

WHAT SIZE COMPUTER SHOULD I GET AND WHAT WILL IT COST?

You can get the hottest new computer system for less than half of what it would have cost just over two years ago, and it is a lot more powerful! You can buy a very nice mid-level computer set-up for around $900 to $1200. A bare bones system capable of running almost every educational program in this book can be had for less than $600. Moreover if you're thinking of buying a used system, there are even better bargains than that! A beginner used system can be had for less than $100. But buyers beware! See the section on used computers for more information.

On the more pricey side, a top-of-the-line system with all the bells and whistles (128 MB of RAM, 60+GB hard drive, DVD drive, and 1000+ MHz processing chip) will run $1300-1800. However by the time you are ready to buy, they will probably be a lot less than that.

Unlike computers of the not-so-distant past, PCs and Macs are designed not to become obsolete in the near future. There are two main reasons why today's computers are not as likely to become obsolete as fast as computers did in the earlier days of home PCs. For starters, today's Macs and many PCs offer better "upgrade paths". This means that at some point later you can add on or replace — at a moderate price — faster, bigger and newer parts. The second reason has to do with the balance between software and hardware. In the earlier years of personal computing, it was far easier for software programmers to push past the speed and processing limits of that generation's computers. For example, they didn't

have to create too much in the way of fancy graphics to choke most of the top-of-the-line computers of the era, and cause those computers to run at a snail's pace. With today's computers having as much RAM memory and as much megahertz horsepower as they do, it takes an incredible amount of programming to choke it. Putting it another way, technology has reached a point where the speed of today's computers has far outpaced the processing needs of most software. Today's typical home computer now has more speed and memory than the multi-million dollar supercomputer of not too many years ago. (Trivia time. Did you know that a modern toy called a Furby has more computer processing power than the computer that was aboard the Apollo 13 spaceship that went to the moon? Hard to comprehend, isn't it?)

Shopping for a computer

Of all the things to consider, the three most important factors in choosing a computer are storage capacity (both hard drive and RAM memory), speed, and brand. If you are reading this in mid-2002, some of these size and speed recommendations may be outdated. Just keep in mind that these numbers can only go up. Lastly, new technology may come out that changes everything. Unfortunately, only the Lord is omniscient in knowing what lies ahead and you will want to seek additional advice at that time.

HARD DRIVE

When you choose a hard drive, get at least a 20 GB (gigabyte) hard drive. 40 GB is not unreasonable and you will not regret getting a huge hard drive- the cost difference is usually negligible. We finally filled up our 10 GB in about a year, but I have installed literally dozens and dozens of educational software programs on our computer- far more than any normal home user would ever install.

If you are planning to manipulate digital pictures (from either a digital camera or digital video camera), music files, or other storage hogging items, consider at least a 40 GB hard drive. Loading MP3 files (music) onto your computer chews up storage space at an insatiable rate.

Other storage options include installing a Zip or Jazz drive for additional back-up space. These are like diskette drives on steroids offering 100, 250 MB disks for additional storage space. You can fill an unlimited number of disks with overflow from your hard drive. Keep in mind though that this type of storage is used primarily for documents and files, not programs or applications themselves.

MODEMS

If you are planning to spend time on the Internet, your choice of a modem will be important. Almost every computer comes with a V.90 56K (56,000 bps: bits per second) phone modem built in. This number signifies the speed at which data will transfer from your computer through your phone line to the Internet. This type of modem connects through your phone line. At this time, 56K is the fastest this type of modem can go. If you want a faster connection, there are other choices available. Most of these require an additional monthly fee to access this type of connection. Of course, as time passes these options will change and new technology may come out.

ISDN

ISDN stands for Integrated Services Digital Network and runs through your regular phone line. It has an additional charge per month and offers exceptional speed.

This is a transmission method that predates both cable modems and DSL but never fulfilled its promise as a universal digital connection utility. Still, ISDN may be the only high-bandwidth service available to people in some rural areas. Basic-rate ISDN's two 64-Kbps channels and software can be combined into one 128-Kbps path or left as two to allow you to use the phone and be on the Internet simultaneously. You must purchase an ISDN modem ($300) and pay your phone company an additional monthly fee. ($40-$70)

Satellite

Some TV satellite companies are now offering Internet access via a satellite dish attached to your roof. DirecTV offers a dish called DirecPC, which accesses the Internet at 400Kbps speeds downloading but only 56Kbps uploading because you still need a phone line to send the information to the Internet. The costs is about $40/month if you use your own ISP (Internet Service Provider) or $50/month if you use them as your ISP. Upfront costs are about $150, plus $20 s/h, plus installation (about $50). Advantages: high speed, no traffic jams. Disadvantage: Still ties-up a phone line, high price. We use a satellite for our TV signals and sometimes during a rain or snow storm, we will lose the signal. I would think this could be a problem with an Internet signal as well.

Cable

This is what our family uses and we love it. The data is transferred through the cable that supplies your local TV signals. Its advantages are super-high speed (2.5-4 Million bps or Mbps), ease of use and the fact that it does not tie up a phone line. We have instant, ever-ready access to the Internet. The cost, about $40/month, includes our Internet service as well so we don't have to spend additional fees on an ISP. Your PC needs an available slot for an additional Network Interface Card (NIC) or a USB connection for an external interface card. Don't worry if you don't have a card, since the cable company can provide one.

We are also able to hook up our laptop, desktop and Mac to the cable modem via a network router via Ethernet cables so all three computers can be on the Internet simultaneously. No fights over tying up the phone line or whose turn it is. The disadvantages of a cable modem are that you must have cable in your neighborhood and house. (Or have it installed in your house. That runs about $50.) If it is not in your neighborhood, you are just out of luck. You must also spend about $300 additionally on a cable modem (it may be plugged into the back of your computer or installed inside), or pay about $6/month to rent one from the cable company. A cable connection operates much like a telephone party line. As more people in your area get cable modems, there will be more traffic and your access speed can drop, sometimes dramatically. Right now that is not a problem for us.

DSL

DSL stands for Digital Subscriber Line and uses existing phone lines to download data at speeds from 128Kbps to a theoretical maximum of 8Mbps. The digital signal piggybacks on the regular phone signal. The beauty of DSL is that you can still make and receive calls on the same phone line. It has an additional charge per month on top of your regular phone line charges but offers exceptional speed. You must purchase a DSL modem ($200-$300) and pay your phone company an additional monthly fee ($40-$125). Not every neighborhood has DSL available. Call your local phone com-

pany to determine availability.

CAUTIONS

As you move to faster Web connections, you should remember that with an "always on" connection you would most likely have a dedicated broadband address. When you're always connected you don't have to dial in through a modem each time you want to access the Net, but the flip side of this is that you're more vulnerable to unwanted intruders and hackers. To keep your PC and all its information safe you'll want to install personal firewall software. Zone Alarm (www.zonelabs.com) is free for personal use and the more feature-rich Norton Personal Firewall (www.norton.com) is $50. Both programs block unauthorized access and record any break-in attempts.

SPEED

As far as speed is concerned, all current new computer speeds are either really fast or really, really fast. As long as you are buying a new, name brand computer, it should have all the speed you will need for most everyday needs. Most new computers come with at least a 700 MHz processor and this is sufficient for most home users. Again, if you are planning to manipulate digital pictures (from either a digital camera or digital video camera), music files, or other storage-hogging items, consider at least a 900 MHz Pentium III or a Pentium 4. The Pentium 4's are just now (spring 2001) coming on the market, so wait until 2002 when the premium is not so cost-prohibitive.

MONITORS

When picking out a computer monitor, get at least a 15-inch Super-VGA color monitor with a .30 mm dot pitch or smaller, with either a Mac or a PC. Never buy a new one with a "dot pitch" .39 or larger. With the price of monitors having come down so much, the price of a 17-inch monitor is not too much more than the price of a 15-inch monitor. If your budget permits, you should consider spending the difference and getting the bigger size. I really can't remember ever hearing anyone say they wished they had bought a smaller monitor. We got our 19-inch monitor for less than $300 and we really like the extra size. It makes it easier for more kids to crowd in and see what's on the screen. (With eight kids, seven of them computer users, this is a good thing!)

Choosing a Mac is simpler

It all boils down to how much speed and memory you can afford. Most features are standard on all Macs. When buying a Mac, you probably want to buy something that is a model or two up from the bottom. This should give you the most bang-for-the-buck. (More on this in a moment.) You definitely want to stay away from the higher-end machines that are designed more for high-end power users, not home users.

If you have no significant computer background, and you are looking for a computer primarily for home use (personal finances, educational use, online services, word processing, desktop publishing, — i.e. letters, newsletters — or even a home-based business) a Macintosh may be a good choice for you. If you have a specific purpose for needing a PC, or have some background of prior PC usage, you may want a PC.

What about laptops?

In the past choosing a laptop over a desktop was prohibitively expensive. Due to competition and technological advances, laptops now rival desktops in speed and performance and are not that more expensive ($300-$500). Laptops now come fully loaded with CD or DVD drives, modems and disk drives. If you think you need the portability of a laptop, consider buying only a laptop and use it as your desktop at home as well, rather than buying two computers. Laptops come with a port to hook-up an external monitor of any size and jacks to plug in speakers, a full-size keyboard and a mouse. I have also used my laptop to play DVD movies on my TV. When choosing a laptop, a brand name is even more important. Laptops get more abuse than a desktop and need to be durable and of high quality. Our recommended brands for laptops are Toshiba, Dell, IBM, and Sony.

Chapter Nine

More on Choosing a Computer

DAN'S 3 SECRETS WORDS OF:

"HOW TO BUY A COMPUTER THAT WON'T BE OBSOLETE IN TWO YEARS"

When I counsel with homeschoolers buying a computer, I often hear the question: "How soon will this computer become obsolete?" or, as the headline implies, "How can I buy a computer that won't be obsolete in two years?" I will reveal the answer in three simple words that everyone will be able to understand.

But, before I reveal Dan's 3 secret words that *(WARNING: Blatant self-endorsement ahead!)* are *well worth the entire* purchase price of this Guide, I might add, we need to understand what is considered "obsolete."

What is meant by obsolete

There are actually two ways to look at the definition.

What is not obsolete

The first way to look at the definition is to consider what it is "not" obsolete. Whether or not a computer becomes obsolete is not a function of brand or speed. Technically, it may be as slow as molasses in a Minnesota winter, but as long as a computer can run most current programs, it works and cannot be considered "obsolete."

There are sort of two levels to a computer being obsolete. The first sign that a computer might be creeping close to obsolescence is that you have a program that you want to run on it, but it won't. The program requires something your computer either doesn't have or doesn't have "enough" of (like RAM memory). At this point, you have to go through the following decision process:

A. How bad do you need to run this program? Can you live without it? Is there another similar program available that would also meet your needs and can run on you computer? (Probably.)

B. Is all that is needed to get the program to run is a minor upgrade to your computer? (Like more RAM or an update to a new operating system?)

(This brings us to the second, more significant level of a computer being accurately considered obsolete.)

What *is* obsolete

C. Would it require a significant rebuild/upgrade of your computer to get new software to work?

In my experience (and opinion) items A and B two don't necessarily qualify a computer as obsolete. Especially if there are only a small number of programs that you can't run on it. On the other hand, if nearly every new program that comes out (not referring here to all that "recycled" stuff) won't run on your computer, then you really need to determine if you need to do either B or C above. Will most the current titles work if you do a minor upgrade or would it take a major overhaul? For more on that, see the section "Should You Upgrade or Replace?" for more details.

For a typical PC, the reasons for becoming obsolete could be any of the following things: insufficient RAM memory, no sound card, older monitor type, no CD-ROM drive, wrong or outdated operating system, insufficient video RAM, inadequate hard drive, or an older, obsolete microchip processor (such as a 386 or 486 chip). Some of these things can be easily upgraded and some cannot; but all these things cost money to upgrade and will still leave you with the rest of the same old machine.

The same as PCs, as long as a Macintosh can run your software, it works and should not be thought of as obsolete. Because of the nature of how Macintosh computers are made, how the operating system runs, and how programs are written, a Macintosh is much less likely to become obsolete due to insufficient RAM memory or wrong or older versions of the operating system. Since the sound cards and video RAM are standard on all Macintosh computers, these things are almost never a factor in its becoming obsolete.

We have an old Mac that is about five years old. It doesn't run much of all the new fancy software out there but it still runs all the older software that we have; and since we are stocked-up on software that works on this computer, it will virtually never become obsolete. My younger kids have rediscovered all this older software and still use this computer a lot. Some of these titles are my perennial favorites: Sammy's Science House, Busytown, PhonicsTutor, Reader Rabbit and more. The only upgrade we did to this computer was adding a huge hard drive — $150. If I decided to upgrade this computer again, it would almost cost more than a new computer. If I wanted to sell it, it would only fetch about $100 with the monitor! So I hang on to it for the younger kids to use.

Now all this brings use back to the premise of our original issue.

How to buy a computer that won't be obsolete in two years.

And the answer is….a drum roll, please...dddddddddd!

"SPEND MORE MONEY." Yup, that's it. Spend more money. Obviously, if you are on a limited budget, spending more money is not always a viable solution. For you, we have two suggestions:

#1) Spend as much as you CAN afford. Or...

#2) Keep saving and buy a better system later.

Because computer prices drop every 3 to 6 months, not only will you have more money for the next model up, it will probably drop lower than what you were originally planning to spend. Between the price drops and your additional savings, your frugalness and sacrifice should reward you well. The flip side of this is to NEVER borrow to buy a computer. By the time you get it paid off, new computers will be faster, for less money than what you paid (and are still paying.)

If your budget is too limited to buy a new computer, then you are faced with your only option of buying a used computer. Obviously, whatever you buy will become obsolete sooner. However, even if you are thinking of going with a used computer, remember that new computer prices drop almost monthly. If you are a patient and careful shopper, keeping an eye out for when the cheapest current models become discontinued, the clearance price might just fall low enough to meet your budget. If you have to go with a used computer keep in mind the tips in the Used Computers section.

Back to the original issue again. In looking at PC systems, here are some specific suggestions, in order of priority, which will help assure that your new computer lasts the longest before it becomes obsolete someday. (Obviously this is assuming you can afford it.) Keep in mind that these are based on prices and standard technologies available the spring of 2001. Prices will drop as the year passes and goes into 2002 and the entry-level standards will be higher and include more memory. Furthermore, no doubt some new "must-have" technology is bound to come out that almost no one knows about at the time of this writing. (Two potential examples that I do already know about are recordable DVD drives and a special new type of CD called DataPlay that is about the size of a quarter. However, it is still too early to tell if these will be "must-have" features.)

This list is not meant to be all-inclusive, nor is this list going to be accurate for years to come. By the very nature of computer technology it can't be. But is a good starting reference point. Here goes.

#1. Get a computer with a DVD drive.

At the time of this writing, there really isn't much software out on DVD yet, but I predict that will change over time. I think this feature is so important that we have a section written specifically about it in a few pages. See it for more details.

#2. More RAM.

RAM memory is the sort of thing that most computer owners eventually end up adding more of to their computer sooner or later. Unless RAM prices really drop unpredictably at some point in the future, it just makes sense to buy more than you need with the original computer purchase. This is especially true if you are having your computer "custom-built" from someone like Dell where every computer is "built-to-order" based on the specs that you have specified in your order. If they are building the computer for you, you don't have to pay any extra installation charge to have more RAM memory; you just pay for the memory upgrade itself. Also, an added benefit is that the price for extra RAM memory is often cheaper than if you were to buy it later and install it then.

As of this writing, we recommend 96 MB of RAM, and if your budget allows you might want to think about getting 128MB. The main reason for this much is "Microsoft." They are known to be very consistent in having programs that are great memory hogs. The operating systems (Windows) that will run your computer are no exception. Every new version of Windows requires about 50% to 100% more RAM memory than the one before it needed. So whatever version of Windows you upgrade to, it is guaranteed to need more RAM than what is needed now.

#3. Get a bigger hard drive.

At a minimum you need at least 10 gigabyte, but 20+ "gig" is much better. Anything over about 40 gigabytes is probably overkill for nearly all basic home users. Why such big hard drives? Well, there is something about hard drives that makes them fill up with the computer version of electronic clutter faster than your garage; and they tend to be a lot harder to empty out when they get full.

#4. More video RAM.

This is a special kind of RAM memory that is dedicated to assisting the computer in drawing all the fancy graphics on the computer screen. Hey, isn't that one of the fun things that computing is all about? Really cool, 3D-style graphics the likes of which used to require multi-million dollar computers to get enough computing horsepower to generate. And now you are doing it with your home PC! Like I said-COOL! Well, all "coolness" aside, there is some absolutely great software with super educational value that also has very high-end style graphics, and therefore requires a lot of video memory. And every year, the "bar" keeps getting raised higher. So, if you want your computer to be able to run some of the better educational software that comes out two and three or more years from now, then get more video memory than you will need today. Just how much is that? Well, 16 MB of video RAM is no longer considered overkill, but I can't really say that you will want any more than that. Another thing to keep in mind is that if you do get a computer with a DVD drive, you will want to make sure you do have at least 16 MB of video

RAM and a 3D graphics card.

The whole concept of buying a computer that will last the longest before it goes obsolete is to go a little beyond shooting for just a "the-most-bang-for-the-buck" type of computer. It is really hard to say which strategy is best, considering the historic trend of dropping computer prices every year; but it is pretty clear that based on that trend, it is a good idea to stay away from both the bottom end and the top end of computer lines when you buy your next computer. Often, buying the second or third down from the top model provides the best compromise of state-of-the-art features, speed, size, long life, and value.

As much as things are always changing, there is one thing that has always remained true when it comes to buying a computer: buy more computer than you need now (both memory and speed). As your usage grows, so will your needs.

Buying a Macintosh

In looking at Macintosh systems, here are some specific suggestions, in order of priority, which will help to assure your new computer lasts the longest before it becomes obsolete someday. (Obviously, this is assuming you can afford it.)

#1. Get the fastest Power Mac with the largest hard drive in your budget (But not the biggest, fastest available!).

#2. If it doesn't come with at least 96 MB of RAM, upgrade it to at least 96 MB. 128 MB would be better.

That's about it. CD-ROM or DVD drive, video RAM, sound card, and modem are standard features most the Power Mac models. Since Macintoshes tend to handle memory better and more efficiently than PCs, less hard drive memory is required.

What about used computers?

Is it worth saving money by purchasing a used computer if you can't get any new software? No it isn't. More on this to come. This is totally different from buying a used car or other used items. Get equipment that will do the job right and will keep up with new software releases for at least a couple of years to come.

When you are coming down to the final decision to buy, just remember Dan's secret three words to preventing premature obsolescence: spend more money. Just remember to keep all this in balance. If you spend over $2000, you are probably paying big premiums for high markup power that is aimed at the high-end, big buck, big budget corporate user—not a homeschooler. I recommend you try keeping it to $2000 or less (including the price of a printer). If you follow these guidelines, you will be the best prepared for making a purchase today that will keep your investment current with the software of the future as long as possible.

Now the WARNING!

That $1000+ computer system that you are looking at (or maybe even just bought!) may be "obsolete" even before two years are up! For a full detailed explanation, see the next section about DVD technology! Don't upgrade your existing computer or buy a new one until you do!

The final purchase

When you are coming down to the final decision to buy, remember this one thing that nearly every computer user agrees on: buy more computer than you need now (both memory and speed). As your usage grows, so will your needs.

Here is another good rule of thumb that has really seemed to hold true over the years: buy the model that is in the middle of the price range. This is what I refer to as getting the most bang-for-the-buck. Stay away from the top-priced models; and don't buy the cheapest model (it will usually be missing something you would want) unless that is all that the budget allows. However, if this is the case, consider waiting a few more months (but don't delay too long). It doesn't take many months before new bigger, faster models will get introduced, the entry-level models discontinued, and today's mid-level models discounted to become the new entry-level model.

I hope I've helped you better understand computers and their differences; and helped you toward some wiser decisions!

DVD: TOMORROW'S "MUST HAVE" TECHNOLOGY

After spending a couple of thousand dollars or more on a new computer system, the last thing you want to read in a computer magazine is a cover article on the next "must have" computer technology that your "just bought" machine doesn't have. Digital Video Disk (DVD) is that technology. Ever found yourself saying, "If I had only known…"? Well, this time you will know.

But first, just what is DVD?

Digital Video Disk is the next generation of CD-ROM technology.

It's like CD-ROMs on steroids! It uses digital technology for crisper, faster, more compressed transfers of data and video images. It uses the same technology as DVD movies, which are quickly replacing VHS tapes, just like CDs replaced records. For some of the same reasons that CDs replaced records, DVDs are replacing current video technology – longer recordings and better quality. These same benefits are why DVD will replace CDs in many areas of computer software as well.

Because of this new technology, just like DVD has done with VHS, DVD will bring video quality on your computer that should exceed today's best VCR/TV systems. Current CD-ROMs are limited to just over 600MB of data per CD. DVDs will store seven to ten times that amount! One of the nice things about DVD drives is they will also be able to read and run all of your current CDs. This means you don't have to worry about losing your investment in your current software that you already have on CD-ROMs.

Better quality, and more of it—but at what price?

DVD technology costs a premium over standard CD-ROM technology, but it is worth it. However, there are some limitations. As of this writing, DVD drives for computers have been out for a few years, but still not received the acceptance they deserve. The technology existed sooner but has been slow coming onto the market. One major delay was due to licensing agreements and standardizing hardware requirements. All the computer manufacturers and software developers needed to agree on compatibility standards. Another delay developed when DVD first became available because most the computers did not have enough "horsepower" to properly handle the additional processing requirements. The long and short of all this means there isn't a whole lot of software available on DVD right now, but we predict that will change over time.

By now you may be asking yourself, "If this computer technology is so great, why hasn't there been better adoption of it?" There have been a number of reasons in addition to those listed above (licensing, standards, and horsepower). One of the biggest is what is known in product marketing as a "chicken-or-the-egg" dilemma. The hypothetical question of "Which came first, the chicken or the egg?" has its own corollary in the business world. (Yes, I know that the whole issue of the chicken-or-the-egg is not doctrinally sound. Allow me to step out of my standard "right-wing-extremist-wacko" persona for a moment to give this explanation from a purely "Capitalist" perspective!) The software companies need a certain "critical mass" of computers with DVD drives out there before they can justify the expense of creating software that takes advantage of the features of DVD technologies. Due to things such as the complexity of photo realistic 3-D graphics and full screen video, DVD technology offers features that push beyond the limits of regular CD storage. As more software companies design better graphics and video into their software, more will turn to DVD as the best media to deliver it. On the flip side of this, if consumers don't see enough super-cool-must-have type software that requires DVDs, then they aren't as likely to feel they need to spend the extra premiums to get DVD for their computers. And in the earliest days of the technology that premium usually ran $700-$1,000 extra in the cost of the computer. This same dilemma exists for most new types of products, not just in the computer industry. However, with the price of DVD drives much lower now, they are becoming much more popular. As such, I expect to start seeing more really cool software coming out in the near future that takes better advantage of the features found only in DVD technology.

Amazingly enough, another reason for the low adoption on DVD technology is actually due to the very same feature that gives DVD its big advantage over CD-ROM storage technology. It is because DVD is such a big electronic storage "bucket" to fill. Think of computer storage like a bucket in which to store the bits and bytes (the "1's" and "0's") that make up the true language that computer programs use to communicate their information and commands. Think of it this way. The "electronic bucket" of a standard computer 3.5" diskette holds the equivalent of 250 pages of text. A CD-ROM can hold around 92,752 pages of text (give or take 10,000 pages or so). Well, a DVD can hold 7 to 10 times the amount of a CD. So if a software program just isn't any larger than what fits on a CD, why bother

putting it on a DVD? This would vastly limit the number of potential machines the program could run on, and thereby extremely limit potential sales and profits. Thus, software companies are currently doing their best to cram what they can onto one CD.

Except for software programs that use massive amounts of either videos or graphics (live-action games, encyclopedias, certain other reference programs, etc.) most programs don't come anywhere near filling up all the available space on current CDs. Like the transition from 3.5" floppy programs, to CD-ROM programs, it will be a while before everything is mainly DVD. The software publishing industry realizes this. They won't be quick to stop making software for the 100,000,000++ computers already with current CD capability. Yes, there will be some fantastic DVD software programs that will hit the market, but we've lived without them this long, so we should be able to live without them for a little bit longer (but not TOO long!!!)

And what about DVD upgrades for your existing machine?

Don't count on it. Most upgrade kits cost $150-$200. That is, if it will even work on your current machine. Due to the high-end video aspects of DVD, many currently owned computers would probably be unable to handle the additional graphics requirements. There will probably be other hardware requirements as well, that will prevent many current computers from effective integration of DVDs. If your computer was built before 1999, it is unlikely to have the system requirements needed to handle DVD. The $150+ upgrade kit will only be the start. You will probably end up doing a major rebuilding of your computer before you are finished, which is not very cost efficient.

Bottom line?

When should you consider adding DVD to your current computer? The answer to these is basically the same as when should you replace your existing computer. When enough of the software programs you need to buy have computer requirements higher than your current computer has. This is even more so when you start finding it difficult to find the software that will run on your existing computer.

If you are already in the market for a computer, as long as you can squeeze it in your budget, you should make sure your next computer has a DVD drive. Odds are you won't need it right away, but eventually it is something you are going to want to have to take advantage of some of the latest-greatest-coolest-must-have software programs in the coming years.

How should all this affect those of you who are thinking of buying a new computer right now?

The answer to this question comes in one of four parts, depending on your situation.

For starters, if you currently have no computer (which is doubtful, considering the fact that you are reading this Guide) then this is what I would advise you: If you can afford a computer with a DVD drive, just get one now. Unless you have no need for a computer, which is doubtful, than you probably have no reason to wait if you can afford it now.

If you have no computer and you can't afford one with a DVD drive yet, you should seriously consider saving some more until you could afford it.

If you have an older computer that can't run most of the new software programs in stores, go ahead, bite the bullet and buy a new computer with DVD. This will allow you to run all the software currently avail-able, and with this new computer, you should have the technology it will take to run the next few generations of software.

This last recommendation is for those of you who already have a half-ways decent computer. If you can still run most the current software, I would say just sit tight. You just might be able to run much of the CD-ROM based software to come out in the few years to come. Any programs that are likely to require greater hardware requirements than today's current entry-level models will probably require DVD technology as well. Wait until you find yourself in that situation I've already covered in which your computer can't run the programs you need, due to your computer's being below the requirements. (However, keep in mind, like I already said, if you can do a minor upgrade to get by, do the upgrade. Don't buy a new computer. More on this shortly.)

Here is another way to look at buying a computer with a DVD drive; you spend $700 on your computer and your neighbors spend $1400 on their computer at the same time you buy yours. Neither of you opts for the DVD option. So next fall you want the new "Captain Bob's Chemist Cadet Quantum Physics Home Study Self-Teaching Ph.D. Course" software program. You find out it only comes on DVD disks. So who's computer became obsolete first? Both did! Your neighbors just have a bigger, better, faster, and more expensive computer that can't run it either (unless, of course, they upgrade to a DVD drive.)

One last thing to keep in mind. When DVDs do become more popular, software stores will start putting all the currently $29-$49 CD-ROM software in the bargain bins to make room for all the hot new DVD titles. More bargains for all of us! ;)

CD-RW

And now, to REALLY get you confused! Do you want or need a CD-RW? Well, first you have to know what one is. A CD-RW is a CD-ROM drive that can also record CDs. The "R" in "CD-RW" stands for "read." This means that it reads and therefore runs all regular CD software just like a regular CD-ROM drive. The "W" stands for "Write." This means that the drive also has the capability to record information onto special kinds of recordable CDs.

Now this begs the question, "If I'm not going to be programming software, why would I need to record CDs?" There are three primary uses to start with. There are even more uses that are only limited by your imagination. The first is related to the first rule of safe computing, "Back-up early and back-up often." A recordable CD is great for doing back-ups, especially for those large files that are too big fit onto a floppy disk.

The second nice feature of recordable CDs is their ability to share things electronically with others. Now, we would never, never, ever advocate that you "copy" commercial software (it's also called "pirating" and it is illegal. The only time it is legal to copy software is for the purpose of backing it up to keep an extra copy for your own use. That is okay.) So, since copying software is illegal, what WOULD you copy to share with others? How about digital photos of your children to send a picture CD to grandpa and grandma? Take it one step farther. Next Christmas, instead of sending out a traditional family Christmas letter, create a multimedia Christmas CD complete with color photos, stories, and even recorded greetings from each family member. Don't worry, your children will come up with even more ideas for you!

The third, and probably the most com-

mon, use of recordable CDs is recording your own customized music CDs. Since I just brought up the issue of pirating software in the previous paragraph, it is only fair that I address the issue here as it pertains to music. However, before I do, I must give you the full semi-legal disclaimer. (Actually, probably more like "barely legal" since I am not, nor have I ever been, a lawyer or had any legal training!) What I am going to cover next is only my understanding of what the law is pertaining to the issue of recording your own music. If you want a truly legal interpretation of what the actual laws are on the matter, you can spend tens of thousands of dollars to get a legal opinion that could probably be overturned by a team of extremely high-priced and overpaid, fancy lawyers working for some multi-gazillion dollar international music company.

So with that disclaimer said, here goes. I will tell you what my opinion is about what I think you legally can and can't do in recording your own music CDs. If you are recording your own music that you already bought and paid for, you can make copies for your own personal use. You may NOT make copies to hand out (or heaven forbid, try to sell) to your friends or relatives. You may not make copies of your friend's CDs for your own use. Maybe, and this is a big maybe, you could do you friend a favor and make him a copy for his own personal use. Is that clear? Hope so. Otherwise, like I said, hire a lawyer, get his opinion, and then hire another lawyer to tell you what the first lawyer said. (Okay, I confess. In case you haven't figured it out yet, I haven't had the most positive personal experience with lawyers in the past.) Anyway, with all that legal mumbo jumbo past us, I will try to sum things up in a slightly different way; even if the high-powered fancy lawyers with their extremely overpriced suits don't know what you are doing, God does. And with God, He sees all and knows our motives. So if you do make copies of things, make sure that what you are doing is legal, ethical, and morally okay.

Back to the issue of why you would most likely want to make copies of music you already own. I will give you the two reasons why I bought a CD-RW to record music CDs (and I love it). The first is that most of the CDs I own have at least one song on them that I can't stand. Either aesthetically I don't like that song from a musical stand-point (personal taste), or it is a song that has too much of a rock and roll influence. (Not that I want to get into it here, but my flesh LOVES rock and roll. Spiritually though, I know God does not. So I have made a conscious choice to eliminate rock and roll for my life and replace it with classical music and Godly Christian music.) Secondly, by recording my own CDs, I can record only the songs I want from any CD and in any order that I want; just like on a cassette tape, only with the quality of a CD. To me, a CD-RW is worth having for that feature alone.

Well, now you might be really unsure of what way to go. The Kihlstadiuses say you should get a DVD drive in your next computer, but this CD-RW thing sounds really cool too. What's a person to do? Decisions, decisions, decisions. And you don't want to spend a thousand dollars, only to wish six months later that you did something different. Well, have I got good news for you. You can have it both ways! Some of the computer manufacturers are making computers with both a DVD drive and a CD-RW drive. If you can afford it, that is probably your best option for getting the best of both worlds!

SHOULD YOU UPGRADE OR REPLACE?

That depends!

Most of the people who don't already have a CD-ROM drive on their computer probably have an older machine that would NOT be very cost efficient to upgrade to CD-ROM. If it doesn't have a CD-ROM drive, it probably doesn't have the other hardware necessary to run CDs, such as at least 1MB video RAM, a 16-bit sound card and large hard drive (for all those massive files that many CD programs like to load onto the hard drive).

In short, unless you have at least a 166MHz Pentium (or generic equivalent) it probably would cost too much to upgrade all the individual components required to run most multimedia CD-ROM programs. What you need for individual components, at bare minimum, are 1MB of video RAM (although 4MB or better is suggested), a 2GB hard drive and a 16-bit sound card. This is especially true in light of some of the deals now available in new computer systems. Today's entry-level Pentium systems (priced under $700 not including monitor) are a bargain compared to the $4000-$5000 price tags similar systems saw when they were first released. Today's computers are many, many times the machines that those were.

Macintosh's

If you have a Macintosh, the decision to upgrade or replace is generally pretty cut and dried and therefore pretty easy to determine. If your Mac doesn't have a Power PC processor and a CD-ROM drive, don't bother doing any upgrades unless they are really cheap to do (like adding a little more RAM or a bigger hard drive, but again, only do it if it is really cheap to add.) Like just mentioned for older Macs, adding more RAM or adding a large external hard drive is usually a good upgrade idea for most Power PC Mac owners. Adding an external hard drive to your Mac is incredibly easy. As I suggested for older PC owners, as long as your Mac can still meet at least the minimum hardware requirements for running most current software, I would recommend you hang on to your Mac. Wait to replace it until you find it too hard to get the software you need that will run on your Mac.

For both Mac and PC owners, our advice to you when you do buy your next computer is to hold onto your old one too. This is especially true if you have a larger family. It will still run all the software it runs now.

USED COMPUTERS

Thinking of buying used?

If you are thinking of buying a used computer (instead of a new one) take this quiz to better understand the potential risks involved.

Question: How much do you save if you buy a $200 used computer instead of a $900 new computer?

Answer: In the chance that you answered $700, let my rephrase the original question another way. How much will you waste if you buy a $200 used computer instead of a $900 new computer and you discover that it won't run most of the current software in the stores? So basically you still need a better computer. (Okay, yes, it is a trick question.)

If you are thinking of buying a used computer, pay close attention to this: many older, cheaper, used computers have computer "brains" (CPUs or chips) smaller than a Pentium (or generic equivalent). DON'T BUY THEM! The owner is selling it because he can't run most of the new software out there—and neither can you! If the owner can't even tell what kind/size of chip it is, even more so, DON'T BUY IT! If you can't afford a cheap, used, bare bones Pentium with 90 MHz for $200-$400 (including monitor, hard drive and CD-ROM), you might want to seriously think about waiting until you can. Believe me, you will be glad you did!

You can buy a decent used color Macintosh for about $400 and up. Make sure it has a Power PC processor with 32 MB of RAM and at least a 1 gig hard drive. This can run almost all Macintosh educational software.

If you are still thinking of buying a used computer, remember this, with the price of new computers having dropped so much in the past couple years, you can often buy a brand new one for only slightly more than someone's used one would cost you. With such great deals on new computer systems priced under $900, it just doesn't make any sense to buy used unless you absolutely can't afford a cheap new one. Computers are NOT like cars in that you would want to go out and find an older used model that has already been nicely depreciated at the expense of someone else.

Remember, you get what you pay for.

A used computer for $200-$300 may seem like a bargain but you may be severely limited in your choice of programs available, especially if it has no CD-ROM drive. If you buy a cheap used computer, you may think you are being a wise steward with your resources, but you will quickly outgrow an underpowered computer and find that all the money you spent was wasted on a machine that will run little or none of the software available. This is a classic case of "Penny wise, but pound foolish." If you have any doubt whatsoever on this issue, just ask any three or four users of older PCs. I have no doubt they will agree with me on this point. Additionally, a computer without good software is usually a waste of money.

One last thing for you to factor if you are still considering the option of buying a used computer instead of buying new: Check into buying a refurbished computer. Sometimes computer manufacturers have some incredible deals on refurbished models or discounts on closeouts of discontinued, bottom-of-the-line models. You might not get a full standard warranty or as much tech support, but whatever it comes with will definitely be better than the warranty and technical support for a used computer (which is none!)

Need more information?

This Guide was printed as a resource to give you enough information to make a wiser purchase decision for your home-school computer uses. We have three suggestions for you if you need more information about buying a computer then what is contained in this Guide. First, talk to any of the people that you know that are highly computer literate. Second, go to your local public library. There are numerous articles in various magazines about buying computers. Due to the nature of tight publishing deadlines, if the magazine is somewhat current, the information should be highly relevant to whatever the current technologies and prices are. Lastly, contact the business from which you plan to buy your computer. However, only contact them after you have done all your homework and you are ready to buy. Once you have settled on your final decision, run it by one of those knowledgeable computer people that you know. Together all this should save you from saying "If I had only known, instead I would have…."

PRINTERS & SCANNERS

Printers:

Ink Jet or Laser: Which is Better For You?

Without going into lengthy detail (which I am well known to do), here is a simple way to determine if you should get an ink jet (or bubble jet as it is sometimes called) printer or a laser printer.

For almost any and every homeschooler's printing need, get a good quality color ink jet printer for around $150. Epson, Hewlett Packard, Apple, and Canon are some of the top names for quality.

If you are printing things out that are being re-printed for publication, i.e. desktop publishing, or you need to print out letters and documents for professional business use, consider a 600 X 600 dpi (dots per inch) black and white only laser printer. Prices range from around $300 and up.

If you need high quality color images for professional use, there are fancier color printers for around $1000 and up that will produce a glossier color image than the standard ink jet printer. There are also special (and expensive) glossy papers available to produce brighter, glossier images than can be done on plain paper. Odds are that if you don't already have one of these fancier printers, you probably don't need it.

A few words about buying a scanner...

First, if you do not know what one is, you probably do not need one. A scanner is sort of like a copying machine that pulls the copied image into your computer where you can use it in articles, flyers, letters, etc.

Second, if you know what one is you still probably do not need one. Most people don't need a scanner as much as they think they do. One mother told me she wanted a scanner so she could use it like a copying machine in her home; she did end up buying one and was fairly satisfied. If you really do feel you need to buy a scanner, here are some tips:

* Buy one at least one or two steps better in quality than you think you need. If you need a scanner, you will need the quality.

* Like computers, scanners keep getting better for cheaper, so don't buy until you need it.

* If you do buy a scanner, unless you already have way too much RAM in your computer, you will probably need more than you have now. Buy more. Buy lots more.

* If you need to scan in photographs, there is an alternative to a scanner. If you take the photos with your own camera, some authorized Kodak photo developers have the ability to take your roll of film and put the images onto a CD-ROM for you. This process is really not too expensive (especially compared to the price of a good a scanner), and it will also produce computerized images that are better quality than any scanner that you can afford. Check with your local authorized Kodak film photofinisher.

* Another idea for getting photos into your computer is that you could buy a good quality digital camera to take the pictures you want put into the computer. What should you look for in a digital camera? I haven't got a clue. But same as with the scanner, you probably want to get something better than you think you need. For better advice, go to the public library and look at some camera magazines or Consumer Reports.

Last thing on a scanner, in case you still feel compelled to get one. What I have recommended for families who wanted a scan-

ner was to consider one of those all-in-one
models. They are a combination scanner,
copier, fax-machine, and printer. Basically,
it is an all-in-one unit. Hewlett-Packard usually offers a good choice.

Chapter Ten

Macs vs. Windows

What we use

Before I go into any details, let me first say that in our home we use two Macintoshes and two PCs. We use most of the computers six days a week, every week of the year. In our previous business, we sold both kinds of computers. We sold both kinds of software. Dan sells software at a software company that makes highly specialized software for factories that only runs on PCs. Lastly, we speak with thousands of other homeschooling families who use PCs, Macs, and some who use both. We aren't just standing on one side of the fence looking over at the other side. We have a good perspective of both sides of the issue.

As I get into the whole issue of Macs vs. PCs, keep in mind the perspective that I will be coming from. If you already own a PC and you are basically satisfied with it (independent from issues of speed and memory limitations of older machines) than we would strongly encourage you to stick with a PC for your next computer. The discussion here is meant for those who don't own a computer yet, those who would like to own a computer but are "computer-phobic," or those who are extremely frustrated by using the PC they already own.

So with that as our perspective, here goes.

WHAT ARE YOUR PLANNED USES FOR THIS TOOL?

PCs Rule

It is a well-established fact that PCs are far more common and popular than Macintosh computers, and that PCs are by far the more popular in the corporate world. Consequently, since most computers used in the world are used in corporations, most of the computers made are PCs.

However, since you are probably reading this to help you choose a computer for your homeschool, those uses probably don't necessarily apply to you for your planned computer needs. If your family's primary uses are going to be educational, and/or personal home use, you might want to also consider a Macintosh as a possible choice.

What is your prior computer experience?

Husbands, consider your wife's computer experience. Before you buy, remember who will be using it the most, and what they will be doing on it. We hear many horror stories from wives of computer wizard husbands who buy a PC, plop it in front them and say, "Here, use this in your homeschool!" Wives are frustrated to say the least. Busy homeschooling moms are not interested in tackling big technical manuals. Husbands — unless you are willing to sit down with your wife and children and teach them how to use Windows — consider whether a Mac might be a better, easier-to-learn choice. Using a Mac, they might be able to be concentrating more on getting their work done, instead of on figuring out how to get their computer to work. Although things have been getting easier to do on a PC than they used to be.

Husbands, if you were a farmer, the best vehicle for your job would be a pickup truck. Imagine how your wife would feel if you told her you were going to town to buy her a vehicle and you came home with another pickup. The first thing in her mind would be visions of bringing home 5 children and all the groceries in the rain. She needs a van or a station wagon! Different jobs require different tools. Choose the best tool for her job!

Farmers use pick-up trucks, but a cab driver never would. Couriers use economy cars, but freight companies use semi-trailers. Moms use station wagons or mini-vans.

Some of the happiest Mac customers are former PC owners or dads who bought a Mac for home but use a PC at work. They can't believe the difference!

Beyond Technology's Promise, a book detailing an exhaustive study on educational computing in the home found, "Where the mothers were comfortable with the machine and actually helped their children, those were the cases where there was really serious computer usage going on for educational purposes. It does show the important role of the mother." This study suggests it is especially important for mothers to model good computer uses, and in those homes where computer education was most successful there were mothers who used the computer and coached the children.

We know from our personal experience talking with thousands of homeschooling moms, that statistically speaking as a group, moms who have Macintoshes know more about their computers, know more about how to use their computers, and use their computers far more that moms who own IBM-compatibles.

I do understand that most of the time a PC will be the best overall choice. Just be aware, in advance, of the longer, frustrating learning curve.

The Quotes

If I simply told you that Macs were best, most trouble-free, and easiest to use; why should you believe me? I am obviously:

a) Biased
b) Ill-informed
c) Have no idea what I'm talking about
or
d) All of the above

So with that out of the way, let's look at what some of the so-called unbiased, neutral parties say.

Popular Mechanics December 2000 issue specifically covering Macs vs. Windows says:

"The Macintosh operating system...is,

has been and will be for the foreseeable future, the easiest operating system to use. This isn't to say that it's the all-around best or the most powerful. But, we can say that using a Mac requires the least amount of computer knowledge. Those who are no more interested in knowing how their computers work than how their car runs will be best served by a Mac." The point here is that you shouldn't have to know how the carburetor or pistons work just to be able to drive your car to the store.

FamilyPC February 2001, also in an article covering the Mac vs. Windows issue:

"Russell Mosemann, Ph.D., a computer science professor at Concordia University in Seward, Neb., uses both Macs and PCs in his work and argues that the Mac operating system and user interface are still easier to grasp than Windows."

Other points to consider when trying to compare Apples to, well, Windows

Troubleshooting and ease of use

PC users like to say that now with Window's ease-of-use the Macintosh has lost its former advantage in the area of troubleshooting and ease-of-use. However, in the real world, the hard cold facts do not back up that assumption. Statistically, for software companies that actually write programs that run on both platforms, the technical support costs per unit sold (factoring in volume differences) are higher on the PC side than they are on the Mac side. PCs have a statistically higher number of problems per unit sold and a statistically longer length of time for technical support staff to arrive at a solution, as compared to identical titles for the Macintosh. The facts of the matter show that PC users do experience a higher rate of problems and a longer time to

resolve them.

Between both of us, Dan and Tammy, we have installed nearly 1000 different software programs on both Macs and PCs. With the Mac, it's rare that a program won't run on the first try after installation. Besides that, of all the educational software programs we've installed over the years, we can recall very few Mac programs that we couldn't eventually get to run (assuming the hardware met the right requirements).

Based on our everyday use, and our review of hundreds of both Mac and Windows software programs, we still come to the same conclusions: the Mac is easier to learn, use, and often more problem free. It is also generally easier to install software and troubleshoot. Isn't that what you want from your computer? You just want to use your computer, without having to try to figure out how to get it working.

But aren't Macs more expensive?

In the past, price differences were definitely more of an issue. Macintoshes were priced at significant premiums to PCs; however, things have changed under Apple's current management. Here is how the February 2001 issue of FamilyPC puts it. "The common perception is that Macs cost much more than their Windows-based equivalents. While this was certainly true a decade ago, it's not always the case today."

But what about the children? They need to learn Windows!

The computer your 13-year-old is using today is a much different animal than he'll be using in the workplace five years from now (see Ten Most Important Computer Skills section). What children need to have is experience with applications — databases, word processors, spreadsheets, accounting software, etc. If the PC is such a superior machine, why has Bill Gates made it his life's ambition to make Windows more like the Macintosh? The greatest advantage a PC gives is more software. So why not buy a Mac? On the other hand, for older teens looking to enter the work force soon, I suggest a PC.

But there's no software for the Macintosh!

Let me dispel the myth that there isn't any software for Macintoshes. It simply isn't true. Most top rated programs come out on both platforms. It is true that most stores primarily carry PC software, with only a small Mac section. That is because most of the Mac software is in the Windows section! If you look at a box of software, you will see that many educational software titles have both the Windows and Macintosh version on the same disk, in the same box, in the PC software section. With some of the new software development tools, developers are able to create software for both platforms simultaneously. Lastly, the new DVD technology offers greater storage for larger, multi-platform programs. This should translate to more software being available for the Mac too.

Referring more specifically to educational software itself, this has traditionally been one of Apple's strong points. To give you an idea of just how strong, take a look at this quote from the February 2001 issue of FamilyPC. "The latest data from Quality Education Data (QED), an educational research firm, finds the split (of Macs vs. PC in public schools) today is almost 50-50." All those Macs need educational software, and since public schools need software, they spend lots of money on it every year. These factors keep the software industry pumping out lots of educational software titles for both Macs and PCs. Additionally,

with the phenomenal success of the iMac's, companies who once considered discontinuing titles for the Mac are changing their mind and are 100% behind producing titles for the Mac. It makes them money!

If you still don't think there is much software for the Macintosh, just look at all the software we list. Most titles are available for both Mac and Windows.

Also keep in mind that there are well over 20,000,000 people using Macintosh computers. Most newspapers are printed using Macintoshes; huge numbers of scientists and engineers use Macs. Obviously, they have software. This book you are reading was created on a Mac

Even if you can't find the exact title you are looking for in a Macintosh version, you can usually find something that can serve the same function.

Why do people like PCs?

It is what is needed for the job. Not because a PC is better or adds up a group of numbers faster. For business users, ease of use and troubleshooting are not the primary issues. They need what works with their business software—easy to use or not. So they buy and use PCs. If it isn't easy, or it has problems, then they hire trained computer specialists (at big bucks, I might add) to deal with it. All part of the cost of doing business.

If you are buying a computer primarily to train your older teenagers to enter the work force, then yes, the PC is probably what you want. (Even if you can't figure out how to use the computer, your teens will!) Over 90% of all computers used in business are PCs. Despite all the PC drawbacks, this fact alone is a pretty good reason to buy a PC if you have older teenage children or if Dad needs to sharpen his computer skills for the job market.

More software. There is no question that there is far more software in general available for the PC than the Macintosh. If you are involved in a profession that requires specialized or custom software, use the machine that successful people in your field use for that software (probably a PC).

Power users prefer PCs. Although many higher-end, serious computer users will admit the Mac is easier to use for most people, they prefer the PC for a variety of reasons. The first would be simply because they are more familiar with it and they feel more comfortable with it. Secondly, the PC is what all their friends and business associates use. Other reasons have to do with the operating system itself, as is discussed in the next section. Lastly, it is what they use at work.

Windows Operating System Strengths

I realize that some of this next section may be a little over the heads of some newer and non-computer users. If so, ask one of your computer savvy friends to fill in the gaps for you.

Pre-emptive multi-tasking.

Many computer users say that "pre-emptive multi-tasking" is probably Window's most significant operating system advantage over the Macintosh. In theory, pre-emptive multi-tasking means (in plain English) that programs run independent of each other and independent of the operating system. The theoretical application of this is that you are able to use the operating system (or a program) while the computer is busy in the background doing some previous command. In recent years, PCs have done this better than Macs have. With the new major operating system upgrade Apple is about to release, "OS X" ("X" representing the Roman numeral for "10"), Apple may take

the lead in that area. Time will tell.

Whereas the Macintosh was the first computer to allow basic multi-tasking, Windows has refined it to be more full-featured and functional. One better feature is supposed to be in the area of computer crashes. Technically, Windows 95 was supposed to let you "escape" a program that had "crashed", without crashing the whole computer, or other programs running at the same time. Real life shows that some times it works that way and some times you just have to turn off the power and restart everything over again. Both Windows and Macintosh still have some struggles in this area and both are getting better in this regard.

Two button mouse.

The extra button on the PC mouse can be used to perform short cut tasks such as cut, copy, paste, resize, etc. This is usually more of a power user feature, since many users don't spend the time to learn the short cuts. I will admit that the more I learn to use both the buttons on my PCs mouse, the more I miss not having two buttons on my Mac. On the other hand, the keyboard shortcut commands on the Mac are far more consistent between nearly every different program on the Mac. With Windows, there is a lot less consistency in keyboard shortcuts between different programs.

HOW & WHICH TO CHOOSE

Now that we have given you the strengths and weaknesses of both, we will present my suggested method of determining which type of computer you should use.

To get a better idea for your family's needs, do the following exercise:

Make a list of all the things that you hope to do with your computer. Add to that list all the things that you would like to do with your computer if you knew how to do it. Next to each item, write either Mac or PC based on which type of computer would be better suited for that task (consider factors such as ease of use, software availability, your knowledge and experience level, etc.). Lastly, sort your list in order of priority, with the most important thing at the top. From this new, resorted list, see which type of computer is listed next to most of the items at the top part of the list. Now your list should give you a strong indication as to whether a PC or a Mac would be better for you, your needs, and your usage.

This next factor might be the second most overriding reason why you should buy a PC instead of a Mac. (The first reason to choose a PC is that more software is available for it.) When you do need technical support, you are significantly more likely to find friends or relatives who are highly knowledgeable PC experts can help you. These two reasons combined should be reason enough for most computer buyers to go with a PC running whatever is the most current version of Microsoft Windows.

With a Mac, it is far more unlikely that you will be able to find a friend or relative who can help you with technical support. Your support will most likely be limited to the company that made the software you are having problems with, or to Apple Corporation. On the other hand, Macintosh troubleshooting is usually significantly easier and generally not needed as much.

On last thought on the choice issue: "But everyone uses PCs!" Okay, well "everyone" sends his or her children to public school too. Don't do what "everyone" else does. Do what's best for your family. If that is to buy a PC, buy a PC. If it is to buy a Mac, buy a Mac.

It is a "PC" world. There is no argument from even the most fanatic of Mac users — it is a "PC" world out there. As just mentioned, "Corporate America" uses PCs; most businesses use PCs; most the people you know who have computers use PCs. So if you buy a Mac, it means going against the flow. It always has. Just like you probably do by homeschooling or in your faith or in your politics.

Pick based on your needs, not the world's needs

Pick what is best for you. This is not an issue of which computer is best for the rest of the world. It is a question of which computer is the best for each individual family's needs. The fact and knowledge that the rest of the world uses PCs does absolutely no good, and is of no help to the homeschooling mom who has no clue what to do next after she turns on the computer. For those who feel that I am stretching the truth on this matter, I challenge you to go out and ask just 10 homeschooling moms about their computing experience. Ask them if they know how to install software, how to backup a file onto a floppy disk, or how to delete a file. These are the most basic of computer commands. Yes, many do, yet our experience with the average homeschool mom is that a significant number of the moms (somewhere between one quarter and one half) cannot do even these bare minimum tasks.

Our goal

Our goal here is NOT to tell people they should buy a Macintosh for their next computer. Our goal is simply to give you the information to know and understand both options before you buy your next computer and to help you best understand the strengths and weaknesses of both. We simply want people to be able to make a fully informed decision based on the facts, not on false assumptions and misinformation. Unfortunately, not many computer salespeople are willing (or are able to spend the time) to do what we just did in this chapter.

The bottom-line

If you were to try to sum up the choice between Macs vs. Window it would be this: you are choosing between easier to learn, easier to use, more trouble free, easier to fix (the Macintosh) or choosing more popular, more mainstream, more tech support, and more software (Windows).

As a general rule, for all these above reasons and more, for those people who have the time, aptitude, and patience to master it, a PC is probably a better purchase than a Macintosh. But if you have never used a computer, have computer phobia, or have consistently had nightmare experiences with using your own PC, at least consider a Mac for you next computer. If you are currently a happy Mac user, you will most likely want to get a Mac for your next computer unless your computing needs have changed and you can't find Mac versions of software to do what you now need to do on the computer. If that is the case, you may need to think about biting the bullet and converting over to "the other side."

(I know, you hard core Mac users cringe at the very thought! Sorry!)

In closing, we want to quote from *Computing For Kids*: "Perhaps the best way to decide is to take your time, study each system in-person at a local store, compare the cost of each to the options each provides (modems, sound card, etc.), and go with whatever system you (and your child[ren]) would be most comfortable with."

Ditto.

Chapter Eleven

More Stuff About Computers

TECHNICAL SUPPORT: FOR BETTER OR FOR WORSE? (SOMETIMES WORSE)

Owning a computer is not like owning a lamp. You buy a lamp, plug it in, turn it on, and it works. Every now and then you need to replace the light bulb. So instead of being compared to a lamp, a computer is better compared to a car. Every now and then it needs a tune-up. Things can and will go wrong. The only people who never have anything go wrong on their computer are people who only use a few programs and rarely add anything new, especially multi-media software.

When a computer is not working right, getting things back to working properly will depend on two main variables: what caused things to go wrong in the first place, and the technical ability of the person doing the troubleshooting. What takes one person five minutes to do may take someone else five hours to do; and then who knows how long to undo everything that was done wrong in the process of trying to fix the original problem. Example: I had a problem with my toilet that I probably would have spent hours messing with and still not get it fixed. A friend of mine who is has an incredible knack for fixing things spent all of 30 seconds and fixed it!

When it comes to troubleshooting, be forewarned: most new computer users make matters worse when they do their own troubleshooting. Computer technical support does not lend itself to tinkering or guessing unless

A) You are willing to run the risk of a potential worst case scenario like having to erase the hard drive and installing everything all over from scratch, or...

B) You have a really good idea of what you are doing.

This does not mean that you should not troubleshoot when it is needed; it does mean that if the manual, book, or person who is giving you instructions is not clear, understandable, and specifically related to exact solutions to your specific problem, then consider finding help elsewhere.

On the other hand, just like some problems with a car, some problems on a computer are just not worth the trouble of getting them fixed. A burned-out light under the dashboard of a car can be an annoyance and inconvenience, but it is rarely worth the effort of removing the dashboard to replace the bulb. In the same manner, if a program or feature of a program is not working, weigh the need for that particular feature against the time, energy, and trouble required to get it working again. When factoring in time, remember that, like tinkering with cars or plumbing, most "fixing" on the computer ends up taking multiples of the time you expected it to take, unless you are fairly certain of what is wrong and what it takes to fix it. Just ask anyone who has owned a computer for more than a year, and uses it regularly. Except for the most skilled computer users out there, most people will simply have to learn to live with a few things that just don't work the way they should or the way they want them to. Even for you Macintosh users!

(Remember before, when I mentioned information in this Guide that goes outside of the content area of educational software? Well, here is another one of those little free-at-no-additional-charge bonus sections. In a perfect computing world, you wouldn't need the information that follows. But alas, we live in a fallen, corrupt world where things can and do go wrong. So with that said, here is...)

A guide to troubleshooting for the computer-challenged

There are four general things that go wrong with computers. Two are related to physical problems with the computer hardware itself and two are related to the software programs on the computer. The very first step in troubleshooting any computer problem is to determine if the cause of the problem is hardware-related or due to problems with the operating system software that runs the computer.

I will deal with hardware first.

In all my experience of troubleshooting computer problems, I have found a very interesting corollary among people troubleshooting computer problems. As a general rule (and I mean very general) the less knowledgeable a person is about computers, the more often they are likely to blame a problem on something physically breaking on the computer. It tends to be just the opposite the more experienced a computer user is. This is especially true in cases where the computer won't even start up. The first thing you might think is that the computer itself broke. However, it is also possible that the software that tells the computer what to do has been corrupted. "Corrupt" is the computer term for "broke."

If your computer won't even start up, try double-checking all the power cords, connections, and power sources.

Without going into any details of actually how to do the next thing you want to try if your computer won't start, I will say it is to try starting it up with a boot disk. Almost every knowledgeable computer user knows what I am talking about; so ask them to explain to you what it is and how to do it. I will also tell you what you are actually trying to accomplish here. It is possible that the computer hardware itself is just fine, but the operating system is corrupt. If the computer will start up using a boot disk, then the problem is probably the operating system. If that is the case, you will most likely want to find either an extremely experienced computer troubleshooter (i.e. Supergeek or Supernerd), or call the company that made the computer for technical support, (Microsoft to work on Windows problems or Apple for a Mac). You do not want to be messing around with the core operating system unless you really know what you are doing.

If the computer won't start up with a boot disk either, call the manufacturer or bring it into a computer repair shop.

Sometimes the computer will start up, but something won't work right. The CD player won't work, or you can't get any sound out of it or whatever. Again this could still be either a hardware or software problem. Here again you will probably want do something similar to the above troubleshooting tips. Call a friend or relative that is a computer expert, call the manufacturer's tech support, or take it into a repair shop. If your computer starts making strange sounds (grinding, high-pitched whining, or whatever) call the manufacturer or else bring it into a repair shop right away. If it is your hard drive going bad, the sooner you get it fixed or replaced, the sooner you will be able to save all the data. I have seen many times (including once on my own computer) where this wasn't dealt with fast enough and everything on the hard drive was lost for good.

Like everything else with moving parts or electronic circuitry, things can and do "just break." The reason it broke probably doesn't matter, because most likely it wasn't anything you did, and there would have been nothing you could have done to prevent it. It happens, so live with it. If something does stop working on the computer, be smart and don't get in over your head trying to fix it yourself.

Here is another free, bonus tip on hardware problems. If you have an older computer (3 or 4 years) that is going wacko (like the date on the computer always goes wrong, no matter how many times you reset it) it is possible you just need to replace the battery. Replacing the battery is especially important to consider if you have a Macintosh. For example, if your Mac keeps resetting the year to 1956, you definitely need to replace the battery. (1956 is the birth year of Apple's cofounder, Steve Jobs. It turns out that Macs are programmed to reset the current date on the computer with the day he was born!)

The next thing I am going to say might shock or surprise some of you. I have spoken to three or four different people who told me their Macs went completely dead but when I told each of them to replace the battery, their computers worked. Now here comes the shocking part. Two of those people had just taken their computers to computer repair shops and been given estimates of very expensive repairs required to fix the exact same problem. One place told them they would have to replace the whole motherboard to fix it. At the time this would have been hundreds of dollars! All it really took was a new battery.

So, I guess it is kind of like repairs with most anything else: every now and then you run into those dishonest people who say the repair costs many multiples of what it really does. In defense of the rest of the computer repair people out there, I will say that I learned about this whole battery thing from an earlier customer of mine who had taken her completely dead Mac into a repair shop where they fixed it by just replacing the battery. She called me to share the good news and, well, I guess I just told you the rest.

The other kind of hardware problem tends to come from installing new stuff into your computer. You don't even want to get me going with the kind of computer nightmare stories I have heard from people having "hardware conflicts." If you have a problem with some new gadget you added to your computer, whether it be a zip drive, digital camera, more RAM or even a software program, the first thing you want to do (assuming here, of course, that you DID consult the manual first!) is call the tech support number (or visit the website) of the company that made the component you are adding. Removing what it was you just added to your computer can also solve many problems. Another quick fix that may work is simply shutting down all components and unplugging them; then, plugging them all back in and restarting your computer.

Software problems

Software problems can usually be divided into two general categories. Problems with the operating system (commonly referred to as the OS – the master computer program that runs everything e.g. Windows) or problems with the applications themselves. I guess there is also sort of a gray area where you have situations where the OS and the application are not playing well together, but I won't really go into that here.

Everything was running fine on your computer until you installed *Captain Bob's Chemist Cadet Quantum Physics Home Study Self Teaching Ph.D.* Course software program. Since then, it seems that all hell has broken loose on your computer. Programs that used to work no longer run. Some programs run, but the sound is gone. There are just all kinds of fun things that might not work right.

If you are fortunate enough, the people who wrote the *Captain Bob's Chemist Cadet Quantum Physics Home Study Self Teaching Ph.D. Course* software program were good enough to also write a decent uninstall program that actually works and to might have a chance of undoing all the damage by uninstalling it. However, odds are that you are still likely to have prob-

lems. So call the folks at Captain Bob's and see what they can do to help you.

Otherwise, call tech support at the company that made your computer, call Microsoft, or (if you are blessed enough to have one) call your computer nerd friend who seems to know how to do it all.

The last major thing that can go wrong with your computer is the operating system itself going bad. Some times this can be fixed by replacing just the files that have gone bad; other times it requires a full reinstallation of Windows (or the Mac OS). Either way, here again you are in one of those situations with which you will really want the help of someone who has experience in this area and really knows what he is doing. Heed the warning in the upcoming section on calling tech support to understand just how important skilled tech support is. There is a lot more at risk than just getting your program running again.

Software installation tips

Here are some tips and suggestions for installing software programs based on more experience than both of us (Dan and Tammy) wish we had.

Read the hardware requirements on the side of the box before opening. Make SURE your system can handle the software's requirements BEFORE you open the box. Once the shrink-wrap is opened, software cannot be exchanged. This is a standard policy with nearly every software retail and mail order company. If your computer does not meet the hardware requirements, do not open the box, it will not run on your computer. Contact the business you bought the software from for their return policy. If they won't take it back, try contacting the software publisher regarding a refund or an exchange for a program that will work.

If, during or after installation, you have

technical difficulties, call the company who made the program. They are the ones who have a paid staff, specially trained in the troubleshooting of the software that they programmed. Please keep in mind that they wrote the programs. Do not try calling the business you bought the program from. The place that sold the program cannot, we repeat, cannot give you any technical support, unless you are paying someone in their repair or tech services department to help you.

If you think you have a defective disk, you will probably need to contact the manufacturer of that disk. The people who sold the software do not make the disks (they buy them, just like you) therefore they do not have the means to offer replacement disks. The store that you bought it from does not manufacture replacement disks. (Besides, they would be making illegal, unauthorized copies if they did make copies!) Some stores will replace defective disk with a full brand new replacement program, but that is not very common.

However, some STRONG words of warning before you send a disk back to the manufacturer! Most so-called "defective" disks are not defective at all! Based on my own personal experience when we had our mail order software business, in nearly every case that someone sent us a so-called "defective disk" it ran just fine on our computers. Almost always, defective disk problems turn out to be a result of either a computer hardware incompatibility problem or an operating system software problem. Thus, no matter how many replacement disks you try, you are most likely to encounter exactly the same error. If you have what you think is a defective disk, try it on a different computer, preferably a newer one. If it won't work on any computer you try it on, then contact the manufac-turer for a replacement.

Don't confuse software bugs for defective disks. There is a difference though it is sometimes hard to detect. A software bug is a mistake in the programming language that causes bad things to happen such as crashes or glitches. As a general rule, if a program crashes every time at the same spot, or when you do the same thing, it is probably a bug. Most likely, the company already knows about it and has a "fix" of some kind. In fact, I remember one company that was having so many problems with a particular release of a program that whenever someone called complaining about problems with it, the company sent the customer out a free copy of the next release (which was much better in both content and quality.)

What to expect when you do call technical support.

A program doesn't work right. You call the technical support line of the company who wrote the program. There is nearly a 100% probability that you will first get put into an automated phone answering system. (I don't remember ever calling for technical support and actually having a real live person picking up the phone and answer the call.) You will have to carefully listen to the selection options and push the appropriate selection on your phone. Now, probably everyone reading this has gone through this process with something before, so you realize that quite often the choices they give you don't always meet your situation. When you finally figure out the right combinations of options, you get to hold for (usually) significant lengths of time and (usually) at your own expense.

Here is a little tip that can sometimes get you through the phone maze a little quicker: if you press "0" on your touch tone phone, or you don't push any numbers, you can usually get through to a living person.

Remember that example of the light bulb burnt out on the dashboard of a car? Well, this is where that analogy really applies. Before you start, realize the potential costs in time and phone bills (not to mention the companies who charge for their technical support!) Decide in advance how much time and money you are willing to invest in this process and if it is even worth it.

PC owners have a love/hate relationship with Microsoft, the maker of Windows. In addition to your long distance costs, Microsoft charges $35 per "incident" to solve your problem. I called Microsoft and they said if they couldn't solve it, they don't charge. I guess that is fair enough.

There are some companies that are nearly impossible to get through to for technical support. They are usually the same companies that sell many inexpensive titles. In the past, for all practical purposes, you wouldn't even want bother trying to get through to them.

Figure it this way, if it is not a toll-free call, plan on spending a minimum of a couple dollars per call on long distance phone charges. But those are the lucky ones. (Here is a little tip: allegedly, the earlier in the day you call, they quicker you will get through.) It is not unheard of for people to run up $30 and $40 phone charges trying to get a problem resolved. I will explain how this usually happens.

Sometimes we would get calls from frustrated customers who were experiencing problems with a particular program. Even though these people usually had the latest, greatest systems, the program they just bought didn't work. They called the software publisher that made the program, and they sometimes spent hours between waiting on hold and getting technical support. Often technical support people will blame the computer manufacturer; the manufacturer will blame the publisher; or they both will blame the operating system (Windows, usually). No one wants to admit guilt. Unfortunately, after multiple times going between the two, some frustrated users ended up never getting it to work right.

You will not experience that sort of thing all the time. It varies by the company, time of day, time of week, and season. (Forget trying to get through to tech support for games or edutainment type programs anytime during the first few weeks after Christmas. Make this note to yourself: if you buy software for your kids for Christmas presents, install it before Christmas and make sure it runs. Otherwise you may have some pretty frustrated kids Christmas morning.) Most tech support experiences I have had were pretty good. Not including all the time on hold, most calls to a software publisher took not much more than five minutes to resolve the problem, and the tech support person knew exactly what to do to solve the problem. (They have probably solved the exact same problem literally over 500 times before!)

The cure can be worse than the problem!

This is the part that I warned you about a few sections section ago: why you can be at more risk than just not getting you program to work. It's those problems that the tech people don't already know the exact solution to, which can get really scary. It is not unheard of for people's computers to never run quite right again after having some tech support person have the computer owner go into the "guts" of the operating system and start messing around, trying things, hoping something works. If they haven't encountered this exact problem before, and they don't know exactly what to do, let them experiment on someone else's time, money, and, more importantly, someone else's computer.

So how do know that they don't know?

Easy. Just ask. Tell them the problem. Then very simply ask them if they have encountered this problem before, if they are familiar with the problem, and have they had experience successfully solving it. If it sounds like they might be "shooting in the dark" in terms of a solution, ask for a more experienced tech support person, call back another time (hoping to get someone more experienced), or look for tech support somewhere else.

The alternative to the telephone technical support.

The Internet. Nearly every software company has a web site. In addition to advertising, one of the main reasons that they maintain these sites is to offer technical support. It is much cheaper for them (and you) to have you read what you need to know, than it is for them to pay someone to talk to you over the phone. You should be able to print out the information you need so you can refer to it while you are doing the troubleshooting on your computer. Somewhere else on that web site is usually posted a list of "Frequently Asked Questions" (FAQs). They will also usually have a section on tips and hints.

Does all this mean that it is a mistake to own a computer, and it is not worth the trouble?

Using the car analogy again, I would say it is no more a mistake than owning a car is a mistake. Sometimes troubleshooting can be quick and easy. Other times it can be a nightmare you wish you could wake up from.

Yes, there are some people out there that just seem to be a little more "computer-challenged" and just never seem to get the swing of things, but I would not go so far as to say that they should never own a computer. Once the operating software is properly set up and their software programs are properly installed and set up, even the "computer-challenged" should be able to run what they need to with few problems. They just need to learn to not push their limits as much, and to try, little by little, to learn more about the basic operations of their computer.

The bottom line to all this is the same as it is with car motors, if the person doesn't know *exactly* what they are doing (and that includes YOU too), don't let them even start trying to tinker! Get someone who knows what they are doing, even if it costs you something. You will be better off in the end.

And so will your computer!

WARNING!
BLATANT SELF-ENDORSEMENT AHEAD! ;-)

THEY DON'T JUST WRITE, THEY SPEAK TOO!

Dan and Tammy Kihlstadius speak at homeschool curriculum fairs around the country. The topics they speak on are similar to those in *The Homeschooler's Software Guide*, but with much more depth of information. They also do question and answer sessions.

Here is just some of what Mary Pride (publisher of *Practical Homeschooling* and author of numerous books on homeschooling) has to say about Dan and Tammy Kihlstadius.

Dear Homeschool Leader:

If you are looking for someone to speak to your homeschool organization on the subject of computers and homeschooling, I can think of no one more qualified, or who would do a better job, Dan and Tammy Kihlstadius, authors of The Homeschooler's Software Guide and home-schooling parents of eight children.

I have known and worked with Dan and Tammy for over eight years. They were the first software columnists for my magazine, Practical Homeschooling. Both meet or exceed the qualifications needed to address this topic at homeschool conventions. I am not aware of any-one who has reviewed and used more educational software for both PC and Mac than Dan and Tammy, or who is more up-to-date on current software titles and computer trends that affect homeschoolers.

You will be glad to know that the Kihlstadiuses are aware of all the many concerns that homeschool parents face when choosing software: not just its educational excellence, but its moral and spiritual wholesomeness. Knowing many programs intimately, Dan and Tammy can recommend titles to fit very specific homeschool objectives. Tammy can recommend dozens of excellent titles at every age level from toddler to college and across every subject area from music to calculus. She is able to give hands-on, real-life suggestions on how to actually use them in your homeschool.

When it comes to experience with homeschool families and their needs, you won't find anyone more able to serve. The Kihlstadiuses have personally counseled with thousands of homeschool families, helping them choose computers and educational software to fit specific educating needs and tight homeschooling budgets. These families have given only the highest appreciation and praise for the work the Kihlstadiuses have done in the homeschool world. I know of no other homeschool family better suited to teach and inform other homeschoolers on how to use a computer in a homeschool.

Yours truly, Mary Pride

If you think that they may have some valuable contributions to make at your state's curriculum fair, contact your state's convention leaders and ask them to invite the Kihlstadiuses to speak!

They can be reached at:

Homeschool Advisor
10424 Ewing Road
Bloomington, MN 55431
952-835-0063
themarket@aol.com

This Guide is copyrighted, 2001

It is illegal to make copies of any page or to reproduce any portion without specific authorization from Dan and Tammy Kihlstadius and Homeschool Advisor. Thank you.

Software to Avoid

This is a partial listing of programs I have run across that I consider a waste of money. Some are worse than others and you may find some acceptable where I have not. I will mention the specific objections and you can judge for yourself. We do not recommend these titles. I have reviewed most of these; others I read the box or other reviews and based my humble opinion on that information.

3-D Wolfenstein — This is an extremely violent and highly addictive virtual reality shoot'em' up arcade game.

Adiboo — magic characters

Adventures of Pinocchio Activity Center — Magic.

Afterlife — You control and design heaven, hell, and the spiritual destinies of an alien world.

Age of Empires- mild violence but my biggest complaint was that my kids got obsessed with it and wanted to play it constantly.

Amazin Blazin — Trivializes the Word of God and teaches little about the Bible.

Amazing Learning Games with Rayman — Arcade game with lots of magic, very little academic value.

Arthur's Teacher Trouble (various titles) — Not necessarily "bad" but is mainly a sight reading cartoon/video.

Big Machines — Boring and cumbersome.

Body Park — Limited education value.

Brainbender Puzzles and Activities: characters are rude, not enough educational value.

Broderbund's First Grade Success Starter — Contains Treehouse and Math Workshop, both of which we don't care for.

Broderbund's Kindergarten Success Starter — Contains James Discovers Math, which we don't care for.

CandyLand — Great music, fun adventure, tons of magic.

Casper Activity Center — Ghosts.

Carmen Sandiego Math Detective: Has a werewolf and a vampire.

Carmen Sandiego Word Detective- Has a werewolf and a vampire.

Charlton Heston's Voyage thru the Bible — Nice, but his paraphrase of the Bible wasn't accurate enough for me, IMHO.

ChessMates — Excellent chess program but has a wizard that teaches, he says "Greetings and Incantations!"

Cluefinders Reading Adventures 9-12: Evil Sorceress

Codehead — in your face attitudes

Connections — Entire premise is new age in nature.

Crayola Magic 3D Coloring Book — Good, but some objectionable material. We will stick with Kid Pix Studio.

DaisyQuest — A magic old wizard teaches phonics and letters.

Darby The Dragon — We don't have a problem with dragons per say, we did have a problem with the magic.

Dino Park Tycoon — Hard to succeed. Graphics not that good.

Dinosoft series — Poor quality, don't waste your money.

Disney's Aladdin: The Fate of Agrabah — "Magic" carpet

Disney's Animated StoryBook Deluxe: The Little Mermaid — Magic

Disney's Animated StoryBook: Hercules — Magic

Disney's MathQuest with Aladdin — Magic

Disney's Animated StoryBook Deluxe: The Little Mermaid

Disney's Action Games – all titles are fun but totally arcade

Disney Activity Centers – nicely done but mostly arcade games and not very educational

Elroy series — Fun but weird and a waste of time.

Ernie's Adventure in Space – Poorly made

Evolution — Need I say more?

Escape From Monkey Island: Insults and magic

Fairy Tale Factory — Magic.

First Grade Success Starter — Contains Treehouse and Math Workshop, both of which we don't care for due to magic.

Broderbund's Kindergarten Success Starter — Contains James Discovers Math, which we don't care for.

Fisher-Price ABC's — Some rock music.

Fisher-Price: Ready for Preschool — Has a magician performing magic, otherwise wonderful program.

Freddi Fish & Luther's Maze Madness — Arcade

game.

Gigglebone Gang World Tour — Lots of myths and folk tales presented as semi-truth, some magic.

Goosebumps-Escape from Horrorland — We don't even have to see the box to know this one is a sure fire thumbs down.

Grammar Gremlins — Has a haunted house theme with gremlins living there.

Grammar for the Real World- you are in a rock band on tour. Too worldly for my tastes.

Great Reading, Math, and Word Adventure — Lots of rock and roll and some violent arcade action. Some haunted stuff. Not to be confused with the Word Adventure from Smartek..

Gus goes to Cyberopolis — Pathetic, waste of money.

Harry and the Haunted House — The house isn't really haunted but it is still a spooky program.

Hollywood — limited in creativity and playability. Too easy to make scary or unedifying scenes. I prefer MECC'c Opening Night.

Incredible Toon Machine — Get The Incredible Machine or Widget Workshop instead, better educational value.

Interactive Math Journey — Magician who performs magic.

James Discovers Math — The number nine activity is in a dark spooky basement with a ghost, a skeleton, spider and genie.

Jonah and the Whale from Parsons Tech — Limited playability.

JumpStart 4th Grade (older version) — We like the rest of the JumpStart series (especially 3rd Grade), but this one was WAY to creepy for our family.

Jumpstart Math for First Graders- Magic

Jumpstrart Reading for First Graders- Magic

Jumpstart Math for 2nd Graders- Magic

Jumpstart Reading for 2nd Graders- Magic

Jungle Quest — Some pagan images, not much educational value.

Kid Keys — Method of teaching typing ineffective and inadequate. Characters irritating and annoying.

Kid Phonics 1 & 2 — Okay phonics but the characters and music is so annoying.

Kids On Site — Rude kids run over their construction supervisors with large machines.

Kids Typing — "Friendly" ghost helps you learn to type faster by levitating objects in a quiet suburban home.

King Arthur through the Ages — Has magic mixed with real history, not very "multimedia".

Lion King (various) — Nice, but Pagan/Far East religious themes.

Lion King Activity Center — Great fun but too much spiritist/new age stuff.

Living Books Series — Whole Language/sight word approach to learning to read. Many characters have bad attitudes.

Madeline's European Adventure — She is chasing a Genie from a magic bottle (we carry some of the other Madeline titles.)

Magic School Bus Explores the Ocean — Too many arcade games, my kids never got to the content.

Mario (in general) — Most titles tend to be okay, but a little more arcade than we care for or lesser educational value.

Mario is Missing — Mindless arcade game.

Mario Teaches Typing — This is an arcade game for the fingers.

Math Blaster Jr. — Has a Magician.

Math Blaster Pre-Algebra- creepy characters in a creepy house

Math Challenge — Limited content.

Math For The Real World — Too worldly for my tastes, you must create a rock music video.

Math Workshop Deluxe — Out of about 30 puzzles, one puzzle is a vampire & another is a ghost rising out of a graveyard.

MayaQuest — Nothing "bad", just could not figure it out.

Mega Math or Turbo Science — Education value mediocre. Characters rude and obnoxious. Graphics are crude at best.

Microsoft Bob — Bob bombed. Most reviewers were less than satisfied with Bob.

Monster Maker Math- Creepy

Mr. Potato Head Saves Veggie Valley — Lots of magic and spells.

Muppet Treasure Island — Fun program but has a ghost.

My First Steps to Math — Limited content.

My Very First Software — Poor quality, limited playability.

My Very First Storybook-Marvin the Ape — lame story.

Nickolodean Brain Bender — Characters have bad attitude.

Nightmare Ned — This one IS a nightmare. Graveyard scenes.

Odell Down Under, Odell Lake — Very eco-correct, mainly arcade-like, limited playability.

Origins of Mankind — They have a different origin then we do (hint: leaves God out of the equation).

Pajama Sam — In one part, Sam mixes potions that make him invisible, smart, levitate, etc.

Putt-Putt and Pep's Balloon-O-Rama — Our children love the Putt-Putt programs, but this one is just an arcade game.

Putt-Putt and Pep's Dog on a Stick — Our children love the Putt-Putt programs, but this one is just an arcade game.

Putt-Putt Travels Through Time — Our children love the Putt-Putt programs, but in this one he meets Merlin the Magician.

Reading Adventures in OZ — Magic.

Reading Blaster — More arcade action than reading practice. Limited depth. Not to be confused with Reading Blaster 2000, which is good.

Reading Blaster Jr. – 1995 version, older program, has magician. New version is great.

Reading Blaster Ages 9-12 a.k.a Reading Blaster 4th Grade- Takes place in a haunted house with creepy but not supernatural characters. Characters become "dehumanized." Educationally speaking, an excellent program.

Reading Blaster Vocabulary, aka Reading Blaster 5th grade – Takes place in a haunted house with creepy but not supernatural characters. Educationally speaking, an excellent program.

Ready for Math with Pooh – Pooh and friend do a "raindance" to bring rain

Rockett series – very worldly teen stuff

Rugrats Totally Angelica: Boredom Buster

Sabrina the Teenage Witch -- witchcraft

Sesame Street's Get Set to Learn — The "Count" performs magic.

Sesame Street Music Maker- annoying rock

Sesame Street Reading Games

Schoolhouse Rock series – my kids spent more time listening to the bouncy rock music than learning anything.

SimAnt — This simulation of being in charge of an ant colony is also violent and the goal is to "take over the human's home."

SimEarth — This simulation program is steeped heavily in evolutionary concepts and premises. You are in charge of a planet and you "design and nurture planets from their creation through the evolution of life." Very mother-earth.

SimLife — Building your own ecosystem is the goal of this simulation. The whole premise is you're in control of all life as God.

Sims – too easy to have your imaginary characters commit sin

Sound It Out Land — Great phonics but too much rock and roll for my tastes.

Spanish for the Real World- has a fortune teller, otherwise good

Spelling Blizzard — Uses the same witch doctor

character as in Yobi's Magic Spelling Tricks.

Stephen Biesty's Incredible Cross-Sections

Stowaway – fascinating CD but has some morbid scenes e.g. amputating a leg with a saw.

Spyro: Year of the Dragon – good but has an evil sorceress

StickyBear at Home — Boring whole language game.

Stickybear's Reading Fun Park — Haunted house with ghost.

Storybook Weaver Classic — Older, crude graphics. NOT to be confused with the newer, better Deluxe version, which we sell.

Streets of Sim City — It involves shooting people.

SuperSolvers Midnight Rescue — The few reading problems there are, are good, but there is too much game between problems.

SuperSolvers OutNumbered — The few math problems there are, are good, but there is too much game between problems.

The Great Word Adventure — Some haunted stuff. Not to be confused with the Word Adventure from Smartek.

Thinkin Things Sky Island Mysteries- boring and has wizard guy

Time Warp of Dr. Brain — Excellent logic games but the premise is based entirely on evolution.

Tonka Construction — Lots of fun, but has a wizard that fills the moat magically

Treasure Mountain, Mathstorm, Galaxy, or Cove — Magic elves, coins and crystals

Treehouse CD — We loved the 3.5" version, but the CD–Rom version contains some objectionable material.

Tuneland — Rock and roll music; not your familiar old melodies in these children's song favorites.

Typing Tutor 7 from Davidson — In one of the drills you "hit" people on the head as you type and watch them scream!

Who Wants to be a Millionaire? — Most of the questions are about pop culture. In other words, pretty useless.

Wishbone — Magic.

Write, Camera, Action — Too easy to create unedifying or scary scenes.

Yobi's Magic Spelling Tricks — Yobi is a witch doctor. Contains "tricksters" which resemble demons to me.

Save Your Money

This is a partial listing of programs that aren't really "bad" per se, but with so many better programs out there, you should consider passing on the ones listd below. Yes, some of these titles have some good features in them, but we trust that you will find the programs in our review section to be better overall in value and/or features. Some of the below are worse than others and you may find some acceptable where I have not. Most of this software is not offensive but that is not worth any more than $5. If you see them in a bundle with other titles, weigh the cost before making the purchase.

3D Minigolf (any version)
American Girl Dress Designer
Animal Planet (Discovery Channel)
Annatommy
Arthur's 1st Grade
Arthur's 2nd Grade
Arthur's Adventures with D.W.
Arthur's Computer Adventure
Arthur's Math Games
Art Explorer
Barbie series
Bear's Imagine That
Bear's Sense of Adventure
Beyond Planet Earth
Bible Time Fun
Bill Nye the Science Guy: Stop the Rock!
Captain Kangaroo Life's First Lessons #1
Captain Kangaroo Life's First Lessons #2
Chicka Chicka Boom Boom
Compton's Learning Real Science
Detective Barbie: Mystery of the Carnival Caper
Detective Barbie: Vacation Mystery
Firefighter
Fisher Price Big Action Garage
Fisher Price Magna Doodle
Fisher Price: Ranger Trail
Flipper
Four Footed Friends
Sesame Street: Get Set to Learn
Gus Goes to Cyberopolis

Gryphon Bricks
Highlights Puzzelmania
Hot Wheels Crash
Hot Wheels Stunt Track Drive
In the Footsteps of Jesus
In the Company of Whales
Jumpstart Baby
Jumpstart 4th Grade
Jumpstart 6th Grade
Harry and the Haunted House
Lionel Trains Presents Transcon!
Little Golden Books: Series
Little Bear Kindergarten
Little Bear Preschool
Little Bear Rainy Day Adventures
Little Bear Toddler
Logic Quest
Matchbox Big Dirt Movers
Matchbox Construction Zone
Mickey Mouse Toddler
My First CDROM Preschool
My First CDROM Toddler
All SofSource/ ProOne Software
MathSoft titles
Mentorom titles
My First Steps to Math
Nordiware titles
P.B. Bears Birthday Party
Ozzie series
Paint, Write, and Play
Phonics Adventure

Phonics Alive
Playskool Puzzles
Planet Earth
Photo Creations
Print Artist Craft Factory
Puzzle Creator 2000
Reading is Fun! Toddler Edition
Reading Search
Road Adventures
Ruff's Bone
Rugrats Movie Activity Challenge
Rugrats Mystery Adventure
Rugrats Adventure Game
School House Rock series
Shiela Rae the Brave
SimCopter
Slam Dunk Typng
SmartStep series
Super 3-D Noah's Ark
Tale of Peter Rabbit
Thinkin Science
Toggle Trouble Math
Tonka Garage
Ultimate Children's Encyclopedia
Ultrakey
Undersea Adventure
Walk in the Footsteps of Jesus
Warplanes
What is a Bellybutton?
Winnie the Pooh Toddler
Winnie the Pooh Kindergarten
Word Stuff
World Geography by KidSoft
Yellowstone Journey

APPENDIX OF SOFTWARE RESELLERS

Company: Home Computer Market
Address: PO Box 385377
City: Bloomington
State: MN
Zip: 55438
Phone: 800-827-7420
WEB ADDRESS:
www.homecomputermarket.com

Company: Great Products
Address: 2813 59th Ave N
City: St. Petersburg
State: FL
Zip: 33714
Phone: 727-403-2772
WEB ADDRESS:
www.greatdiscountsoftware.com

Company: Sunday School Software
Address: 4369 Brickwood Drive
City: Hilliard
State: OH
Zip: 43026
Phone: 800-678-1948
WEB ADDRESS:
www.sundaysoftware.com

Company: Timberdoodle
Address: E 1510 Spencer Lk Rd
City: Shelton
State: WA
Zip: 98584
Phone: 360-426-0672
WEB ADDRESS:
www.timberdoodle.com

APPENDIX OF SOFTWARE PUBLISHERS

Company: 4:20 Communications.
Address: PO Box 421027
City: Minneapolis
State: MN
Zip: 55427
Phone: 888-420-READ
WEB ADDRESS: www.phonicstutor.com

Company: A.D.A.M. Software, Inc.
Address: 1600 RiverEdge Parkway
Suite 800
City: Atlanta
State: GA
Zip: 30328
Phone: 800-755-2326
WEB ADDRESS: www.adam.com

Company: AbleSoft
Address: 8550 Remington Avenue, Suite E
City: Pennsauken
State: NJ
Zip: 08110
Phone: 609-488-8200
WEB ADDRESS: www.ablesoft-inc.com

Company: Alliance for Technology Access
Address: 2175 East Francisco Blvd, Suite L
City: San Rafael
State: CA
Zip: 94901-5521
Phone: 415-455-4575
WEB ADDRESS: www.ataccess.org

Company: Alpha Omega Publications
Address: 300 North McKemy Avenue
City: Chandler
State: AZ
Zip: 85226-2618
Phone: 800-622-3070
WEB: www.home-schooling.com

Company: American Education Corporation
Address: 7506 North Broadway Extension
City: Oklahoma City
State: OK
Zip: 73116-9016
Phone: 800-222-2811
WEB ADDRESS:www.amered.com

Company: Barnum Software
Address: 3450 Lake Shore Ave., Suite 200
City: Oakland
State: CA
Zip: 94610-9805
Phone: 800-553-9155
WEB ADDRESS: www.thequartermile.com

Company: BibleSoft
Address: 22014 7th Avenue South
City: Seattle
State: WA
Zip: 98198-6235
Phone: 206-824-0547-
WEB ADDRESS: www.biblesoft.com

Company: Bolchazy-Carducci Publishers, Inc.
Address: 1000 Brown St., Unit #101
City: Wauconda
State: IL
Zip: 60084
Phone: 800-392-6453 -
WEB ADDRESS: www.bolchazy.com

Company: Boxer Learning, Inc.
Address: 105 West Main Street
City: Charlottesville
State: VA
Zip: 22902
Phone: 800-736-2824
WEB ADDRESS: www.boxerlearning.com

Company: Cognitive Concepts
Address: 990 Grove Street
City: Evanston
State: IL
Zip: 60201
Phone: 888-328-8199
WEB ADDRESS: www.cogcon.com

Company: Cognitive Technologies Corporation
Address: 4884 Cloister Drive
City: Rockville
State: MD
Zip: 20852
Phone: 800-335-0781
WEB ADDRESS: www.cogtech.com

Company: Cubic Science, Inc.
Address: 19433 East Walnut Drive South
City: City of Industry
State: CA
Zip: 91748
Phone: 800-383-6363
WEB ADDRESS: www.cubicsci.com

Company: The Discovery Channel
Address:
City: Bethesda
State: MD
Zip: 20814-3579
Phone: 800-678-3343
WEB ADDRESS: www.discovery.com

Company: Disney Interactive
Address: 19433 East Walnut Drive South
City: Glendale
State: CA
Zip: 91201
Phone: 800-900-9234
WEB ADDRESS: www.disneyinteractive.com

Company: DK Multimedia
Address: 95 Madison Avenue
City: New York
State: NY
Zip: 10016
Phone: 888-342 5357
WEB ADDRESS: www.dk.com

Company: Dole Food Company
Address: 100 Hegenberger Road, Suite 100
City: San Mateo
State: CA
Zip: 94402
Phone: 800-472-8777
WEB ADDRESS: www.dole5aday.com

Company: Don Johnston, Inc.
Address: 26799 West Commerce Drive
City: Volo
State: IL
Zip: 60073
Phone: 800-999-4660
WEB ADDRESS: www.donjohnston.com

Company: Edmark (IBM Corp.)
Address: P.O. Box 97021
City: Redmond
State: WA
Zip: 98073-9721
Phone: 800-426-0856
WEB ADDRESS: www.edmark.com

Company: Educational Insights
Address: 16941 Keegan Ave.
City: Carson
State: CA
Zip: 90746-1307
Phone: 800-995-4436
WEB ADDRESS: www.edin.com

Company: Encore Software
Address: 5420 W. 83rd Street
City: Los Angeles
State: CA
Zip: 90045
Phone: 310-342-0610
WEB ADDRESS: www.encoresoftware.com

Company: Fairfield Language Technologies
Address: 165 S. Main St.
City: Harrisonburg
State: VA
Zip: 22801
Phone: 800-788-0822
WEB ADDRESS: www.trstone.com

Company: Forest Technologies
Address: 735-A Industrial Dr.
City: Cary
State: IL
Zip: 60013
Phone: 800-544-3356
WEB ADDRESS: www.foresttech.com

Company: Grammar Key
Address: PO Box 33230
City: Tulsa
State: OK
Zip: 74153
Phone: 800-4800-539
WEB ADDRESS: www.home-school.com/Mall/GK/Grammar.html

Company: Harmonic Vision
Address: 68 East Wacker Place, 7th floor
City: Chicago
State: IL
Zip: 60601
Phone: 800-474-0903
WEB ADDRESS: www.harmonicvision.com

Company: Hasbro Interactive
Address: 1027 Newport Avenue
City: Pawtucket
State: RI
Zip: 02862
Phone: 800-683-5847
WEB ADDRESS: www.hasbro-interactive.com

Company: Houghton Mifflin Interactive/Sunburst
Address: 120 Beacon Street
City: Somerville
State: MA
Zip: 02143
Phone: 617-503-4800
WEB ADDRESS: www.sunburst.com

Company: Idea Maker
Address: 80 South Redwood Rd. Suite 212
City: North Salt Lake
State: UT
Zip: 84054
Phone: 888-974-8322
WEB ADDRESS: www.startwrite.com

Company: Jump! Music
Address:
City: Mountain View
State: CA
Zip: 94040
Phone: 800-289-5867
WEB ADDRESS: www.jumpmusic.com

Company: Knowledge Adventure
Address: 4100 W. 190th St.
City: Torrance
State: CA
Zip: 90503
Phone: 800-542-4240
WEB ADDRESS: www.knowledgeadventure.com

Company: The Learning Company
Address: 500 Redwood Blvd.
City: Novato
State: CA
Zip: 94948
Phone: 800-543-9778
WEB ADDRESS: www.learningco.com

Company: Logo Computer Systems Inc.
Address: PO BOX 162
City: Highgate Springs
State: VT
Zip: 05460
Phone: 800-321-5646
WEB ADDRESS: www.lcsi.ca

Company: Logos Research Systems
Address: 715 SE Fidalgo Ave
City: Oak Harbor
State: WA
Zip: 98277-4049
Phone: 800-875-6467
WEB ADDRESS: www.logos.com

Company: Lucas Learning
Address: PO Box 10667
City: San Rafael
State: CA
Zip: 94912
Phone: 888-887-7909
WEB ADDRESS: www.lucaslearning.com

Company: Memlok
Address: 420 Montwood
City: La Habra
State: CA
Zip: 90631
Phone: 800-373-1947
WEB ADDRESS: www.memlok.com

Company: NavPress
Address: P.O. Box 35002
City: Colorado Springs
State: CO
Zip: 80935
Phone: 800-366-7788
WEB ADDRESS: www.navpress.com

Company: Online Bible
Address: 127 N. Matteson St.
City: Bronson
State: MI
Zip: 49028
Phone: (517) 369-2195
WEB ADDRESS: www.onlinebible.org

Company: Oregon Institute of Science & Medicine
Address: 2251 Dick George Rd.
City: Cave Junction
State: OR
Zip: 97523
Phone: 541-592-4142
WEB ADDRESS: www.oism.org

Company: Scholastic, Inc.
Address: 555 Broadway
City: New York
State: NY
Zip: 10012-3999
Phone: 212-343-7100
WEB ADDRESS: www.scholastic.com

Company: School Zone Interactive
Address: 1819 Industrial Drive
City: Grand Haven
State: MI
Zip: 49417-9937
Phone: 800-253-0564
WEB ADDRESS: www.schoolzone.com

Company: Scientific Learning
Address: 1995 University Avenue, Suite 400
City: Berkeley
State: CA
Zip: 94704
Phone: 888-665-9707
WEB ADDRESS: www.scientificlearning.com

Company: Simon & Schuster Interactive
Address:
City: New York
State: NY
Zip: 10020
Phone: 888-793-9972
WEB ADDRESS: www.ssinteractive.com

Company: Smartek
Address: 7908 Convoy Court
City: San Diego
State: CA
Zip: 92111
Phone: 800-858-9673
WEB ADDRESS: www.wordsmart.com

Company: Soleil Software, Inc.
Address:
City: Palo Alto
State: CA
Zip: 94303
Phone: 800-501-0110
WEB ADDRESS: www.soleil.com

Company: Steck-Vaughn Company
Address: PO Box 26015
City: Austin
State: TX
Zip: 78759
Phone: 800-531-5015
WEB ADDRESS: www.steck-vaughn.com

Company: Sumeria, Inc.
Address: 100 Eucalyptus Drive
City: San Francisco
State: CA
Zip: 94132
Phone: 415-586-3820
WEB ADDRESS: www.sumeria.com

Company: Sunburst Communications, Inc.
Address: 101 Castleton Street
City: Pleasantville
State: NY
Zip: 10570 - 3498
Phone: 800-338-3457
WEB ADDRESS: www.sunburst.com

Company: Sunday School Software
Address: 4369 Brickwood Drive
City: Hilliard
State: OH
Zip: 43026
Phone: 800-678-1948
WEB ADDRESS: www.sundaysoftware.com

Company: Topics-Entertainment (CounterTop Software)
Address: 1600 SW 43rd St.
City: Redmond
State: WA
Zip: 98052
Phone: 425-895-9811
WEB ADDRESS: www.topics-ent.com

Company: Transparent Language, Inc.
Address: 9 Executive Park Drive
City: Merrimack
State: NH
Zip: 03054
Phone: 888-245-1829
WEB ADDRESS: www.transparent.com

Company: Waypoint Software
Address: 3200-1322 Old Winter Garden Road
City: Ocoee
State: FL
Zip: 34761
Phone: 407-522-3766
WEB ADDRESS: www.waypointinc.com

Company: World Book, Inc.
Address: 233 N. Michigan Ave.Suite 2000
City: Chicago
State: IL
Zip: 60601
Phone: 800-967-5325
WEB ADDRESS: www.worldbook.com

Company: Zane Publishing
Address: 2425 Arbuckle Street
City: Dallas
State: TX
Zip: 75229
Phone: 972-488-9263
WEB ADDRESS www.zane.com

Index of Software Titles